Followership Development and
Enactment among the Acholi of Uganda

Followership Development and Enactment among the Acholi of Uganda

A Seamless Paradigm for Relational Leadership

DAVID WESLEY OFUMBI

WIPF & STOCK • Eugene, Oregon

FOLLOWERSHIP DEVELOPMENT AND ENACTMENT AMONG THE ACHOLI OF UGANDA
A Seamless Paradigm for Relational Leadership

Copyright © 2019 David Wesley Ofumbi. All rights reserved. Except for brief quotations in critical publications or reviews, no part of this book may be reproduced in any manner without prior written permission from the publisher. Write: Permissions, Wipf and Stock Publishers, 199 W. 8th Ave., Suite 3, Eugene, OR 97401.

Wipf & Stock
An Imprint of Wipf and Stock Publishers
199 W. 8th Ave., Suite 3
Eugene, OR 97401

www.wipfandstock.com

PAPERBACK ISBN: 978-1-5326-6220-1
HARDCOVER ISBN: 978-1-5326-6222-5
EBOOK ISBN: 978-1-5326-6223-2

Manufactured in the U.S.A.   JULY 22, 2019

Contents

List Of Tables | vi
List of Figures | vii
Abstract | ix
Acknowledgments | xi

1   Introduction | 1
2   Pivotal Eras in Followership Perception | 7
3   The Case—Exemplary Followership Of The Acholi People In The Northern Ugandan Conflict Resolution (1985–2012) | 64
4   Methods and Procedures | 100
5   The Findings—Human Dignity | 119
6   Findings on Followership Development: Root Factors | 154
7   Findings on Followership Enactment: Fruit Actions | 254
8   Discussions and Summary | 264

Appendix A—Demographic Data on Participants | 291
Appendix B—Interview Guide | 293
Bibliography | 295

List Of Tables

Table 1: Summary of Perceptions of Followership | 63

Table 2: Statistics on the Impact of War in the Acholi Subregion 1986–2006 | 88

List of Figures

Figure 1: Human Dignity Emanates from Interactions Between Root Factors and Fruit Actions | 120

Figure 2: Followership Development Tree | 121

Figure 3: Followership Enactment Staircase | 122

Figure 4: Tree Growth Circle Depicting a Seamless Mental Model | 255

Figure 5: Three Mental Models | 275

Abstract

The industrial era organizations used individualistic and dualistic leadership theory, which regarded followers as objects of leaders' influence to socialize them into passive followership irrespective of context and outcome. Consequently, organizations focused on leadership and condemned active followership as a toxic behavior that sabotages organizational processes and outcomes. However, the emergence of relational leadership theory in the information era, which regards followers as subjects of their own behaviors, has heightened the demand for active followership throughout organizational ranks, roles, and relationships. Nonetheless, followership studies are still in their infancy. For instance, whereas scholars like Robert Kelley, Ira Chaleff and Barbara Kellerman identified followership identities, roles and behaviors, and Melissa Carsten et al. established factors influencing followership development and enactment, how factors influence followership development and enactment remains unknown. For that matter, we do not know how followers develop and enact active followership. Thus, using a qualitative research paradigm as well as grounded theory case study approach, interview data collected from thirty-nine participants on how they understand their followership identity, roles, and behaviors; factors influencing how they develop and enact them; and how such factors influence the way in which they develop and enact them, yielded substantive information, which upon analysis generated a theory of followership development and enactment. Per the findings, whereas in the West active followership is attributed to the dawn of information era characterized by a fast-expanding global economy, improved technology and highly educated workforce, among the Acholi people active followership is the outgrowth of human dignity, which emanates from context-specific seamless continuous interactions between layers of convert factors and overt actions hereafter referred to as root factors and fruit actions respectively. It is enacted through a context-specific seamless consensus-building process of observation, analysis, and response. The study advanced followership theory by offering a theory of followership development and enactment anchored in a seamless paradigm that can be used to expand leadership theory beyond individualistic and dichotomous tendencies that absolutized the differences among leadership variables despite their seamlessness, and exclusivistic Western methodological and empirical paradigm.

Acknowledgments

My doctoral faith journey (2012-2017) which led to this publication epitomizes the African life ethos I have held since childhood: that we are human because we belong. I am because we are, and since we are therefore I am. In my case, this bond of belongingness encompasses vertical absolute dependence on God and horizontal self-independence and interdependence.

Therefore, first, I owe it to God who created me in his image as a cocreator so that I may relate to him, myself, the others, and the rest of creation to incarnate God while enhancing human and ecological wellbeing.

Second, to my family: my wife Anne Opande Nyarangi, our daughters Tehilah and Taleesa, our Uganda and Kenya family and friends, our American family and friends (especially Delia Ohara and Herb Johnstone posthumously), Karen and Gil Gleason, Reverend Lois Mueller and Dr. J. Alfred Smith, Sr. You covered me with the canopy of love and support I needed to pursue this journey.

Third, I owe a debt of gratitude to the faculty and my peers at Biola University. Specifically, I would like to thank President Corey, Drs. Rich Starcher, Tom Steffen, Leanne Dzubinski, Kenneth Nehrbass, Rhonda McEwen, and Stephen Chan, and my friends Daniel Low, Francis Nwobu, Habutamu Umer, Jane Rhoades, and Ivan Chan, to mention just a few. I would also like thank Patrick Kiruki who designed all the images I used to illustrate the findings. This book could not have been completed without your support.

Lastly, I owe it to myself for steering the course this far on the firm shoulders of my vertical absolute dependence on God and horizontal self-independence and interdependence. To God be the glory.

1

Introduction

THE indispensable role leaders play in organizational management prompted the emergence of leadership theory.[1] Central to the theory is the assumption that leaders are the subject of leadership, and other factors like followers are objects of leaders' influence. This theory shone exclusive light on leaders and leading for over a century at the expense of followers and following.[2] For instance, in Africa, it is implied in Chinua Achebe's observation that a crisis of poor leadership is the foremost challenge of the continent,[3] which accelerated leadership development programs across sectors as a panacea.[4] Thus, slogans like "everything rises and falls on leadership" have won axiomatic acceptance.[5]

However, during my educational interaction with Christian leaders in East Africa, paradigm-changing experiences challenged my understanding of leadership as a unidirectional influence of leaders on followers. First, most leaders were reluctant to apply knowledge and skills that they thought would provoke opposition from their followers. On the other hand, northern Ugandan leaders narrated how the Acholi people influenced the Ugandan government to adopt a peaceful approach to settle the region's conflict despite the latter's preference for a military option.

---

1. Taylor, *Principles of Scientific Management*.
2. Heckscher, "Defining the Post-Bureaucratic Type," 98–106; Hurwitz and Hurwitz, *Leadership is Half the Story*.
3. Achebe, *Trouble with Nigeria*.
4. Ogbonna, "Followership Imperative of Good Governance," 65–80.
5. Maxwell, *21 Indispensable Qualities*, ix.

Consequently, I began exploring and analyzing the phenomena of the flow of influence in leadership processes and outcomes because followers could not hold viable alternative viewpoints if they were merely passive recipients of leaders' influence. Second, I felt disoriented when I realized that despite the explicit evidences of active followership in both encounters, I did not have a language to describe it or the competency to nurture it because I knew of neither a study nor a training program on it. Nonetheless, following prolonged research on the flow of influence and how it has been applied in leadership, I developed the curiosity to explore leadership as a context-specific human collaborative phenomenon driven by factors that are simultaneously independent and interdependent, which inspired me to pursue followership from the perspective of followers.

Most studies on followership have been conducted in North America in the context of business, schools, churches, and governmental departments.[6] Virtually no study on active followership has been undertaken in Africa despite the topic's popularity.[7] Moreover, contextual factors heightening interest in it in North America and Africa are different.[8] So far, it is difficult to relate followership phenomena in North America to the increasing agitation for active followership, especially in Africa.[9]

For example, despite the extensive literature available on northern Ugandan conflict, no study has examined the role of the Acholi active followership in the region's conflict resolution as a unique countercultural phenomenon. The omission is not accidental. First, African indigenous cultures have been generally associated with a high-power distance and authoritarian sociocultural environment in which subordinates are socialized into passive followership.[10] This saying among the Busoga, "*Omwami kyankoba zena kyenkoba*" ("What the chief has said is what I go with"), which presumes passive followership, typifies it.[11] Second, the colonial powers in

---

6. Baker, "Followership," 50–60.

7. Ogbonna, "Followership Imperative of Good Governance," 65–80; Oyetunji, "Relationship between Followership Style," 179–87; Thomas-Slayter, "Structural Change, Power Politics," 1479; Zoogah et al., "Determinants of Strategic Followership," 137–48.

8. Hughes et al., *Leadership*; Osaghae, "Limits of Charismatic Authority," 29–44; Rajan and Wulf, "Flattening Firm"; Zoogah et al., "Determinants of Strategic Followership," 137–48.

9. Carsten et al., "Exploring Social Constructions of Followership," 543–62; Ogbonna, "Followership Imperative of Good Governance," 65–80; Oyetunji, "Relationship between Followership Style," 179–87.

10. Gyekye, *African Cultural Values*; Hofstede, *Cultures and Organizations*; Ndongko, "Management Leadership in Africa," 97–102.

11. Kanungo, "Culture and Work Alienation," 3–6; Oloka-Onyango, "'New-Breed' Leadership, Conflict," 29–52.

Sub-Saharan Africa created paternalism in the modern sector, which entrenched a dependency culture between leaders and followers.[12] Therefore, the current grounded theory case study offers a window for understanding active followership in an African context. It explores how followers develop and enact followership identity, roles, and behaviors in the leadership process and outcomes. It uses the case of active followership among the Acholi as manifested in the northern Ugandan conflict resolution between 1985 and 2012.

PROBLEM STATEMENT

Whereas some studies in North America have established followership identity, roles, and behaviors,[13] and identified factors influencing their development and enactment, none has examined how they do so.[14] Furthermore, few studies on followership have been conducted in the African context, and none has touched upon the process of followership development and enactment. Therefore, the process of followership development and enactment is unknown, especially in an African context.

PURPOSE STATEMENT

The purpose of this grounded theory case study is to understand how northern Ugandan Acholi followers, during the troubled period between 1985 and 2012, developed and enacted followership identity, roles, and behaviors as they negotiated conflict resolutions with national leaders.

RESEARCH QUESTION

The central question guiding this grounded theory case study is: How did northern Ugandan Acholi followers, during the period between 1985 and 2012, develop and enact followership identity, roles, and behaviors as they negotiated conflict resolutions with national leaders? Its subsequent questions are: (1) How did the followers understand and describe their

---

12. Abudu, "Work Attitudes of Africans," 17–36; Ajulu, *Holism in Development*; Hughes, *Africans in the British*; Komakech, *Reinventing and Validating the* Cosmology; Mamdani, *Citizen and Subject*.

13. Chaleff, *Courageous Follower*; Kellerman, *Followership*; Kelley, *Power of Followership*.

14. Carsten et al., "Exploring Social Constructions of Followership."

followership identity, roles, and behaviors? (2) How did the followers describe factors influencing the ways in which they developed and enacted followership identity, roles, and behaviors? (3) How did the followers describe the ways in which factors influenced the development and enactment of their followership identity, roles, and behaviors?

DEFINITIONS

"Followership" herein refers to conceptualized and operationalized "characteristics, behaviors, and processes of individuals acting in relation to leaders" toward a common goal in a context.[15]

Followership schema in the current study refers to "generalized knowledge structures that develop over time through socialization and interaction with stimuli relative to leadership and followership,"[16] or the cognitive framework that followers use to make meaning of their followership identity, roles, and behaviors in the leadership process.

"Variables" herein refers to different dimensions of factors like culture and followership style that influence how followers develop and enact followership in leadership processes and outcomes.

"Active followers" herein refers to employees who choose followership identity, roles, and behaviors in support of leaders and teams toward common organizational goals. In other words, it is "followers [who] have the ability to influence leaders and contribute to the improvement and attainment of group and organizational objectives."[17]

"Followership identity" herein refers to the orientation followers adopt in their relationship to leaders while pursuing a common goal. The possible orientations include active, passive, and toxic followership. This study explores active followership.

"Followership role" herein refers to the part followers play based on their followership identity. For example, followers who choose active followership play roles like initiation and self-management.

"Followership behavior" herein refers to the ways followers act in relationship to leaders toward accomplishing a goal like being either obedient or disobedient.

---

15. Uhl-Bien et al., "Followership Theory," 83–104.

16. Carsten et al., "Exploring Social Constructions of Followership," 546–62; Fiske and Haslam. "Social Cognition is Thinking," 143–48; Fiske and Taylor, *Social Cognition*.

17. Crossman and Crossman, "Conceptualizing Followership," 484–97; Kellerman, *Followership*.

SCOPE

This grounded theory case study focuses on how followers develop and enact followership identity, roles, and behaviors. Data was gathered from the *Kacoke Madit* archives in London and libraries in Uganda, as well as interviews with thirty-nine prominent Acholi people in Uganda and the Diaspora, particularly London and North America, who played seminal roles in northern Ugandan conflict resolution. Hence, this qualitative grounded theory case study was limited to the Acholi people of Uganda.

LIMITATIONS

This study cannot be generalized beyond the Acholi people because of the nature of Acholi culture, northern Uganda conflict, and the unique role the Acholi people played in Ugandan political history. However, its findings may be transferable beyond the prominent Acholi people who played a seminal role in the region's conflict resolution.

Second, this study focuses on the relationship between the Acholi people as an ethnic group and the Ugandan government, and therefore it may not adequately represent other organizational relational dynamics like the relationship between followers and leaders who come from different social backgrounds. It may not also tell us how the Acholi people react to leaders in other places where they don't enjoy strong ethnic consciousness and accountability.

SIGNIFICANCE STATEMENT

A fuller understanding of how followers develop and enact followership identity, roles, and behaviors in an African context is critically important in leadership studies for several reasons. First, leaders and followers in the Acholi subregion in particular and Uganda in general could use the findings to develop a cognitive model to reduce and perhaps even eliminate dualistic tendencies that bifurcate leadership and followership into absolute active-passive categories.[18] Managerially, leaders and followers could use the findings to broaden their understanding of the dynamic process of human influence in organizational processes and outcomes by adding follower constructs and behaviors to the current typologies of leader constructs and behaviors.

18. Burns, *Leadership*.

They could also use the findings to establish the rationale and criteria for creating appropriate contextual variables and schemas that enhance active followership without compromising commitment to leaders and organizational goals. They could also use the findings to create "a contextual infrastructure that motivates people to work together for the common good of their community, for leaders to return respect, honor and dignity back to followers, and for followers to feel a personal sense of fulfillment in being a follower" beyond reward.[19] The participants could use the findings to inform their response to national politics and government policies, thereby enhancing possibilities of socioeconomic transformation through followership.

Academically, this study serves as a seminal work in African literature on active followership and expands literature on followership in general globally, which can be used to establish a platform to enhance cross-cultural leadership research, education, and practice instead of the monocultural approach that characterizes the Western model. It also generates an understanding of how followers develop and enact followership identity, roles, and behaviors in leadership processes and outcomes.

Last but not least, African scholars and the educated elite could use insights from this study to inform their demand for active followership, particularly in the church and the marketplace, to redress leadership failures in Sub-Saharan Africa.[20] For instance, many African Christian scholars[21] concur with the framers of the Lausanne Covenant that Christians "have sometimes pursued church growth at the expense of church depth, and divorced evangelism from Christian nurture,"[22] and Christian nurture from socioeconomic transformation.[23] Thus, the church is clamoring for a discipleship model that empowers the body of Christ beyond leaders, and a leadership model that acknowledges the complementary role of followers beyond the four walls of the church[24] to "mobilize and equip the whole church to take the whole gospel to the whole world."[25]

---

19. Lundin and Lancaster, "Beyond Leadership," 18.
20. Ogbonna, "Followership Imperative of Good Governance," 65–80.
21. Hanciles, "Conversion and Social Change," 157–80.
22. Stott, "Education and Leadership," 1.
23. Ntamushobora, "From Transmission to Transformation."
24. Allen, *Future Church*.
25. Stott, "Education and Leadership," 1.

2

Pivotal Eras in Followership Perception

CONSIDERING the purpose of this study, the current chapter is designed to establish followership perceptions since the emergence of leadership theory and their impact on followership development and enactment. The perception of followership identity, roles, and behaviors has undergone several changes since the emergence of leadership theory. Knowledge of these changes is important in understanding the dynamics of leadership processes and outcomes. For instance, it sheds light on factors that have blurred the line between leaders and followers.[1]

This chapter categorizes the pivotal changes in followership perception into three eras: (a) followership antecedents (1888–1987); (b) followership theory (1988–2010); and (c) followership development and enactment (2010–present). In the first section, I will discuss the etymology of followership and emergence of negative connotation, earlier theorists, and theories, including why they failed to win a foothold in both the public media and organizations. In the second section, I will discuss the rationale for followership theory and its dynamics, and the recent interest in followership development and enactment. In the third section, I will discuss the efforts made so far toward establishing the dynamics of followership development and enactment.

While followers and following are always inseparable from leaders and leading,[2] leadership research, education, and practice have tended to focus

---

1. Hurwitz and Hurwitz, *Leadership Is Half the Story*.

2. Kelley, *Praise of Followers*, 142–48; Malakyan, "Followership in Leadership Studies," 6–22; Taylor, *Principles of Scientific Management*; Uhl-Bien et al. "Followership Theory," 83–104.

solely on the latter. Whenever followers are mentioned, they are rendered homogenous objects of leaders' influence,[3] or constructors of leadership.[4] The preoccupation with leaders and leading was influenced by the dualistic mental model, which places the locus of leadership in individual leaders.[5] Thus, leadership has been regarded as a unidirectional influence of leaders on followers.[6] Furthermore, leadership theorists and practitioners ignored studies that called for the exploration of followers' own perceptions of followership or followership theory for over a century.[7]

However, over two decades ago, the dawn of the knowledge era—which is characterized by a fast-expanding global economy, improved technology, and highly educated workforce[8]—led to a flattened organizational structure. Consequently, it created a greater need for collaboration across sectors.[9] For example, whereas in 1980 only 20 percent of work was done by teams, in 2010, teamwork levels stood at 80 percent.[10]

Consequently, studies on followership as a discipline sprang up.[11] So far, there is general agreement that the relationship between leaders and

3. Bass and Bass, *Bass Handbook of Leadership*..
4. Meindl, "On Leadership," 341; Meindl et al., "Romance of Leadership," 78–102.
5. Northouse, *Leadership*, 5.
6. Angucia, "Children and War in Africa"; 77–95; Follett, *Essentials of Leadership*; Hollander, "Processes of Leadership Emergence," 19–33; Hollander, *Leadership Dynamics*; Kelley, "Rethinking Followership," 5–15; Uhl-Bien and Pillai, *Romance of Leadership*; Yukl, *Leadership in Organizations*.
7. Berg, "Ressurrecting the Muse," 27–52; Fairhurst, *Power of Framing*; Fairhurst and Uhl-Bien, "Orgainzational Discourse Analysis," 1043–62; Frye et al., "Embracing Spiritual Followership," 243–60; Herold, "Two-way Influence Processes," 224–37; Hollander, "Processes of Leadership Emergence," 19–33; Hollander, "Essential Interdependence of Leadership," 71–75; Hollander and Webb, Leadership, "Followership and Friendship," 163–67; Kelley, "Leadership Secrets from Exemplary Followers," 193–201; Prasad, "Beyond Analytical Dichotomies," 567–95; Sanford, "Authoritarianism and Leadership"; Uhl-Bien et al., "Followership Theory," 83–104.
8. Baker et al., "Fluid Nature of Follower," 73–88; Boyett and Conn, *Workplace 2000*; DeRue and Ashford, "Who Will Lead?," 627–47; Kelley, *Power of Followership*; Shamir, *From Passive Recipients*; Uhl-Bien and Ospina, "Paradigm Interplay in Relational Leadership," 536–80.
9. Kunnath, *Followership*.
10. Aboukhalil, "Rising Trend in Authorship"; Hollenbeck et al., "Beyond Team Types and Taxonomies," 82–106.
11. Baker, "Followership," 50–60; Baker et al., "Fluid Nature of Follower," 73–88; Chaleff, *Courageous Follower*; DeRue and Ashford, "Who Will Lead?," 627–47; Hurwitz and Hurwitz, *Leadership is Half the Story*; Kelley, *In Praise of Followers*, 142–48; Kelley, *Power of Followership*; Shamir, *From Passive Recipients*; Uhl-Bien and Ospina, "Paradigm Interplay in Relational Leadership"; Uhl-Bien et al., "Followership Theory," 83–104.

followers is reciprocal. Thus, "leaders and followers live in a relational world, 'a world in which leadership is co-created in systems of interconnected relationships and richly interactive contexts.'"[12] For that matter, the art of "leadership resides in the context of the interactions between leaders and followers"[13] rather than merely in a fixed position occupied by an individual at the top of an organization.[14]

The relational view of leadership voided "the unidirectional and dichotomous tendencies inherent in hierarchical structures and its authoritarianism."[15] Consequently, leadership scholars and practitioners began to accord equal attention to the development and enactment of both leadership and followership.[16]

Nonetheless, followership studies have barely begun and are still overshadowed by monumental bottlenecks.[17] So although relational leadership is gaining increasing publicity,[18] there is still little information on followers and following compared to what we know about leaders and leading.[19]

For instance, whereas some researchers have conducted empirical studies to support followership theory, none examined the process of followership development and enactment.[20] Moreover, only 30 percent of followers in formal organizations in North America and Europe are ready to adapt to the dynamic changes sweeping across human organizations and relationships that call for active followers. On the other hand, 70 percent of followers in the same region still lack the capacity for active followership that the knowledge era demands.[21]

The situation in other parts of the world is worse. For instance, research shows that only 12 percent of followers in Africa identify themselves

12. IBM Global CEO Study, "Capitalizing on Complexity," 935.
13. Northouse, *Leadership*, 5.
14. DeRue and Ashford, "Who Will Lead?," 627–47.
15. Friedman, *World Is Flat*, 15.
16. Bradbury and Lichtenstein, "Relationality in Organizational Research," 551–64; Kunnath, *Followership*; Zoogah, *Strategic Followership*.
17. Bjugstad et al., "Fresh Look at Followership," 304–19; Carsten et al., "Social Consturction," 546–62; Crossman and Crossman, "Conceptualizing Followership," 481–97; Kelley, "Rethinking Followership," 5–15; Meindl et al., "Romance of Leadership"; Uhl-Bien et al., "Followership Theory," 83–104.
18. Potter et al., "Leading the New Professional," 145–52.
19. Zoogah, *Strategic Followership*.
20. Densten, and Gray, "Links between Followership," 69–76; Uhl-Bien et al., "Followership Theory," 83–104.
21. Brown and Thornborrow, "Do Organizations Get ther Followers?," 5.

as active followers.[22] Second, organizational systems and cultures in Africa are not conducive to the development and enactment of active followership.[23] Altogether, studies show that leadership theorists and practitioners still marginalize followership[24] and therefore many organizations still either attribute the contributions of active followers to leaders or mistake them for insubordination.[25] At the same time, the realities of leadership limitations have overtaken the larger-than-life image previously attributed to leaders. For instance, globally, leaders' failure rate now ranges between 50 percent and 75 percent and their tenures have been steadily declining over the last ten years.

Furthermore, theoretically, seminal studies on it were observational.[26] So most studies on it are empirical research undertaken in different sectors to validate followership theory.[27] For instance, although followership theory is almost three decades old, studies on followership development started in 2010, and none has explored how followers develop and enact followership theory.[28]

Conceptually, leadership theory and practice bifurcated leadership and followership into absolute active-passive categories due to the dualistic tendencies that limited leadership to individual characteristics and actions of leaders.[29] The exclusive focus on leadership sabotaged efforts toward recognizing followership as a discipline.

The status quo undermines the understanding, the development, and the enactment of leadership as an intentional, interdependent, dynamic, and contextual process between a "person in the role of leader and one or

---

22. Oyetunji, "Relationship between Followership Style," 179–87.

23. Ndongko, "Management Leadership in Africa," 89–123.

24. Bjugstad et al., "Fresh Look at Followership," 304–19; Lapierre and Carsten, *Followership*.

25. Rost, "Followership," 53–66.

26. Lapierre and Carsten, *Followership*; Lipman-Blumen, *Allure of Toxic Leaders*.

27. Alcorn, "Dynamic Followership," 9–33; Barrs, *Shepherd and Sheep*; Brown and Thornborrow, "Do Organizations Get the Followers?," 5; Caesar, "Impact of Followership"; Chai, "Leading as Followers"; Dale, "Leadership-followership," 23–28; Dixon, "Exploration of the Relationship"; Frye et al., "Embracing Spiritual Followership," 243–60; Habecker, *Other Side of Leadership*; Havins, "Examination of the Relationship"; Huizing, "Importance of Ritual"; Ricketson, "Development of the Biblical Followership"; Tanoff and Barlow, "Leading and Followership," 157–67.

28. Carsten and Uhl-Bien, "Follower Beliefs," 210–20; Medcof, "Followers and Followership"; Uhl-Bien et al., "Followership Theory," 83–104.

29. Fairhurst, *Power of Framing*; Frye et al., "Embracing Spiritual Followership," 243–60; Kelley, "Leadership Secrets from Exemplary Followers," 193–201; Prasad, "Beyond Analytical Dichotomies," 567–95.

more persons in the role of follower."[30] A review of the changes in followership perception will enhance organizational desire and capacity to develop and engage active followership effectively.[31]

FOLLOWERSHIP ANTECEDENTS: THE ROMANCE OF LEADERSHIP

The dominant modern leadership theories were established during the industrial era, which has been replaced by the information era.[32] Organizations in the former era regarded followership as either nothing or a path to leadership. So organizations socialized followers to render blind obedience to leaders and refrain from movement toward active followership, even when such efforts were in the best interest of leaders and their organizations.[33] Therefore, "too often followers were expected to be agreeable and acquiescent and were rewarded for being so when in fact followers who practice knee-jerk obedience were of little value and were often dangerous."[34] Followers were pejoratively classified as either conformists and underachievers who were incapable of anything apart from the influence of leaders, or disobedient troublemakers who were bent on disrupting and sabotaging organizational process.[35]

The negative stereotypes associated with followership forestalled the emergence of followership theory for over a century despite the demand for it[36] because organizations developed a unidirectional leadership construct and structures to manage, control, and direct followers, instead of a relational construct and structures that could have enhanced active

---

30. Hinrichs and Hinrichs, "Comparing Followers and Subordinates," 89–108; Ricketson, *Follower First*.

31. Graen and Uhl-Bien, "Relationship-based Approach to Leadership," 219–47; Hosking et al., *Management and Organization*; Katz and Kahn, *Social Psychology of Organizations*; Rost, *Leadership for the Twenty-first Century*; Seeley, *Followership*; Yukl, *Leadership in Organizations*; Zoogah, *Strategic Followership*.

32. Collinson, "Dichotomies, Dialectics and Dilemmas," 36–55; Meindl, et al., "Romance of Leadership"; 78–102; Uhl-Bien et al., "Complexity Leadership Theory," 109–38.

33. Henman, "Leadership"; Taylor, *Principles of Scientific Management*.

34. Bennis, "Art of Followership," xxv.

35. Meindl et al., "Romance of Leadership," 78–102.

36. Bennis, *Managing the Dream*; Hoption et al., "Submitting to the Follower Label," 221–30; Latour and Rast, "Dynamic Followership," 102–10; Yukl et al., "Forgotten Follower," 374–86; Yukl and Van Fleet, "Theory and Research on Leadership," 148–66.

followership.³⁷ The leadership bias romanticized leaders as the organizational engines that ignite other factors at the expense of relational dynamics inherent within organizations. In the next section, I will discuss the etymology of the word "follower" and the emergence of its negative image thereafter.

Etymology of Followership

The word "follower" was derived from "Old High German *fallaziohan* which meant to assist, help, succour, or minister to."³⁸ The definition corresponds to the Old High German root of the term "leader" which meant, "to undergo, suffer, or endure."³⁹ For a long time, it meant "'to go or be in full number' as in a crowd"⁴⁰ or being one of or among a group of people. For example, "follower" was used of people attending a public gathering addressed by a king. In such cases, the term "follower" carried positive connotations, which accorded followers prestige.⁴¹

Thus, in its original setting, followers were complementary to leaders and followers' collaboration with leaders was esteemed. For that matter, the relationship between leaders and followers was symbiotic.⁴² In that setting, "to be accorded the status of follower was considered an honor associated with a level of prestige such as when King Arthur chose the knights of the roundtable or when Jesus chose his disciples."⁴³ This view is supported by leadership evolutionary theory, which suggests that the bureaucratic leadership structures that characterized the industrial era are comparatively recent in human history.⁴⁴ Therefore, the shift of preference from dualistic hierarchies to flat structures that recognize the reciprocal agency of leaders and followers is not unprecedented.⁴⁵

However, over time, the word "follower" developed a negative connotation in the evolution of leadership as a phenomenon of human efforts toward achieving a common goal. In the following section, I will discuss

---

37. Hersey and Blanchard, *Management of Organizational Behavior*.
38. Kelley, *Power of Followership*, 34.
39. Kelley, *Power of Followership*, 34.
40. Kelley, *Power of Followership*, 34
41. Kelley, *Power of Followership*, 34.
42. Burns et al., *Encyclopedia of Leadership*.
43. Kelley, *Power of Followership*, 34.
44. Fairhurst and Uhl-Bien, "Organizational Discourse Analysis," 1043–62.
45. Ashforth, "Experience of Powerlessness in Organizations," 207–42; Fairhurst and Uhl-Bien, "Organizational Discourse Analysis," 1043–62.

how the emergence of leadership theory created negative connotations that characterized followership for over a century.

Etymology of Modern Leadership Theories

The emergence of the word "leadership" as a concept referring to the interaction between leaders and followers to achieve a common goal is recent. Prior to it, "words meaning 'head of state,' 'military commanders,' 'prince,' 'proconsul,' or 'king' were common in most societies; these words were used to differentiate the ruler from other members of society."[46] According to Ralph M. Stogdill, "[the] preoccupation with leadership as opposed to headship based on inheritance, usurpation, or appointment occurs predominantly in country with an Anglo-Saxon heritage."[47] While

> The Oxford English Dictionary 1933 noted the appearance of the word 'leader' in the English language as early as 1300, the word 'leadership' did not appear until the first half of the nineteenth century, in the writings about the political influence and control of the British Parliament.[48]

Otherwise, the study of the subject of leadership goes back to the origin of humanity. The earliest leadership literature was preoccupied with theoretical issues with special focus on types of leadership and their impact on phenomena in society.[49] Unlike their contemporary counterparts, the earlier theorists ignored the interaction between followers and leaders.[50]

Evolution: Followership is Either Nothing or a Path to Leadership

The evolutionary perspective attributes the negative connotation associated with followership to evolutionary game theory.[51] In this theory, ancestors used natural selection hypothesis according to evolutional psychology to apply what worked in the past to new situations. With regard to leadership,

46. Stogdill, "Personal Factors Associated with Leadership," 35–71.
47. Stogdill, "Personal Factors Associated with Leadership," 35–71.
48. Bass and Barrett, *People, Work, and Organizations*, 7.
49. Stogdill, "Personal Factors Associated with Leadership," 35–71.
50. Bass and Barrett, *People, Work, and Organizations*, 6.
51. Maynard Smith, *Evolution and the Theory*.

they selected and retained leadership traits because they solved yesterday's problems.[52]

In this case, whenever a tribe encountered an adaptive challenge that required coordination, cooperation, and innovative thinking, it would defer the leadership role to one of them and the rest of the community chose to follow. In return, the community claimed for itself passive followership and attributed to leaders exceptional qualities that set them apart from the rest of the community.[53] Consequently, they defined followers' passivity by what followers were incapable of doing in comparison to what leaders did. Followers' passivity created implicit expectations that leaders rather than followers are responsible for making tough decisions, solving problems, and ultimately realizing organizational outcomes.[54]

The preindustrial conceptualization of leadership and followership influenced the industrial era organizational culture. For instance, according to Charles Heckscher,[55] "although our world has become so complex and the problem of survival and prosperity have changed, our thinking about followership and followers has not."[56] Thus, just like the preindustrial era, leadership theories in the industrial era focused on leaders' emergence and accomplishments. Whereas leadership qualities were believed to be both inborn and acquired,[57] followership was regarded as a step toward leadership rather than its complement as Michael R. Mitchell noted: "Followership is a commitment to change, a willingness to be transformed into the image, style, and behavior of the leader."[58]

In the next section, I will discuss the preindustrial sociological, psychological, and philosophical perspectives and concepts of followership that account for modern leadership theories that subjected followership to leadership.

Sociological Perspective on Followership

Sociology examines human social behaviors and actions, social structures, and institutions. It focuses on understanding societies, social structures,

---

52. Van Vugt et al., "Leadership, Followership, and Evolution," 182–96.
53. Van Vugt et al., "Leadership, Followership, and Evolution," 182–96.
54. Meindl, "Romance of Leadership," 285–98; Meindl, et al., "Romance of Leadership," 78–102.
55. Heckscher, "Defining the Post-Bureaucratic Type," 14–62.
56. Heckscher, "Defining the Post-Bureaucratic Type," 14–62.
57. Clinton, *Short History of Modern Leadership*, 87.
58. Mitchell, *Leading, Teaching, and Making Disciples*, 45.

organizations, and group influence on a collective level. The earliest management theories were advanced by sociologists like Karl Marx[59] and Fredrick Taylor.[60]

Karl Marx's Influence on Modern Leadership Theories

Karl Marx (1818–1883) argued that while organizational leaders should maintain power and authority, followers should simply follow orders blindly. In Marx's theoretical framework, the industrial economy and society were zero-sum games where the benefits reaped by one party were the direct outcome of the losses of another.[61] In this context, leaders reaped power, status, and superiority from subordinates who were considered uneducated, ineffectual, and lacking in initiative. On the other hand, followers often engaged in strikes and attempts to sabotage, such as providing less effort, less initiative, and little commitment. In response, leaders subordinated followers. During the industrial revolution, which started in the seventeenth century, leadership theorists used Marx's theory to frame human relationships in organizations.[62]

Fredrick Winslow Taylor's Influence

Taylor (1856–1915) advanced a theory of scientific management in which he sought to improve the efficiency of workers after he was convinced that workers were not performing to their optimum potential for the benefit of factory owners. He developed his theory based on the assumptions that workers are lazy, uneducated, and unskilled, and thus should be strictly managed and supervised. Taylor illustrated his theory in a conversation he had with a follower he was motivating to work harder and produce greater output as a dutiful worker:

> You will do exactly as this man tells you . . . from morning to night. And what's more, no back talk. Do you understand that? When this man tells you to walk, you walk; when he tells you to sit down, you sit down, and you don't talk back to him.[63]

---

59. McLellan, *Karl Marx*.
60. Taylor, *Principles of Scientific Management*.
61. McLellan, *Karl Marx*.
62. Child, *Industrial Relations*.
63. Volti, *Sociology of Work and Occupation*, 30.

Leadership theorists used Taylor's writings to develop the idea that followers are incapable of planning, directing, and controlling themselves without the direct influence of leaders. Psychological perspectives reinforced the sociological perspectives.

Psychological Perspective on Followership

The field of psychology examines human behavior at both the individual and group levels, focusing on how individual perceptions, traits, motives, cognitions, and attributions affect behavior. The foremost psychological theory in leadership is Trait Theory, which explores personal characteristics that distinguish leaders from nonleaders.[64] The theory came out of study of the Great Man Theory, which posits that leadership traits can be determined by exploring leaders throughout history.[65] It assumes that leaders are born rather than made, and that when one lacks the characteristic needed to be a great leader, such a person is relegated to the rank of follower.

The earlier theorists who advanced this point of view were Thomas Carlyle and William James.[66] They argued that history should be understood by examining the conquest of great men—heroes who influenced society through their superior intelligence, creativity, and self-confidence. The traits were considered inherent and thus could not be developed or transferred.[67] The theory led to the emergence of an implicit theory of followership, which consigned followers to nonleadership roles because of their presumed ineptitude and inability to influence leadership processes and outcomes.[68]

The psychological perspective centers leadership in the leader as an individual and not in the context of the reciprocal relationship between leaders and followers. This view was deeply ingrained in leadership theory to the extent that it prevailed against all the earlier voices that held other views about leadership.[69]

---

64. Bass and Bass, *Bass Handbook of Leadership*.
65. Carlyle, *On Heroes, Hero-Worship*.
66. Carlyle, *On Heroes, Hero-Worship*.
67. Galton, *English Men of Science*; Locke and Kirkpatrick, *Essence of Leadership*.
68. Stogdill, "Personal Factors Associated with Leadership," 35–71.
69. Follett, *Essentials of Leadership*; Follett, "Management as a Profession," 7–17.

Philosophical Influence on Followership: Darwinism

Industrial-era worldviews influenced followership perception. One such worldview is attributed to Charles Darwin's notion of the survival of the fittest, which he modeled after the acrimonious relationships among the ancient Greek gods. In ancient Greece, a god gained supremacy over other gods through conquests. According to Greek mythology, "to struggle and compete is natural, good, and right. The winners, by definition, are leaders; the losers are everyone else"[70] or subordinates. The superordinate-subordinate paradigm associated with the gods became one of the cardinal cultural values leadership theorists infused into the terms "follower" and "leader." Darwin's paradigm created false hierarchical prototypes that portrayed followers as passive recipients of leaders' influence. Darwin's viewpoint was both a reflection and justification of his society: "the 19th century England which was reeling on imperialism and material progress."[71]

Thus, leadership theories, like any human dynamics, are socially constructed in a context.[72] Modern leadership theories were founded when follower passivity of the preindustrial slave labor and landlord-tenant relationships were still very strong.[73] For example, follower passivity of the preindustrial slavery era directly influenced industrial-era management theories such as Theory X—a belief that workers are inherently lazy, that they find work distasteful, and they are motivated solely through money.[74] In this theory, man is a machine, "a mechanism with a shadowy entity of a mind attached to it."[75] The mind and the well-being of the workers were not of concern to employers. Theory X, like its subsequent theories, entrenched unidirectional organizational structure, which emphasized leaders' superiority and followers' subordinance.[76] Altogether, sociological, psychological, and philosophical perspectives created dichotomous tendencies that characterized leadership theories during the industrial era.

---

70. Kelley, *Power of Followership*, 40.

71. Kelley, *Power of Followership*, 40.

72. Carsten et al., "Exploring Social Constructions of Followership," 543–62; Uhl-Bien and Pillai, *Romance of Leadership*.

73. Hampton, "Deification of Man."

74. Brown, *Social Psychology of Human Industry*; Henman, Leadership.

75. Brown, *Social Psychology of Human Industry*, 16.

76. Meindl et al., "Romance of Leadership."

Dominant Tendencies During the Industrial Era

Tremendous changes of historical importance preceded the dawn of the industrial era. According to Laura Lynn Hampton,

> this tumultuous time witnessed the end of feudalism, [slavery], voyages to the Orient, the discovery of a New World, the invention of movable print, the revival of Greek and Roman culture, the beginning of modern science, the emergence of nationalism, the weakening of the Roman Catholic Church, and the groundswell of new religious beliefs.[77]

Eighteenth-century writers referred to these social phenomena as the Renaissance. It marked a human attempt to understand the universe anew based on the influence of Platonic dualism, which gave birth to individualism and dualistic tendencies. Philosophically, the emphasis shifted "away from Aristotle [who examined things inductively, particular to universal] and back toward the Neo-Platonism [that was deductive, universal to particular] in the Age of the Fathers"[78] In science, it led to a major intellectual movement in Western civilization that gave birth to humanism.[79] Humanism is a philosophical and ethical theory that places man, rather than God, at the center of the universe. It exalts human reason above revelatory knowledge, scientific facts above faith convictions, and the human mind above humans' emotional bodies. In other words, it secularized science and mystified religion. Whereas science dealt with the empirical world using mechanistic analogies, religion was relegated to otherworldly matters. The leading voice in this change was René Descartes.

THE IMPACT OF RENÉ DESCARTES' (1596–1650) PHILOSOPHY ON FOLLOWERSHIP

Descartes was a French philosopher and the father of modern Western philosophy whose work gave birth to modernity theories that shaped the industrial era. Among other things, Descartes used logic and scientific methods to argue for the "separation of 'the rational mind' from the 'emotional body'" based on his famous argument, "for I consider the mind not as a part of the soul but as the thinking soul in its entirety."[80] Having replaced theocentric

---

77. Hampton, "Deification of Man," 40.
78. Hampton, "Deification of Man," 45.
79. Bufford, *Human Reflex*, 30; Berger et al., *Homeless Mind*.
80. Hampton, "Deification of Man," 40.

authority with anthropocentric authority, he established the human rational mind as the subject of human autonomy over the human emotional body as the object of the former. For instance, "leadership studies have traditionally focused on leaders' minds to the neglect of their bodies, treating leadership as an inherently cerebral and disembodied process, concerned with decision-making, strategy, vision and (changing) 'minds.'"[81] In this case, the effectiveness of leaders in their inspirational and motivational roles is a mental task, and workers' roles are emotional, bodily tasks that are subservient to leaders' mental roles. So "[w]hile followers' bodies are often centrally implicated in the outcome of such processes, leaders and their practices are assumed to be almost entirely disembodied."[82] Descartes's influence created individualism and dualism.

Individualism

Individualism undergirded the industrial era's leadership theories. Most organizations during the industrial era constructed human relationships on dialectical terms whereby an individual figure was placed at its center, a system was set in the background, and communities were incidental.[83] Individualism focused on the cognitive traits of charismatic individuals who were accorded superior status above the rest of the community in the same way the rational mind was separated from the emotional body.

Individualism was entrenched in organizations through hierarchical structures in which followers were treated as passive recipients of the leaders' influence. As a result, the theorists focused on simplifying and rationalizing organizational structures and processes aimed at maintaining stability and certainty.[84] On the human side, leaders depersonalized workers by prioritizing their machine side over their human side.[85] Once depersonalized, workers were reduced to machines whose emotional selves became alienated from the machine selves. Managerially, "corporations promised life-long job security to employees in exchange for their loyalty, obedience, and hard work."[86] Under such contractual arrangement, organizations attributed their success to leaders' actions.[87] The negligence of the followership role

81. Collinson, "Rethinking Followership," 179–89; Gardner, *Changing Minds*.
82. Collinson, "Rethinking Followership," 179–89.
83. Collinson, "Rethinking Followership," 179–89.
84. Ilinitch et al., "New Organizational Forms and Strategies," 211–20.
85. Collinson, "Rethinking Followership," 179–89.
86. Baker, "Followership," 50–60.
87. Berg, "Resurrecting the Muse," 27–52.

conditioned followers to be dependent to the extent that when the situations changed later, "leaders found that their followers were ill equipped to take initiative or to collaborate with their superiors" without reorientation.[88]

Furthermore, in the wake of the growth of companies into complex corporations, leadership theorists and practitioners made no effort to develop a complex method of understanding organizational complexities. Instead, leadership was singled out as the key factor in understanding organizational success and failure.[89] These oversimplifications entrenched the "concept of leadership, which has assumed a romanticized, larger than life role as a result."[90]

Consequently, leadership research, education, and practice preoccupied themselves with leadership based on the assumption that the nature of leadership determines the success and failure of an organization. In this environment, followers' roles in organizational dynamics were marginal when compared with the leaders' roles. Hence, organizations focused their attention on developing leadership skills that make a leader successful.[91] The exclusive emphasis on leaders ignored the relational dynamics in human organizations. Thus, "whereas knowing what people do individually is important, one cannot adequately understand social structures, without exploring what people do in relationship to the other participants."[92] In addition, individualistic approaches distort reality because distinctive "boundaries are not fixed perimeters, but rather, are sets of functions that dynamically interpenetrate one another."[93] In essence, individualism that romanticized leadership created an asymmetrical wedge between leaders and followers.[94] In the next section, I will discuss dualism and its impact on organizational culture during the industrial era.

Dualism

The industrial era was characterized by dualistic tendencies in human thinking and relationships, which prioritized differences and similarities over interconnections and interdependence or either/or categories rather

---

88. Berg, "Resurrecting the Muse," 27–52.
89. Smith and Dyer, "Rise and Transformation," 28–51.
90. Meindl and Ehrlich, "Romance of Leadership," 91–109.
91. Maxwell, *21 Irrefutable Laws of Leadership*.
92. Courtright et al., "Interaction Patterns," 773–802.
93. Cilliers, *Complexity and Postmodernism*, 135.
94. Meindl et al., "Romance of Leadership."

than both/and categories.[95] For that matter, in the "study of leadership, 'dualisms pop up everywhere.'"[96] For instance, some of the dichotomies in leadership theories include

> transformational/transactional; leadership/management; leaders/followers; leaders/contexts; born/made leaders; task/people orientation; theory X/theory Y; one best way/contingent; organic/mechanistic, autocratic/participative; forceful/enabling; saviors/scapegoats; charismatic/quiet; and essentialist/ constructionist.[97]

The dualistic tendencies created a dichotomy between leadership and followership. Throughout the industrial era, leaders were perceived as active and heterogeneous, whereas followers were regarded as homogenous and passive recipients of leaders' influence. So while leaders oversaw planning, managing, and controlling the leadership process, followers were subjected to passive dependence.[98]

The challenge with dichotomous tendencies in leadership theories "is not so much the creation of distinctions per se, but rather the tendency both to overstate them by neglecting underlying inter-relationships and to create unwarranted asymmetries between them."[99] James M. Burns noted that, "leader-follower bifurcation is one of the most serious failures in the study of leadership."[100] For example, even though Burns was conscious of its damaging effects, he acknowledged that it was "exceptionally difficult" to make any linkage between leadership and followership in his own study and life:

> I think my book is overly dichotomized . . . I tried to present the conceptual frameworks of transformational leadership and transactional leadership as a contrast as though there is no connection between them. I now think this is wrong. There is a stronger connection between transformational leadership and transactional leadership than I led readers to believe. I think we have a spectrum. A few leaders operate wholly on the transactional side and a few leaders operate wholly on the transformational side, but most work on both sides of that spectrum and combine transformational leadership and transactional leadership. I do not know why I did not see the mixture there.[101]

95. Frye et al., "Embracing Spiritual Followership"; Senge, *Fifth Discipline*.
96. Harter, "Leadership as the Promise," 77–87.
97. Harter, "Leadership as the Promise," 77–87.
98. Smith, "Followership Behaviors."
99. Burns, *Leadership*, viii.
100. Burns, *Leadership*, 3.
101. Burns, "Structure of Moral Leadership," 87.

Burns' admission of the negative influence of dualism illustrates how dichotomous thinking minimizes the complex nature of leadership that requires relational analysis and approach.[102] Whereas "analytical categories of difference"[103] are necessary, leadership scholars can use systems thinking and strategic essentialism—proposed by Peter Senge and Ajnesh Prasad, respectively—and the seamless mental model the Acholi people espouse to conduct research and engage in discourse without entrenching their bifurcating tendencies.[104] (Systems thinking is a mental model that regards entities as systems in which the parts influence each other within a whole. On the other hand, strategic essentialism advocates for the development of complex systems to understand complex organizational structures rather than simplifying them.) Systems thinking offers followers agency because it allows leadership theorists and practitioners to use analytical categories of difference to subvert their assumptions that polarize classes of difference into absolute opposites.[105] On the other hand, strategic essentialism advocates for the development of complex systems to understand complex organizational structures. Therefore, the impact of dualistic tendencies that were heightened by the renaissance and the economic boom after the Second World War prevented leadership theorists and practitioners from ever according followers an active role in leadership processes and outcomes.

Rationale for Dichotomous Thinking

Leadership dynamics are complex and elusive. Burns contends that "leadership is one of the most observed and least understood phenomena on earth."[106] While commenting on the challenges inherent in leadership studies Jeffrey Pfeffer concurred that, "persistent ambiguities make leadership difficult to research as well as challenging to enact."[107] In their attempt to simplify the ambiguities, researchers have always employed dichotomous thinking and approaches which ignore the dynamic nature of leadership processes and outcomes. For instance, rather than analyzing the complex, interconnected, and ever-changing nuances of leadership theory and

---

102. Hollander, "Essential Interdependence of Leadership," 71–75.

103. Alcoff, "Objectivity and Its Politics," 835–48.

104. Prasad, "Beyond Analytical Dichotomies," 567–95; Senge and Sterman, "Systems Thinking and Organizational Learning," 137–50.

105. Alcoff, "Objectivity and Its Politics," 319; Prasad, "Beyond Analytical Dichotomies," 567–95.

106. Burns, *Leadership*, 2.

107. Pfeffer and Press, *Ambiguity of Leadership*, 5.

practice, leadership researchers examine the constituent dynamics independently. In such cases, they absolutize the distinctions among leadership variables into immutable polarities. According to David Collinson, "Dichotomization also involves simultaneous and asymmetrical processes of privileging, marginalizing, and excluding. Furthermore, it tends to narrow down the range of concepts, issues, and variables as well as limiting and fixing their causal direction."[108] Thus, theorists ignore ambiguous dynamics such as power, authority, tensions, paradoxes, and contradictions. The polarizing dialecticisms that characterize leadership communication literature are experienced as choice points within the research process. Overall,

> Like a camera angle, research methodologies offer a view of our subjects that inevitably precludes other angles and views. In both theory and methods, the buy-in process by researchers over time produces dominant versus marginal perspectives, mainstream versus emerging research, the *au courant* (up to date) versus the passé (out of date).[109]

Therefore, in their attempt to simplify leadership, researchers and practitioners preferred a traditional hierarchical organizational ethos that is centered on planning, controlling, and managing. However, the impact of global forces like eroding competitiveness, explosive technological, political, and environmental change, and the dissolution of market and national boundaries have exposed the ineffectiveness of the rigid and dichotomous tendencies associated with traditional hierarchical organizational structures and systems.[110]

In the emerging organizational environment, effectiveness is predicated on "versatile, agile and ambidextrous practices that require a capacity to deal with uncertainty, unpredictability, paradox, simultaneity, and ambiguity in more subtle ways.[111] In the new context, tensions and paradoxes act as catalysts for creative thinking and innovations, without which postmodern organizations cannot survive the tidal wave of changes in the twenty-first century. So rather than dichotomizing distinctions into either/or categories,

---

108. Collinson, "Dichotomies, Dialectics and Dilemmas," 36–55.

109. Fairhurst, *Dualisms in Leadership Research*, 379; Reuther and Fairhurst, "Chaos Theory," 236–56.

110. Fisher-Yoshida and Geller, Transnational Leadership Development.

111. Collinson, "Rethinking Followership," 36; Barge, "Pivotal Leadership and the Art," 56–78; Wilkinson, *Ambiguity Advantage*; Yukl and Lepsinger, "Why Integrating the Leading," 361–75.

organizations adopt a both/and mindset to establish the creative balance that stimulates innovation and progress without compromising stability.[112]

In summary, individualistic and dichotomous tendencies romanticized leadership at the expense of followership during the industrial era. However, in the twenty-first century, leadership is being reconceptualized as an emergent property of group interaction.[113] In the next section, I highlight the traces of the pervasive influence of the romance of leadership during the industrial era.

Traces of the Romance of Leadership in the Antecedent Theories

The romance of leadership dominated research, education, and practice for over a century, and its traces are ingrained in all the leadership theories developed during the industrial era. The antecedent leadership theories fall into three categories: leader-centric, follower-centric, and relational. Although all the antecedent theories underwent tremendous adjustments toward embracing active followership, the romance of leadership entrenched dichotomous tendencies that objectified followership as passive recipients of the leaders' influence. Each case emphasized leadership development and its subjugating influence over followers.

SIMPLICITY THEORIES: LEADER-CENTRIC

Leadership theories started as a simple explanation of organizational process and outcome through the lens of a leader. In the industrial era, theorists and practitioners gave little attention to other variables, and when they did, the focus was on leaders and leading. Leader-centric theories viewed leaders as the only active agents affecting group and organizational outcomes.[114] Whereas status, power, influence, and prestige belonged to leaders, followers were socialized to a passive followership schema.[115] The dominant theories identified under this approach include:

---

112. Collins and Porras, *Built to Last*.

113. Fisher-Yoshida and Geller, *Transitional Leadership Development*; Prasad, "Beyond Analytical Dichotomies," 567–95.

114. Hollander, "Essential Interdependence of Leadership," 71–75; Meindl et al., "Romance of Leadership," 78; Yukl and Van Fleet, "Theory and Research on Leadership," 374–86.

115. Hirschhorn, "Leaders and Followers," 177–96.

"Great Man" Theory: 1841–1904

The phrase "great man" defined the concept of leadership in the nineteenth century. Leadership theorists and practitioners believed that leaders were born and not made. Hence, leadership qualities were inherent. Second, men with those unique qualities were few. Such qualities were identified in highly capable leaders like Alexander the Great, Hitler, and Churchill. Therefore, efforts were devoted to studying individuals who had achieved tremendous success in the history of their communities. During this era, one was either a leader or a nobody.

The central architect of the Great Man Theory was Thomas Carlyle, who in his book, *On Heroes, Hero-Worship and the Heroic in History*, attributed to leaders extraordinary intellectual ability without which societies would not solve any problems.[116] According to Carlyle, these leaders deserved to rule without question. Although subsequent theorists quickly challenged the Great Man Theory, its image of a leader as a larger-than-life individual outlived its demise. For instance, Robert Kelley reported that Donald Kennedy, the former president of Stanford University, exemplified its influence in his speech: "We do so out of faith that [leaders'] capacity for wise and compassionate leadership is the best possible guarantee of the survival of everything we think is important."[117] In this era, there were no leadership theories other than the larger-than-life leaders and their followers because leadership talents and skills were assumed to be inborn.[118]

Traits Theory: 1904–1948

Building on the pervasive influence of the Great Man Theory, psychologists in the early twentieth century, advanced Traits Theory based on the argument that there are necessary traits a leader needs in order to attain a leadership position and to effectively influence followers toward the realization of a desired outcome.[119] Among other things, they focused on identifying specific inherent physical, social, and personal unique features that set apart leaders from nonleaders.[120] Their research was preoccupied with

---

116. Carlyle, *On Heroes, Hero-Worship*.
117. Kelley, *Power of Followership*, 14.
118. Galton, *Hereditary Genius*.
119. Dinh and Lord, "Implications," 651–60; Hogan et al., "What We Know about Leadership," 493–504; Stogdill, "Personal Factors Associated With Leadership," 35–71.
120. Allen, *Management and Organization*; Bernard, *Introduction to Social Psychology*.

those people who had exhibited extraordinary leadership and attributes that set them apart from the rest.[121] Although this theory did not last for long just like the one before it, it nonetheless entrenched further the romance of leadership without moderation.

Behavioral Theories: 1948–1967

After the Second World War, leadership theorists sought for those behaviors that influenced followers toward specific goals. Key studies under this category carried out at Ohio State University and the University of Michigan focused on behaviors related to task and initiation of structure in work environment (directive and goal-oriented behaviors—initiation), as well as those behaviors that focused on leader/follower relationships (relationship-oriented behaviors—consideration).[122] Although theorists believed these behaviors could be acquired, their ideas were conceived under the framework which viewed leaders as the levers that cause followers to act.[123] The theory retained the larger-than-life leader image in the leadership process.

Contingency Theories: 1967–1980

In these theories, followers received recognition as one of the variables a leader needs to manipulate in order to achieve an organizational goal.[124] However, its construct favored leaders at the expense of followers. For example, whereas followers were involved in the decision-making process, their involvement was limited to complying with the chosen course of action.[125] There was no focus on the relational dynamics between leaders and followers apart from the leaders' relational abilities to influence followers' effective participation in leadership processes and outcomes. The leader was still the prime mover.

---

121. Horner, "Leadership Theory," 4.

122. Judge et al., "Forgotten Ones?," 36–51; Komarn, "Consideration, Initiating Structure," 349–61.

123. Uhl-Bien et al., "Followership Theory," 83–104.

124. Fielder, *Theory of Leadership Effectiveness*; Hersey and Blanchard, *Management of Organizational Behavior*.

125. Vroom, and Jago, "On the Validity," 151–62; Vroom and Yetton, *Leadership and Decision-Making*.

Complexity Theories: 1980–1986

In the complexity era, leadership theorists recognized the complexity and fluidity of leadership phenomena, and as such they started to explore other elements of leadership that they had hitherto ignored. Three prominent approaches characterize this era: leader-centered, follower-centric, and relational.

Leader-Centered Views

In this category, theorists viewed factors of leadership through the lens of the leaders for the purposes of enhancing the effectiveness of leaders as the prime movers. Some of the dominant theories are charismatic and transformational leadership.

Charismatic Theories

People like Max Weber, Rabindra Kanungo, and Robert House advanced charismatic theory. In this category, leaders were regarded as people with charisma, which referred to " special personality characteristic that gives a person superhuman or exceptional powers and is reserved for a few, is of divine origin, and results in the person being treated as a leader."[126] Leadership qualities include display of confidence and ability to persuasively articulate vision. These qualities inspire high expectations in followers and instantaneous following.[127]

Servant Leadership

Robert Greenleaf introduced and popularized servant leadership based on Hermann Hesse's novel, *Journey to the East*. Vexed with the big-man syndrome that had hitherto pervaded leadership prototypes, Greenleaf introduced a servanthood image to reverse the lens.[128] According to Greenleaf, the hallmark of authentic leadership depends upon a leader's willingness to serve others. Thus his theory refocused leadership to followers above

---

126. Weber, *Economy and Society*.

127. House, "Path-Goal Theory of Leader," 321–39; Kanungo, "Culture and Work Alienation," 795–815.

128. Greenleaf, *Servant Leadership*.

organizational goals.[129] However, it is still leader-centered because it locates leadership in the leader rather than in the reciprocal interaction between leaders and followers.

Transformational Leadership

James V. Downton introduced transformational leadership, but James MacGregor Burns developed it further. Other theorists like Bernard Bass expanded Burns' works. It focuses on the process where a leader inspires and empowers followers to develop and maximize their potential. So it attributes to the leader the role of inspiring and motivating followers to commit themselves to the desired goals. The central point of the theory is that leaders transform nonperformers into star performers.[130] Thus, followers are objects of leaders' influence.

Whereas the theory has some focus on the leader-follower relationship, it does not designate followers as active agents who initiate things in the organization on their own accord. Therefore, like the previous theories, it projects leaders as the catalysts of the followers' actions. In this theory, followers are unable to make independent contributions in organizational processes and outcomes without the catalytic role of the leaders. The objective image of followers is expressed in such a statement: "Any leader who has only followers around him will be called upon to continually draw his own resources to get things done."[131] Ultimately, the argument here is that "the bottom line for the follower is what a leader is capable of."[132] All these negative stereotypes painted followers as inconsequential in leadership processes and outcomes. For that matter, there was no need to focus on followers when there were leaders over them. Under this theory, it was inconceivable to think of active followership as a complementary role to that of the leadership role. However, since the end of the twentieth century, globalization forces have blurred the distinction between leaders and followers. These changes influenced new perceptions that drew attention to follower-centric theories.

---

129. Patterson, "Servant Leadership Roundtable," 1–13.
130. Burns, *Leadership*; Bass and Riggio, *Transformational Leadership*.
131. Maxwell, *Developing the Leaders around You*, 10.
132. Maxwell, *21 Irrefutable Laws of Leadership*, 51.

Follower-Centric Theories

The follower-centric approach emerged to counter the leader-centric orientation to leadership. It adopted a bottom-up approach in which followers were regarded as influential agents in the leadership process. Therefore, followers were examined to determine the effectiveness of leaders.[133] Under this approach, leadership is a social construction in which the leadership is "generated in the cognitive, attributional and social identity processes of followers."[134] Although the theory is about followers, its view of followers focuses on leaders. That is, the theory uses the perspectives of followers to develop effective leaders.

Romance of Leadership

Faced with the increasing complexity of organizational culture following the influences of technological innovations and globalization processes, James R. Meindl and his colleagues attacked Western culture for examining organizational performance by only studying leaders.[135] They argued that the exclusive focus on leaders exaggerates leaders' actions and influence. According to their conclusion: "Leadership has assumed a romanticized, larger than life role."[136] Instead, they believed that followers socially construct leadership.[137] However, while this approach shifted leadership focus toward followers, it was still talking about leaders through the eyes of followers rather than followership from the perspective of followers.

Implicit Leadership Theories

This theory was advanced by Dov Eden and Israel Uri Leviatan; James S. Phillips and Robert G. Lord; and Michael C. Rush, Jay C. Thomas, and Robert G. Lord. They pointed out "that followers have beliefs and schema for leader behavior that influence the extent to which they attribute effectiveness and normative evaluations such as 'good' or 'bad' to a leader."[138] In return, followers apply these "schemas to encode leadership information,

---

133. Crossman and Crossman, "Conceptualizing Followership," 481–97.
134. Uhl-Bien et al., "Followership Theory," 86–104.
135. Meindl et al., "Romance of Leadership."
136. Meindl et al., "Romance of Leadership," 79.
137. Bligh and Meindl, "Charting the Language of Leadership," 562–74.
138. Rush, "Implicit Leadership Theory"; Phillips and Lord, "Causal Attributions and Perceptions," 143–63; Eden and Leviatan, "Implicit Leadership Theory," 736–41.

which serves as essential elements of organizational sense making." Followers form their implicit leadership theories through socialization and past experiences.[139] Hence, this theory was seen as a step toward a followership focus because it attributed to followers their decision to follow leaders.[140]

Social Identity Theory of Leadership

Social identity theory examines intergroup behaviors. It stipulates that people develop self-consciousness from the group where they belong.[141] Hence, followers' prototypical behaviors influence leadership behaviors. For example, Michael A. Hogg[142] discovered that, "Followers empower individuals as leaders—they create a status differential between the leader and the rest of the group and set up conditions conducive to the use (and abuse) of power."[143] Implicit leadership theories and social identity theories gave rise to the relational views of leadership in which leadership is regarded as a reciprocal transaction between leaders and followers.

Relational Views

The relational approach assumes influence reciprocity between leaders and followers. It focuses on the study of the process by which followers engage and influence leadership processes and outcomes.[144] It faults the leader-centric approach because it focuses on explicit behaviors while ignoring the implicit dynamics that drive leadership.[145] The relational approach focuses on how leadership variables engage each other and why each is influenced by the corresponding actions of the others.[146] It depicts followers as active and dynamic agents.[147] Relational views started quite early in leadership research, but they were overshadowed by the romance of leadership until the end of the twentieth century. In the next section, I will discuss the major views under this category.

    139. Epitropaki and Martin, "Implicit Leadership Theories," 293–310; Schyns and Meindl, *Implicit Leadership Theories*.
    140. Sivasubramaniam et al., "In the Eyes," 27–42.
    141. Hogg and Reid, "Social Identity, Self Categorization," 89–106.
    142. Hogg, "Social Identity Theory of Leadership," 184–200.
    143. Hogg, "Social Identity Theory of Leadership," 184.
    144. Oc and Bashshur, "Followership, Leadership and Social Influence," 919–34.
    145. Lord and Brown, "Leadership, Values, and Subordinate Self-concepts," 133–52.
    146. Uhl-Bien et al., "Followership Theory," 83–104.
    147. Lord, "Four Leadership Principles."

Power With

Mary P. Follett, who is referred to as "the prophet of management,"[148] is perhaps the earliest theorist to see the relational influence between leaders and followers.[149] While she acknowledged the hierarchical leadership paradigm, she rejected the idea of unidirectional influence. Instead, she asserted that leaders and followers take orders from each other. She rejected as overexaggerated the idea that prefers leaders over followers in the discussion of the relationship between managers and followers.[150] While advancing her theory of "power with," she called for the recognition of the reciprocal relationship between leaders and followers.[151] Follett argued that, "we need to understand that authority is an 'intermingling of forces' between leaders and followers wherein a self-generating process of control is created."[152] She called for the empowerment of workers to take up full responsibility for their own work. She believed that both management and workers have a common interest in the survival and prosperity of an organization. Consequently, she called for separate research in the field of followership. However, Follett's ideas were not adopted in leadership research, education, or practice for several decades.[153]

Hollander's Relational Approach

Edwin P. Hollander discovered that leadership is a role developed and enacted in a relational process. He faulted the view of leadership as a position.[154] He was particularly concerned about the lack of interest in followers and the underlying processes of leadership dynamics.[155] He also pointed out the "failure to distinguish leadership as a process from the leader as a person

---

148. Graham, *Mary Parker Follett*, 1.
149. Follett, "Leader and Expert," 220.
150. Follett, *Essentials of Leadership*.
151. Follett, *Essentials of Leadership*.
152. Follett, *Essentials of Leadership*, 40; Follett, "Leader and Expert," 220–43; Follett, "Management as a Profession," 7–17.
153. Follett, "Management as a Profession."
154. Hollander, "Essential Interdependence of Leadership," 71–75; Hollander, "Legitimacy, Power and Influence," 27–47; Hollander, "Conformity Status and Idiosyncrasy Credit," 117–27; Hollander, "Style, Structure and Setting," 1–9; Hollander, "Leadership and Power," 485–538; Hollander, "On the Central Role," 39–52.
155. Hollander, "Essential Interdependence of Leadership," 71–75; Hollander, "Leadership, Followership, Self and Others," 43–54.

who occupies a central role in that process."[156] Consequently, he called for the understanding of "leadership as an influence relationship between two or more people for attainment of mutual goals in a group situation."[157] However, like Follett, his views were not immediately adopted in mainstream leadership theory.

LEADER-MEMBER EXCHANGE THEORY

This theory stipulates that leadership is a transaction between leaders and followers.[158] It focuses on leader-follower relationships toward a common outcome.[159] It states that leaders build relationships with in-group persons—those who are engaged beyond formal job requirements—and the out-group persons—those who are engaged within formal contractual obligations. These relationships depend on an exchange in which the leader engages more with the in-group than the out-group. While the earliest work on the theory supported subjugating hierarchy in organizations,[160] the latest work recognizes active followership.[161]

Although it includes followers in a relational process, it is still leader-centric because it privileges leaders as the initiator of the transaction.[162] Second, it assumes that the relationships are built upon the desire for an exchange as offered by the leader. The theory ignores what followers want to offer beyond the material rewards leaders offer. In that regard, it limits followership to followers' participation in leadership processes and outcomes at the expense of followers' rights of and demand for ownership. Hence, it reduces followers' stakes to existential needs that leaders supply at the expense of the followers' identity and quest for self-consciousness and fulfillment. People do not necessarily work only to meet their existential needs. They also work from a sense of who they are for the purpose of self-fulfillment beyond monetary gains.[163] Thus, leader-member exchange theory ignores

---

156. Hollander and Julian, "Contemporary Trends in the Analysis," 387–97.
157. Hollander and Julian, "Contemporary Trends in the Analysis," 387–97.
158. Graen et al., "Effects of Leader-member Exchange," 109–31; Graen and Scandura, "Toward a Psychology," 175–208; Liden et al., "Leader-member Exchange Theory," 47–119.
159. Graen and Uhl-Bien, "Relationship-based Approach to Leadership," 219–47.
160. Dansereau et al., "Vertical Dyad Linkage Approach," 46–78.
161. Uhl-Bien et al., "Implication of Leader-member Exchange," 137–86.
162. Uhl-Bien et al., "Implication of Leader-member Exchange," 137.
163. Clinton, *Leadership Emergence Theory*.

the follower identity as the platform for developing a leadership model that accords leaders and followers equal attention.

Toxic Triangle

The toxic triangle is an environment that abets destructive leadership.[164] It is concerned with bad organizational output that emanates from a combination of bad leaders, followers, and atmospheres. Understanding toxic leadership requires a systems approach that looks at multiple factors which combine to abet it rather than only leadership behaviors. The followers who breed toxic leaders fall into three categories: susceptible followers, conformers, and colluders.[165] Conformers are those followers who go along with destructive leaders out of fear. On the other hand, colluders are followers who deliberately support toxic leaders for personal gain. The authors' import is to watch out for toxic leaders, susceptible followers, and unhealthy conditions that nurture toxic triangles.

In summary, although leadership theory has undergone many changes, the greater-than-life image of leaders outlived all theories for over a century. The longevity of the larger-than-life syndrome was sustained by dualistic tendencies. However, when the knowledge era emerged amidst the tumbling of corporate giants like Enron, the resultant pressure swayed leadership researchers and practitioners to appreciate and enact a relational approach in the leadership process. Thus, the change of focus from leader-centric approaches to relational approaches has been mainly reactionary rather than proactive. The ideal relational leadership theory needs a thorough analysis beyond expedient cultural imperatives. In the following section, I will discuss the emergence of followership theory since the last quarter of the twentieth century, and factors that stalled research interests in followership development and enactment.

FOLLOWERSHIP THEORY: A CONSTRUCT WITHOUT EMPIRICAL EVIDENCE

Unlike the industrial era, which was characterized predominantly by individualism and dualism, the knowledge era, within which followership theory was founded, is marked by flexibility, interdependence, and

---

164. Padilla et al., "Toxic Triangle," 176–94.
165. Padilla et al., "Toxic Triangle," 176–94.

interconnectedness.[166] In this era, the asymmetrical wedge between leadership and followership was reversed,[167] and the leadership spotlight that focused exclusively on leaders for a century steadily broadened to include followers among other factors that influence leadership processes and outcomes.

The fulcrum of leadership phenomena "resides in the context of the interactions between leaders and followers," which forms a symbiotic system throughout the leadership process.[168] Leadership is no longer seen as individual acts by leaders, and followership is no longer seen as what followers do as passive recipients of leaders' influence. Rather, leadership is regarded as a "relationship wherein leaders and followers collaborate in a particular context because they are mutually invested in a direction and because they are inherently interdependent in a common process."[169] There is consensus that the traditional boundary between leaders and followers is a myth. In this new era, organizations cannot survive "without responsible individuals who could be productive as both leaders and followers."[170]

Therefore, followership has gained recognition as an active role in leadership processes and outcomes.[171] For instance, when corporate hierarchies flattened workforces and eliminated middle managers over the past two decades,[172] corporations asked followers to assume leaders' roles to increase organizational efficiency against the pressure of emergent market forces.[173] Second, in the church there is increasing clamor for organizational structure that supports member development and participation beyond leaders and a ministry paradigm beyond the four walls of the church and denominational barriers.[174]

The acknowledgment of followership as a distinct discipline in leadership studies began when leadership theorists realized that the romance of leadership distorted the meaning of leadership.[175] Instead, theorists discovered that leaders and followers both perform leadership and followership

---

166. Senge and Sterman, "Systems Thinking and Organizational Learning," 137–50.
167. Bennis, *Managing the Dream*.
168. Northouse, *Leadership*, 5.
169. Rost, "Followership," 53–66.
170. Smith and Dyer, "Rise and Transformation," 28–51.
171. Lundin and Lancaster, "Beyond Leadership," 777–80.
172. Rajan and Wulf, "Flattening Firm."
173. Hughes et al., *Leadership*.
174. Allen, *Future Church*.
175. Burns, *Leadership*.

roles interchangeably.[176] These discoveries necessitated the establishment of followership as a distinct essential discipline in leadership research, education, and practice.[177]

In this section, I will discuss the evolution of followership theory by highlighting factors that led to its recognition as a distinct discipline that is complementary to the leadership role. I will also show how the theory simultaneously stalled and abetted interest in the development and enactment of followership identity, roles, and behaviors.

Exogenous Factors That Influenced the Recognition of Followership Theory

The postindustrial economy is influenced by factors like globalization and technology.[178] For instance, the "technology that was meant to simplify work has in fact networked the world, diminished distance and boundaries and created relationships where none previously existed."[179] In this economy, "knowledge is a core commodity and the rapid production of knowledge and innovation is critical to organizational survival."[180] While in the industrial era organizations preoccupied themselves with management of physical products,[181] postindustrial organizations focus on managing intangible products like knowledge, where "The goal is to cultivate, protect, and use difficult-to-imitate knowledge assets as compared to pure commodity-instigated production."[182]

Likewise, instead of seeking to simplify the process of adaptation, organizations in the new era gain competence by adapting complex structures based on the law of requisite variety originally suggested by William

---

176. Ciulla, *Ethics of Leadership*; Gronn, "Leadership"; Hackman and Wageman, "Asking the Right Question"; Rost, *Leadership for the Twenty-first Century*; Williams and Miller, "Change the Way You Persuade," 65–73.

177. Dvir and Shamir, "Follower Development Characteristics," 327–44; Hollander, "Legitimacy, Power and Influence," 27–47; Howell and Shamir, "Role of Follower," 96–112; Sy, "What Do You Think?," 73–84.

178. Halal and Taylor, *Twenty-first Century Economics*; Hitt, "Presidential Address," 218–24.

179. Fisher-Yoshida and Geller, Transnational Leadership Development *Development*, 40.

180. Bettis and Hitt, "New Competitive Landscape," 7–19.

181. Boisot, *Knowledge Assets*; Schneider, "Stakeholder Model of Organizational Leadership," 209–20.

182. Nonaka and Nishiguchi, "Introduction," 3–9.

Ross Ashby,[183] and which Bill McKelvey & Marcel H. Boisot adopted and renamed the Law of Requisite Complexity.[184] That is, "it takes complexity to defeat complexity—a system must possess complexity equal to that of its environment in order to function effectively"[185]

Furthermore, the dominant organizational theories during the industrial era sought stability and avoided uncertainty.[186] They also focused on micromanagement of workers to attain leadership goals.[187] However, in the postindustrial era, leadership is regarded as a complex phenomenon based on group dynamic process.[188]

In America, successful post-World War II "corporations promised lifelong job security to employees in exchange for their loyalty, obedience, and hard work."[189] In such cases, leadership theorists and practitioners ignored both the leader-follower relationships and the active role of followers. However, following corporate restructuring due to the downsizing trends of the 1980s and 1990s, employees adopted a new psychological contract when they were entrusted with traditional leadership roles like decision-making and initiative-taking.[190] Since then, organizations have invested in high-quality workers with higher leverage to manage the ever-changing business terrains that require high skills to retain customers.[191] Therefore, postindustrial era technology puts people rather than organizations in control. Brain power and customer choice drive the market.[192] The new employee status as partners has endeared them to work beyond a mere sense of duty and material reward.

The impact of technological revolution and globalization processes has effected new changes in organizational structures and processes. For instance, postindustrial organizations have adopted complex approaches to

---

183. Ashby, *Design for a Brain*.

184. McKelvey and Boisot, "Transcendental Organizational Foresight."

185. Uhl-Bien et al., "Complexity Leadership Theory," 109–39.

186. Ilinitch et al., "New Organizational Forms and Strategies," 211–20.

187. Bass, *Leadership and Performance*, 321–39; Zaccaro and Klimoski, "Nature of Organizational Leadership," 3–41.

188. Heifetz, *Leadership Without Easy Answers*; Heifetz and Linsky, *Leadership on the Line*; Parks, *Leadership Can be Taught*.

189. Smith and Dyer, "Rise and Transformation," 28–51.

190. Hall, *Modernity*; Potter et al., "Leading the New Professional," 145–52; Rousseau, "Psychological and Implied Contracts," 121–39.

191. Offermann, *Leadership Followership Focus Group*; Useem, "Corporate Education and Training," 292–326.

192. Baum, "Competing in the 21st Century."

understanding organizational complexities.[193] Some of the specific changes are as follows.

Flexible Role Orientation

The high competition associated with the information era requires flexibility. For example, whereas effective production during the industrial era was based on mastering specific skills and procedures,[194] production in the information era requires creativity and innovation to cope with current organizational dynamics.[195] For that matter, organizations without a flexible role orientation can't flourish in the new era.

Universal Information Access

The information era has lowered bureaucratic cultures in organizations.[196] For instance, the internet allows followers to access information previously reserved for leaders and to develop a social network of support beyond leaders.[197] Thus, "leaders are no longer the exclusive source of vital information about their companies or fields; therefore, they can no longer expect to be followed blindly by their now well-informed, more skeptical ranks."[198] The universal information eroded the justification of the romance of leadership. Therefore, organizations have expanded the role of workers beyond the contractual employee status to partner status with full ownership rights and obligations.

Horizontal Organizational Structure

Technology altered the nature of competition and strategy, and thus introduced a new organizational culture. Theorists look at technology epistemologically. That is, "it is not something that somehow exists outside of people's brains. Like science, culture, and art, technology is something that

---

193. Smith and Dyer; "Rise and Transformation," 28–51.
194. Ilgen and Hollenbeck, "Structure of Work," 165–207.
195. Webster, "Chicken or Egg?," 53–67.
196. Williamson, *Economic Institutions of Capitalism*.
197. Brown, "New Followership," 68; Cross and Parker, *Hidden Power of Social Networks*.
198. Brown, "New Followership," 68.

we know, and technological change should be regarded properly as a set of changes in our knowledge."[199]

The traditional managerial mindset that limited leaders' roles to planning, managing, and directing followers is irrelevant in the new era.[200] For instance, "To have strategic flexibility, firms must use a flexible process of strategic decision making to maintain flexibility in the deployment of critical resources."[201] The flexible role orientation has introduced a learning-oriented culture that has flattened organizational structure.[202] Unlike hierarchical structures, flattened structures decentralize decision-making.[203] Consequently, these changes blur the traditional distinction between leaders and followers.[204]

New Form of Authority

The impact of globalization and technological innovations on corporate hierarchies "flattened" workforces. In response, corporations replaced middle managers with effective followers to increase efficiency.[205] Consequently, a paradigm shift occurred in the perception of leadership dynamics that highlighted the significance of followership in organizational success.[206]

The flat organizational structures prompted corporations to expand the role of followers and to reconsider how people work, what skills they need, and what kinds of careers they expect. According to Larry Hirschhorn, organizations expect people to bring all their faculties to their jobs.[207] As a result, organizations have adopted a new concept of authority and culture in which superiors and subordinates acknowledge their co-dependence. The flat structure has emboldened followers to assume full ownership of their own initiatives and participation, and created a culture whereby the patron-client relationship between leaders and followers counts as a leadership failure.

199. Mokyr, *Lever of Riches*, 52.
200. Bettis and Hitt, "New Competitive Landscape," 7–19; Bettis and Prahalad, "Dominant Logic," 5–14.
201. Sanchez, "Strategic Flexibility in Product Competition," 135–59.
202. Mitroff et al., *Framebreak*.
203. Halal, "From Hierarchy to Enterprise," 69–83; Mitroff et al., *Framebreak*.
204. Fisher-Yoshida and Geller, *Transnational Leadership Development*.
205. Hughes et al., *Leadership*; Rajan and Wulf, "Flattening Firm."
206. Rosenbach and Pittman, "Performance and Relationship Questionnaire."
207. Hirschborn, "Leaders and Followers."

Leadership Failures in Africa

In Africa, leadership failure is influencing the demand for effective followership.[208] Many have lost confidence in their leaders to fulfill the rising expectations for holistic transformation and development despite the "large followership leaders have built" since the 1960s.[209] African scholars no longer surrender the communal nature of their society and societal responsibility of their people,[210] the burden of effective and accountable leadership, and the quality of socioeconomic and spiritual transformation to the whims of "leaders no matter how exemplary, messianic, heroic, or revolutionary they may be."[211] Instead, Africans increasingly demand an acknowledgment of the reciprocal relationship between followership and leadership, relevant literature on followership, and of the development of effective followership that can stand up to, for, and with leadership.[212] That is, followers that "have the ability to influence leaders and contribute to the improvement and attainment of group and organizational objectives."[213]

Leadership failures have become apparent elsewhere. Barbara Kellerman argues that, despite being preoccupied with the romance of leadership as the sole source of power and money, achievement, and change, leaders of every stripe are in disrepute.[214] Statistically, leadership failure rates average between 50 and 75 percent.[215] The leaders' ineffectiveness is partially attributed to the preoccupation with leadership at the expense of the group dynamics associated with the processual nature of leadership. For that matter, leaders should rely on the willful cooperation of followers to succeed.[216] Therefore, active followership is necessary because it enhances a horizontal organizational culture in which the acceptance of a leader's authority and the legitimacy of the direction and vision of the leader is the proactive prerogative of the followers.[217] In the next section, I will discuss the evolution

208. Ogbonna, "Followership Imperative of Good Governance," 65–80.
209. Osaghae, "Limits of Charismatic Authority," 29–44; Oloka-Onyango, "'New-Breed' Leadership, Conflict," 29–52.
210. Ntarangwi, *Jesus and Ubuntu*.
211. Osaghae, "Limits of Charismatic Authority," 29–44.
212. Osaghae, "Limits of Charismatic Authority," 29–44.
213. Crossman and Crossman, "Conceptualizing Followership," 481.
214. Kellerman, *End of Leadership*.
215. Hurwitz and Hurwitz, *Leadership is Half the Story*.
216. Bjugstad et al., "Fresh Look at Followership," 304–19; DePree, *Leadership Jazz*; DePree, "Leadership Quest," 69.
217. Hansen, "Management's Impact on First Line," 41–45; Kellerman, *End of Leadership*; Rajan and Wulf, "Flattening Firm."

of followership theory and highlight why leadership scholars did not explore the process of followership development and enactment in leadership processes and outcomes.

Followership Pioneer Theorists

Until Susan D. Baker published her article, followership theorists assumed that interest in followership theory originated from Kelley's 1988 article, "In Praise of Followers," and his 1992 book, *The Power of Followership*. But following Baker's 2007 article, "Followership: The Theoretical Foundation of the Present Construct," consensus emerged that interest in followership studies originated from Mary Follett's appeal to consider followership as a complementary role in leadership process that demands an independent study.[218] Follett was followed by Fillmore H. Sanford,[219] and from then on, many people added their voices to the debate prior to Kelley.[220] However, it was Kelley who won press with his publication, *In Praise of Followers*.

Hollander and his colleagues were among the earlier voices in followership studies. Hollander was critical of the traditional view about followership. In the following quote, he brought up the dominant assumption about followers, and responded:

> It is commonly assumed that a cleavage exists between those who lead and those who follow, and that being a follower is not being a leader. Only some members of a group have leadership qualities . . . and stand out as leaders. Followers are treated essentially as "non-leaders," which is a relatively passive residual category.[221]

In their first study, Edwin P. Hollander and Wilse B. Webb noted that leadership and followership are mutually inclusive. When Edwin P. Hollander and James W. Julian[222] examined the then-prevailing literature to advance George C. Homans's work on social exchange processes,[223] they concluded that leadership is a reciprocal process between leaders and followers.

---

218. Follett, "Leader and Expert," 220–43.
219. Sanford, "Authoritarianism and Leadership."
220. Hollander and Webb, "Leadership, Followership, and Friendship," 163–67.
221. Hollander, "Processes of Leadership Emergence," 20.
222. Hollander and Julian, "Contemporary Trends in the Analysis," 387–97.
223. Homans, *Human Group*.

Furthermore, Hollander, argued that followership and leadership are roles rather than the people serving those roles.[224] Leaders and followers play both roles interchangeably. In addition, leadership behaviors are not unique to leaders. Hollander's theory of the reciprocal influence between leadership and followership was corroborated by Herold's empirical study, which laid the foundation for the body of literature on the subject of reciprocity of influence between leaders and followers.[225] Although other voices spoke and wrote on the subject, their works did not have much impact on followership theory because they were "leadership studies that incorporate data about followers."[226] For example, although David R. Frew developed the first instrument for measuring followership importance to leaders, his study focused on leadership qualities followers admired in their bosses.[227]

Another study that made a significant contribution to followership theory was undertaken by Joseph A. Steger, George E. Manners, and Thomas W. Zimmerer. The study proposed a followership model. In their findings, they concluded that "a hierarchical structure was a given, and the only question was how much freedom the organization gave a manager to reward or punish subordinates."[228] Second, they pointed out that power was a managerial tool that managers use according to follower behaviors. However, although Steger et al. referenced followership, their study focused on the role of followers in leadership performance.

In his attempt to simplify leadership contingency theory, William E. Zierdan called upon managers to elevate subordinates by incorporating their attitudes and feelings in organizational decisions.[229] Dean Tjosvold, Robert Andrews, and Hales Jones explored the relational dynamics between leaders and subordinates to understand qualities that make the former cooperative and competitive. Their study suggested that followers and leaders should share common goals:

> To improve their own success, to improve subordinates' reactions to their leadership, to increase subordinates' satisfaction, and to build morale leaders should emphasize common goals held by leader and subordinates, help subordinates achieve their goals, encourage subordinate learning and development,

---

224. Hollander, "Processes of Leadership Emergence."
225. Herold, "Two-way Influence Processes," 224–37.
226. Wortman, "Strategic Management," 371–83.
227. Frew, "Leadership and Followership," 90–97.
228. Steger et al., "Following the Leader," 22–28.
229. Zierdan, "Leading through the Follower's," 27–46.

exchange information and resources, and share the rewards of their combined efforts.[230]

Unfortunately, all the antecedent followership studies were using followers' lenses to study leadership. None of them looked at how followers viewed followership because both leaders and followers developed a larger-than-life image of leaders, which influenced them to attribute organizational successes and failures to leaders.

Theoretical Antecedents to Active Followership

Like leadership theory, theorists in other disciplines like sociology and psychology influenced early followership researchers. Some of the specific theories that influenced the emergence of followership theory were social exchange and small group theories.[231]

Social Exchange Theories

These theories examine the relational exchanges between an individual and a group that is characterized by mutual obligations and benefits. The members maintained the exchange as long as they continued to get mutual benefits.[232] The originators included Homans,[233] whose work was followed by that of Hollander, as well as Hollander and Julian. In their work, they called for the inclusion of "an entire interpersonal system" in understanding the performance of leaders.[234] Burns built on their transaction model to develop transactional leadership theory, which examined followers' leadership schema. The theory recognized leadership as an act, which involves an exchange with another.[235]

---

230. Tjosvold et al., "Cooperative and Competitive Relationships," 111.

231. Baker, "Followership," 50–60.

232. Bass, *Bass and Stogdill's Handbook*; Homans, Human Group; Homans, *Social Behavior*.

233. Homans, *Human Group*.

234. Hollander, "Processes of Leadership Emergence," 19–33; Hollander and Julian, "Contemporary Trends in the Analysis," 387–97.

235. Burns, *Leadership*, 20.

Leader-Member Exchange Theory

Leader Member Exchange (LMX) theory was developed by George Graen, Terri Scandura, Mary Uhl-Bien, and others. Their theory, which looked at the relationship between followers and leaders discovered that when leaders and followers developed good relationships, informal bonds replaced formal contractual bonds. In this case, they operated on mutual trust devoid of subjugating influence.[236] When mutual trust reduces the distance between leaders and followers, it makes the organization structure flat. However, although LMX theory shifted the focus from the leadership domain to the relationship domain,[237] it remains leader-centric because it portrays the leader as the catalyst of the exchange.

Attribution and Small Group Theories

The theories offered an alternative framework for examining leader–follower relationships. They called for the need to understand leaders' and followers' schemas of leadership rather than merely the former's attributes and conduct. They suggested that leaders and followers had leadership schemas about leaders and their behaviors and attributed the romance of leadership to the failure to understand business systems when corporations grew and became complex after World War II.[238] They noted that in that context, theorists attributed "organizational success or failure to something more easily understandable—a person, in particular a leader, to whom was attributed control and responsibility as well as the performance of entire industries."[239] Thus, managers used this larger-than-life image of leaders to understand and manage organizations. Edwin P. Hollander and Lynn R. Offermann used the same theories to examine leadership schemas followers use to determine their response to leaders. These theories influenced research interests in leader-follower relations.[240]

---

236. Graen and Uhl-Bien, "Relationship-based Approach to Leadership," 219–247; Schriesheim et al., "Folly of Theorizing," 515–51.

237. Howell and Shamir, "Role of Follower," 98–112.

238. Bass, *Bass and Stogdill's Handbook*.

239. Meindl et al., "Romance of Leadership," 78–102.

240. Hollander and Offermann, "Relational Features of Organizational Leadership," 83–97.

Leadership Studies Within the Field of the Social Sciences

Social scientists studied the behavior of members of small groups as a microcosm for understanding larger groups.[241] However, in the field of management, insights about group dynamics gleaned from social sciences were restricted to the interaction between superordinates and subordinates. The theorists maintained a sharp distinction between leader and supervisor, which other theorists like Jill W. Graham used to draw similar distinctions between followers and subordinates.[242] Altogether, these voices and theories generated common themes in followership literature.

Themes in Followership Literature

When leadership scholars on followership concluded that the imbalance between leadership and followership studies constitutes the "most serious failure" in leadership studies,[243] they called for the need to treat the two variables as "co-equal." They noted that leadership and followership were not discussed as "co-equal concepts" partly because the discussion on followership by itself was rare.[244] Ronald Gilbert noted that there was little management literature on followership compared to leadership and attributed the imbalance to the "romance of leadership" and "dependence on the leader's 'ability to motivate.'"[245] even though it has now been established that active followers motivate themselves[246] Both Stephen Lundin and Lynne Lancaster, as well as Andrew Brown and W. T. Thornborrow, confirmed the paucity of literature in the field of followership and added that most of the literature on followership is "written mostly by American authors who wrote from an American perspective."[247] David N. Berg drew our attention to the "overwhelming emphasis" on leadership within corporations and schools at the expense of followership.[248] Kent Bjugstad et al. regarded it as

---

241. Homans, *Social Behavior*.
242. Graham, "Chapter 3 Commentary," 73–79.
243. Burns, *Leadership*, 3.
244. Heller and Van Till, "Leadership and Followership," 405–14.
245. Gilbert, "Building Highly Productive Work Teams," 449–54.
246. Hughes, *Keeping Your Job*; Strebel, "Why Do Employees Resist Change?," 86–92.
247. Lundin and Lancaster, "Beyond Leadership"; Brown and Thornborrow, "Do Organizations Get, the Followers?" 5–15.
248. Berg, "Resurrecting the Muse," 27–52.

an "understudied discipline,"[249] and Rob Goffee and Gareth Jones noted that "the analysis of followership has barely begun."[250] Altogether, these scholars identified common themes in the leadership-followership relationship upon which followership theory was later established. In the following section, I will discuss the themes.

Roles, Not Positions

The idea that followership and leadership are roles was initially suggested by Margret Mead.[251] In later research, Hollander noted that, "a role is a set of behaviors which are appropriate for a position which an individual fills."[252] Thus, leaders and followers share qualities. Trudy Heller and Jon Van Till noted that, "leadership and followership are best seen as roles in relation."[253] Kelley stated that followership and leadership were interchangeable roles between followers and leaders.[254] Thus, the distinctions between leadership and followership were not intelligence or character, but rather the roles played by each party.[255] Ira Chaleff noted that the difference between leadership and followership disappears when followers perform traditional leadership roles like planning.[256] Berg gave empirical evidence from his workshop, where participants concurred that as managers, they perform both roles in their organizations.[257]

Therefore, management scholars and practitioners now concur that leadership and followership are flexible roles that apply to leaders and followers equally in organizations.[258] However, none explored how followers construct their roles until Melissa Carsten et al. identified some of the factors influencing role construction.[259]

---

249. Bjugstad et al., "Fresh Look at Followership," 304.
250. Goffee and Jones, "Art of Followership," 22-26.
251. Mead, "Problems of Leadership," 7-12.
252. Hollander, "Processes of Leadership Emergence," 19-33.
253. Heller and Van Till, "Leadership and Followership," 406.
254. Kelley, *In Praise of Followers*.
255. Kelley, "Leadership Secrets from Exemplary Followers," 193-201.
256. Chaleff, *Courageous Follower*.
257. Berg, "Resurrecting the Muse," 27-52.
258. Hurwitz and Hurwitz, *Leadership is Half the Story*.
259. Carsten et al., "Exploring Social Constructions of Followership," 543-60.

Active, Not Passive

The relationship between followership and leadership roles within an organization has evolved over the years. Initially, followers were generally regarded as passive objects of leaders' influence.[260] However, toward the close of the twentieth century, the followership role gained active status. Scholars now argue that since leadership is a reciprocal interaction between followers and leaders, followership is an active role. They called for a comprehensive theoretical framework that goes beyond individualistic approaches to interactional processes.[261]

The change of mind is accredited to many theorists such as Chester I. Barnard, who pointed out that leaders derive their authority from followers through followers' cooperation and assent.[262] In the same train of thought, William Litzinger and Thomas Schaefer theorized that followers' rights to grant or withhold obedience act as a series of checks and balances to leaders. They argued that active followers follow leaders only when leaders follow organizational goals.[263] In addition, building on Barnard's idea, Theordore L. Hansen stated that active followership requires effective leadership.[264]

Thus, all these studies concluded that followers are active and not passive recipients of leaders' influence. Henceforth, the long-held view that followers are passive recipients of leaders' influence is not feasible in the postindustrial era.[265] However, there are still no studies on how followers develop and enact followership because both the seminal and most of the subsequent empirical studies focused on establishing and supporting followership theory.

---

260. Alcorn, "Dynamic Followership," 9–33.

261. Grant et al., *Sage Handbook of Organizational Discourse*; Grant and Hofmann, "Role Expansion as Persuasion Process," 9–31; Phillips, and Oswick, "Organizational Discourse," 1–47; Putnam and Fairhurst, "Discourse Analysis in Organizations," 78–136.

262. Barnard, "Theory of Authority," 92–104.

263. Litzinger, and Schaefer, "Leadership through Followership," 78–81.

264. Hansen, "Management's Impact on First Line," 41–45.

265. Fisher-Yoshida and Geller, *Transnational Leadership Development*, 14.

Common Goals

Followers and leaders share common goals. Scholars who advance this argument included Follett,[266] Burns,[267] and Robert P. Vecchio.[268] For instance, for Follett, followers and leaders pursue a common goal in their respective roles. On the other hand, Burns wrote that leadership and followership roles are "inseparable functions."[269] Hollander called on leaders to occupy followers with "mutually satisfying and productive enterprises." [270] For Vecchio, followers and leaders are interconnected and are therefore two sides of the same coin in terms of leadership processes and outcomes.[271]

Relationality

Leadership and followership are relational variables. Following the earlier writings of theorists like Follett and Mead, followership theorists have reached a consensus that leadership and followership are interconnected roles that call for more studies to examine the relationship between them.[272] Using the both/and category rather than either/or, the following followership theorists described the relationship as interdependent: Hollander and Webb, [273] Hollander and Julian, and Burns.[274] Others included, Herold, Frew, Heller and Van Till, Gilbert, and Berg.[275] Earl H. Potter et al. stated that the two roles are interrelated and equal.[276] On the other hand, like Thane S. Pittman, et al. stated that the leader-follower relationship is a partnership.[277]

---

266. Follett, "Management as a Profession," 1–17.
267. Burns, *Leadership*.
268. Vecchio, "Effective Followership," 114–33.
269. Burns, *Leadership*, 20.
270. Hollander, "Essential Interdependence of Leadership," 71–75.
271. Vecchio, "Effective Followership," 114–33.
272. Mead, "Problems of Leadership," 7–12; Folllett, "Leader and Expert," 220–43.
273. Hollander and Webb, "Leadership, Followership, and Friendship," 163–67; Hollander, and Julian, "Contemporary Trends in the Analysis," 387–97; Burns, *Leadership*.
274. Hollander and Julian, "Contemporary Trends in the Analysis," 387; Burns, *Leadership*.
275. Herold, "Two-way Influence Processes," 224–37; Frew, "Leadership and Followership"; Heller and Van Til, "Leadership and Followership"; Berg, "Resurrecting the Muse," 27–52.
276. Potter et al., "Leading the New Professional," 145.
277. Pittman et al., "Followers as Partners," 107–20.

For his part, Kelley added that followers and leaders play their roles independently and interdependently.[278]

Recently, leadership scholars like Jane M. Howell and Boas Shamir noted that "understanding followers is as important as understanding leaders."[279] Building on Howell and Shamir's work, William Gardner, et al. designed a prototype of "authentic leadership and followership," which prioritizes the role of self-consciousness in role performance.[280] All in all, leadership is a relational process that involves active participation of both leaders and followers.

Neither Inherent Nor Homogenous Possessions

Followership development and enactment in the knowledge era is not optional. First, the passive followership characteristics and behaviors leadership scholars attributed to followers during the industrial era are not inherent possessions of followers.[281] Instead, like leaders, followers are made and follower dynamics like characteristics, role orientations, and behaviors are context specific.[282] Hence, there are no universal followership dynamics. Instead, follower identities, roles, and behaviors are products of the relational process of interactions among the various factors involved in leadership processes and outcomes in a particular context. Likewise, followers are not homogenous. Studies show that followers have multiple followership identities and role orientations that are context specific.[283] Each followership perception and role orientation is enacted in response to other factors at play in organizations in their respective contexts.[284] Therefore, a clear understanding of followership identities and how they are developed and enacted in each specific context is necessary. So far, no study has explored the process of followership construction and enactment.

---

278. Kelley, *Power of Followership*.
279. Shamir and Howell, "Role of Followers," 96–102.
280. Gardner et al., "Can You See?," 343–72.
281. Carsten et al., "Exploring Social Constructions of Followership," 543–60.
282. Lapierre and Carsten, *Followership*.
283. Homans, *Social Behavior*.
284. Medcof, "Followers and Followership."

Actual and Ideal Behaviors

Followers' actual behaviors are not necessarily their ideal behaviors.[285] In the industrial era, leadership theorists and practitioners treated followers according to their actual behaviors rather than ideal behaviors that ought to characterize active followership. Most of the actual behavioral typologies of followers associated with the industrial era misrepresent ideal followership.

In summary, followership and leadership are complementary factors in leadership processes and outcomes. Thus, a focus on followership should recognize the relational nature of the leadership process, which prioritizes interdependence over compartmentalization based on the assumption that leadership and followership are distinct entities with flexible boundaries that enhance interdependence.

Types of Followers and the Need for Followership Development

Leadership scholars are still exploring why followership received little attention in leadership literature. Augustine O. Agho argued that initially both leadership practitioners and theorists assumed that followers follow instinctively.[286] However, in the information-era organizational culture of reciprocal leadership,[287] followers and leaders perform leadership and followership roles interchangeably.[288] Thus, active followership is imperative when attempting to enhance leaders' and followers' competencies.[289]

Followership theorists categorize followership styles and behaviors into two groups: descriptive and prescriptive. The descriptive category is concerned with actual followership styles and behaviors as they occur, while the prescriptive category is concerned with ideal followership behaviors, which depict how followers ought to behave in a particular context.[290]

The earliest typologies of subordinate behavior were suggested by Abraham Zaleznik, who studied follower/leader and follower/follower relationships using the continuum of power and conflict in the context

---

285. Bjugstad et al., "Fresh Look at Followership," 304–19.
286. Agho, "Perspectives of Senior-level Executives," 159–66.
287. Johnson, *Ethics in the Workplace*.
288. Horsfall, "Real Leaders Make a Difference," 80.
289. Bjugstad et al., "Fresh Look at Followership," 304–19; Dixon and Westbrook, "Followers Revealed," 19–25; Russell, "Leadership and Followership," 145–55; Wortman, "Strategic Management," 371–83.
290. Crossman and Crossman, "Conceptualizing Followership," 481–97.

of dominating/submissive relationships. In his analysis, he found out that followers respond to leaders' power through either absolute submission or dominant defiance.[291] Therefore, according to his finding, followers either support or undermine leader authority.

Two decades later, Kelley differentiated between followers based on their level of dependency and critical thinking. Dependent or uncritical passive followers hold back personal opinions and contribute little to the organization. Conformists are followers who perform within comfort zones.[292] Exemplary followers, or star followers, are normative followers who contribute initiatives and support their peers, leaders, and organization beyond contractual obligation. They exercise critical thinking that can turn them into alienated followers when organizational conditions are not favorable. Alienated followers are normally star followers-turned-disengaged followers who see themselves as victims of organizational shortcomings. They focus on what they do not like in an organization, rather than on its future. Finally, Kelley identified pragmatists as "better safe than sorry" followers who "want to do good but are not willing to stick their necks out, or worse fail."[293] They confine themselves to contractual obligation.

Kellerman categorizes followers according to their level of engagement.[294] Isolates are followers who are completely detached from the leader, other followers, and the organization. Their stance entrenches leader-centric image of leaders. Bystanders are observers who have resolved to remain neutral to the status quo. Participants care enough to engage or disengage from the leader, group, or organization, but their engagement or disengagement is limited to their self-defined interest. Activists harbor a strong feeling for the leader and they act enthusiastically. They care deeply about people and group processes to the extent of undermining or even unseating their leaders. Diehards are followers who are totally committed to a cause and they spare nothing including their own lives to fulfill it.

Ira Chaleff cast a courageous follower image that is essential for the reciprocal relationship between follower and leaders.[295] Chaleff's follower typologies include implementer, partner, individualist, and resource. Implementers constitute the majority of followers in organizations who faithfully do their leaders' biddings. Partners are those followers who show total

---

291. Zaleznik, "Dynamics of Subordinacy," 119–31.

292. Kelley, *Power of Followership*; Kelley, "Rethinking Followership," 5–15; Kelley, "Leadership Secrets from Exemplary Followers," 193–201.

293. Kelley, "Leadership Secrets from Exemplary Followers," 193.

294. Kellerman, *Followership*, 97; Kellerman, "What Every leader Needs," 84–91.

295. Chaleff, *Courageous Follower*.

support to their leaders, but they are not hesitant to oppose them when necessary. Individualist followers express their minds and feelings, but they are usually marginalized because of their propensity to withhold engagement. Finally, resource followers are those workers who commit themselves according to formal organizational expectations which are commensurate with their needs.

Follower behaviors fall into three categories. The first consists of the least desirable followership behaviors with low levels of production. These are described using words like "detached,"[296] "estranged,"[297] "indifferent,"[298] "subservient,"[299] and "segregated."[300] Some of these follower typologies characterize ideal followers in the industrial era.

The second category is identified as ideal followers described by words like "active," [301] "performer,"[302] and "partner."[303] These adjectives depict behaviors followers should exhibit rather than their actual behaviors. Followers who portray these behaviors make both performance initiatives and relationship initiatives to improve their relationships with leaders by building trust, courageous communication, and negotiating through differences. In performance initiatives, exemplary followers perform diligently and proactively embrace change.

The third category is made up of moderate followers who are described as "conformists," "pragmatists," "bureaucrats," "donkeys," "game players," "contributors," and "participants."[304] Followers in this category are partially committed. They lack the motivation to participate beyond contractual obligation as well as the backbone to challenge leaders' unethical behaviors. Unfortunately, most followers today fall under this category.[305]

So far, studies show that courageous followership behaviors permeate the entire organization. For instance, in their study, Gene Dixon and Jerry Westbrook discovered that courageous followership permeates the entire

---

296. Zaleznik, "Dynamics of Subordinacy."
297. Kelley, *Power of Followership*.
298. Steger et al., "Following the Leader."
299. Potter and Rosenbach, "Followers as Partners," 91–102.
300. Kellerman, *Followership*.
301. Kelley, *Power of Followership*.
302. Steger et al., "Following the Leader."
303. Potter and Rosenbach, "Followers as Partners," 91.
304. Thody, "Followership in Educational Organizations," 141–56.
305. Brown and Thornborrow, "Do Organizations Get the Followers?," 5–15; Oyetunji, "Relationship between Followership Style," 179–87.

organizational hierarchy.[306] Second, the conceptual understanding and acknowledgment of exemplary followership is greater at the senior levels of organizational hierarchy.

In the current era, where there is an increasing demand for corporate social responsibility and business ethics,[307] the lack of active followership breeds toxic leadership.[308] Hence, firms need active followers with a strong self-follower identity.[309] Robert G. Lord suggests that followers with a strong self-follower identity possess the capacity for exceptional performance beyond contractual obligation.[310]

However, since active followership calls for whistle-blowing in response to organizational ethical hazards like bad leadership,[311] followers can suffer severe consequences for their actions.[312] Thus, ideal behaviors represent significant career risks.[313] For that matter, theorists have called for organizations to respect divergent opinions, and for followers to prepare themselves for the cost of courageous followership.

In summary, although the current follower actual behaviors necessitate development of ideal followership behaviors, there are no adequate resources. First, all seminal works on followership lacked empirical evidence.[314] Second, most of the subsequent empirical studies were undertaken to support the basic followership assumptions. None examined the process of followership construction. While lesser than a dozen studies identified factors influencing followership development and enactment, none examined the actual process.[315] Therefore, the process of the development of followership identities, roles, and behaviors is still unknown. In addition, most of followership studies examined organizations in Northern America from an American perspective. Thus, followership perceptions and experiences

---

306. Dixon and Westbrook, "Followers Revealed," 9–25.
307. Johnson, *Ethics in the Workplace*.
308. Henrich, "Follower Propensity to Commit Crimes," 69–76.
309. Avolio and Reichard, "Rise of Authentic Followership," 325–37; Gardner et al., "Can You See?," 343–72; Collinson, "Dichotomies, Dialectics and Dilemmas," 36–55.
310. Lord, "Followers' Cognitive and Affective Structures," 255–66.
311. Goffee and Jones, "Art of Followership," 22–26; Johnson, *Ethics in the Workplace*.
312. Alford, "Whistleblowing as Responsible Followership," 237–54; Johnson, *Ethics in the Workplace*.
313. Crossman and Crossman, "Conceptualizing Followership," 481.
314. Chaleff, *Courageous Follower*; Kellerman, *Followership*; Kelley, *Power of Followership*.
315. Huizing, "Importance of Ritual"; Hurwitz and Hurwitz, *Leadership is Half the Story*.

from other contexts, such as Africa, are not only lacking, but might be altogether different. Since followership development and enactment are context specific, there is need for research from other contexts besides followership development.

FOLLOWERSHIP DEVELOPMENT AND ENACTMENT

Leadership theorists have included followers in their studies for a long time. However, the emphases in those studies were either leader-centered or multiple leadership-centered. In the former, the focus was on either followers' perspectives of leaders and leaders' behaviors or leaders' perspectives of followers and followers' behaviors. In the leader-centered paradigm, the focus was on rotational leadership among team peers.[316] While the leader-centered approach is a bottom-up approach, the multiple leadership approach is team-based with fluid roles.[317] Both approaches were reactions to the leader-centric approach to leadership in which the locus of leadership was in an individual atop the organizational hierarchy, and was exercised as a top-down influence over subordinates through direction, control, and management.[318]

Whereas leader-centered and multiple leadership-centered approaches expanded leadership beyond the constraints of individualized hierarchical roles, they don't tell us anything about followers' own perspectives of followership. How followers view followership and how they develop and enact it are essential because first, followers develop and enact their own followership identity, roles, and behaviors,[319] and second, there is need for adding effective follower constructs and behaviors to the current typologies of leader constructs and behaviors because the followership role in the postindustrial era is reciprocal to the leadership role.[320]

---

316. Avolio and Reichard, "Rise of Authentic Followership," 325–37; Crossman and Crossman, "Conceptualizing Followership," 481.

317. Gronn, "Leadership," 267–90; Kerr and Jermier, "Substitutes for Leadership," 375–403; Shamir, *From Passive Recipients*.

318. Mumford et al., "Charismatic, Ideological and Pragmatic Leadership," 144–60; Sashkin, "Transformational Leadership Approaches," 171–96.

319. Carsten et al., "Exploring Social Constructions of Followership"; Howell and Shamir, "Role of Follower"; Hughes, *Keeping Your Job*; Strebel, "Why Do Employees Resist Change?," 86–92.

320. Potter et al., "Leading the New Professional," 145–52.

Therefore, since there is an increasing demand to know how followers develop and enact their own followership identity, roles, and behaviors,[321] this study was designed to explore the process of followership development and enactment. In the next section, I will discuss the lenses used in followership studies, and the different types of followership identities, role orientations, and behaviors.

Lenses Used in Followership Studies

The study of followership explores the dynamics of followers and following in leadership processes and outcomes. Leadership process, according to a connectionist view, is "a dynamic system involving leaders [or leading] and followers [or following] interacting together in context" toward a common goal.[322] In this context, there are two ways of looking at followership: first, a role-based approach in which followership refers to a rank or position and the focus is on the role, or second, followership as a social process in a specific context and the focus is on relational interactions among leadership variables.

In a role-based approach, followership is either a role between followers and leaders or a rank between a subordinate and a manager.[323] The constructionist approach looks at leadership as a reciprocal phenomenon cocreated in mutual interaction.[324]

A role-based approach examines how followers influence a leader's attitude, behavior, and outcome. It looks at follower dynamics as independent agents, and leader dynamics as dependent or moderator variable.[325] In the constructionist approach, followership and leadership emanate from relational interactions.[326] In this approach, leaders and followers accept and cooperate with each other's roles and exchange them where necessary.[327]

---

321. Carsten et al., "Exploring Social Constructions of Followership," 543–62.

322. Uhl-Bien and Ospina, "Paradigm Interplay in Relational Leadership," 537–80; Shamir, "Leadership Research or Post-leadership Research," ix–xxxix.

323. Katz and Kahn, *Social Psychology of Organizations*.

324. DeRue and Ashford, "Who Will Lead?," 627–47; Fairhurst and Grant, "Social Construction of Leadership," 171–210; Fairhurst and Uhl-Bien, "Organizational Discourse Analysis," 1043–62; Shamir, "Leadership Research or Post-leadership Research," ix.

325. Shamir, "Leadership Research or Post-leadership Research," ix.

326. DeRue and Ashford, "Who Will Lead?," 627–47; Uhl-Bien and Ospina, "Paradigm Interplay in Relational Leadership," 537–80; Fairhurst and Uhl-Bien, "Organizational Discourse Analysis," 1043–62.

327. Fairhurst and Uhl-Bien, "Organizational Discourse Analysis," 1043.

Hence, followership is a process of relational interaction between followers and leaders. Furthermore, in the constructionist model, followers develop and enact followership as either followers or subordinates.[328] In that case, follower and employee are not synonymous due to the degree of the freedom of responsibility.

Whereas earlier scholars like Barbara Kellerman, John Kelley, and Ira Chaleff looked at followership through role-based lenses,[329] recent scholars have started to view followership through constructionist lenses, thereby promoting studies on followership development and enactment.[330]

Follower Identity

Follower identities are important because they determine the quantity and quality of follower commitment and contribution to organizational processes and outcomes. Followers develop and enact followership either from a role-based approach or a constructionist approach. In the former, followership and leadership are associated with holding a formal hierarchical position. In the latter, followership and leadership refer to a relational interaction toward a common goal.

Role-Based Identities

A role-based follower identity examines how followers relate with leaders to accomplish organizational goals.[331] The primary focus is on follower dynamics. It considers how follower dynamics interact to promote a desired outcome.[332] So far, theorists have identified several follower identities as follows:

---

328. Collinson, "Rethinking Followership," 179.

329. Kellerman, *Followership*; Kelley, *Power of Followership*; Chaleff, *Courageous Follower*.

330. Carsten et al., "Exploring Social Constructions of Followership," 543–62.

331. Carsten et al., "Exploring Social Constructions of Followership"; Oc and Bashshur, "Followership, Leadership and Social Influence," 919–34; Sy, "What Do You Think?," 73–84.

332. Graen and Uhl-Bien, "Relationship-based Approach to Leadership," 219.

Dominance-Submission and Activity-Passivity Categories

Zaleznik, while studying the dynamics of subordinance, separated followers into two types based on the continuum of dominance-submission and activity-passivity. From these two categories, he developed four types of followers: impulsive subordinates, compulsive subordinates, masochistic subordinates, and withdrawn subordinates.[333] His typologies were meant to enable leaders to provide direction for subordinates who aspired to leadership positions. It was clearly a leader-centric view of follower identity.

Dependent-Independent and Passive-Active Categories

Robert Kelley's typology categorizes followers into two groups based on the continuum of dependent-independent and passive-active. From these he identified four typologies of followers that range from active followers who initiate their own action, to passive followers who follow leaders blindly. In this typology, ideal followers are active and exhibit a courageous conscience.

Courageous Follower Categories

Chaleff identified ideal followers that he called courageous followers. While Kelley used the descriptive method in his approach, Chaleff was prescriptive. He built his theory on the assumption that leaders need followers who perform beyond mere obligation. Courageous followers give accountability and hold leaders and other followers accountable to uphold organizational integrity and performance. So courageous followers must have moral courage to steer the course of the organization.[334]

Engagement Categories

Kellerman categorized followers into five groups based on levels of engagement which range from reeling and doing to being passionately committed and deeply involved. They are isolated, bystanders, participants, activists, and diehards. She built her views based on a conviction that the level of commitment determines the quality of follower. Her typologies portray followers as active agents of change, which was contrary to the traditional

---

333. Zaleznik, "Dynamics of Subordinacy," 167.
334. Chaleff, *Courageous Follower*.

typologies that portrayed followers as being passive recipients of leaders' influence.[335]

Toxic Categories

Jean Lipman-Blumen identified three toxic follower typologies that encourage bad leadership: benign followers, the leader's entourage, and malevolent followers.[336] These categories of followers are driven by selfish motives which create corrosive culture within an organization.

Independent Categories

Jon P. Howell and Maria J. Mendez view followership as a reciprocal role to the leadership role. The independent role involves a high level of autonomy and a high competence that complements the leader's role.[337] An ineffective independent role connotes followers whose purposes do not mesh with those of their leaders. A shifting role connotes followers playing both leader and follower roles within a team context. For example, collaborative teams where members step into leadership and followership roles alternatively based on their expertise.

Constructionist-Based Identities

In the constructionist-based approach, followership and leadership are regarded as a dynamic relational process. It "considers how leaders and followers develop and enact leadership and followership in asymmetrical relational and social interactions."[338] The interactions are not limited to formal roles.

Granting and Claiming Identities

According to Scott D. DeRue and Suzan J. Ashford, followership identities are developed in mutual interactions where followers grant a leader a leadership role and they reciprocate by playing the followership role. The grants

---

335. Kellerman, *Followership*.
336. Lipman-Blumen, *Allure of Toxic Leaders*, 237–51.
337. Howell and Mendez, "Three Perspectives on Followership."
338. Fairhurst and Uhl-Bien, "Organizational Discourse Analysis," 1043–62.

and claims must be reciprocally supported. Here, the identity-claiming and granting processes show that leadership and followership constructs are context-specific and work in hierarchical or relationship structures.[339] In that case, leadership and followership are shared rather than fixed roles. Second, a leadership position does not translate into leadership unless there are corresponding changes to granting and claiming.

Construction Process

David Collinson uses a post-structuralist approach to examine follower identities. His view is based on human interrelatedness.[340] Therefore, people's actions must be examined relationally[341] to understand the dynamics influencing their self-consciousness.[342] Collinson envisaged three possible identities: the conformist self, the resistant self, and the dramaturgical self. Whereas the first category "works with prescribed ideal-type behaviors,"[343] the second category is oppositional in nature. The dramaturgical self is manipulative. Therefore, Collinson noted that followership development and enactment are complex processes that require followers' active participation. So he condemns the leadership approach that depicts followers as merely employees who respond mechanically.

Discursive Process

On the other hand, Fairhurst and Uhl-Bien discussed the discursive process. In this approach, followers are regarded as actors who "engage, interact, and negotiate with leaders to influence organizational understanding and produce outcomes."[344] DeRue and Ashford, "examine influential acts of organizing (e.g. influence attempts and responses) and the 'language games' played by those acting in leader and follower roles."[345] The critical role of followership is implicit in their model.[346]

339. DeRue and Ashford, "Who Will Lead?," 635.
340. Burkirtt, *Social Selves*; Layder, "Understanding Social Theory."
341. Giddens, *Constitution of Society*.
342. Foucault, *Discipline and Punish*, 133–87.
343. Collinson, "Rethinking Followership," 183.
344. Fairhurst and Uhl-Bien, "Organizational Discourse Analysis," 1024.
345. DeRue and Ashford, "Who Will Lead?," 627–47.
346. Fairhurst et al., "Inertial Forces and the Implementation," 168–85; Fairhurst et al., "Manager-Subordinate Control Patterns and Judgments," 395–415; Larsson and Lundholm, "Talking Work In a Bank," 1101–29.

Coproduction Process

In his approach of coproduction, Shamir's relational view accords followers' active roles. He regards leadership as a joint effort between leaders and followers. The approach gives followers' roles an active status because followers coproduce leadership.[347]

Role Orientation

Followers hold multiple role orientations.[348] In their empirical study, Carsten et al.[349] explored follower role perception and factors influencing its development and enactment; their findings affirmed follower roles identified by Kelley, Chaleff, Kellerman, and Shamir.[350] In their case, schema application is context specific.[351] Second, followers' developmental characteristics determine their ability and inclination to influence leadership processes and to enact their schemas.[352]

According to Parker et al., "Even within the same job, employees will have different beliefs regarding what their role is about."[353] On the other hand, Louise E. Davis and Gerald J. Wacker observed that workers define their roles in broad terms, which include "restrictive views about their roles; a phenomenon described as the 'job myopia' or 'that's not my job' syndrome."[354] According to Daniel R. Ilgen and John R. Hollenbeck, "Roles contain both 'established task elements' that are constructed by the organization as well as 'emergent task elements' that occur as a result of social factors, including the job-holder who can self-generate these elements."[355]

According to Amy Wrzesniewski and Jane E. Dutton, "people craft and shape their job to achieve meaning and identity in the work place."[356] For example, nurses might see "their work as being about total patient care,

---

347. Shamir, *From Passive Recipients*.
348. Carsten et al., "Reversing the Lens"; Parker et al., "That is Not My Job," 899–929.
349. Carsten et al., "Exploring Social Constructions of Followership," 543–60.
350. Kelley, *Power of Followership*; Chaleff, *Courageous Follower*; Kellerman, *Followership*; Shamir, *From Passive Recipients*.
351. Carsten et al., "Exploring Social Constructions of Followership," 543.
352. Howell and Shamir, "Role of Follower," ix–xxxix.
353. Parker et al., "That is Not My Job," 904.
354. Davis, and Wacker, Job Design, 431.
355. Ilgen and Hollenbeck, "Structure of Work," 165–207.
356. Wrzesniewski and Dutton, "Crafting a Job," 179–201.

rather than merely the delivery of high-quality technical care."[357] Therefore, role orientation depends on how people understand "their work role, rather than their affective reactions to that role."[358] It is about how a follower "defines their work role, such as how broadly they perceive their role; what types of tasks, goals, and problems they see as relevant to their role; and how they believe they should approach those tasks, goals and problems to be effective."[359] Thus, followers' roles vary in perception according to context.

Follower Behaviors

Followership theorists have identified followership behaviors according to different categories that range from the level of obedience, resistance, and proactivity. In the following section, I will discuss them.

Obedience and Subordination

Traditionally, followers exhibit obedient and deferent behaviors in their respective roles.[360] However, following the shift from production economies to knowledge economies, followers have the latitude to employ resistance and proactive behaviors to advance organizational goals.[361]

Passive, obedient, and deferent behaviors are associated with management theory that views leadership in terms of hierarchy and authority.[362] Hierarchy legitimizes leaders as authority figures with exceptional capacities.[363] This assumption relegates followers' roles to one of blind subordinance[364] because of the larger-than-life image given to leaders.[365] This view is reflected in Carsten et al.'s finding where followers understood their job to be obeying orders. Although organizations are prone to socializing

---

357. Wrzesniewski and Dutton, "Crafting a Job," 179.
358. Parker, "From Passive to Proactive Motivation," 447–69.
359. Parker et al., "That is Not My Job," 904.
360. Carsten and Uhl-Bien, "Ethical Followership," 49–61.
361. Grant and Ashford, "Dynamics of Proactivity at Work," 3–34; Tepper et al., "Personality Moderators of the Relationship," 974–83; Tepper et al., "Subordinates' Resistance and Managers' Evaluations," 185–95.
362. Barnard, *Functions of the Executive*; Taylor, *Principles of Scientific Management*.
363. Weber, *Economy and Society*.
364. Heckscher, "Defining the Post-Bureaucratic Type," 14–62.
365. De Cremer and Van Dijk, "When and Why Leaders," 553–63; De Vreis and Van Gelder, "Leadership and the Need," 277–304; Ravlin and Thomas, "Status and Stratification Processes," 966–87.

followers as subordinates, recent studies show that assigning someone a subordinate role can affect their performance negatively.[366] When followers are socialized into passive subordination, they see themselves as ineffective and leaders as being more capable.[367]

Resistance

The romance of leadership overshadowed research on active followership.[368] Theorists ignored the fact that not all followers obey passively. Thus, studies on active followership received little attention until recently.[369] According to the latest studies, resistance or active followership occurs due to bad leadership and follower acquiescence. Generally, managers consider all forms of resistance as being dysfunctional or malfunctional. The former is true where there is poor relationship, and vice versa. Carsten et al. and Shamir noted that followers with strong coproduction resist bad leadership.[370]

Proactive Behaviors

According to Adam M. Grant and Suzan J. Ashford, proactive behaviors are "anticipatory actions that employees take to impact themselves and/or their environment."[371] Followers regard them as behaviors "that can be applied to any set of actions through anticipating, planning and striving to have an impact."[372]

Some leaders still regard proactive behaviors as insubordination.[373] However, proactive behaviors examine how employees respond in order to create change. Follower behaviors are context specific. Therefore, leaders

366. Hoption et al., "Submitting to the Follower Label," 221–30.

367. Burger, "Replicating Milgram," 1–11; Carsten and Uhl-Bien, "Ethical Followership," 49–61; Henrich, "Follower Propensity to Commit Crimes," 69–76; Milgram, "Some Condition of Obedience," 57–76; Milgram, *Obedience to Authority*.

368. Padilla et al., "Toxic Triangle," 176–94; Hollander and Julian, "Contemporary Trends in the Analysis," 387–97.

369. Tepper et al., "Personality Moderators of the Relationship," 974–83; Tepper et al., "Subordinates' Resistance and Managers' Evaluations," 185–95.

370. Carsten et al., "Exploring Social Constructions of Followership," 543–62; Shamir, "Leadership Research or Post-leadership Research."

371. Grant and Ashford, "Dynamics of Proactivity at Work," 3–34.

372. Grant and Ashford, "Dynamics of Proactivity at Work," 9.

373. Bolino, "Citizenship and Impression Management," 82–98; Frese and Fay, "Personal Initiative," 133–87; Grant et al., *Getting Credit for Proactive Behavior*; Whiting et al., "Effects of Message, Source," 159–82.

need moderating tools to leverage proactive behaviors to enhance greater organizational output.

Summary

In this chapter, the major eras in followership perception are followership antecedent, followership theory, and followership development and enactment. While in the followership antecedent era the romance of leadership stifled studies that called for active followership, in the followership theory era, the theoretical nature of seminal studies simultaneously abetted and stalled research interests in followership development and enactment. However, in the followership development and enactment era, efforts toward followership development and enactment have picked up pace despite remaining in their infancy. For instance, while we know some of the factors influencing followership development and enactment, we still do not know how they do so. That is, we don't know how such factors influence followership development and enactment.

The organizational environment is ripe for followership development. However, for this to happen, organizations must support followers to develop and enact active followership by developing a systems culture in which qualities of followers' participation depends on organizational dynamics that demand and support it rather than only followers. Table 1 gives a summary of the chapter.

Period	Romance of Leadership Era: 1888-1987	Theory Without Empirical Data Era: 1988-2009	Development Era: 2010-
Seminal theorists	Taylor, Descartes, Marx, Follet, Hollander, Carlyle	Kelley, Chaleff, Kellerman, Baker	Uhl-Bien, Carsten, Hurwitz, Zoogah
Mental model	Dualism, individualism "Either/or"	Systems thinking "Both/and"	Seamless thinking "One in all/all in one"
Context	Slave trade, industrial revolution, Renaissance	Globalization, WWII, information technology, economic depression	Intensity
Lens	Hierarchy, fixed position, subordinance	Teams, role, relation	Relational interaction in context
Perception	Nothing or path to leadership	Actual follower behavior among others	Normative behavior
Focus	Larger than life image	Complementary role	Human nature
Area of concentration	Euro-America	Scanty in other areas	Scanty
Theoretical paradigm of inquiry	Euro-American	Same	One African

Table 1: Summary of Perceptions of Followership

3

The Case
Exemplary Followership Of The Acholi People In The Northern Ugandan Conflict Resolution (1985–2012)

UGANDA is susceptible to abrupt violent changes of government. So far, it has experienced eight coup d'états since it attained its independence from Britain in 1962, and yet there is still no sign of a peaceful transition of government. The 1986 coup sparked the northern Uganda conflict that raged on for over two decades.[1]

The northern Uganda conflict has attracted wide attention since Jan Egeland, the former United Nations Under-Secretary General for Humanitarian Affairs and Emergency Relief Coordinator, described it as "northern Uganda is the most forgotten crisis in the world."[2] However, unlike the war, the role of the active followership of the Acholi people in its resolution has been ignored. Using active followership, the Acholi people created a narrative of peaceful approach to conflict resolution, which overcame the Ugandan government's narrative of military solution to armed conflicts.

In the next section, I will highlight three instruments that entrenched armed conflicts in Uganda: (a) ethnic stratification and profiling; (b) militarization of politics; and (c) externalization of state legitimacy. Thereafter, I will apply the three instruments to northern Ugandan conflict and discuss

---

1. Adupa, "Conflict Continuous"; Omara-Otunnu, "History of Political Crisis"; Whitmire, "Creation and Evolution."
2. Allen, Trial Justice, 73.

how the role of the Acholi people in its resolution is a countercultural case of active followership.

THE HISTORICAL CONTEXT OF THE CONFLICT

Historically, armed conflicts and politics are inseparable in Uganda. The marriage between armed conflicts and politics stems from the impact of British colonial rule on state formation and operation.[3] Britain colonized Uganda to protect its interest in the Upper Nile Basin against France and Italy and the source of the Nile River against Germany.[4] The British colonial policy in Uganda militarized, ethnicized, and foreignized the state legitimacy.[5] While some people deny that the damaging effects of the colonial legacy still affect the East African subregion,[6] overwhelming evidence reveals, "the past always bleeds through after it has been forgotten, willfully repressed, or covered over by the present" unless it is holistically readdressed.[7] By stressing the importance of the past or historical consciousness, this study is not advancing the cause of a victim mentality that underestimates the self-determination of individual Africans to achieve progress. Instead, it is underscoring the interrelatedness of human existence where the past, present, and future overlap.[8]

Before the 1885 Berlin Conference that precipitated the European scramble for and partition of Africa, Uganda was "composed of tribes categorized into kingdoms (tribes under a king), chieftainships [tribes under chiefs without a king] and cephalous tribes under heads with neither kingdoms nor chiefs."[9] When Britain declared Uganda a British protectorate in 1894, the tribes in Uganda were involved in intertribal wars of political expansion, amalgamation, and preservation of their respective heritages.[10] According to Walter Rodney, these wars were neither unique to Uganda nor signified any "evidence of innate inferiority or backwardness. That was the state in which the [region] found itself—a point along a long road that others

---

3. Hutchful, "Military and Militarism in Africa."

4. Adyanga, "Modes of British Imperial Control," 48; Girling, *Acholi of Uganda*.

5. Adupa, "Conflict Continuous"; Adyanga, *Modes of British Imperial Control*; Kalu, "African Christianity"; Mamdani, *Citizen and Subject*; Perkins, *Beyond Charity*.

6. Miller, *Against All Hope*, 31.

7. Smith, *Siblings by Choice*, 56.

8. Atkinson, "Evolution of Ethnicity," 19–43; Mbiti, *African Religions and Philosophy*; Smith, *Siblings by Choice*; Bloch-Hoell, "African Identity."

9. Mung'oma, "Revitalization in the Church," 4.

10. Rodney, *How Europe Underdeveloped Africa*.

had traversed and along which [it] was moving."[11] In other words, the wars signified normal political development that characterized the process of state formation the world over. However, when Britain colonized Uganda, it turned "the normal political conflicts of the pre-capitalist African situations into weaknesses" that undermined the indigenous efforts to attain national identity and unity to develop and consolidate into a viable and legitimate government that reflects the dynamic ethnic diversities in Uganda.[12]

One of the damaging legacies of the British subjugation and rule is the ethnicization of Ugandan politics, which created mistrust and suspicions that have stirred up armed conflicts since the colonial era.[13] In the next section, I will discuss how the British colonial policy ethnicized Ugandan politics.

Ethnicization of Ugandan Politics

According to the social identity theory, social identity "provides a framework that gives meaning to events, objects and people."[14] It influences the daily lives and interactions of people implicitly and explicitly, regardless of whether they recognize it or not. For instance, it shapes human perceptions of who people are, how they interact with others, and how they view the world around them. It has the potential to both unite and divide people depending on what aspects of it people emphasize. When people emphasize their differences at the expense of their similarities, social identity can lead to open conflict.[15] Therefore, "identity conflicts are, and will remain for decades to come, the most important source of international violence and war in the world" as long as people prioritize their differences over similarities.[16]

The potential threat social identity poses to peace is neither exaggerated nor dismissible. Recent history is awash with examples of social identity-caused conflicts. For example, in Rwanda, "the administration forced Hutu men to kill their Tutsi wives before they go to kill anyone else—to prove they

---

11. Rodney, *How Europe Underdeveloped Africa*, 181.

12. Kanyogonya et al., *Sowing the Mustard Seed*, 188; Rohner et al., "Seeds of Distrust."

13. Nannyonjo, "Conflicts, Poverty and Human Development," 473–88.

14. Gioia, "From Individual to Organizational Identity," 17–32; Gudykunst, *Bridging Differences*.

15. Samovar et al., *Communication between Cultures*, 5.

16. Kaufman, "Social Identity and the Roots," 1.

were true Interahamwe."[17] Other examples include the Holocaust, where people killed those they considered their enemies on the basis of race.[18] Therefore, it is imperative to explore how a misperception about social identity can degenerate into conflict.

According to Stuart Hall, identity-based conflicts emanate from how humans identify the "other," especially in the contexts of nationality and ethnicity. Social identity degenerates into conflict because of the strength of attachment people accord to the groups in which they belong, and how other people are stratified and profiled as the "other."[19] The process of stratifying and profiling other people as the "other" is based on "the possession in common of rich legacy of memories, the desire to live together and the will to perpetuate the heritage that one has received in an undivided form."[20]

In this process, people take deliberate acts "to reduce the humanity of the enemy and to prepare a social web of support for behavior that is basically cruel, immoral, and normally disapproved."[21] The process also involves ascribing to oneself a sense of purity and a symbolic image with which to identify, while at the same time projecting an imagined impurity on the "other."[22] Furthermore, in ethnic profiling, people carry out "basic value orientation" which acts as "the standard of morality and excellence by which performance is judged."[23] Some scholars distinguish between identity-based conflicts and interest-based conflicts. For example, Karina Korostelina argues that identity-based conflict deals with basic needs and values. Such identity conflicts are categorized by "existential needs, values, safety, dignity, control over destiny and are rooted in complex and multidimensional psychological, historical, and cultural factors."[24] Among the existential needs are participation, consistency, security, recognition, and distributive justice. She further argues that identity-based conflicts occur in situations where a group feels oppressed, victimized, or marginalized and has been denied the necessities of recognition, security, and equity. A group's

---

17. Mamdani, *When Victims Become Killers*, 4.
18. Gass, "Kind of Killing," 75–82.
19. Hall, *Modernity*, 611.
20. Hall, *Modernity*, 615.
21. Gass, "Kind of Killing," 75–82.
22. Williams, "Class Act," 401–44.
23. Barth, "Ethnic Groups and Boundaries," 9–37.
24. Korostelina, "Identity Salience as a Determinant," 100–50.

readiness for conflict with the out-group is a function of intergroup bias and inter-group discrimination, and depends on calculations of possible risks to vested interest and the possibility of strong opposition from out-group. The determination to engage in conflict is catalyzed by the salient identity of the in-group in response to the perceived risk and loss threat from the outer-groups.[25]

According to Korostelina's "Four C Model," there are four steps in identity-based conflicts: comparison (we-they perception); competition (conflicts of interest among counterpoised communities); confrontation (transformation of conflict of interest into moral confrontation between the virtuous "us" and demonized "other"); and counteraction (discrimination, violence, genocide).[26] For Edward. E. Azar, identity-based conflicts are "distinct from traditional disputes over territory, economic resources, or East-West rivalry . . . revolve around questions of communal identity."[27]

The aforementioned qualities of identity-based conflicts have some common features with the legacy of British rule in Uganda in general, and northern Uganda conflict in particular. In the next section, I will discuss how the colonial policy ethnicized politics in Uganda.

When Britain declared Uganda a British protectorate in 1894, it embarked on systematic social, economic, political, and military maneuvers to consolidate its rule over the territory.[28] Having defeated other European and Arab competitors, the British government and the Kabaka of Buganda signed the 1900 Buganda Agreement, which deemed all the other tribes in the territory that became Uganda in 1926 to be part of Buganda.[29] Thereafter, Britain used the policy of indirect rule to colonize the rest of the tribes without any due regard for their respective cultural identities, consent, or interests[30] Under the agreement, Buganda was granted a semiautonomous status and the Buganda region became the "citadel of the [colonial] establishment."[31] The colonial administration divided the country into southern and northern Uganda along tribal lines. The south was composed

25. Korostelina, "Identity Salience as a Determinant," 107.
26. Korostelina, "Identity Salience as a Determinant."
27. Azar, "Analysis and Management," 16.
28. Girling, *Acholi of Uganda*; Whitmire, "Creation and Evolution."
29. Adupa, "Conflict Continuous"; Omara-Otunnu, "History of Political Crisis."
30. Buganda Kingdom, "Uganda Agreement of 1900"; Adyanga, "Modes of British Imperial Control."
31. Mutibwa, *Uganda Since Independence*, 9.

of the Bantus and the north was composed of the Nilotes, including the Acholi of northern Uganda.

Britain used the ethnic divide, which is a relic of the since-discredited racial anthropology of European colonialism in Africa that the postcolonial African leaders subsequently adopted. In the judgment of the British colonial administration, the tribes from the south were superior to the tribes in the north because of their physical features, attributes, and political organization.[32]

Whereas the colonial administration trained southerners to take up clerical and administrative offices, northerners were drafted into the army, police, and prison forces, and also recruited as sugarcane plantation workers in the south.[33] The colonial administration also used the same rationale to allocate other resources. For instance, while southerners grew coffee, which was less labor intensive and highly profitable, northerners grew cotton, which was labor intensive and less profitable.[34]

The British colonial system of indirect rule entrenched a culture of ethnic stratification and profiling as the characteristic emblem of the people and politics of Uganda, to the extent that by the time Uganda attained its independence from Britain in 1962, the country was already polarized along ethnic lines.[35] The danger with ethnic stratification is that prior to British subjugation and rule, indigenous cultures were neither ethnicized nor tribalized because the evolution of indigenous societies into distinct ethnicities was not yet complete. Second, "such a process is never complete."[36] For instance, in the precolonial period, the Acholi people were made up of both foreigners who did not claim the Acholi ancestry (*Lobang*, "commoners") and the bona fide Acholis (*Lokar*).[37]

So in essence, "the Acholi are today, as they were at the beginning of the twentieth century, in their always unfinished process of coming to be."[38] Therefore, the failure to recognize that identity formation is a continuous process inclined the British colonial administration and subsequent post-independent regimes to look at culture and cultural identity as static

32. Adyanga, "Modes of British Imperial Control"; Atkinson, "Evolution of Ethnicity"; Natulya, "Exclusion, Identity and Armed Conflict"; Olango, "Christian Leadership in Relation."

33. Natulya, "Exclusion, Identity and Armed Conflict"; Whitmire, "Creation and Evolution."

34. Oloya, *Child to Soldier*.

35. Adupa, "Conflict Continuous"; Kitching, *On the Backwaters*.

36. Atkinson, "Evolution of Ethnicity," 20.

37. Girling, *Acholi of Uganda*; Whitmire, "Creation and Evolution."

38. Atkinson, "Evolution of Ethnicity," 20.

features of a group rather than dynamic relational phenomena with many patterns and processes of change that link and overlap the past, present, and future.[39] Furthermore, the colonial administration restricted interethnic movements.[40]

Hence, the colonial approach to social identity stagnated the process of authentic identity formation in Uganda because it introduced the perception of ethnicity as static identities limited to time and space. For that matter, the ethnic and tribal identities in Uganda are political identities imposed on Ugandans along tribal lines rather than organic social identities that reflect dynamic diversity and the aspirations of Ugandans. Therefore,

> the colonial project of classifying and highlighting cultural differences rather than similarities fragmented indigenous people into 'bantus,' 'nilotes,' 'hamitic' and so forth, thereby planting the seeds of intolerance, suspicion, and present day ethno-cultural conflicts.[41]

For example, following the British model, southerners have always referred to northerners as *Bamanawanga* ("outsiders"), as backward, primitive, and warlike because of their ethnicity and place of origin.[42]

The condescending attitude of southerners toward northerners that characterized the colonial era was formally introduced into post-colonial Ugandan politics in 1966.[43] Following status, territorial, and economic disputes that started during the colonial era, the Bugandan Kingdom—acting in the interest of the Buganda region through its parliament—gave the Ugandan government, which was then headed by a northerner, a seven-day ultimatum to vacate Bugandan soil in exchange for Bugandan independence.[44] When the Ugandan government, acting in the national interest of the Republic of Uganda, defied the directive to vacate Bugandan soil, the Bugandan Kingdom staged an armed uprising to enforce its order to the Ugandan government. In response, the Ugandan government quashed the uprising and abolished the Buganda Kingdom. The king was forced into exile in Britain where he died a few years later.[45] Nevertheless, the Buganda factor still dominated Ugandan politics. For example, later on, the

39. Atkinson, "Evolution of Ethnicity."
40. Rohner et al., "Seeds of Distrust," 217–52.
41. Oloya, *Child to Soldier*, 69.
42. Finnström, "Wars of the Past," 200–20.
43. Adupa, "Conflict Continuous"; Adyanga, "Modes of British Imperial Control"; Dwyer, "Acholi of Uganda."
44. Dwyer, "Acholi of Uganda."
45. Oloya, *Child to Soldier*, 80.

Buganda region supported the Luwero-Triangle guerrilla war (1980–1986) that culminated in the overthrow of the northerner-led regime and consequently the northern Uganda conflict.[46]

The Buganda Crisis had a direct effect on northern Uganda conflict. First, it ethnicized and militarized Ugandan politics. Since 1966, all the major political differences in Uganda have been settled through armed conflicts along tribal lines and northern Ugandan conflict was not an exception.[47] For instance, to counter northerners' dominance of the army, southern elites joined the army to attain and retain political power. When they fused politics and the army, they intensified the militarization of politics along ethnic lines. For example, during the northern Uganda conflict, southerners understood the conflict as a war against northerners "rather than a war for democracy."[48] In fact, the president's own war propaganda portrayed the Acholi people as *maadui*, meaning "enemies," and subsequently declared the entire Acholi subregion a war zone.[49] Therefore, the conclusion by the Women's Commission that the "current conflict in northern Uganda has its roots in ethnic mistrust between the Acholi people and the ethnic groups of central and southern Uganda" is incontestable.[50]

Second, the Buganda Crisis set a tone of revenge for the suffering that southerners experienced under northerner-led regimes between 1962 and 1985. Since northerners dominated the Ugandan army under northerner-led regimes, the latter blamed their suffering on the former. Therefore, when southerners overthrew the northerner-led regime in 1986, they took it upon themselves to avenge the murder of over 300,000 members of their kindred and loss of property.[51] According to social identity theory, as evidenced in the verbal declaration of southerners, the northern Uganda conflict was ultimately both the defeat of and revenge against northerners by southerners rather than merely a change of government. In addition, the overthrow of the northerner-led regime reinstated the colonial status the British accorded southerners. In return, northerners regarded the overthrow of the northerners-led regime as a deliberate scheme by southerners to exterminate them based on the verbal and nonverbal behaviors of the National Resistance Army/Movement (NRA/M) soldiers.[52] While describing the nature

46. Finnström, *Living with Bad Surroundings*.
47. Adupa, "Conflict Continuous."
48. Finnström, *Living with Bad Surroundings*, 74.
49. Leggett, *Uganda*; Olara-Otunnu, "Secret Genocide," 44–46.
50. Women's Commission, "Against All Odds," 81.
51. Whitmire, "Creation and Evolution."
52. Dolan, *Social Torture*; Olara-Otunnu, "Secret Genocide," 44–46.

and effects of the war, Jan Egeland, the former UN Under-Secretary-General for Humanitarian Affairs confirmed that northern Uganda conflict was not a conventional war: "This is not a normal guerrilla war between rebels and a government. This is a war on, and with children, and against children."[53]

Egeland's analysis is supported by many unprecedented heinous atrocities government soldiers committed against the Acholi people. For instance, "killing of civilians some of whom were buried in latrines and mass graves or burnt alive in their grass-thatched huts in Pabo, Anaka, Angako, Pagoro sub-counties; and suffocating prisoners in pits dug in the ground in Burcoco and Palenga sub-counties."[54] Furthermore, most of the atrocities were against Acholi customs. For example, according to Acholi customs, children and women were to be treated with utmost respect during conflicts.[55] However, during the northern Uganda conflict, women, children, and property were not spared. According to Bishop Baker Ochola, the:

> 'worst thing about' the NRA soldiers was having forced [carnal knowledge] of women one after the other. Men and women were collected during what they [NRA] called a "screening exercise to flush out" the rebels [The Lord's Resistance Army, LRA] from the community. The men and women were then put in separate groups. Then in the evening, the NRA soldiers started [to have carnal knowledge of] the women in the compound. One woman could be [raped] by up to six men; and this went on for three days.[56]

Some of the atrocities were inconceivable in the Acholi culture. For instance, the raping of men in public is anathema to them. The Acholi people invented the word, *tekgungu,* meaning "as soon as one kneels one is raped from behind," to describe the brutality of rape the National Resistance Army (NRA) committed in Alero, Amuru, and Guruguru.[57]

Therefore, when the atrocities intensified, the Acholi people unanimously interpreted the verbal and nonverbal behaviors of NRA/M as the latter's intent to exterminate the Acholi people. For example, Olara A. Otunnu, an Acholi and the former Under-Secretary General of the United Nations and Special Representative for Children and Armed Conflict, believed that

---

53. Allen, *Trial Justice*, 64.
54. Isis-WICCE, "Women's Experiences of Armed Conflict," 24.
55. Adupa, "Conflict Continuous"; Speke, *Journal of the Discovery.*
56. Buijs, "Arms to Fight," 60.
57. Oloya, *Child to Soldier*, 1.

the northern Uganda conflict was a "silent genocide" that was "systematically destroying a people"[58]—the Acholi. According to Otunnu,

> The truth is that reports of indisputable atrocities of the LRA are being employed to mask more serious crimes by the government itself. To keep the eyes of the world averted, the government has carefully scripted a narrative in which the catastrophe in northern Uganda begins with the LRA and will only end with its demise. But, under the cover of the war against these outlaws, an entire society, the Acholi people, has been moved to concentrated camps and is being systematically destroyed—physically, culturally, and economically[59]

Olara-Otunnu's synthesis of northern Ugandan conflict was echoed by Father Carlos Rodriguez, a Catholic missionary priest who witnessed the atrocities: "Everything Acholi is dying."[60] NRA/M ideologists, soldiers, and the president confirmed these interpretations. According to Kajabago Karusoke, the principle government ideologist, "those people [Acholi] are not human beings; they are biological substances . . . that should be eliminated."[61] Major General James Kazini, the then-army commander who blamed the war on the Acholi, added his own twist: "if anything it is the local Acholi soldiers causing the problem. It's the cultural background of the people here: they are violent. It's genetic."[62] Finally, the president of Uganda, a southerner, branded the Acholi people as "culturally backward" and likened them to "'grasshoppers in a bottle,' in which 'they will eat' each other 'before they find' the way out."[63]

Two things stand out on the conduct of NRA/M in the northern Ugandan conflict: First, the verbal and nonverbal behaviors of NRA/M violated fundamental tenets of Acholi social identity. Second, the meaning the Acholi people attached to the aforementioned behaviors prompted their counterresponse in self-defense of their human dignity. In the next section, I will discuss how the British colonial policy of subjugation and rule militarized Ugandan politics.

58. Otunnu, "Secret Genocide," 44
59. Olara-Otunnu, "Secret Genocide," 44.
60. Olara-Otunnu, "Secret Genocide," 44.
61. Omara-Otunnu, "Causes and Consequences of War," 1.
62. Finnström, "Wars of the Past," 200–20.
63. Omara-Otunnu, "Struggle for Democracy in Uganda," 1.

Militarization of Ugandan Politics

Britain colonized Uganda as a British Protectorate in 1894 to protect its interest in the Upper Nile basin against other imperial powers like France, Italy, and Germany.[64] According to Sir William Harcourt, a Liberal cabinet member, Britain did not have interest in Uganda in and of itself except for the importance of the source of the River Nile, and for the control of its stake in the Upper Nile basin. In the following excerpt, Harcourt expressed his opposition to the colonization of Uganda:

> They went there, as Sir Percy Anderson says, because their hands were forced by the Germans. It was from jealousy and "earth-hunger" that they occupied a place which was of no value and which they cannot hold. We are to effect the reconquest of Equatoria and occupy the Albert Lakes and the whole basin of the Upper Nile. Why? For fear of the French, the Germans and Belgians, etc. etc. This is jingoism with a vengeance. We are to have a "Wacht am Nile," and our drum and fife band is to play ... It is because I am deeply opposed to the policy of annexation and conquest and international rivalry that I view our committal to the first stop with the greatest dread.[65]

Therefore, the lack of concern for the interests of the indigenous people of Uganda implied that the British occupation and rule was a military expedition that required the full measure of military force to enforce it. For example, between 1890 and 1900, Britain established formal control of Uganda through aggressive wars of conquest that subjugated indigenous people to the British colonial hegemony along tribal lines.[66] In Buganda, it started with a religious war between the Protestants and Catholics that established the Anglican paramountcy over the Buganda monarchy because of the support of Britain. Britain deposed and exiled the king in 1897, following the latter's contestation of the forceful abrogation of his sovereignty and reign. The colonial administration replaced the king with his infant son, Daudi Chwa, who governed with the help of indigenous regents.[67] For that matter, Britain enforced its conquest, occupation, and rule by the threat of military force such as what Captain Lugard did during the signing ceremony of the 1890 agreement between Britain and Buganda, as reflected in the following quotation:

64. Girling, *Acholi of Uganda*.
65. Gardiner, *Life of Sir William Harcourt*, 192.
66. Omara-Otunnu, "History of Political Crisis."
67. Adyanga, "Modes of British Imperial Control."

A warm discussion arose on many points; then the chiefs were signing, but the King [Mwanga] held back and giggled and fooled; he demanded time. I replied by rapping the table and, speaking loudly, said he must sign now. I threatened to leave the next day . . . and possibly go to his enemies, the Wa Nyoro [sic]. I pointed to him that he had lost the southern half of his Kingdom to the Germans by his previous delay, and that he would lose yet more if he delayed now. He was, I think scared at my manner, and trembled visibly, and was on the point of signing when a rabble with guns . . . threatened to shoot the first man who signed, shouting that they were selling the country . . . This man knew perfectly well that the object of the Treaty was to sign away the land that belonged to them.[68]

The colonial administration replicated the same approach in the other parts of the country, and by the end of 1926, when Uganda officially became a country, all the indigenous authorities and their subjects were subjected to British colonial rule. The British reliance on the armed forces to attain and maintain political power over the indigenous authorities and their subjects, without honoring the latter's interests, introduced a culture of reliance on the military as the exclusive factor in the political management of the state. Since then, state elites in Uganda have "relied heavily upon the military and police enforcers"[69] as the main source and guarantor of political power. In effect, the military has become the agent of the state. It also set a precedent and a framework for an elitist type of state, which is composed of agents of the state and members of the ruling classes. In this context, the state marginalizes the interests of the citizens, and brands their efforts to demand for their interests as subversive. Hence, ordinary citizens who constitute the majority of the population are socialized to play a passive role in the political process.[70]

Furthermore, the military "has in Africa replaced political parties as Africa's most important political institution."[71] Eboe Hutchful argues that there is a thin line between the military and civilian government. For instance, when elites from southern Uganda realized the centrality of the military in attaining and maintaining political power, they joined the army to control both the army and the state as military politicians. For that matter, there is no separation between the military and the state.[72] The relationship between the two suggests that the military and the state cannot

68. House of Commons. "Hansard," 6.
69. Luckham, "Armaments, Underdevelopment, and Demilitarisation," 179–245.
70. Kougniazondé, *Militarization and Political Violence*.
71. Luckham, "Armaments, Underdevelopment, and Demilitarisation," 179–245.
72. Luckham, "Armaments, Underdevelopment, and Demilitarisation," 179.

function without the other. In that context, the decision to go to war or to use the army to quell internal opposition usually depends on the level and the extent of the militarization of politics. The deeper the military culture, the greater the inclination to perceive and respond to any internal divergent challenge with maximum military force.[73]

Second, the British colonial administration established the military as a sociopolitical institution that was independent of the masses. Its purpose was to protect the colonial interests of Britain. Prior to the colonial subjugation and rule, the indigenous tribes did not have standing armies. The security matters of each ethnic group were vested in the hands of all the able-bodied men.[74] However, when the colonial administration established the military as an independent sociopolitical institution responsible for the state's interests, it created a culture in which military intervention became a primary tool in political processes. Thus, "the greatest contributor to the legitimation of violence in our society is the maintenance of a massive, powerful military establishment, committed to the use of force, not as last resort, but as a central instrument" in conflict resolution and governance.[75]

In Uganda, the NRA/M demonstrated its preference for military solution to political challenges when it breached the 1985 Nairobi peace agreement it signed with the Acholi-led regime, in which they had agreed to form a broad-based government of national unity. When NRA/M violated the 1985 Nairobi peace accord, it betrayed both the trust of the Acholi people and the hope for national unity. This breach entrenched a culture of mistrust and suspicion, which ignited the northern Ugandan conflict.[76]

Third, the British promotion of conflict and violence to attain and consolidate power legitimized the use of armed violence in state political processes which do not cater to the interests of the masses. So just like the colonialists,

> the postindependence African State is a ruthlessly efficient bureaucracy, which organizes its survival by cultivating conflicts, promoting mistrusts among different nationalities, and pitting various groups against each other in its attempts to subdue the uncooperative ones.[77]

---

73. Kougniazondé, *Militarization and Political Violence*.
74. Mutibwa, *Uganda Since Independence*.
75. Kelman, "Violence without Moral Restraint," 25–53.
76. Nkurunziza, "Insurgency in Northern Uganda," 314–28.
77. Kougniazondé, *Militarization and Political Violence*, 40.

In this context, national security is synonymous with state security and its many abuses. For example, African states often use the ideology of national security as a pretext that "helps its supporters to mobilize and prepare the citizenry, not only to accept its validity, but also to consent to all sacrifices that may become necessary in due course of action."[78] National security ideology is a ploy the state uses to destroy its adversaries while enhancing and strengthening the power base of its proponents.[79] For instance, the Acholi people accused the government of creating the Internally Displaced People's camps mainly to weaken rather than to protect them against the LRA atrocities.[80]

Fourth, the British colonial administration set a precedent for the culture of political propaganda in which the real causes of war are camouflaged.[81] The colonial administration used a colonial policy discourse that hoodwinked both the British citizens and Ugandans into believing that the colonial project was aimed at protecting Uganda against other European contenders, when in fact the so-called protection benefited only Britain. In the same manner, the Ugandan government used the post-Cold War conflict discourse to camouflage its interests against the interests of the Acholi people.[82]

The post-Cold War conflict discourse portrays most conflicts as internal and bipartisan, and asserts that the motivations for such conflicts are apolitical and at times irrational. That is, conflicts are categorized as two-party wars that are either internal or external.[83] Third parties are regarded as mediators rather than generators of conflicts.[84] Likewise, motivations for conflicts are attributed to economic factors like greed[85] and horizontal economic inequalities,[86] barbarianism characterized by a breakdown of social order, and precolonial tribal enmities and irrational primitivism that had been suppressed by the Cold War.[87] Other factors, according to Robert D.

78. Lopez, "National Security Ideology," 76–90.

79. Hutchful, "Military and Militarism in Africa," 47.

80. Acholi Religious Leaders Peace Initiative, *Let My People Go*; Nibbe, "Effects of a Narrative."

81. Tindifa, "Listen to the People."

82. Kougniazondé, *Militarization and Political Violence*, 40; P'Lajur, "Challenge of Reporting."

83. Ramsbotham and Woodhouse, *Humanitarian Intervention in Contemporary Conflict*.

84. Kelman, "Informal Mediation," 64–96.

85. Collier and World Bank, *Economic Causes of Civil Conflict*.

86. Stewart, "Horizontal Inequalities as a Source," 105–36.

87. Keegan, *War and Our World*, 66.

Kaplan, include the "breakdown of state monopoly of violence, the growth of informal and parallel economies, a thinning down of civil order, and the fear of the consequences of inactions on law and order."[88]

Generally, several solutions are suggested to resolve such conflicts: the first solution suggested by Edward N. Luttwak is that such conflicts should be left to burn out.[89] The second, and most popular, is third-party intervention through

> aid and development programs allied to stronger alliances to other nations which strengthen the economic structure of such States and help to neutralize insecurities against which their governments constantly battle.[90]

These approaches try as much as possible to detach conflicts from wider global dynamics and any possibility of political explanations.[91] However, according to Oliver Ramsbotham and Tom Woodhouse, international social conflicts are issues

> which are neither inter-state conflict . . . nor contained within the resources of domestic conflict management . . . There are many other terms for this level of conflict, most commonly 'internal conflict' or 'civil war,' but these do not capture the further twin characteristics of ISCs: (a) that they are rooted in relations between communal groups within state borders (the social component), and (b) and that they have broken out of the domestic arena and become a crisis for the state itself, thus automatically involving the wider society of states (the international component.[92]

The post-Cold War conflict discourse is further compounded by the Western discourse on good governance and democracy, which "coincided with the end of the Cold War and the need to find alternative mechanisms and legitimations for implementing a neo-liberal economic agenda driven by the West."[93] Western discourse on good governance and democracy constructs the whole area of the globe as "objects to be transformed rather

---

88. Keegan, *War and Our World*, 24.

89. Luttwak, "Give War a Chance," 36–44.

90. Keegan, *War and Our World*, 73; "Branch, Political Dilemmas of Global Justice."

91. Dolan, *Social Torture*, 3; Okumu-Alya, "Regional Dimensions of the War"; Tindifa, "Listen to the People."

92. Ramsbotham and Woodhouse, *Humanitarian Intervention in Contemporary Conflict*, 87.

93. Abrahamsen, *Disciplining Democracy*, 24.

than as subjects with a history and with their own power to transform the world and react to changing circumstances."[94] The discourse is

> implicated in power relationships and serves to perpetuate international relations of dominance and subordination. It does "not take a sufficient account of the interconnectedness of the States and political forces in the global era, and that they maintain a strict internal/external dichotomy that is no longer an accurate or useful description of the world.[95]

In these discourses, security is synonymous with military action. However, according to Robert McNamara, former U.S. Secretary of Defense and former president of the World Bank

> In modernizing society, security means development. Security is not military hardware, though it may include it; security is not military force, though it may involve it; security is not traditional military activity, though it may encompass it. Security is development and without development, there can be no security.[96]

The Ugandan government scripted northern Ugandan conflict according to the tenets of the post-Cold War conflict discourse and the Western discourse on good governance and democracy. It portrayed the conflict as purely an internal issue driven by barbarism.[97] For it to popularize its propaganda, the government censored alternative news about the war for over a decade with the complicit support of the international community. Thus, the world knew virtually nothing about the war and most especially the squalid conditions of its victims until Jan Egeland declared it as the most forgotten human crisis in the world. According to a local journalist who monitored the war, there was

> lack of information, concealment of information, propaganda and misinformation, between the warring parties and the affected community. In order to suppress information, the government [of Uganda] downplays any negative image and was not interested in exposing what was going on in the war zone.[98]

---

94. Abrahamsen, *Disciplining Democracy*, 20.
95. Abrahamsen, *Disciplining Democracy*, xi.
96. Kennedy, *Rise and Fall*, 509.
97. P'Lajur, "Challenge of Reporting"; Sturges, "Information and Communication," 204–12.
98. P'Lajur, "Challenge of Reporting," 72.

However, following the courageous intervention of the Acholi people, the world became aware of the true causes of the war, its antagonists, the conduct, and its impacts on the Acholi people, the country, and the Great Lakes region.[99]

Externalization of State Legitimacy

Britain used the policy of indirect rule in Uganda to protect its interests in the Upper Nile basin. Structurally, indirect rule was composed of "different organizations of power in rural and urban arenas under a single central hegemonic authority."[100] In the rural areas where most Africans lived, the British used indirect rule through the traditional chiefs who pledged absolute allegiance to the British colonial administration at the expense of indigenous traditions. Under the colonial administration, the traditional authorities collected taxes, passed local ordinances, and determined punishments for violations of colonial laws. The traditional chiefs were accountable to the colonial administration rather than their own people. For that matter, the policy of indirect rule undermined the authority of indigenous people and their traditional system of governance. Therefore the British supplanted the indigenous popular authority with an external source of authority by appointing, managing, and directing the traditional authorities.[101] According to Mahmood Mamdani, the British colonial policy of indirect rule through the traditional chiefs abrogated the popular (clan) legitimacy and institutional constraints of peers or people—a phenomenon he referred to as "decentralized despotism."[102]

On the other hand, in urban areas, the minority African elite lived under direct colonial rule alongside minority Europeans and Indians. However, while African elites enjoyed all the other rights and privileges accorded to their European and Indian counterparts, they were racially differentiated in the enjoyment and exercise of civil rights and privileges, as well as access to high-level administrative posts. Furthermore, African elites were also exempted from customary laws and domination of traditional chiefs. The rural-urban divide and racial segregation in urban settings set the tone for the independence struggles and the subsequent state formation and operation.[103] For example, for African elites, independence meant freedom from

---

99. Okumu-Alya, "Regional Dimensions of the War."
100. Adyanga, "Modes of British Imperial Control," 3.
101. Adyanga, "Modes of British Imperial Control.".
102. Mamdani, *Citizen and Subject*, 43.
103. Mamdani, *Citizen and Subject*.

indigenous customs and authorities, as well as freedom to have civil rights and access to high-level administrative posts.[104]

Mamdani refers to dichotomized and differentiated treatment of races in urban and rural areas as the bifurcation of African states. In the postcolonial era, the rural-urban divisions led to the consolidation of diffused and concentrated power in the executives of the state,[105] and the strengthening of a decentralized despotism under local chiefs.

Mamdani's analysis of the British colonial system of indirect rule shows that the colonial system of administration is responsible for the abrogation of the authority of local citizens to determine the political processes of their countries and their rights to active participation in them. For that matter, it is not an exaggeration to conclude that the Ugandan state is an "artificial animal,"[106] because it is alien to the indigenous African cultures and customs. The colonial legacy wrestled power away from the people and instead concentrated it in the state.[107] This process externalized power at two different levels. First, the imperial control externalized the legitimacy of the Ugandan state, whereby Ugandan leaders owed their legitimacy to the external authority rather than indigenous authority. Second, as long as the Ugandan leaders adhered to the demands of the external authority, their conduct toward their own people was not subject to any local restraint because they did not need the consent of their own people to remain in power.

In Kwame Nkrumah's analysis, the phenomenon of externalizing the legitimacy of the state political power is perpetuated by neocolonialism. According to Nkrumah,

> The essence of neo-colonialism is that the State which is subject to it is, in theory, independent and has all the outward trappings of international sovereignty. In reality, its economic system and thus its political policy is directed from outside . . . Neo-colonialism is also the worst form of imperialism. For those who practice it, it means power without responsibility and for those who suffer from it, it means exploitation without redress.[108]

In Uganda, neocolonialism, which has characterized the political life of all the post-independence regimes, is an extension of colonialism. For instance, when Kabaka Mwanga of Buganda denounced the British assumption of the Bugandan sovereignty, he was deposed and exiled in 1897.

104. Adyanga, "Modes of British Imperial Control."
105. Mamdani, *Citizen and Subject*, 108.
106. Mamdani, *Citizen and Subject*, 107.
107. Bayart, "Civil Society in Africa."
108. Nkrumah, *Neo-Colonialism*, ix.

The colonial administration replaced Mwanga with his son, Daudi Chwa, a minor, who governed with the assistance of regents. Subsequently, Kabaka Chwa signed the 1900 Buganda Agreement with Britain under Sir Harry Johnston, sub-Commissioner to Uganda, which consolidated the British informal control over Buganda by externalizing Kabaka's legitimacy. The same policy applied to the Obote I and II regimes, whereby the overthrow of his regimes were sanctioned and supported by external powers.[109]

In the same manner, the current Ugandan government concealed the truth about the conflict with the complicit support of the international community until the Acholi people marshalled enough local and global support to unearth the true causes of the war, the antagonists, and its impacts on the Acholi people, the country, and the Great Lakes region. In the next section, I will discuss the nature of northern Ugandan conflict, the Acholi culture, and the impact of their intervention.[110]

ACHOLI COUNTERCULTURAL INTERVENTION

The Acholi intervention led to the peaceful resolution of the northern Uganda conflict. Initially, the government developed a military narrative that localized the conflict as an Acholi affair to justify its propaganda that the Acholi people deserved the war and the suffering they underwent. The government developed its narrative according to the global perception of conflicts in Africa, which favors military solution to political conflicts. As a result, the government gained the legitimacy to use a military approach to resolve the conflict. However, the Acholi people mounted a successful counternarrative that legitimized a peaceful approach to conflict resolution. The Acholi people overcame the culture of ethnic stratification and profiling, militarization of political conflicts, and the externalization of the state legitimacy in which the state socializes followers (the citizens) to a subservient passive role. In this context, followers risk undertaking an active role at the cost of their careers, civil liberties, properties, and lives.[111]

The intervention of the Acholi people is countercultural. Historically, when the British colonial administration established its control over the Acholi people and eventually integrated them into the Uganda Protectorate, the Acholi cultural system was one of the first casualties of the colonial

---

109. Adupa, "Conflict Continuous."

110. Nibbe, "Effects of a Narrative"; Okumu-Alya, "Regional Dimensions of the War."

111. Hutchful, "Military and Militarism in Africa."

administration.[112] Among other things, the British introduced a centralized system of governance that subjugated the Acholi chieftain to the jurisdiction of the central government. Since then, one of the legacies of the colonial rule in Uganda is the coexistence of the modern sector represented by the state and the traditional sector represented by local traditional institutions.[113] Under the aforementioned political setup, the state is supposed to control and empower traditional sectors, but instead the former exercises absolute control over the latter.[114] Although the colonial administration reinstated the sovereignty of local administrations in the 1962 constitution, the post-independence regimes of Milton A. Obote and Yoweri K. Museveni abrogated it using their respective constitutions of 1967 and 1995. Furthermore, culturally, all the previous regimes spared the Acholi cultural values and beliefs except the prolonged armed conflict under the Museveni's regime.[115]

Nevertheless, contrary to the norm whereby the state exercises absolute power over the traditional sectors, the Acholi people still managed to influence the Ugandan government to pursue peaceful approach to conflict resolution.[116] In particular, the nature of the conflict and the Acholi culture—among other factors—motivated the Acholi people to play an active role in the conflict's resolution.[117] Therefore, the Acholi people's active role in northern Ugandan conflict resolution is unique in Ugandan political history. For that matter, a proper understanding of northern Ugandan conflict resolution calls for explication of the intervention of the Acholi people. In the next section, I will discuss the nature of the conflict and the active role of the Acholi people despite the Ugandan government's vehement opposition.

Northern Ugandan Conflict

The northern Ugandan armed conflict is a complex subject given the nature of the global perceptions of conflict in the post-Cold War era and the culture of armed violence in Uganda since the colonial era. For example, the Ugandan government and the international community used a script,

112. Adupa, "Conflict Continuous."

113. Ajulu, *Holism in Development*, 105.

114. Ghai, "Participatory Development"; Holmquist and Ford, "Kenya," 97–111; IBRD, "Tenth Annual Review"; Thomas-Slayter, "Structural Change, Power Politics," 1479–85.

115. Onyango-Ku-Odongo, *Central Lwo During the Aconya*.

116. Allen, *Trial Justice*; Eriku and Kwo, "Museveni Apologizes for Army Atrocities"; Okello, "Kacoke Madit."

117. Komakech, *Reinventing and Validating the Cosmology*.

which reduced the conflict to a war between the Ugandan government and the LRA, where the focus was on the atrocities committed by the latter. However, given the Acholi people's knowledge of the role of the state, culture and conflict dynamics, they unearthed facets of the conflict that the government propaganda glossed over.[118] After a thorough analysis of the conflict in accordance with the Acholian cultural tenets of truth-telling and inclusiveness, they identified and pointed out the government's crimes of commission and omission in the Acholi subregion and the global factors related to it.[119]

Therefore, following their input, consensus emerged that the northern Ugandan conflict was multilayered and multifaceted. In particular, they identified five main characteristics about the conflict. First, it was a war between the Ugandan government and the Lord's Resistance Army (LRA). Second, it was the LRA atrocities against the wider Acholi population. Third, it was a proxy war between the Ugandan and the Sudanese governments through their support of the respective rebel groups in each other's countries. Fourth, it was an ethnic conflict driven by the north/south divide in Ugandan politics since the colonial era. Finally, it had an international nuance and flare such as the animosity between the Ugandan government and the other neighboring countries, and America's support for the SPLA rebels of Southern Sudan.[120] The Acholi analysis and response was informed by the history of political conflict in Africa.[121]

The northern Ugandan conflict started in 1986 following the overthrow of the military junta, the Uganda National Liberation Army (UNLA), led by General Tito Okello Lutwa, an Acholi and a northerner, by the National Resistance Army/movement (NRA/M) led by General Yoweri K. Museveni, a southerner. The overthrow of the Okello regime marked a turning point in Uganda's political history. It shifted both the political and military power from northerners to southerners.[122] The northerners had monopolized both security forces and politics since 1962, when Uganda attained its independence from Britain. Hence, many theorists[123] concluded that the Acholi people responded to recapture the political power they had lost. According to the loss of power hypothesis, "other reasons, such as the loss

118. Onyango-Ku-Odongo, *Uganda*.

119. Fiechter, "Role of Traditional Justice"; International Crisis Group, *Northern Uganda*; Onyango-Ku-Odongo, *Uganda*.

120. Nkurunziza, "Insurgency in Northern Uganda," 315.

121. International Crisis Group, *Northern Uganda*.

122. Nkurunziza, "Insurgency in Northern Uganda," 318; Parliament of the Republic of Uganda, *Report of the Committee*, 7.

123. Parliament of the Republic of Uganda, *Report of the Committee*, 7.

of military power that was considered as a humbling experience and the economic implications of the military defeat, merely facilitated this desire."

However, after further analysis I herein argue that the ethnic stratification and profiling, culture of military violence, and externalization of state legitimacy, which caused deep-seated mistrust and rivalry between northerners and southerners, sparked the conflict. First, the high level of mistrust intensified after Museveni's NRA/M soldiers used the 1985 Nairobi peace talks, initiated by the Okello regime, as a pretext to reorganize the NRA for combat operations that eventually toppled the Okello regime six months after they had signed the 1985 Nairobi peace agreement.[124] The disregard for the peace overture the Okello regime extended to Museveni's NRA/M, and the breach of the power-sharing agreement between the two antagonists portrayed the Museveni's NRA/M as a cunning group that believed in violence and violent means for achieving political goals.[125] The mistrust is rooted in the colonial legacy in which southerners regarded northerners as an inferior and warlike group. As such, southerners blamed the Acholi people without verifiable proof for the abuses meted out on them by the previous governments because the Acholi people were the majority in the UNLA. Therefore, when southerners overthrew the northerner-led government, they took it upon themselves to revenge and avenge the suffering they experienced under the previous regimes and to reinstate their dominant position over northerners.[126]

As I pointed out earlier, some of the abuses they meted out on the Acholi people were beyond mere revenge. So in response, the Acholi people mobilized every able-bodied adult male to forestall what they interpreted as the southerners' plot to wipe out the Acholi threat to their hold on military and political power.[127] The Acholi people responded to save the future of the Acholi community, which was on the verge of extinction at the hands of the NRA/M.[128]

For instance, when I visited the Internally Displaced People's camps in Gulu in 2002, 2007, and 2008, I discovered that the Acholi people were preoccupied with neither their condition before the war nor their suffering during the war, but rather with the impact of the conflict on the future of the Acholi people. In my conversations with elders, I learned that the fears

---

124. Nkurunziza, "Insurgency in Northern Uganda," 315; Komakec, "Making Peace (Peacemaking) in Uganda"; Prisca, "Analysis of the Rebel War," 335–45.
125. Gordon, "Complementarity and Alternative Justice," 621–702.
126. Komakec, "Making Peace (Peacemaking) in Uganda."
127. Omara-Otunnu, "Causes and Consequences of War."
128. Afako, *Northern Uganda*.

of the Acholi people were focused on the negative impact of the war on the underlying fabric of the Acholi community and their ability to build a new future. For example, in a conversation with an elder, I lamented the squalid conditions under which the people were living in the Alero camp, but the elder cut me short with a rejoinder, "Young man, our problem is not the living conditions in this camp or even the losses we have incurred. Our biggest question and worry is this: if this war ends today, shall we rebuild our community again?"[129] This sentiment is reflected in the data concerning the conflict and its impact on the Acholi people.[130]

The northern Uganda conflict was destructive and costly. The Civil Society Organisations for Peace in Northern Uganda (CSOPNU), in its report released in 2002, found that the war cost Uganda $1.33 billion between 1985 and 2002.[131] In the following quotation, Macleod Baker Ochola II, the former Anglican bishop of the Kitgum diocese and a proponent of the Acholi peaceful method of conflict resolution, described the social cost of the war:

> Amin's terror affected the military, the civil servants, but it did not really affect ordinary people. That's the difference with this government—our cattle, granaries and houses. The cattle rustling of the Karimojong was the first step in a process that has left the Acholi people deep in the pit of poverty.[132]

From 1997 onward, when the government of Uganda issued a military order for the forceful displacement and misplacement of the Acholi people into the Internally Displaced People's (IDP) camps, 1.5 million people were living in forty IDP camps all over the Acholi subregion.[133] The camp conditions shattered the Acholi people's lives both economically and socially. For example, they were denied access to their land and for the entire thirteen-year period they lived in IDP camps. They were rendered beggars who survived on humanitarian relief from international agencies such as the World Food Program.[134] They lost over 285,000 cattle to Karamojong warriors in connivance with the NRA.[135] The war tore the social fabric of the Acholi community. One resident of the Paicho camp summed up his life in the camp:

129. Ofumbi, *Identity and Transformation*, 111.

130. Acholi Religious Leaders Peace Initiative, *Let My People Go*, 17; Afako, *Northern Uganda*, 80.

131. Nyongesa, "$300b Lost in Conflicts Yearly."

132. Leggett, *Uganda*, 29.

133. Fiechter, "Role of Traditional Justice," 11.

134. Acholi Religious Leaders Peace Initiative, *Let My People Go*, 13.

135. Doom and Vlassenroot, "Kony's Message," 5–36.

> I used to have a yearly harvest of twelve bags of rice, which I would use for paying children's education. Now I wake up in the morning, I can't go to my fields and my only choice is to spend the whole day doing nothing.[136]

The United Nations confirmed the Acholi people's pessimism about the war that threatened their social fabric and their existence as a people:

> The most disturbing aspect of this humanitarian crisis is the fact that this is a war fought by children on children—minors make up almost 90 percent of the LRA's soldiers. Some recruits are as young as eight and are inducted through raids on villages . . . Those who attempt to escape are killed. For those living in a state of constant fear, violence becomes a way of life and the psychological trauma is incalculable.[137]

Between 20,000 and 25,000 children were abducted by the rebels, and over 10,000 are still unaccounted for, while 1,500 are still in the bush with the LRA.[138]

The Acholi people's fears were based on concrete evidence. For instance, the entire population in northern Uganda was devastated by displacement, abductions, murder, and other atrocities. A summary of the destruction is given in Table 2.

The war resulted in devastating and widespread human rights violations as well as the destruction of the Acholi socioeconomic and political infrastructures. Thousands of people were brutally abducted, killed, maimed, injured, raped, traumatized, displaced, and misplaced. Most importantly, the conflict eroded the Acholi social fabric due to the breakdown of families and community life. Most Acholi elders were worried that they might lose their heritage regardless of when the war ended:

> A life of dependence and destitution breeds lack of respect to parental authority, they don't get any help from their parents. If children are not provided for by their parents, they will try to fend [for] themselves. Therefore, there are so many children from camps who join the Local Defense Units at the age of 13 or 14, since they have nothing to do and the perspective of earning 40,000 shillings a month is attractive. If things continue this way

---

136. Acholi Religious Leaders Peace Initiative, *Let My People*, 14.
137. Fiechter, "Role of Traditional Justice," 11.
138. Fiechter, "Role of Traditional Justice."

we are going to lose a whole generation that has been born or brought up in the camps.[139]

The impact of the war bred feelings of hopelessness, powerlessness, disenfranchisement, voicelessness, frustration, anger, and protest, which they demonstrated in the their voting patterns in the 1996, 2001, and 2006 presidential elections, where the incumbent president consistently lost to the main presidential challengers by huge margins.[140]

Catastrophe	Number affected	Percent
Acholi population displaced	1.8 million	94
Children abducted	25,000	6.6
Children dying each week, from all causes	1000	5
Cattle stolen	380,191	95
Schools destroyed	737	60
Children not attending school	250,000	75
Students who drop out after elementary school, before entering high school*	133,000*	98.5*

Table 2: Statistics on the Impact of War in the Acholi Subregion, 1986–2006

Note. Based on Civil Society Organizations for Peace in Northern Uganda, "Counting the Cost," 7–8; Nampindo, "Impact of Conflict," 13–15; Ofumbi, "Significance of the Humanity," 114.

*Includes only Kitgum district. All other figures include both Gulu and Kitgum districts.

Second, northern Ugandan armed conflict was multifaceted and multilayered. It required a different approach from the one the Ugandan government used in order to understand and address it.[141] For example, the perpetrators and the victims of the war were mostly family, friends, and neighbors. Most of the LRA combatants who carried out atrocities against their own relatives were victims of abduction and forceful indoctrination and socialization into the rebel ranks at a very young age. Second and perhaps most important, northern Ugandan conflict was part of a spiral of military violence that has characterized Ugandan politics and history since the colonial period. Unfortunately, since the Ugandan government censored

139. Acholi Religious Leaders Peace Initiative, *Let My People Go*, 30.
140. Doom and Vlassenroot, "Kony's Message," 23.
141. Tan, "Reconciliation as Political Ethic."

news about the conflict in favor of propaganda that portrayed the LRA as bandits and terrorists without any rational political objectives save for committing heinous crimes like killings, miming, abduction, and looting, it was very difficult to establish the nature and scope of the conflict and its impacts. However, after the bold and courageous intervention of the Acholi people, the international scope of the conflict was unearthed. For instance, it became apparent that the conflict was partially a proxy war between the Ugandan and Sudanese governments and the other neighboring countries given the Ugandan government's sponsorship of cross-border aggressions in the region.[142]

It was also discovered that the conflict was rooted in the culture of ethnic stratification and profiling, military violence, and the externalization of state legitimacy. As a result, when the Acholi people unearthed the complex nature of the war, they concluded that the solution to the northern Uganda conflict required a holistic analysis of Uganda's political history since the colonial era, as well as the global systems that prefer dichotomous approaches to systems approaches, which consider interrelations among things rather than merely their differences and similarities.

Furthermore, the conflict was based on diversionary propaganda driven by the post-cold war conflict discourse, Western discourse on good governance and democracy, and culture of military violence in Uganda.[143] Therefore, following the active participation of the Acholi people, multinational forums were formed which culminated in the Juba Peace talks and agreement that in turn led to the decongestion of the IDP camps and resettlement of the Acholi people to their homes in 2009.[144]

Finally, it was an ethnicized conflict, which was fought along the historical ethnic divide that pitted southerners against northerners. It was also characterized by the "bifurcation of State" built on paternalism and externalization of the state legitimacy whereby people were subjected to taxation without the freedom of participation in their own governance.[145] In the next section, I will discuss the origin of the Acholi people and their culture, which informed their active followership.

142. Lord's Resistance Army Disarmament and Northern Uganda Recovery Act of 2009.

143. Ramsbotham and Woodhouse, *Humanitarian Intervention in Contemporary Conflict*.

144. Baines, "Accountability, Reconciliation, and the Juba"; Baines, "Peace Process in Northern Uganda"; Finnegan, "Forging Forgiveness," 424; Riano-Alcala and Bainesy, "Archive in the Witness."

145. Oloya, *Child to Soldier*; Omara-Otunnu, "Struggle for Democracy in Uganda"; Onyango-Ku-Odongo, *Uganda*.

The Acholi-Self and the "Other"

The Acholi people "are part of cattle keeping Luo-speakers who migrated from their homeland along the Nile River in Southern Sudan in the sixteenth century and settled in different parts of East Africa."[146] The Acholi people have experienced some changes in their culture. "Prior to colonialism, the people known today as the Acholi referred to themselves as *An-loco-li*, which means 'I am a human being.'"[147] But during and after the colonial era, it also meant "black."[148] In its original version, the label *An-loco-li* transcended both ethnic and geographical boundaries even though the "Acholi people had a collective identity encapsulated in cultures and customs that governed their existence for thousands of years."[149] However, when Britain colonized Uganda, "the Acholi people developed a distinct ethnic identity that characterizes them as 'northerners' or dark people, something that sets them apart from the people in the 'South' commonly referred to as southerners."[150]

Economically, the Acholi survived as cattle herders and as mixed agricultural farmers. During the northern Uganda war, they lost their cattle to Karimong warriors who were conniving with the NRA/UPDF soldiers, and access to their land when the government forced them into IDP camps where they ended up living for over 15 years.[151] Before the war, the Acholi people practiced hunting during the dry season. Due to the escalation of the war, the Acholi people transformed their skills of hunting wild animals into hunting human beings, a new development that abetted unprecedented violence in the Acholi subregion.[152]

Politically, the Acholi people belong to different domains, each composed of designated villages formed along family lines. A chief known locally as *Rwot*, who is also the head of his own domain, heads the chiefdom.[153] However, although the *Rwot* is the head of a chiefdom, and due to that title is the most important political and social figure, he nonetheless shares his powers and responsibilities with the heads of other domains and

---

146. Atkinson, *Roots of Ethnicity*, 74.
147. Atkinson, *Roots of Ethnicity*, 78; Tutu and Abrams, *God Has a Dream*.
148. Doom and Vlassenroot, "Kony's Message," 10.
149. Ofumbi, "Significance of the Humanity."
150. Ofumbi, "Significance of the Humanity."
151. Doom and Vlassenroot, "Kony's Message," 12.
152. Acholi Religious Leaders Peace Initiative, *Let My People Go*, 15.
153. Girling, *Acholi of Uganda*; Ogot, *History of the Southern Luo*.

the constituents of the respective lineages.[154] Among other things, the *Rwot* is the "link between the living and the dead. It [is] his duty to offer sacrifices to the ancestors on behalf of his people" as well as to preside over reconciliation rites.[155] The *Rwot* rules through consensus whereby major decisions in each domain are derived from the interests of its constituent villages. There are no centralized judicial or executive bodies, which control the activities of the Acholi people. The respective lineages enjoyed shared authority and a fair amount of autonomy until the introduction of colonial and post-colonial centralized forms of administration, which usurped the powers of the latter.[156] Although the indigenous political structure is still intact, its functions have been taken over by the representatives of the central government.

Religiously, "the Acholi world is a spiritual community, densely populated with spirits, forces and powers."[157] The spiritual life of the Acholi people rested upon chiefdoms under respective *Rwot*. Each chiefdom had its own shrine and priests under a *Rwot*.[158] There are elaborate rites associated with different communal events, issues, and life stages of the Acholi people. With regard to war, guardian spirits and human messengers, known as *nebi*, guard and guide the community accordingly.[159] The Acholi traditional religion was not static. The Acholi people's religion permeates "their thought and behavior and, by extension, define[s] both the nature of communication and the information content of communication in its native ground" as well as their general lifestyle.[160] It is therefore not a coincidence that the wars in Acholi land had spiritual characteristics and appeal.

In times of conflict, the Acholi people first sought for peace and reconciliation among the warring parties. They never practiced capital punishment. Even murderers were rescued from the wrath of bereaved relatives by taking them to stay with uncles or aunts during the period of grief. Later on, the uncle or aunt would bring such a person back to the community to confess their sins and to pay reparation for the murder.[161] For any conflict at a clan level, the Acholi people had reconciliation rituals and processes for restoring broken relationships. The gravity of the sin committed dictated the procedure.

154. Atkinson, *Roots of Ethnicity*, 78.
155. Lapat, "Role of the Structures," 52.
156. Atkinson, "Evolution of Ethnicity."
157. Doom and Vlassenroot, "Kony's Message," 17.
158. Girling, *Acholi of Uganda*, 105.
159. Sturges, "Information and Communication," 204–12.
160. Sturges, "Information and Communication," 206.
161. Lapat, "Role of the Structures," 80.

Acholi Culture and War

An overview of how the Acholi people culturally regard war is necessary in order to understand why they pursued peaceful options to conflict resolution despite Ugandan government opposition. Culturally, the Acholi are a peaceful people. Unlike imperial kingdoms such as Buganda and Bunyoro in the south, the Acholi used diplomacy at all times to settle conflicts and opted for war as a last resort.[162] The Acholi sanctioned war only to defend their homesteads (*Gwooko Dog Paco*), which represented their heritage. The Acholi rules of engagement in the situation of a justified war prohibited plunder of any nature and the use or abuse of children and women by both sides of the war.[163] In an event of external aggression, which defies all diplomatic efforts, all able-bodied adult men are mobilized to defend their ancestral homestead as a matter of necessity and as a preemptive strike against an enemy about to attack. It is therefore not true that the Acholi are militaristic as alleged by Heike Behrend.[164] In fact, the Acholi never engaged in any war without establishing a just cause for it. The process of establishing the basis of a just war is known as *lapir*. The principles of *lapir* do not authorize unsanctioned aggression against enemies for any reason.[165]

Source of the Acholi Traditional System of Conflict Resolution

In this section, I will discuss why the Acholi people preferred a peaceful approach to conflict resolution over the military approach the Ugandan government espoused. I will also identify the impact of the Acholi method of conflict resolution on northern Ugandan conflict. The Acholi traditional system of conflict resolution is rooted in Acholi life views and practices.

For the Acholi people just like their other counterparts in Sub-Saharan Africa, human life and community is centered on harmony, which refers to human "connectedness" and interdependence.[166] Harmony is encapsulated and reflected in the term "referred to as *Ubuntu* or 'human beings.'"[167] In their context, "*Ubuntu* recognizes that the entire creation is the mental expression of the divine or the entire creation is a thought in the mind of

---

162. Oloya, *Child to Soldier*, 70.
163. Onyango-Ku-Odongo, *Central Lwo During the Aconya*, 100.
164. Behrend, *Alice Lakwena*, 39.
165. Omara-Otunnu, "Causes and Consequences of War."
166. Gitari, "Claims of Jesus," 119; Tutu and Abrams, *God Has a Dream*.
167. Doom and Vlassenroot, "Kony's Message," 10.

the creator."[168] It connotes the recognition of the transcendence and the immanence of the divine, which forms human "understanding that a person is a person because he/she recognizes the humanity of others."[169] Thus, harmony (vis-à-vis human connectedness and interdependence) is the essence of life and the highest goal of a community, which is expressed in the daily routines of life.[170]

In this context, "spiritual life permeates the whole of their lives and it expresses itself through rituals, songs, dances, myths, proverbs, stories, and riddles just to mention a few."[171] Overall, "the Acholi people derive their identities and their behaviors from their spirituality and in return their identity and their behaviors inform and shape their spirituality."[172] In Dallas Willard's language, Acholi spirituality is "'embodied spirituality' where faith is not removed from everyday life. It is the relationship of our embodied selves that has the natural and irrepressible effect of making us alive to the Kingdom of God—here and now in the material world."[173] In other words, "[f]or the Acholi people, the whole of life is a sacred act of expressing and growing into the image of God."[174] According to John S. Mbiti, "Acholi spirituality is a living spirituality that is written on the lives of its people."[175]

Thus, among the Acholi people, harmony is expressed in the following proverb: "I am because we are, and since we are therefore I am."[176] This proverb encourages the Acholi people to esteem the sacredness of life in everyone. For example, Desmond Tutu and Douglas Adams wrote that Africans "know that they are diminished when others are humiliated, diminished when others are oppressed, diminished when others are treated as if they were lesser than who they are."[177]

Relating to conflict, "the Acholi people believe that violence mars human identity, which in return destroys the capacity to create the harmony required to build a mutual community."[178] Therefore, unlike the Western modernist epistemology of justice, which defines a wrong as a crime

---

168. Ofumbi, "Significance of the Humanity," 1.
169. Ofumbi, "Significance of the Humanity," 1.
170. Komakech, *Reinventing and Validating the Cosmology*.
171. Ofumbi, "Significance of the Humanity."
172. Mbiti, *Introduction to African Religion*, 24.
173. Willard, *Spirit of the Disciplines*, 31.
174. Ofumbi, "Significance of the Humanity," 1.
175. Mbiti, *Introduction to African Religion*, 126.
176. Ofumbi, "Significance of the Humanity," 1.
177. Tutu and Abrams, *God Has a Dream*, 26.
178. Ofumbi, "Significance of the Humanity," 1.

remedied through punishment upon an establishment of guilt, the Acholi epistemology of justice "prefers the notion of 'wrong' to 'crime' and 'restoration' to 'retribution.'"[179] Second, a wrong among the Acholi people is accorded a social rather than an individual dimension. That means that the community rather than the individual alone is responsible for responding to a wrong. This is due to their "mindset in which the worst evil is to live in complete disregard of the humanity of others,"[180] and the worst punishment is exclusion from society. This is important to them because the Acholi mindset "is built upon a sense of a moral universe, which is predicated upon God's love and power to transform the worst of the human situation to the best of what it should be despite all the evidences that seem to be to the contrary."[181]

Tutu and Abrams contend that, "in this mindset, neither evil nor injustice nor oppression nor lies have the last word."[182] For that matter, "This mindset endears the Acholi people to see others as humans who are capable of being human no matter what their condition might be."[183] In this regard, justice in Acholi is restorative rather than retributive.

Impact of Acholi Countercultural Response

The Acholi people's countercultural response was responsible for the resolution of northern Ugandan conflicts in many ways. For instance, their peaceful approach overcame mistrust among the stakeholders. In the next section, I will highlight the impact of Acholi active followership.

Kacoke Madit and Media Attention

In the Acholi community, conflicts are common and are regarded as challenges that require a theoretical foundation and inclusive structure for community involvement to resolve them. The community forum that deals with community challenges is called *Kacoke Madit,* which means "big meeting." Each big meeting is structured according to the nature of the case at stake. The Acholi use a community ritual known as *Mato Oput* among others to

---

179. Komakech, *Reinventing and Validating the Cosmology*, 129.
180. Ofumbi, "Significance of the Humanity," 1.
181. Ofumbi, "Significance of the Humanity."
182. Tutu and Abrams, *God Has a Dream*, 26.
183. Ofumbi, "Significance of the Humanity," 1.

resolve conflicts.[184] As a precondition for reconciliation and peace, *Mato Oput*—(drinking the bitter roots of the Oput tree) requires crime perpetrators to narrate the whole truth about a crime, acknowledge guilt and pledge to refrain from acts of aggression.[185] The victims too have a responsibility.

When the Acholi established that the Ugandan government was deliberately misinforming the world about the conflict, they established and shared with the international community the facts about the war despite government news censorship. Prior to that, the world did not know anything about the conflict.

However, following the successful Acholi campaigns to disseminate information about the war, the web of ignorance and silence that had characterized the conflict was broken.[186] For example, in 2002, the Acholi people invited Jan Egeland to northern Uganda.[187] Following his own assessment of the humanitarian conditions in the camps, and declaration, more international stakeholders such as the Carter Peace Center, Human Rights Watch, and the U.S. Congress joined the effort to identify the facts about the war and to find solutions.[188] For example, two years later, the U.S. Congress passed the Northern Uganda Crisis Response Act. The act, among many other things, called for improvements in the professionalism of Ugandan military personnel stationed in northern Uganda, and for the Sudanese government to stop its support of the LRA rebels. Also, the Human Rights Watch discovered that Ugandan government soldiers and LRA rebels had committed gross human rights abuses in northern Uganda.[189]

Therefore, when the local and international news media gained interest in the human rights violations in northern Uganda, the historical and regional scope of the conflict became apparent to the international community. Consequently, the international community influenced the Ugandan government and the LRA to pursue a peaceful option to resolve the conflict.

Voices of the Acholi People

The Acholi sociopolitical system is decentralized. Members of the Acholi community are involved in all major political processes and decisions

184. Komakech, *Reinventing and Validating the Cosmology*.
185. Komakec and Ahmed, "Quest for Governance, Conflict Transformation"; Ojera, "Northern Uganda"; Pain, "*Bending of Spears*."
186. Okello, "Kacoke Madit"; Poblicks, "Kacoke Madit."
187. Allen, *Trial Justice*, 73; Associated Press, "Northern Uganda."
188. Nkurunziza, "Insurgency in Northern Uganda," 325.
189. Human Rights Watch, "ICC."

affecting their lives. In a similar manner, during northern Ugandan conflict, the Acholi people demanded platforms for the Acholi people to participate in the conflict resolution. For instance, the Acholi people demanded that all the programs the government created to address northern Uganda conflict be relocated from Kampala to northern Uganda. Second, they demanded that the government appoint Acholi people to head all those programs to enhance the popular participation of the Acholi. As a result, all government programs handling northern Ugandan conflict resolution, such as the Amnesty Commission and the Northern Uganda Social Action Fund (NUSAF), were relocated to Gulu. Second, the government filled the top leadership of the programs with people from the Acholi subregion.[190]

Therefore, the popular participation of the Acholi people in the search for peace in northern Uganda marked a turning point in the conflict's resolution. Their efforts overcame the government propaganda that had confined the conflict to the LRA. Second, the Acholi people galvanized the global support, which in turn subordinated the state to the interests of the Acholi community.[191]

Amnesty Act and Amnesty Commission

The efforts to end armed conflict in northern Uganda encountered numerous obstacles. One of the philosophical obstacles was the dispute over how to end the war. On one hand, President Museveni preferred military solutions to political and armed conflicts.[192] Consequently, the Ugandan government opted for the supremacy of a military solution to political conflict. On the other hand, globally, the international community prioritized a retributive judicial approach over a restorative judicial approach, which the Acholi people espoused.

However, following their cultural system of conflict resolution, the Acholi people opted for a peaceful resolution to political conflict. After overcoming the government's deliberate efforts to discredit their relentless pursuit for peace, the Acholi people managed to galvanize international consensus that a peaceful option was the only viable solution to the conflict.[193] Consequently, the Ugandan government, under intense pressure from the international and local communities, adopted the Acholi traditional method of conflict resolution. For example, it passed and enacted

190. Ofumbi, "Significance of the Humanity."
191. Atkinson, *Roots of Ethnicity*, 4.
192. Obote, "Notes on Concealment of Genocide."
193. Allen, *Trial Justice*, 85.

the Amnesty Act through the Parliament in 1999 and 2000 respectively. To implement the act, the government created the Amnesty Commission, headed by an Acholi. Following the enactment of the Amnesty Act, over 500 rebels renounced rebellion and applied for amnesty in the first week alone. By 2003, over 5,000 rebels had renounced rebellion and applied for amnesty.[194]

Therefore, when the Ugandan government embraced a reconciliatory tone and included the Acholi people in the governance of their own affairs, the latter also changed their attitudes toward the state. For instance, in 2011, a considerable number of people voted for the incumbent president for the first time since 1986. As a result, many Ugandans believe that the Acholi gesture of support for a southerner was perhaps the beginning of the process of national healing and reconciliation that will bridge the gap between the south and the north, as well as subordinate the state's interests to those of the citizens.

Peace Talks and Traditional Justice System

The government of Uganda had indeed pursued and signed peace accords with different rebel groups in Uganda in the past. Some of the peace talks included the 1985 Nairobi peace agreement between the UNLA and the NRA; the June 3rd 1988 Peace Agreement between the Uganda People's Defense Army/Movement (UPDA/M) and the NRA/M; the July 14, 1990 Addis Ababa Peace Agreement signed between the UPDM and the Uganda People's Movement (UPM); and finally, the 1993/94 Betty Bigombe aborted peace efforts that were sabotaged by the government's seven-day ultimatum to the rebels to surrender.[195]

However, there are remarkable differences between the former peace talks enumerated above and the Juba peace talks. For instance, all the previous peace talks benefited the antagonists and their supporters rather than the victims of conflicts. The opposite is true about the later peace talks. For example, in the 2006 Juba peace talks, all the stakeholders were involved in the initiation as well as the peace talk's proceedings. The inclusive representation bound the antagonists to the tenets of the agreement they signed in 2008. Although Kony and President Museveni never signed the final document, the cessation of hostilities following the accord enabled over one million people to resettle in their land in 2009.[196]

194. Allen, *Trial Justice*, 75; International Crisis Group, *Northern Uganda*.
195. Westbrook, "Torment of Northern Uganda," 211.
196. Fiechter, "Role of Traditional Justice," 11.

After the Juba peace talks, the neighboring governments of the Sudan, the Democratic Republic of Congo, and the Central African Republic formed a joint military and diplomatic effort to flush out the LRA from their respective territories. The military protocol they signed sanctioned a joint cross-border operation under which the Uganda army got the permission to pursue the LRA beyond the Ugandan borders. Since then, the LRA has neither crossed the border nor attacked targets in Uganda.[197]

Most importantly, the government and the international community formally recognized the Acholi traditional system of conflict resolution.[198] The Ugandan government adopted it as an alternative justice system alongside the conventional justice system. It set up a special division of the High Court of Uganda to try the initiators of human rights violations while other offenders are tried through the traditional justice system.[199] The Acholi traditional systems of conflict resolution is distinct from the transitory justice system adopted to resolve conflicts in places like Rwanda, South Africa, and Yugoslavia[200]

Socioeconomic Transformation

In Acholi, security is synonymous with development and holistic well-being rather than the mere absence of war. They demanded peace in order to secure a prosperous Acholi by the Acholi people. Based on their demands, the government disbanded the Internally Displaced People's camps and allowed the people to return to their former homes that no longer existed.

SUMMARY

The northern Ugandan conflict was part of the spiral of political armed violence that has plagued Uganda since the colonial era. Although the Ugandan government censored news about the conflict, the courageous response of the Acholi people highlighted its multilayered and multifaceted nuances which enhanced holistic, communal, participatory, proactive, and restorative approaches to its resolution. The active followership of the Acholi people overcame the culture of ethnic stratification and profiling,

---

197. Fiechter, "Role of Traditional Justice," 12.

198. International Crisis Group, *Northern Uganda*; Komakec and Ahmed, "Quest for Governance, Conflict Transformation."

199. Human Rights Watch, "Justice for Serious Crimes."

200. Okumu-Alya, "Regional Dimensions of the War."

political violence, and the externalization of state legitimacy. Instead, it created a culture in which citizens now actively participate in the political process of their governance. However, while we know the role the Acholi people played in the conflict's resolution, nothing is known about how they developed their active followership.

4

Methods and Procedures

IN this current chapter, I will describe my research design—philosophical assumptions, research paradigm, and research approach—as well as the procedures I followed regarding data collection and storage, data analysis, and reporting of the research findings. I will also address validation issues and ethical challenges that emerged during the study.

PHILOSOPHICAL ASSUMPTIONS AND INTERPRETATIVE FRAMEWORKS

The philosophical position and interpretative framework I adopted for this grounded theory case study were based on the research problem and qualitative research paradigm. Qualitative researchers acknowledge that researchers' personal biases color their research. Therefore, as the primary data collection instruments, it is imperative for qualitative researchers to spell out an elaborate methodology that enables them to know and articulate their biases so they can design mitigating measures to undergird the authenticity of their study.

Consequently, I state here the philosophical assumptions and interpretive framework that guided this qualitative grounded theory case study research process and outcome. Overall, the interpretive framework that undergirded this study is social constructionism anchored on "systems thinking" and relational leadership theory. Systems thinking is a mental model that regards entities as systems in which the parts influence each other within a whole.[1] It is an interpretative framework that considers interrelationships among different variables rather than merely distinctive similarities and differences. It is "a discipline that prioritizes the holistic picture over compartmentalized entities. As a framework, it focuses on "patterns of change rather than static 'snapshots.'"[2] On the other hand, the relational approach is processual. It regards variables like followers and leaders as byproducts of a process rather that distinct entities in and of themselves.[3]

Therefore, while I believe ontologically that objective reality exists independent of human experience, epistemologically I affirm that independent objective reality is experienced subjectively.[4] In that regard, objective reality and subjective reality are mutually inclusive. In the same vein, axiologically I believe that both the data I collected and the findings from the analysis are interpreted views. Therefore, in this study, I primarily uncovered the processes by which followers develop and enact active followership. I explored it through participants' subjective, in-depth understanding of the research problem in relation to the context in which they were situated in order to develop a complex understanding of the phenomenon.

Therefore, I did not use philosophical assumptions and interpretative frameworks as distinct entities with fixed boundaries. Nevertheless, I still categorized each of the philosophical assumptions and interpretative frameworks according to their distinctive features that integrate them into the whole. So while I chose social constructivism as the ideal interpretative framework for the research topic under study, I did not necessarily preclude relevant insights from other interpretative frameworks. For example, I used critical theory to uncover the consciousness that governed leadership theory during the industrial era, which is important because the knowledge of such consciousness creates the impetus to develop or acquire an alternative understanding, which calls for appropriate actions to change the status quo.[5] This approach is consistent with the purpose of this study in that I sought to uncover and interpret how participants developed and enacted followership identities, roles, and behaviors, a process that calls for examining the linkages and interactions among systems of variables.[6]

1. Senge and Sterman, "Systems Thinking and Organizational Learning," 137–50.
2. Senge, *Fifth Discipline*, 1.
3. Hosking and Bouwen, "Organizational Learning," 129–32; Hosking et al., *Management and Organization*; Hosking and Fineman, "Organizing Processes," 583–604.
4. Hiebert, *Missiological Implications of Epistemological Shifts*; Starcher, "Qualitaive Research in Missiological Studies," 54–63.
5. Crotty, *Foundations of Social Research*.
6. Merriam, *Qualitative Research*.

RESEARCHER'S PERSONAL BACKGROUND

I am a Ugandan, born and raised in Uganda. I was brought up by my Christian maternal grandparents, who lived a countercultural lifestyle that has impacted my life and ministry orientation. In the pursuit of a countercultural lifestyle, I have viewed most human social problems as stemming from the spiritual roots of social structures and practices. This point of view followed a conversation I had with my grandfather in which he explained that whereas people establish social structures and practices for the good of a society, over time, social structures and practices develop a life of their own whereby, instead of them serving the society, the society starts to serve them. Using many examples, he cautioned me never to regard a culture as either good or bad, but rather as something that is either dead or alive, which requires discernment and skill to make it serve you without you serving it.

Therefore, when I went to northern Uganda over ten years ago to facilitate a leadership workshop, I was struck by the stories the leaders shared about how the Acholi people used their culture of peaceful conflict resolution to influence the Ugandan government to adopt a peaceful approach to resolving the conflict that had plagued the region for more than a decade. In their stories, I recognized active followership, which influenced me to use their example as a case to explore how followers develop and enact active followership. Although I come from a tribe that shares the same Luo ancestry with the Acholi people, my interest in the Acholi people had nothing to do with their ethnicity. Nevertheless, my Luo ethnic background resulted in my building an instantaneous rapport with my research participants.

RESEARCH PARADIGM: QUALITATIVE RESEARCH

A research paradigm must be congruent with the researcher's biases, theoretical framework, and the research topic.[7] Overall, there are three social science research paradigms: quantitative, mixed methods, and qualitative.[8] My rationale for using qualitative research paradigm was as follows.

First, it was designed to provide an in-depth understanding of a problem. It is focused on a few participants with the aim of developing "a complex picture of the problem under study comprising multiple perspectives, different factors involved in the situation, and a larger picture of what emerges."[9] My goal was to uncover and interpret participants' subjective,

---

7. Joseph A. Maxwell, *Qualitative Research Design*.
8. Creswell, *Qualitative Inquiry and Research Design*.
9. Creswell and Plano, *Designing and Conducting Mixed Methods*, 25.

in-depth understandings of how followers develop and enact followership identities, roles, and behaviors in leadership processes and outcomes. Therefore, I conducted an inductive study that accorded me the flexibility "to move back and forth between the themes and the data until [I established] a comprehensive set of themes that explain the complex patterns that emerge from the analysis."[10]

Second, since I was the primary research instrument in this study, I interacted with participants face-to-face over time to gather comprehensive data using multiple sources such as interviews, documents, audiovisual recordings, and artifacts.

Third, for me to explore the dynamic relationships among the different variables and construct patterns that explain how followers develop and enact followership identities, roles, and behaviors in the leadership process, I inductively engaged the deeper thoughts and behaviors of the participants and the context in which they responded.

Finally, my research design was emergent. That is, all phases of the research process were driven by the dynamic interactions between the researcher and the participants in the context of the research problem. In this case, the research question, forms of data collection, and participants changed considering my interaction with the participants situated in the context of the phenomenon. In such a complex process, I chose qualitative research methodologies and data collecting strategies to create an in-depth understanding of the problem.

RESEARCH APPROACH: GROUNDED THEORY CASE STUDY

I called my approach grounded theory case study because I used the former to collect and analyze the data and the latter to locate the research arena in a context bound by time and space. A case study is appropriate when a particular case requires study because of its uniqueness (i.e., an intrinsic case study). It is also appropriate when there is an issue and the case is used as an instrument to understand it (i.e., an instrumental case study).[11] Mine is an instrumental case study in which I explored the Acholi people's active followership in the northern Ugandan conflict resolution between 1985 and 2012 in order to understand how followers develop and enact followership identities, roles, and behaviors in leadership processes and outcomes.

10. Creswell, *Qualitative Inquiry and Research Design*, 43.
11. Stake, *Art of Case Study Research*.

However, in order to advance a new theory within followership studies, I used grounded theory methods and procedures to collect and analyze data.

DATA COLLECTION STRATEGIES AND PROCEDURES

In this section, I will discuss the data collection strategies and procedures I used in this qualitative grounded theory case study, including sampling procedures, site and participants, and the case. In the next section, I will discuss criteria for case selection.

Sampling Procedure

Because this was a qualitative study using grounded theory case study methods, I needed participants who could "purposefully inform an understanding of the research problem and central phenomenon in this study."[12] I identified and contacted participants from among the Acholi people who pioneered and coordinated the active followership role of the Acholi people during northern Ugandan conflict resolution. Their exceptional knowledge of the phenomenon and willingness to share their in-depth understanding with me allowed me to formulate a robust theory.

Site and Participants

In a qualitative case study, the researcher makes two levels of sampling choices: first, the researcher must get a case or cases, which are significant. Second, the researcher must select participants, activities, and documents to interview, observe, and analyze respectively within the selected case or cases.[13] In this study, I selected the case, participants (see Appendix A for a list of participants by pseudonyms), and documents, which I will discuss in the next section.

The Case Study

The current qualitative grounded theory case study is an explanatory, instrumental case study designed to understand a specific problem—how

---

12. Joseph A. Maxwell, *Qualitative Research Design*, 97.
13. Merriam, *Qualitative Research*, 81.

followers develop and enact followership identities, roles, and behaviors in leadership processes and outcomes.[14] I used the case of the active followership of the Acholi people in the northern Ugandan conflict resolution between 1985 and 2012.

When the northern Ugandan armed conflict started in 1985, many prominent Acholi people fled their ancestral homes and country. Many were granted asylum in Europe, North America, and other parts of the world, from whence they formed a forum of the Acholi people in the diaspora known as *Kacoke Madit* (big meeting) to advocate for a peaceful solution to northern Ugandan conflict.[15] According to my preliminary contacts, the architects of *Kacoke Madit* settled in Europe and North America, and all the archival records of their activities are stored in London. The Acholi at home also formed different local forums like the Acholi Parliamentary Group, Acholi Religious Leaders Peace Initiatives, and the Acholi Traditional Leaders forum, among others, to lobby for the adoption of the Acholi traditional method of conflict resolution as the only viable solution to the northern Ugandan conflict.[16] The original members who formed the aforementioned groups are still alive and were available to participate in this case study. Therefore, I chose the participants from among the Acholi people who pioneered and coordinated the active followership role of the Acholi people during the northern Ugandan conflict resolution.

Criteria for Participant Selection

Generally, in qualitative case study research, there are three criteria to determine case selection: accessibility, direct replication, and variation.[17] However, since this was research for a single case study, I used the criteria of accessibility and variation. The third criterion, direct replication, does not apply in my case because it is mainly used in multiple case studies.

Accessibility

The participants I contacted to get information from for this case study were all accessible. The participants were comprised of Acholi individuals, men

---

14. Creswell, *Qualitative Inquiry and Research Design*; Stake, *Art of Case Study Research*; Yin, *Case Study Research*.
15. Poblicks, "Kacoke Madit."
16. Acholi Religious Leaders Peace Initiative, *Let My People Go*.
17. Foss and Waters, *Destination Dissertation*.

and women who pioneered and coordinated the exemplary followership role of the Acholi people in the northern Ugandan conflict resolution between 1985 and 2012. I selected the participants from among those Acholi individuals who initiated *Kacoke Madit*, the Acholi Parliamentary Group, the Acholi Religious Leaders Peace Initiative, the women's forum, the Lord's Resistance Army (LRA) returnees, Acholi journalists, and the Acholi Traditional Leaders forum, because they have in-depth understanding of the phenomenon by virtue of their shared interest and participation in the peaceful resolution of the northern Ugandan conflict, even though each group might have examined it from different viewpoints.

I established contact with the key people who in turn connected me to the other participants in both the diaspora and Uganda. For example, I met and discussed my research problem with the person who coined the term *Kacoke Madit*, and he introduced me to the Acholi community in London where the *Kacoke Madit* archived records are stored. In Uganda, I talked with several participants who expressed support for this research. I also found gatekeepers in Uganda who hosted me and made all the necessary arrangements for me to access information on the Acholi people's exemplary followership in the northern Ugandan conflict resolution.[18] Therefore, I wrote up a summary of the purpose of this research where I articulated its significance to the participants to arouse their enthusiastic participation in the study. Once I composed a brief write-up of my research, I initiated a dialogue with some of the participants to develop a rapport with them as the launching pad for the actual interviews.

Variation

I selected research participants from each of the groups mentioned above because they represent different viewpoints on the research problem. Their participation ensured adequate variation in this case study.[19] I interviewed a total of thirty-nine participants.

Participants' Demographic Data

The thirty-nine participants were selected from nine different groups: members of parliament (MP); nongovernmental organizations (NGOs); cultural leaders; elders; religious leaders; women; the diaspora; rebels (LRA); and

---

18. Creswell, *Qualitative Inquiry and Research Design*.
19. Creswell, *Qualitative Inquiry and Research Design*.

journalists (press) that played pivotal roles in the conflict resolution participated in this study. Appendix A contains a summary of their demographic data.

Data Collection Strategy

In this section, I will discuss the details of my data collection sources, which included interviews, documents, and audiovisual materials. In the interview section, I will discuss the interview protocol, and data recording and storage strategies pertaining to the qualitative grounded theory approach.

Data Sources

I used multiple data sources—namely interviews, archival records, documentation, and audiovisual materials[20]—which I used to explore the process, meaning, and understanding of how followers develop and enact followership identities, roles, and behaviors in leadership processes and outcomes.[21]

Interviews

According to Burt Yin, "Interviews are one of the most important sources of case study information."[22] Interviews were, indeed, my primary source of data. Each interview took between forty and sixty minutes due to its semi-structured nature. The location of the interviews depended on the schedule and venues participants preferred.

Interview Protocol

I conducted one-on-one, semi-structured interviews with each participant. In each interview, I used open-ended questions to explore the participants' points of view about the phenomenon. I contacted the participants through my local connections in order to inform them of the research project, ask for their permission to participate in the study, and so we could agree on the time and venue for the interviews. In cases where a participant could

---

20. Yin, *Case Study Research*.
21. Merriam, *Qualitative Research and Case Study*.
22. Yin, *Case Study Research*, 84.

not arrange for an interview in his or her office, I arranged for an alternative venue that was convenient for the participant in question. During the interviews, I observed the participants' body language and compared it with their verbal opinion on the phenomenon and the context. According to Yin, "the opportunity to make . . . observations is one of the most distinctive features in doing case studies."[23] Appendix B is a copy of the guide I used for the interviews.

Data Recording and Storage

I recorded each interview on a digital voice recorder and wrote down field notes of valuable comments and situations that arose during the interviews, in addition to insights gained thereafter. Following that, I transcribed the recordings verbatim and arranged them in appropriate files with labels that identified each participant's excerpts. I also typed the field notes and transferred them to my personal computer, and then backed them up to an external hard drive. Further, I stored all the data in NVivo, which is password-protected data analysis software. Finally, I stored all the electronic devices I used in a safe place to guarantee the safety of the data.

Documentation and Audiovisual Materials

I collected archival records and audiovisual material from the *Kacoke Madit* archives in London through their website, and documents from different locations in Uganda. Documents included such things as conference papers, policy papers, invitation letters and meeting agendas, newsletters, publicity materials, and reports. Audiovisual material included the *Kacoke Madit* website, recorded conference presentations, and community meeting proceedings, among others, produced about the northern Ugandan conflict resolution. Where possible, I asked for the soft copies of the above documents, which I then stored on my hard drive safely. In situations where the soft copies were not available, I made photocopies and stored them in secure, special files.

Data Analysis

In this section, I will explain the methods I used to analyze the data: the relationship between data collection and data analysis; coding procedures;

23. Yin, *Applications of Case Study Research*, 11.

and memo writing in relation to the qualitative research paradigm using grounded theory analytical methodology.

According to John W. Creswell,[24] qualitative data analysis goes together with data collection, interpretation, and report writing. In the same vein Joseph A. Maxwell reiterated that, "The researcher begins data analysis immediately after finishing the first interview or observation."[25] Concurrent analysis enables the researcher to refine data collection strategies in light of the preceding interviews. According to Kathy Charmaz, coding in grounded theory is the process whereby "we take segments of data apart, name them in concise terms, and propose an analytic handle to develop abstract ideas for interpreting each segment of data."[26] In other word, coding is used "to 'fracture' the data and rearrange them into categories that facilitate comparison between things in the same category and that aid in the development of theoretical concepts."[27] Here in below are the different types of coding.

Initial Coding

Initial coding involves labeling concepts, as well as defining and developing categories according to their properties and dimensions. It enables researchers to identify important ideas, points, or thoughts of interest in the text.[28] The identification can be based on either the "researcher's prior idea of what is important or on an inductive attempt to capture new insights."[29] This stage involves asking questions such as, "What is this data a study of?"[30] and, "What does the data suggest, from whose points of view among others?"[31] Initial or open coding stays close to the data, to the point of sometimes even using words in the text to identify concepts or emerging categories.[32] This process is important because to build concepts from a textual data source, researchers need to open the text and expose the meaning, idea, and thoughts in it.

24. Creswell, *Qualitative Inquiry and Research Design*.
25. Joseph A. Maxwell, *Qualitative Research Design* (2005), 95.
26. Charmaz, *Constructing Grounded Theory*, 45.
27. Joseph A. Maxwell, *Qualitative Research Design*, 107; Strauss, *Qualitative Analysis for Social Scientists*.
28. Siedman, *Interviewing as Qualitative Research*, 100.
29. Joseph A. Maxwell, *Qualitative Research Design*, 107.
30. Glaser, *Theoretical Sensitivity*, 100.
31. Joseph A. Maxwell, *Qualitative Research Design*, 107.
32. Charmaz, *Constructing Grounded Theory*.

Focused Coding

The purpose of focused coding is to identify recurrent patterns and multiple layers of meaning, and to sketch out variations and interrelationships among subthemes within the general topic. It often enables researchers to revise the general topic, regroup excerpts, or reorient the overall approach. It implies "using the most significant and/or frequent earlier codes to sift through large amounts of data. It requires decisions about which initial codes make the most analytical sense to categorize your data incisively and completely."[33] Therefore, it is deductive rather than inductive. It enables the researcher to identify more complex analytical codes after shifting through the initial codes. The goal of focused coding is to determine how adequate the codes are. Since coding in this case study was an emergent process, progression to focused coding was not a linear process. In such a case, new events shed light on earlier events including the researcher's preconception of the topic.[34] In the next section, I shall discuss the connecting strategies built in the last two of the four coding procedures mentioned above.

Connecting Strategies: Axial and Theoretical Coding

According to Barney G. Glaser, theoretical coding precludes axial coding. Therefore, I synthesized axial coding and theoretical coding into a connecting analytical strategy.[35] I used axial coding procedures to "relate categories and subcategories, specified the properties and the dimensions of a category, and reassembled the data that I fractured during the initial coding to give coherence to the emerging analysis."[36] At this level, I examined the connections between categories and subcategories at a conceptual rather than descriptive level. In other words, I linked categories with subcategories and examined the interrelationships among them or the influence each category had on another.[37] Thereafter, I used theoretical coding procedures to conceptualize "how the substantive codes related to each other as hypotheses to be integrated into a coherent theme/theory," which explained how followers develop and enact followership identity roles and behaviors in leadership

---

33. Charmaz, *Constructing Grounded Theory*, 57.
34. Yin, *Case Study Research*.
35. Glaser, *Theoretical Sensitivity*.
36. Charmaz, *Constructing Grounded Theory*, 60; Strauss, *Qualitative Analysis for Social Scientists*.
37. Strauss and Corbin, *Basics of Qualitative Research*.

processes and outcomes.[38] In the next section, I will discuss memo writing in relation to the data analysis process.

Memo Writing

According to Charmaz, memo writing is the pivotal intermediate step between data collection and writing drafts of papers. "Writing successive memos throughout the research process keeps you involved in the analysis and helps you to increase the level of abstraction of your ideas."[39] Furthermore, "memos provide ways to compare data, to explore ideas about the codes, and to direct further data-gathering."[40] Therefore, I wrote memos throughout the research process to capture major insights, issues, and questions that emerged, which furthered the data gathering and data analysis processes.

Validation Strategies

Validity, in principle, is concerned with questions that research proposal and report readers seek answers to, like: "How will we know that the conclusions are valid?"[41] In other words, does the evidence reflect the reality on the ground? However, validity as used by qualitative researchers does not refer to an objective truth that is used to measure the accuracy of the research processes and outcomes. Instead, researchers in qualitative research use validity as "a ground for distinguishing accounts that are credible from those that are not."[42]

Therefore, in qualitative research, a researcher must identify the specific threats to validity and develop ways to mitigate their adverse effects. Generally, in qualitative research there are two types of validity threats: researcher bias and reactivity.[43] Regarding researcher bias, all researchers are inclined to personal interests that influence their theories, goals, beliefs, preconceptions, data selection and analysis, and research outcome.[44] Reactivity, on the other hand, refers to the influence of the interviewer on

---

38. Glaser, *Theoretical Sensitivity*.
39. Charmaz, *Constructing Grounded Theory*, 72.
40. Charmaz, *Constructing Grounded Theory*, 12.
41. Przeworski, and Salomon, *Art of Writing*, 2.
42. Joseph A. Maxwell, *Qualitative Research Design*, 122.
43. Merriam, *Qualitative Research in Practice*.
44. Merriam, *Qualitative Research in Practice*.

interviewees. The goal of the knowledge of such influence is not to control the influence of the interviewer on interviewee, but rather to understand the influence, how it occurs, and how it affects the inferences the interviewer draws from the interview.

In qualitative research, common validation strategies include member checks, rich data, peer review, and triangulation. However, validity threat attenuation measures are specific to respective research approaches and research issues in each research project. In my case, I will discuss validity protocol measures in relation to qualitative case study.

Potential Reactivity

In a qualitative case study, an ethic of caution is mandatory for the researcher to minimize undue influence on the interviewees. I exercised caution through the following measures.

First, I shared my research problem with the participants to arouse their interest in the study and to solicit their enthusiastic participation as informants who understand the significance of the study, rather than mere respondents volunteering information to the researcher.

Second, during the interviews, I avoided using leading questions. Instead, I prepared research questions and interview protocol that guided the interview sessions. During the interviews, I also asked follow-up questions where necessary in relation to the research questions and phenomenon being studied. The purpose here was to allow the participants, rather than the questions or the researcher, to direct the interview.

Third, I shared with the interview data, analysis, and findings with the participants to ensure they were adequately represented throughout the research process.

Fourth, I applied the mental model I adopted for this study to minimize undue influence on interviewees. According to systems thinking's central assumption that regards variables as systems that influence each other within a whole rather than distinct entities, a research study like this case study is considered a system in which the researcher's role and that of the interviewees are interconnected and complementary. The complementarity enabled the participants to identify with the study beyond merely providing information to the researcher. In my case, participants expressed interest in the study outcomes, which are highlighted in the significance statement.

Triangulation

Since I sought to understand participants' subjective perspectives on the phenomenon within a constructivist framework, I anticipated getting multiple perspectives and alternative explanations that might otherwise not fit my personal biases.[45] Multiple perspectives call for gathering extensive data from multiple sources to gather comprehensive information as the basis for a holistic interpretation of the phenomenon that mitigates against personal bias.[46] Therefore, I guarded against personal biases through data triangulation and theory triangulation.

Data Triangulation

Since instrumental case study requires extensively rich and thick description of the case and data from multiple sources, I triangulated data from the different sources to guard against personal biases in my interpretations.[47] For example, I cross-checked case description data with the interview data to make sure that participants told me their own understanding of the phenomenon rather than merely what they thought I wanted to hear. In the same manner, I cross-checked field notes data with data from other sources to ensure that my observation did not misrepresent either the context or participants' interpretation of the phenomenon. Therefore, the cross-data triangulation enhanced holistic interpretation across data sources and thus mitigated any personal biases that might have occurred at any stage of data collection.

Perspective Triangulation

The northern Uganda conflict is a complex phenomenon that is bound to generate multiple perspectives and approaches to understanding it. This is evident in the composition of the strategies the Acholi people used to address it. Therefore, I needed to triangulate the different perspectives that emerged to achieve a holistic interpretation of the phenomenon. This approach is congruent with a constructivist approach, which advocates for multiple views and approaches to a phenomenon because in a constructivist

---

45. Creswell, *Qualitative Inquiry and Research Design*.
46. Merriam, *Case Study Research in Education*.
47. Joseph A. Creswell, *Qualitative Inquiry and Research Design*.

approach, "knowledge is made up largely of social interpretations rather than awareness of an external reality."[48]

Member Checking

Member checking refers to a process whereby the researcher regularly asks participants to examine and give feedback on the researcher's observations, findings, and interpretations to ensure accuracy and palatability. It is particularly aimed at capturing how well the researcher has captured the participants' perspectives of the phenomenon being studied. In case of any discrepancy, the participants are asked to make the necessary corrections which can include either alternative language or interpretations.[49] Hence, I regularly invited participants to opine on the data and conclusions to ensure that their views were well represented throughout the entire process of the research study.

Searching Out Discrepant Evidence

A researcher can easily ignore discrepant evidence. Therefore, "identifying and analyzing discrepant data and negative cases is a key part of the logic of validity testing in qualitative research."[50] First, as a researcher, I was conscious of my own temptation to ignore data that did not support my preferred theories, beliefs, and perceptual lenses, and consequently developed the self-discipline to examine the data and conclusions for any issues or concepts that contradicted my aforementioned biases. According to Joseph Maxwell, contrary views enable the researcher to modify his/her construct or search for further evidence to clarify the research findings or conclusions. However, since I used systems thinking as my interpretative framework, I regarded discrepant evidence as an integral component of the perspectives I needed to examine in order to develop a holistic understanding of the phenomenon.

According to Maxwell,[51] a researcher can compare the variant opinions of the participants to detect and examine discrepant evidence. In my study, the participants represented different points of view concerning the phenomenon.

48. Stake, *Art of Case Study Research*, 170.
49. Stake, *Art of Case Study Research*.
50. Joseph A. Maxwell, *Qualitative Research Design*, 127.
51. Joseph A. Maxwell, *Qualitative Research Design*.

Audit Trail

According to Sharan B. Merriam, a researcher needs an audit trail replete with details about data collection, analysis procedures, emerging themes, and critical decision-making yardsticks in the research method in order to enhance validity.[52] I therefore kept a research journal where I recorded all the important details about the progress of the study. It contained the records of the major themes and interventions I applied, and the outstanding issues that needed further interventions.

Thick, Rich Description

A typical case study write-up requires extensive description of the case and its context, in addition to other components like the research problem, the methods, and confirming and disconfirming evidences.[53] A rich description provides abundant, interconnected details about the case or a theme depending on the specifics of a study. According to Creswell, "with such detailed description, the researcher enables readers to transfer information to other settings and to determine whether the findings can be transferred because of shared characteristics."[54]

In this case study, I provided a thick description of the case—the role of the Acholi people in northern Ugandan conflict resolution, and the setting as well as the themes that emerged from participants' multiple perspectives on how followers develop and enact their followership identities, roles, and behaviors. I also gave equal priority to the concrete description of the case, its context, research problems, methods and procedures, emergent themes, interpretations, and lessons learned.

Ethical Considerations

Ethical issues are critical to the authenticity of a researcher's credibility in the research world.[55] Creswell contends, "Ethical issues in qualitative research can be described as occurring prior to conducting the study, at the beginning of the study, during data collection, in data analysis, in reporting

---

52. Merriam, *Qualitative Research in Practice*.

53. Erlandson et al., *Doing Naturalistic Inquiry*; Lincoln and Guba, *Naturalistic Inquiry*; Merriam, *Case Study Research in Education*; Stake, *Art of Case Study Research*; Yin, *Case Study Research*.

54. Stake, *Art of Case Study Research*, 252.

55. Merriam, *Qualitative Research*.

the data and in publishing a study."[56] Ethical issues include concerns such as: (a) reciprocity between researcher and participants, (b) confidentiality, (c) disclosure of sensitive information, (d) participants' safety, and (e) handling of research data, analysis, and publication.[57]

Therefore, an authentic study must integrate ethical issues into the research design to provide ethical guidance to the researcher. The ethical integrity in this qualitative grounded theory case study was anchored by a transparent process that created and sustained trust between the researcher and participants, researcher and readers, and the participants and the public interests they represented. The ethical threats I anticipated and thus dealt with are discussed below. I addressed whichever ethical issues emerged at each level of the research process as follows.

Ethical Issues Prior to the Research

Since the participants in this case study are comprised of high-profile members of the Acholi people, accessibility and the interview venue could have posed ethical challenges because their public status dictates their public relations protocol and the measures needed to safeguard their security. Therefore, I established direct contacts with them and secured their consent to participate in this study, and thereafter made appointments with them to discuss their venue preferences. For those that were not comfortable to host the interviews in their respective offices, I consulted with them to identify alternative venues.

Second, for me to develop a reciprocal relationship of trust with participants, I ensured that the research questions conveyed the research problem and also recognized and honored participants' autonomy and interests. Therefore, I designed an interview question guide and thereafter pilot-tested it to find out how well the questions would work during the real interview.[58] I also developed a rapport with the participants, which enabled us to cultivate an environment of mutual interactions during the interview.

---

56. Creswell, *Qualitative Inquiry and Research Design*, 147.

57. Creswell, *Qualitative Inquiry and Research Design*, 174; Merriam, *Qualitative Research*; Weis and Fine, *Speed Bumps*.

58. Joseph A. Maxwell, *Qualitative Research Design*.

Ethical Concerns in Data Collection

Before commencing the interview, I furnished participants with clear and concise information about the research topic and the interview protocol. In my introductory remarks, I pledged to avail the research data and the findings to the participants. Thereafter, I welcomed them to feel free to request the transcript and findings whenever they so wish. I also prudently stated in the interview protocol that I was there to learn from them as a gesture of my appreciation of their expertise on the research problem and willingness to offer me the opportunity to learn from them. The goal here was to boost eagerness and enthusiasm in the participants to participate in the interview devoid of any apprehension.

Where possible, I sent the interview guide in advance to give participants ample time to read and internalize them. Thereafter, I asked them to sign the consent form and give it back to me as a sign of their voluntary consent to participate in the interview. Above all, I also pledged to the participants that I would adhere to the confidentiality code stipulated in the interview protocol, and also reiterated that their participation in the interview was entirely voluntary. At this stage, the central goal in my preliminary interaction was to build trust and collegiality with the participants.[59]

Ethical Concerns in Data Analysis and Writing

Ethical issues in data analysis and write-ups are no less demanding than in the preceding stages of research. At the data analysis and write-up stage, I adhered to the case study protocol that calls for thick description, confidentiality, validating procedures, respect for alternative voices, sufficient evidence, and engaging narrative among others.[60]

First, I respected the participants by representing their voices in my analysis and write-up. I also consulted with them to check for the accuracy of their input and sought their opinion where further clarification was needed. This demonstrated to them my commitment to their interest in the research study and an appreciation of their participation as well.[61] However, while I guarded against writing anything that would shine a negative light on the participants, I sought to tell the truth in a manner that respects the participants and the true nature of the findings.[62]

59. Creswell, *Qualitative Inquiry and Research Design*, 147.
60. Yin, *Case Study Research*.
61. Creswell, *Qualitative Inquiry and Research Design*, 147.
62. Creswell, *Qualitative Inquiry and Research Design*, 147.

Second, I allowed discrepant evidence to emerge rather than ignoring it or deliberately omitting it from the analysis or write-up so that readers may draw their own conclusions based on the thick description of the case and embedded evidence. This is important because how a researcher treats discrepant evidence has a huge bearing on the authenticity of research processes and outcomes.

Furthermore, I adhered to writing a case study report that is complete by giving equal attention to both the phenomenon under study and the case in its natural context. I followed the saturation principle, which recommends cessation of analysis when further data analysis and interpretations fail to yield new interpretations.[63]

---

63. Yin, *Case Study Research*.

5

The Findings
Human Dignity

IN this study, I asked thirty-nine participants who played a seminal role in the northern Ugandan conflict resolution to discuss how they developed and enacted their followership identities, roles, and behaviors in response to Uganda government policy and their approach to the conflict. On one hand, the responses were not new to me. They identified factors such as culture and characteristics like courage. Additionally, some were initially reluctant to identify themselves as followers, due to the pejorative stigma associated with the word. On the other hand, their responses revealed new insights about followership. Per my analysis, followership is the outgrowth of the self-consciousness of and commitment to human dignity. It emanates from context-specific, seamless, continuous interaction between layers of root factors and fruit actions and is enacted through a context-specific, seamless, consensus-building process of observation, analysis, and response. These latter insights were new to me and have enhanced my understanding of followership theory. I was surprised when the participants wondered why active followership should not be followers' normative behavior since it is an enactment of human dignity.

Data analysis yielded six major themes categorized into two facets, which generated this theory. The unifying concept that synthesized the way participants developed and enacted their followership identities, roles, and behaviors is self-consciousness of and commitment to human dignity, hereafter summarized as human dignity. The two critical facets are: (a) root factors, which are divided into three subsections: core values, characteristics, and exogenous factors; and (b) fruit actions, which are categorized into three subsections: observation, analysis, and response (see Figure 1).

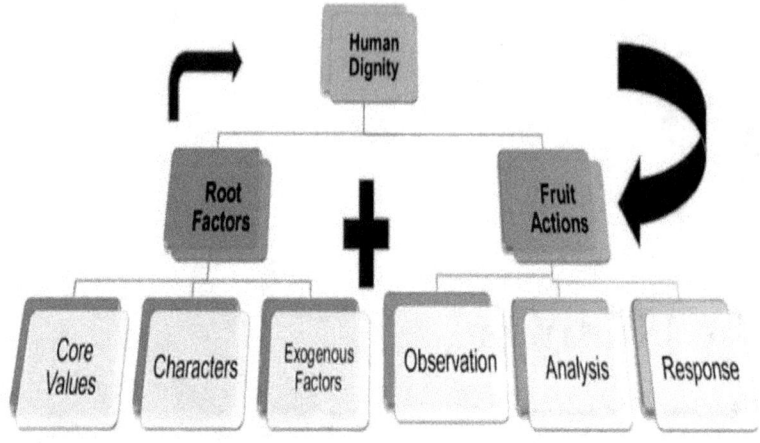

Figure 1: Human Dignity Emanates from Interactions Between Root Factors and Fruit Actions and It In Turn Influences Fruit Actions

Therefore, this theory proposes that followers develop followership identities, roles, and behaviors, due to their own self-consciousness of and commitment to human dignity. Human dignity, in the context of leadership, encompasses the agency to nurture and actualize human potential to thrive, reverence for the inherent worth of all humans, and unfettered access to equal opportunities for all. It emanates from context-specific, seamless, continuous interactions between layers of root factors (core values and characteristics that inform and are informed by exogenous factors) and fruit actions (a consensus-building process of observation, analysis, and response). Thus, followership development and enactment occur in the context of daily life encounters focused toward a common goal relative to other contexts across time and space. The idea of a specific context, relative to other contexts across time and space, connotes tapping resources from the precedents in one's own experiences and that of other people to understand and respond to a challenge at hand. So, whereas development of followership identities, roles, and behaviors is influenced by a context-specific, continuous, seamless interactions of human dignity, root factors, and fruit actions, the enactment of followership identities, roles, and behaviors is a consensus-building process of observation, analysis, and response influenced by human dignity based on root factors as illustrated in the tree and staircase images in Figure 2 and Figure 3, respectively. These images embody human relational nature, which makes human life and actions seamless phenomena. Followership development and enactment processes are discussed in detail in chapter 6 and chapter 7, respectively.

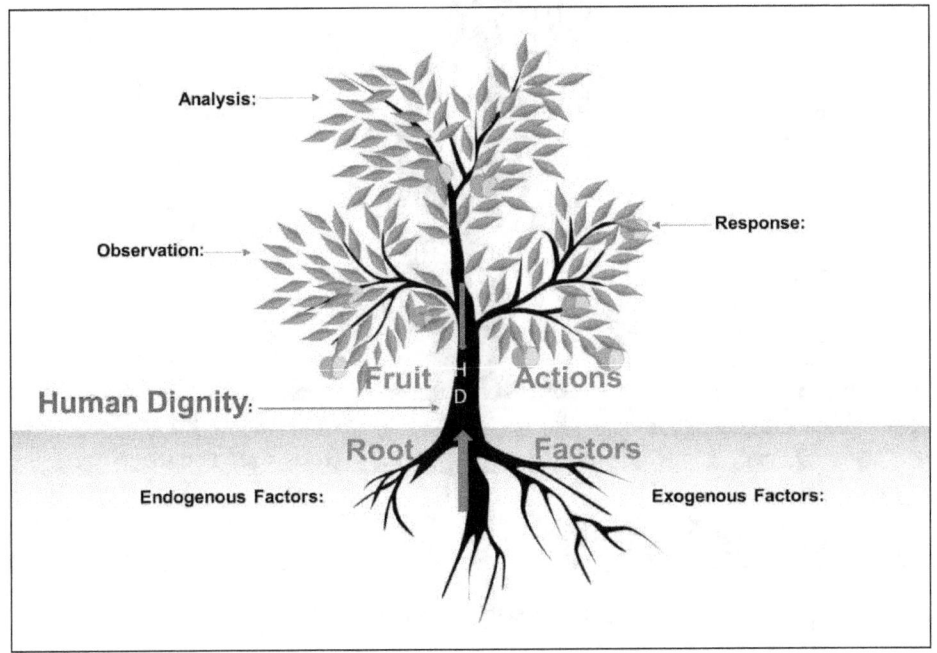

Figure 2: Followership Development Tree

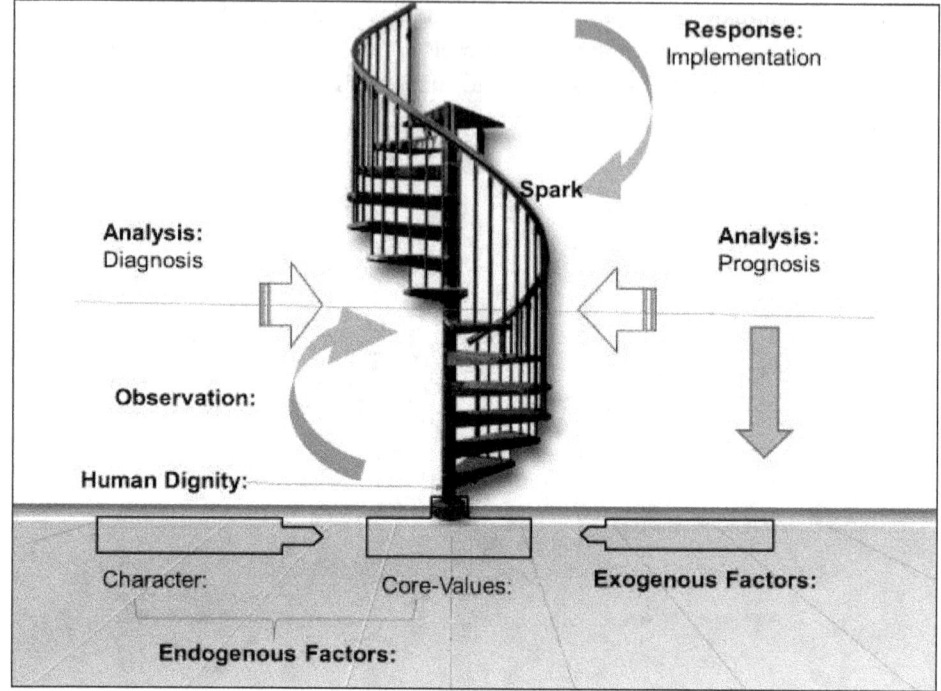

Figure 3: Followership Enactment Staircase

The findings are divided into three chapters: human dignity, followership development, and followership enactment. This chapter reports the findings on human dignity, which comprises the agency to nurture and actualize inherent human potential to thrive, reverence for the inherent worth of all humans, and unfettered access to equal opportunity for all. Chapter 6 reports the findings on followership development, subdivided into three subsections, and chapter 7 reports the findings on followership enactment, subdivided into three sections. Chapter 8 presents the discussions and summary.

"Human dignity" is an ambiguous phrase subject to multiple meanings.[1] However, per the data analysis, the Acholi people regard it as the intrinsic essence of humanity, which is integral to human self-consciousness, expectations, obligations, and well-being. It governs the social fabric upon which the Acholi well-being is built. As OL—an elder, cultural and elected leader, and academician—noted in his conversation with the Save

---

1. Arend et al., *Human Dignity and the Future*; Chan, "Concept of Human Dignity," 274–82.

the Children Uganda country director, the Acholi people value and guard their dignity at any cost, even potential physical harm:

> The lady of Save the Children Uganda, who was the country director here, wanted to know more about the war and I told her that, you know, "This is not something you will understand easily. But for us it is easier to pay the price of death than to allow our dignity to be taken away. That is why some people don't understand why people would accept to suffer like that and for such a long time. But, for us, everything is nothing [without our dignity]." (OL)

Thus, human dignity constitutes the central pillar of the Acholi heritage from which every generation responds. According to OO1, a member of parliament, "[In the] initial migration from Khartoum, slightly over 25 kilometers, we had so many encounters and the society had to make [many resolutions] in the way they developed values. I think [human dignity] is more of a genetic aspect." The inference here is that the consciousness of and commitment to human dignity are developed in the context of daily-life encounters over a long period, and are so ingrained in the Acholi cultures that they dictate their societal ethos and responses. As YA, an elder and a cultural leader noted, "Our culture is very rich; it is the constitution of our tribes." However, in their context, culture is neither given nor static. Instead, it is relevant and dynamic. Therefore, each encounter takes into consideration attendant factors, as OA2, a Roman Catholic prelate, described:

> Our being together made us always to sit and reflect. You know, talk of strategy, we never learned peace in school. I mean we never learned peace talks or such kind of things, never! But we were doing them by common sense, common sense, yah! The reality of facing critical things like these made us to think very hard and it helped us to pick the right ways of doing things. It became protective for us because we were not interested in seeing either side lose. That was not our interest. Of course, if we had [partiality] in our mind, we would have been dead. (OA2)

The Acholi people use different adages to describe their regard for human dignity. Some of the popular phrases include *Cham moo ni* ("Eat your own butter") and *Abedo rwot ki ioda* ("I am a chief in my own house"). These adages signify the inherent individual autonomy and authority culture ascribed to everyone. However, as OO3, a retired Anglican bishop, explained in the excerpts below, individual authority and autonomy in the Acholi cultures are interdependent attributes derived from a common human identity rather than absolute individualism as in Western cultures. In the following excerpts, MA, an elder, and OO3, a retired religious leader, described these adages.

> We don't want anybody to belittle us. An Acholi, even if he or she is poor, does not want to be belittled by others. Never! When I say *cham moo ni* ("eat your butter"), you understand? *Ingeyo oceyo*, ("do you know Aframomum?")—it is a kind of fruit we get from the bush, the red type. We collect it during dry season, and you squeeze with water, and then you bring *moko kwon* ("millet flour") or sweet potatoes, and then you mix, and you call it *rwot loya gi moo* which means *rwot* ("chief") has got cows that can give him milk and out of milk he can get butter. He only defeats me that way. But the taste is the same. Now you can see, an Acholi will never, never, never, never accept anybody to belittle him. No! However poor he/she might be, and that is actually the inborn spirit that we have. (MA)

In the same vein, OO3 described another adage they use to refer to human dignity:

> You know, the Acholi people have a saying, *Arwot ki ioda* ("I am a chief in my own house"). There is a stool we had in homes those days. Even if a president comes to my home, he cannot sit on it; he will sit on a mat because I am a chief in my house. You cannot take over my chieftain. I like that culture of respect, culture of authority. And you know, the level of authority, if you are in somebody's house, he is the chief, you just respect, whether you are a bishop, you must sit where he shows you, even a close friend does not take over the chair. Now, if people know where authority is and they know that the authority is wrong, an Acholi will not spare you, he will challenge you with the authority he has as a person. That is in our culture. Even your own brother that you are looking after will tell you, "Because you are looking after me, you want to treat me like that?" That authority, where we got it from I don't know, which makes us so autonomous, but not the individual autonomy of the Western style of individualism, no, no. As much as you are a chief in your own house, you are a nobody without the rest of the community. So you move with the people—the communality of the people, the communal life we live in common. People know that when you are alone, you are nothing. So what we agree on in our homes, that is what we go with. Not me my dear is nothing. (You cannot make decisions alone.) That is what we call politics. Politics is *todero* ("under the granary"). You conduct politics under the granary,

and if people agree on something under several granaries, then you are in business. (OO3)

The Acholi's high sense of human dignity predates the modern Acholi and is known beyond the Acholi subregion. Foreigners who interacted with the Acholi people before and during the colonial era attested to their uncompromising regard for inherent human dignity. The earliest European explorers expressed profound shock at their egalitarian views and practices. For example, according to OR1, a member of parliament,

> When Europeans started coming here, they reached out and wanted to conquer areas and sign agreements with chiefs and betray the people. Sir Samuel Baker, an explorer, came and wanted to meet the chiefs. So the chiefs asked who that person was, and they were briefed that he was an explorer, perhaps representing interests of other countries. The chiefs sent their representatives to meet with Baker. In sending their representatives, the idea was about protocol: that you know, the chiefs cannot meet that guy. The level of protocol is different, but we can send our representatives. So Baker was amazed and wrote it in his notebook [*Sir Samuel Baker: His Life and Adventures, 1880*]. He asked, "Where are the chiefs?" People were quiet until at one point they told him that actually, the chiefs have sent their representatives because they feel that they are the equivalent of Baker. So they can discuss the issues and report back to the chiefs the same way Baker was going to take the report to his boss. So that has been the nature of the Acholi people, the dignity. The Acholi people value their dignity. They would not compromise their dignity for any material or monetary benefit, they would not. So these are some of the values I am talking about, that the dignity of the people is paramount, more than anything else. (OR1)

In another encounter, while on an African tour, Winston Churchill witnessed the commitment of the Acholi people to their intrinsic human dignity in the way they structured seating arrangements at their public meetings. In one of the meetings organized in his honor, Churchill noted that the seats were arranged in a circular manner, rather than hierarchically. OJ, a prominent member of parliament, recollected Churchill's accounts of his experience in Acholiland.

> There is a book (*My African Journey*) written by [Winston Churchill]. In it he says that everywhere he went, he was received like a royal, put on a pedestal higher than everybody else that made him look higher than everybody else. But when he

came to Acholiland, they made him sit in a ring with all the rest. Everybody was in a ring. Nobody was above the other. And in his conclusion, he said the Acholi people believed that everybody is the same. Nobody whether white or not are the same. We sit at the same level. We are all human beings. (OJ)

Administratively, John R. P. Postlethwaite, the first British colonial administrator, failed to establish a centralized system of governance in the Acholi subregion because the Acholi cultures vested autonomy and authority in ordinary people rather than in an individual or a group of individuals as in cultures with hierarchical systems of governance. OO2, an elder and academician who witnessed and wrote about the establishment of colonial administration in Uganda, recollected the experience.

> The first provincial commissioner, Emin Pasha, was not the only European who failed to understand the natural [consensus] democracy of the Acholi people. The first British administrator, John Rutherford Parkin Postlethwaite, who had planned to use Acholi chiefs to establish a hierarchy in Acholi, like the one established by George Wilson in Buganda, could not easily identify any ruler who could rule the Acholi from the armpit of the British colonizers. The galaxy of the Acholi chiefs he found in power were democratically elected. They had no power to make any decision single-handedly. Before the British took over the political control of the Acholiland, no single person or a group of persons could take a political decision on their own. The Acholi absence of chiefs who could be made paramount chief follows. (OO2)

In his own admission, Postlethwaite described the challenges he encountered when he tried to introduce the hierarchical system of governance the British preferred in Acholiland:

> In many parts of the country [Acholiland], it was extremely difficult to locate anyone who could be treated as a chief and gradually entrenched in that position. However, this was done as it was essential to the carrying out of my determination that from the outset we would administer the Acholi through, and not despite, their chiefs.[2]

However, OO2 noted that the British colonial administration and the post-colonial regimes eventually circumvented the indigenous leaders by appointing charismatic individuals who enjoyed the popular support of

---

2. Postlethwaite, *I Look Back*, 106.

the masses to execute their agenda—the trend that gradually entrenched centralized hierarchy—which had been distorting and contesting with the Acholi egalitarian system for supremacy in Acholiland:

> In the east of the district he became so discouraged by the absence of any real chief with definitive permanent tribal authority. The absence of a real chief in the recognized sense of the word was in fact a blessing in disguise as no hierarchy chieftainship had to be recognized and a well-chosen outstanding Acholi was usually accepted by the tribe on the DC's instigation.[3]

Otherwise, culturally in Acholiland, the indigenous leadership construct undergirds human dignity. Leaders embodied and amplified the collective voices and identity of the people. A leadership role neither subjugated nor dispossessed nor negated the inviolable authority and autonomy the Acholi culture accords everyone. For instance, during the conflict, the religious leaders interpreted the children's action of sleeping in bus parks to avoid abduction by the rebels as a dramatic mouthpiece to rebuke their elders and cry for help. OO3, the founder of the Acholi Religious Peace Initiative, narrated that they responded to the children's plea by embodying and amplifying this action by sleeping in the parks for four nights along with the children.

> At the same time, they [night commuter children] were appealing to the rest of humanity. There are organizations, which are formed in the names of the children, why are they not here to take care of us? Why? Why? So they were communicating these things in the way they acted. So we understood and said, "Let us go there and amplify it. Let the world hear it from us the adults." (OO3)

Thus, a leader is regarded as a chairman, the first among equals, whose primary role is to summon people to exercise their powers and then to execute the collective will of the people. Leadership is also regarded as an identification role. It is the embodiment and expression of a people's collective identity, aspirations and obligation, rather than the exclusive executive authority and power vested in the person holding a position of leadership. One becomes and is recognized as a leader, first, because he or she exemplifies the Acholi cultural core values, and second, because he or she is sensitive to the self-consciousness, aspirations, obligations, and well-being of the Acholi people and can offer stewardship for the people to fulfill those values. Nobody is recognized as a leader merely because he or she is holding an office. Thus, OF, a prominent member of the Acholi cultural institution

---

3. Postlethwaite, *I Look Back*, 106.

(*Ker Kwaro Acholi*) and an academician, argued leadership "is an embodiment of the community. It is a horizontal role, which involves the whole society," rather than a vertical executive role. In this setting, problem solving is communally oriented. In the following excerpt, OF continued explaining that the leadership construct is horizontal and collectivistic:

> Followership and leadership in the Acholi traditional social setting (*Ke Kwaro Acholi*) are not as rigid as this conceptualization [relational view of leadership]. I thought it is not only a relational role. It is also seen as an identification role—a practice that promotes collectivism that brings people together. As we are saying, it is not vertical. It is horizontal, so that you come together as in those days [before the war], which they are trying to bring back. (OF)

For that matter, after understanding the Acholi systems, the British colonial administration allowed the Acholi systems to coexist with the British system in governing the Acholi people. According to OO2, "During the British time, we had power. We had a dual system, which allowed the Acholi system and the British system to coexist. For example, we had the British courts as well as the traditional court system."

However, whereas the British entrenched Acholi egalitarian values in the postcolonial constitution (autonomy of the local governments), the subsequent post-independence, indigenous regimes abrogated it through the 1966 and 1995 constitutions which were in favor of the centralized hierarchy. Nonetheless, the Acholi people still attribute the introduction of the centralized system of governance in Acholiland to the British. According to OO2,

> When the British came here, they established what I call paternal governance, saying, "Oh, I will do this for you." Before the British, we did not have that. When the British came, they levied taxes on everything and yet turned around and claimed that they were doing things for you. (OO2)

It is not an understatement to conclude that human dignity is the preeminent attribute that undergirds the leader-follower relationship among the Acholi people. It defines, as well as drives, Acholi self-consciousness, expectations, obligations, and well-being. It is demonstrated in Acholi egalitarian life views and cultural artifacts like circular houses, dances, and seating arrangements, among other things. Above all, this view of human dignity accords everyone the status of a subject, rather than an object of their leaders' influence. In the next section, I will discuss the three ingredients of human dignity which influenced the Acholi people's response to the Ugandan government's policies and approaches to the northern Uganda conflict: potential, worth, and opportunity.

Potential

Inherent potential is one of the key components of human dignity in the Acholi culture. The Acholi people believe that God endowed everyone with the inherent capacity to thrive, a capacity which remains dormant until it is nurtured and activated. They unlock this potential through songs, dances, games, formal and informal education, ceremonies, rituals, folklore, community meetings, and chores, among other things. As YA, an elder and cultural leader, observed, "The Acholi people cannot be like the story of the chicken and a tree whereby they wait for the wind to shake the tree with their mouth wide open waiting for the seeds that fall down." Instead, they depend on their inherent potential to respond to whatever challenges they encounter in life, because they see this ability as the fundamental mark of being human rather than merely a skill for material well-being. Thus, they pride themselves on taking self-initiative and personal responsibility, rather than waiting for these to be imposed on them from above. OG1, a cultural and elected leader, explained that self-initiative decentralizes leadership and flattens structure, which in turn enhances popular ownership and participation toward the common good:

> That is why I will say that despite all the government programs here, if you look at them, you will realize they address the same thing. Ten previous programs addressed the same thing. Is it because of nomenclature, the names are different, or what? Different names, but same programs. And the moment you have not localized the leadership of a project, the moment we have not domesticated the structure of a project, be rest assured that the community will take it as a foreign thing, it has come from somewhere, it is a government thing, name it. And they have been naming these things by the organizations that sponsor them. (OG1)

The pride in self-initiative enhances their identity and potential contrary to teaching them dependence. As WO, a religious and an elected leader, described in the following excerpt, the abdication of the responsibility of self-initiative is tantamount to forfeiture of human identity and potential. So dependence is one of the worst forms of abuse to the Acholi people:

> You know, some of our proverbs also help to consolidate our sense of independence, because if you depend entirely on somebody, you cease being a human being. Because what you can do is being in partnership. But you cannot be totally dependent on somebody. Acholi will not accept that. And that is why most of the projects here are failing. World Vision came here and gave people goats, but when the goats fall sick, they will call World Vision. World Vision, your goat is sick and yet you have already given out the goats and that is a person's goat but because you said you are the one who gave out the goat. The Acholi people want to work for their own things, and they can be independent. But if you give them, they will call you on phone, "Come and see your cow is sick." And if you give them, they will slaughter it. That is why the government project of restocking cattle has failed. Why? People will slaughter them. Our independence is based on pride, you take pride in what you do, you don't take pride in what is given freely. The war tried to destroy [our pride], but it failed. That is why up to now, Acholis are independent. If they say, "I want to do this," he will do it. Once an Acholi says yes, it is a yes and he can't change it. (WO)

The Acholi sense of dignity, which prides itself in self-initiative is expressed in many adages written throughout their responses. For example, in the following excerpt, OW, a religious leader, said that they express their sense of self-initiative through adages such as *Olomadilo matelo*, which means "self-reliance is not an option":

> So, it is embedded in our cultures. Our cultural setting gives that mandate because we have many proverbs like *Abedo rwot ki ioda* ("I am a chief in my own house"). We have also a proverb which says, *Olomadilo matelo* ("that a big man or a hero is pulled by the skin of his or her back") and there are many proverbs like that. This means that if I don't do it by myself, nobody else will do it. That is what gives us power. So if you and me can agree, then we can move, then we can make decision, instead of just getting orders from above coming down to us here. It does not work that way. So our cultural setting gave us the independence. (OW)

The Acholi belief in the potential for self-initiative as a mark of humanity doesn't negate external input. Rather, this belief enhances their commitment to inviolable human life, interdependence, and interrelationship. Thus, this belief vehemently discourages and opposes any form of cheap favors, threats, or overt abuses that threaten the Acholi resolve to nurture and actualize their inherent potential to thrive. In the following quotation

YA described how the Acholi people applied the Western education system to transform their society without compromising their heritage:

> I think even prior to the war, education came and helped our people to look at things from a wider perspective. And even our people who are learned started using the new knowledge and married it with our culture to help inform and form the character of our people. That is why we have many literatures written by people like Okot P'Bitek and Ochitti. They helped because they liked the good things from the Western cultures and African cultures. We discard bad things from both cultures. This also helped in shaping who we are. But even education; because for us here we say that you can go to school but the books cannot get a problem out of you (education is more than merely obtaining a certificate). We say that you read but you have not learned. The knowledge from school has not transformed your life. Because they want to see how you apply that knowledge in the day-to-day life. Are you respectful? Do you work as a team with people? Because when you are educated, and you begin to isolate yourself from the people, you become an outcast. Here you need to be part and parcel of the community life, like attending community functions. That one gives you your true image in the community. (YA)

However, during the northern Ugandan insurgency, all the Acholi processes of nurturing and enacting their inherent potential to thrive were disrupted for over a decade. So following a thorough analysis of the war propaganda, its conduct, and impacts, the Acholi people concluded that the war was primarily a form of genocide against their way of life. In the excerpt below, RO, an elder who received an international award in recognition of her role toward the conflict's resolution, likened the Acholi people to prey caught between the jaws of a predator:

> Acholiland was engulfed in the conflict that they had never seen before. And we looked at it as a destructive sort of conflict. Destructive in a way that the war was being fought in people's compounds and targeting ordinary people. Our understanding of war is that when two people are fighting amongst themselves, civilians should be protected, but the nature of that war was completely different. That was the motivation for most people to do something about it, because all of us collectively realized that if we don't do anything then that was the process of finishing us off, and we looked at the war, as many people say, it was a design to finish off the Acholi. (RO)

RO's account of the war corresponded with the poor living conditions I witnessed in the Internally Displaced People's camp at the peak of the northern Ugandan insurgency where I encountered an elder. Before I could complete my sentence of sympathy over the squalid condition of the camp in Alero, the elder cut me short with a rejoinder, "Young man, our problem here is not what you see or what we have lost because of this war. Our problem rather is this: In case this war ends today or tomorrow, shall we rebuild our Acholi society again?" In other words, the war was primarily destroying the software of the Acholi social fabric. The elder's apprehensions about the war were echoed by YA, an elder and cultural leader, as he explained his motivation for participating in the conflict resolution. He asked, "Can we really continue like this as Acholi and still remain human beings in our area?" There are several ways the conflict inhibited the development and enactment of Acholi potential.

First, the war stalled all the enculturation programs and activities the Acholi people used to develop and exercise their potential. According to OO4, a former member of parliament and an elder, the Acholi local community ceased to function as a normal human community "after the Ugandan government forcefully rounded them up and took them to the concentration camps where it abandoned them in abnormal conditions" for over a decade. Consequently, JC, a member of the Acholi diaspora based in London, observed that the younger Acholi generation, which grew up in the camps, did not develop the Acholi cultural identity because they neither participated in the initiation ceremonies nor enjoyed family and community guardianship and tutorship:

> You see, we are a generation that grew up in Uganda before the war erupted. We were supported within a family system whether you had parents or not. We had collective responsibility. We had members of extended family. Children listened to folklores at the fireplace in the evening. In that environment, the nurturing environment where elders pass these stories to you about what happened in the past; that kind of education helped us. But during the war, people were running up and down in the camps, and in that case, the people wanted the war to end so that the next generation should grow up the way we did. The war had changed that. (JC)

Second, the nature of the war and its impact destroyed all the cultural institutions and structures the Acholi used for enculturation. For instance, OF, an academician who pioneered the Peace Center at Gulu University, said that the cultural leaders and elders abandoned their cultural functions in the camps because they were under constant attack from both the rebels and government forces and attendant challenges like diseases and famine. Thus, for over a decade, the life conditions in the camps exacerbated moral degeneration and work ethic, especially among the generation that was born and raised there:

> The elders and leaders lost their places. They could not sit together. The granary was no more (a granary symbolized a community business meeting as well as their food store). The youthful generation lost respect for the chiefs and elders, including their own parents. I tried to go to my parents' village to contribute toward development. I bought bulls, ox ploughs and goats. Elders are not there now. But they started slaughtering the goats immediately I left and after one month the project collapsed. The mindset has changed. The war, through this internal displacement, distorted culture. The language changed. For example, "*Mzee* has decided" meaning "*Mzee* (elder) has died" (new slang). There is over drinking. The young people tell you they don't want to work together with the educated. (OF)

On both personal and collective levels, the Acholi community suddenly became destitute when the Ugandan government forcefully displaced the entire community from their homes, misplacing them in camps without notice. For over a decade, the entire Acholi community survived on donations from relief agencies. This is the first time in their existence as a people they have had to rely on others to provide their necessities. The younger generation resorted to illicit behavior due to the lack of constructive engagement opportunities in the camps; many of them were either abducted or killed by warring factions. Those who survived abduction and death joined the ranks of the night commuter children who trekked to town every evening to seek shelter in places like the bus parks and hospitals that lacked adequate protection and the care they deserved. RO, a global peace award winner, narrated that the forceful displacement from their homes and misplacement in the Internally Displaced People's camps by the Ugandan government, which reduced her to living the life of a pauper, was the most painful experience in her life:

> That was all I had, and I had to run away from that place. And I walked several miles for several days to reach my sister's home which was somewhere in Bwadira before I could go to my own home in Paico where my husband's home was. So that experience became, at the end of the day, really the motivating factor for me, because initially I was the one affected and I knew what

> it meant to become a destitute whole of a sudden. Because that is what happened to me. From a high school teacher, I was now reduced to a beggar. And I was just an ordinary person without anything on me and I was looking up to people to give me clothes, to give me food, to give me everything I needed in life with my children and that was the most painful experience for me. For a person who had been self-reliant, and I was actually economically independent, and now to be degraded to that level was very painful. So as the war continued to affect more and more people, including me, because I got displaced many times from Paico where I ran to and from Samuel Baker where I relocated to teach I had to run away to town [because of the war]. In town, I could not stay because I had nothing. (RO)

Furthermore, the war sowed seeds of despondency and apathy in the community, which nearly cost them the spirit of innovation and ingenuity. For the first time in the history of the Acholi people, the participants witnessed a very high level of detachment from community affairs among the community members. This loss of the desire to participate in community affairs threatened the existence of Acholi cultural values. In the following excerpt, OO6, a member of the Acholi diaspora based in Canada who coined the term *Kacoke Madit*, described an incidence of detachment that he witnessed:

> I think if we are talking about informing, the Acholi people have a culture of being active in confronting whatever situation, whether it was hunger or war and perhaps even disease. Since time immemorial, people sat down, people did not wait for directive to come from above: that this is the way we should handle this issue. So this process of *pedo pinyi* ("sitting down") worked even at family level, whether there was a fight or disagreement over land and property and so on. It required people to sit down. The notion that nothing could be done or people should do nothing was inconceivable. But I should tell you something I saw when I went to Uganda, after a very long time in March of 2000, to do some research around child soldiers, to illustrate this in vivid way. When we arrived in Gulu on March 15, a member of Gulu council had passed away and her body was being buried in one of the camps where her family lived. The then chairman of the Gulu council said, "Why don't you accompany me? It is dangerous out there. There are all kinds of ambushes, let us go to Pagaki." So we went there and when we reached, the burial ceremony was in progress, but what struck me was how so many Acholis were aloof in the camp; they were inattentively sitting right there near

where the funeral was taking place and I was extremely alarmed of what was taking place. That is, people were not concerned about what was going on. I was completely alarmed because I had never seen something like that. I noted it down and I asked the chairman about it later." (OO6)

On the other hand, the Acholi people encountered many deliberate maneuvers intended to lure them into practices that would compromise their dignity with respect to honest gain. On many occasions, they were enticed by money, the loss of a job, or torture at the hands of others. However, given their strong sense of cultural resilience, many of them upheld their resolve to adhere to their cultural belief in the inherent human potential to thrive. In the following excerpt, OR1, a member of parliament, narrated a story about a lady who declined cheap favors from a senior army commander who enjoyed direct contact with the president. This excerpt underscores their confidence in the inherent potential to thrive:

> I remember I went to the village with one of the President's generals, who is his kin. It was during the hard times when people were in the camps. And there was a woman who got up and asked a question. She said, "S, S, S; it is good you have come, go and tell your kin, why do you want to subject us to suffering here in the camp? Why do you put us here to live without food? Why do you allow our children to die here? Why do you humiliate us to this kind of thing and all these kinds of things as if you are not a government? Go and tell your kin, why is he doing this to the Acholi people? If the war was in his region, would he do the same? Would he match people to camps and not give them food, and not give them medicine, and allow their children to die?" S replied and said, "Now this woman, called Aryem, is now my best friend. You have been honest since I came here. I have not had honesty like that." So before we left, S got an envelope with 500,000 shillings, which is a lot of money in the rural area. So he called the lady, "You come here. You have become my friend; I have this envelope for you." Then the lady asked, "What is that?" S said, "It is money to help you buy clothes and other things." She said, "No, I did not ask you the questions for money. I don't want that money." Now this is a woman who was in rags; she would definitely need that money. But because of the issues of dignity, she could not compromise what she asked with monetary value. She said, "No, I don't want your money." She humiliated S., so when we came to town, he asked me, "Why are you the Acholi so proud? Look at that woman, her buttocks are empty, she did not have clothes, and yet she refused my money." I told him, that

for us, "We don't envy people's things. We value what is ours. We don't go for what does not belong to us. And that is where you people misunderstand us, because we are honest. We tell you the truth. Because when you asked that woman, 'What do you want me to do?' She told you that take me back home, because if I go there, I will cultivate and get my food and money and I would sustain myself. But this money of yours, no!" (OR1)

For his part, OO2 narrated how he declined an assignment which the topmost government officer asked him to undertake in exchange for colossal monetary benefits. It is worth noting here that, at that time, OO2 was the director of a public department under the top government officer. Second, unlike many of his colleagues in charge of public offices, OO2 told me that he did not amass wealth. But the allure of monetary benefits and job security could not compromise his pride in the Acholi way of honest gain:

> When he saw me, he said, "Oh, I have to meet OO2 first." Our meeting lasted two hours. Then he started by saying that we are talking as sons of Uganda forget about all these things [referring to a letter he had written critical of government failures in northern Uganda]. He assigned me a very difficult thing to do. He told me that his secretary should give me some money, a lot of money in dollars for which I was not required to account because it was security matter. But I refused. So I left. That was the last time I met him. Again, he wrote to me and I said I will see if I can do something. You know if I received that money, I was expected to do something, and I thought I was not in a position to do something like that. Did I tell you Kony comes from my clan? We share the same ancestral shrine with Kony's mother. (OO2)

Furthermore, during the insurgency, the Acholi people were deprived of all basic human rights and subjected to extreme suffering that nearly cost them their dignity. OL, an academician, summarized the plight of the Acholi people:

> We paid a high price. So many of our people were decimated, either under Lakwena or Kony or UNLA or even UPDA. So many were disenfranchised as Ugandans. They lost jobs, they lost houses, property. Of course, the suffering that we endured in the IDP [Internally Displaced People's] camps, at one time, 1000 were dying a week. Those are terrible physical prices we paid, but when we reflect on it, we preserved our dignity and say that was worth it. (OL)

However, as OL observed, threats and overt abuse never broke the confidence of the Acholi people in their potential to thrive. For instance, when the northern Uganda brigade commander put NM—an academician, politician, and a prominent lawyer—at gun point to discourage him from gathering evidences of the atrocities committed against the masses by the government security forces and the rebels, NM reminded the military officer of the source of his authority without any fear:

> This place was highly militarized. The first challenge was that I was facing threats from army officers. Many times, guns were pulled on me. There was a certain colonel here called Colonel S. One time he pulled out a pistol and said, "You know, you are not going to Parliament, you are going to the mortuary." So I told him, "Well, it really does not matter, because the matters of life and death are matters that are in the hands of God. (NM)

Despite all the suffering they underwent, OO1, a member of parliament, said that the Acholi people never resorted to begging, because of their pride in human potential to thrive, whereby it is better to die than subject oneself to a life of dependence.

> So, the Acholis still remain the central Luo. So we should have the traits of most of the Luos around the world. So the resolve is more about genetics. I would give it close to 70 percent. People were in the camps, but you would not find any Acholi begging on the streets of Kampala—not even one. It is something someone should carry out a research about. Not even one and you . . . there are certain services that are still not there in Gulu, but you will not find anyone begging on the streets. (OO1)

During my interviews, I affirmed the Acholi resolve to thrive through their inherent human potential. In my conversation with the local people in Gulu, I learned that when the Ugandan government disbanded the camps and finally allowed the Acholi people to resettle in their land, they resumed supplying food crops to the World Food Program after only six months:

> This resettlement process of the Acholi people from the IDP camps allowed us to start prospering in our homesteads. People are now digging. We can now see Mukwano, the businessman coming over here to buy our produce. Sudanese are coming here to buy food stuff because we have them now. We had the opportunity to plant them, but before that we were all beggars. We were all dependents. I would like to say that we are now getting back to our independent status.

OL, a professor, concluded that when they realized the war was disrupting their efforts to nurture and actualize their inherent human potential, they responded in subversion to the war that was meant "to subjugate [them] to a psychological surrender into a war not just for power but a fight for psychological survival, a fight to uphold their dignity and a fight to reject the debasement of the Acholi people and their society." They relied on their cultural norms (in which it is preferable to die than be mentally enslaved) to demand for a space for mutuality and dialogue, which paved a way for a peaceful approach to conflict resolution.

The war was an affront to their human dignity, which accords everyone inviolable individual autonomy and authority, whereby human relationships are built on mutuality rather than subjugation. The war threatened their existence as people. So, their struggle to end it was not motivated by the desire to capture power, but rather to regain their human dignity. In the following excerpt, OL narrated that the conflict contained all the ulterior factors that would provoke a spontaneous response.

> The key element that would provoke us to respond the way we did had to be in place. The rest was not an assembly or conference or negotiated decision process. I mean, like, during those early days, if a lion attacks a *kraal*, the owner would blow his horn and sound a war cry, and nobody would ask who is doing this. No, you respond and sort out the rest of the issues later. The immediate thing is an instinctive thing that you must respond. You don't have to rationalize your response, but you will respond. I think it is now ingrained in us, having evolved as a people of a particular community. (OL)

Therefore, they likened their response to a reflex action of lifting one's leg when it steps into the fire because the war violated all the tenets of their human self-understanding, expectations, obligations and well-being, encapsulated in their cultural core values, characteristics, and exogenous factors.

Worth

The cultural mental model, which defines and drives Acholi self-consciousness, expectations, and obligations, endears them to many, friends and foes alike. In their mental model, everyone is endowed with an inherent worth, which supersedes all other categorizations and classifications such as position, gender, and race. Consequently, everyone is accorded inviolable autonomy and authority commensurate with their inherent worth. There is an established conscientious standard on how they ought to treat everyone and how others ought to treat them. For instance, a leader is considered as the first among equals—*primus inter pares*, or one among the people and leadership is considered as a role among other roles in human organization toward a common goal. Thus, as OO5, the former Under Secretary General at the UN, states below, leadership is a role rather than a position or status which subjugates, dispossesses, and negates the authority and autonomy inherent in human worth:

> So, among the central Luo or the Luo in general, it is more of a kind of an equality culture. The hierarchy is very faint, it is very thin. It is not as strong as in highly hierarchical societies. Of course, you know that the Luo have their king, the *rwot*, but the *rwot* is relatively an ordinary person. It is really sort of a kind of what the British call *Primus Inter Pares*, (the first among equals). You know, he is somebody who is answerable to the population. The population can challenge the *rwot*; they can depose the *rwot* and replace with another, the son, or whatever. The *rwot* does not have the absolute power that a king has. He is still the *rwot*, he is still the king and he is still highly respected, but the *rwot* cannot rub shoulders over the people [exercise authority over people unilaterally]. (OO5)

Generally, the Acholi people strongly oppose any values and behaviors that violate the inherent human worth which their culture accords to everyone. According to MA, a respected elder and a retired teacher, the Acholi people commit themselves to new relationships or ideas after ascertaining that the values and conduct of the people in question are congruent with theirs. While their hesitation to commit to new relationships or ideas has often been mistaken for stubbornness, the Acholi people consider it an inevitable procedure to safeguard their values.

> And for that matter, we are naturally very observant. Even a powerful man may come from another clan, you observe him, if he has that talent of yours, you befriend him, and you take him as real brother, and if possible, your offspring even marries his. If we learn that a certain tribe is more powerful, we observe them very carefully, why are they more powerful than us and you befriend them. Befriending in such a way that you don't give yourself wholly to him to understand you. You observe first, and this is it. (MA)

This cautious response to new ideas undergirds the Acholi sense of dignity. For instance, in the following excerpt, OO3, a retired religious leader, said that it has taken the Acholi people a long time to embrace Christian teaching on monogamy because the people who introduced Christianity to them did not address the cultural values associated with polygamy:

> We don't have mass wedding here. I don't think they have understood it. The question of one man, one wife. Because even the first Christian, when he believed in Christ and became a catechist, his people chased him away because he is going to kill the clan to be with only one wife, he is going to kill the clan. No, we cannot tolerate this. Where will we get children? This makes the Acholi people sometimes I feel very difficult to deal with, but at the same time, I feel that it is very easy to deal with them if you make them understand what you intend to do. (OO3)

During the conflict, the Acholi people observed the government war policy and conduct in northern Uganda for a considerable period, and after a thorough analysis they concluded that the government approach to the conflict was a strategy designed to debase and subjugate the Acholi community. According to OF, an academician, the regime conducted itself as an adversary rather than a government. For instance, it trampled upon people's dignity instead of upholding it.

The overt denigrating attitude and conduct of the National Resistance Army/Movement (NRA/M) regime toward the people from northern Uganda that sparked the conflict began during the 1985 Nairobi peace talks. The Nairobi peace talks between the Tito Okello military junta and the Museveni's rebel group, the NRA/M were called immediately after Okello overthrew the Uganda People's Congress (UPC) government which had been led by Dr. Milton Obote. The Acholi overthrew the Obote regime to initiate a peaceful solution to the military conflict in central Uganda. However, according to OL, an academician, during the peace talks, the Acholi people noticed gestures of condescending attitudes in the language and conduct of the NRA delegates. To them, this was a forewarning of the nature of the group they were dealing with, as well as the dangers this group posed to the Acholi community. When the Museveni group violated the peace accord which they had signed to form a government of national unity to pursue a military approach to conflict resolution, OL observed that the Acholi people felt that "Museveni stabbed them in the back after the long negotiation in Nairobi."

The betrayal injured the Acholi dignity and their culture of sincerity. So rather than using the Nairobi peace forum to build the capacity for mutual trust and respect, the Acholi people started to prepare themselves for the worst, which began unfolding immediately after the NRA violated the peace accord. In the following excerpt, OL says the betrayal of the Acholi magnanimity by the Museveni group sowed a seed of discord that triggered the northern Uganda conflict:

> Well, I can tell you that when there was this struggle between the Acholi and Langis when Obote was still in power; at that time, I was a student in Nairobi. But even when the Luwero conflict was ongoing, as members of the Uganda People's Congress, we used to meet and talk about some of these things even in the system and the fact that there was a need for dialogue and to find a common ground. But when the war intensified after the overthrow of the Obote regime and there was this Nairobi peace process, I was in Nairobi and I would go and monitor what was going on and try to understand of course at the level I was in [a student]. I was not able to advise, but it allowed me at least to understand the nature of M regime. You could detect deceitfulness. You could detect arrogance, you could detect despicable attitude toward us. Looking down on us and that told you that this is not somebody you could trust. That told you that this is somebody you have to watch. That told you that there was trouble ahead. So subconsciously we were all preparing for the time when we would be challenged, when there would be trouble, when we would be called upon in our different capacities to respond and we did that. When Museveni took over power, the guys ran into exile. Many of them used to hold meetings in Kenya, although I was convinced that a military counter-intervention was not the right thing, given that we had just been disorganized from an institutional setting. If it had been in our powers some of us would have given the regime time to settle in, but that did not happen. So that war was a deliberate strategy of Museveni; for example, in Agago, where I come from, people collected guns and handed over 3,000 to the government when it reached there. Our desire was not war. We knew that when you go for war, you either lose or win and when you lose you concede. (OL)

When the NRA/M eventually overthrew the Okello Junta in 1986 in a military coup, the Acholi people conceded defeat and were ready to work with the new regime. LK, a member of parliament and researcher, recounted that the Acholi people welcomed the NRA soldiers in Gulu without a fight and responded positively to government orders to return any guns in their possession. However, despite the peaceful overtures, in northern Uganda the NRA/M soldiers and leaders talked and conducted themselves as an occupying force rather than a liberating army and government.

> On arrival in the north, the NRA was taken very suspiciously based on what they had been told before, and of course as time went on, these fears manifested themselves in terms of the dishonesty that the NRA started displaying. There was a battalion called 135th battalion; that battalion went to northern Uganda and began to behave in a manner that demonstrated that they were not people's army. And that is what drew heavy suspicion. The soldiers who were in the army disserted and decided that the only thing they could do was to defend themselves. That is what laid the foundation of what was called the UPDA, which was led by Brigadier. Odongo Lateki, who was an officer in the Obote and Okello regimes. (LK)

In the following excerpt, NM, a decorated icon of the Acholi culture and a human rights lawyer, narrated that the NRA/M regime focused its war propaganda, policy, and conduct against the Acholi people as a community indiscriminately. Thus, when its narrative, which incriminated the whole of the Acholi community, gained local and international support, the Ugandan government declared northern Uganda a war zone and governed it under covert military decree. The Ugandan government explicitly portrayed the Acholi people as a barbaric, warlike people who were the enemy of civilization and Uganda. In this setting, the government dispossessed the Acholi people of their human dignity by subjecting them to unprecedented suffering. In addition, the government exempted its personnel from any possible prosecution because of the atrocities they meted out on the Acholi people, because they believed the Acholi people deserved them and that these actions would civilize them:

> The first time I came to contest for a political position here, I was 26 and I came here to Gulu and I told the people, that "Look, the government in Kampala has decided to blame, we the people of northern Uganda, for everything that has gone wrong in Uganda. We must reject that paradigm because every tribe has got good people and bad people. Second, we must reject the stigmatization of our community; third, we must reject this heaping of the collective guilt. If there are people in Acholiland who committed crimes in Uganda, they should be held responsible individually. (NM)

LB, a former rebel commander, explained that the NRA/M regime pursued a military and political policy of revenge and sectarian tendencies against the Acholi people. Its soldiers committed unprecedented mass murders and other heinous atrocities across the Acholi subregion. The government excessive abuses forced the Acholi community to defend themselves against a government that turned itself against the people without any provocation.

> Unfortunately, the advancing soldiers of NRA; most of whom were recruited from Luwero where there was bitter war. So they came when they were very bitter for revenge. So when they came, they started doing bad things to our people. But for fighters, we were tired. We had gone to Sudan with all our equipment and said, "No, let us not fight. Let us see what he is going to do. If he is not violent as Id Amin, let him rule. If he wants some of us to go back in the army, we shall join him, and if not, we shall stay at home." So people were staying there in Southern Sudan. But reports started coming to us, "We are being killed." Then we started seeing massive people running and we said, "This is serious." So some of our officers said, "No, this time our people are not going to be butchered like during Id Amin. This time we have to resist it." That is how the war started. (LB)

The government abuses against the Acholi people were intolerable. For instance, the president violated the protocol on how the Acholi people reprimand their leaders. As religious leader ON noted, while the Acholi people consider a leader as an ordinary person, they esteem their leaders enough to spare them public rebuke as a reflection of the cardinal restorative values embedded in their culture rather than the retributive overtones and attitudes they read in the president's public outbursts. On many occasions, the president and his subordinates denigrated Acholi leaders in public to the dismay of the Acholi people:

> I was able to talk to the President in a calm atmosphere. You know, if I take activist approach, I was told the government would have resisted. But if you have your facts, you can challenge the President; you can argue with him. There was time, for example, when the President came here on Women's Day and he attacked one of the MPs [member of parliament], a local MP from here, and yet, that MP, he appointed him on the presidential peace team to talk with the rebels, but he attacked him in the rally so much. So after the rally, he invited us leaders to meet him in the barracks and we discussed what we discussed. Fortunately, I was asked to pass a vote of thanks. Before the vote of thanks, I raised my disappointment. And I told him, that, "Mr. President, I am so much disappointed with you today. I am angry with you. You know why? How can you attack a MP of the people in a rally like that? This man you appointed in your

presidential peace commission, if you know he is not performing, why don't you deal with him at your level? Why attack him in a rally?" And the MP was there and he responded after. And the President said, "I am sorry; I was misled." Now if I had challenged him in public, he would have bungled me together with that MP. (ON)

Economically, OG1, a member of parliament, noted that the Acholi people noticed that Ugandan government development programs were meant to hoodwink them, since all the programs focused on hardware components rather than the software that could address the root causes of human challenges in northern Uganda. Additionally, the composition of the staff and location of the program offices favored people from southern Uganda. Given the historical regional economic imbalances already entrenched in Ugandan politics, they concluded that the government policy of hostility against the Acholi people was a strategy to solidify the ethnic disfranchisement in favor of southerners.

> And when we looked at these, they are only targeting the hardware component of development because they don't have the time to look at the software component of development. They want the hardware component, where there is money, because in the software component, sometimes you may not interact with money and it is not tangible. It can only be tangible as a process, long-term process. But the hardware component, because you want accountability, you put up medical structure somewhere, but you go inside, no drugs, no personnel to run. Go to the schools, put up nice building, nice desks, everything, but the children are walking barefooted, they don't have pencils, books, teachers are not motivated. They sit in the class and do nothing. The students enjoy the ambiance, the beauty of the class, they are comfortable, they walk home, they eat, but when the results come, no first grade [equivalent to an A grade]. Hospital, you are admitted, there is no emergency care. You go to Gulu referral hospital, you will be shocked. You will die; no facilities completely. So the nitty gritty software component of these government projects is what the community wanted to see not the structure. I would have loved to be committed under a tree but with a proper care. (OG1)

The government's political and economic priorities were inconsistent with Acholi values. The Acholi people prioritize quality over quantity. For instance, they would be happy to be treated without facilities if there was equipment, but there wasn't. So for a people who prioritize the software components of life over hardware elements, the Ugandan government's overt and covert hostilities against their community violated the Acholi core cultural value of fairness, which demands honoring humans' inherent worth. In the Acholi cultures, the regime's intent to subvert the Acholi cultural values was tantamount to witches dancing on the grave of a victim they had bewitched. Thus, the regime's ignorance of the Acholi people's cultural values blinded them to errors of judgment and conduct, which cost the country lives, time, and resources, and marred their public image.

As a response, the Acholi stood up against the deficiencies of a regime bent on trampling on their worth as a people. They stood up to defend their conscientious expectation and obligation to the humane treatment of fellow humans. The government took up the prerogative to think that it had the powers and duty to debase and subjugate the Acholi people without taking the time to understand that any policy and strategy used to debase and subjugate people is inherently self-defeating.

Opportunity

The Acholi people's dedication to and urge for equal opportunity comes from their cultural identity, which is built on collective self-understanding, expectation, responsibility, and well-being. It is expressed in consensual procedures, which prioritize everyone's unique contributions and interests. Their communality insisted that you are stronger together when everyone's unique features, obligations and interests are embedded in the collective identity, responsibility and interest. Collectivity, in their context, is greater than the sum of the individual parts because everyone reflects the whole, which is greater than the sum of their parts. Thus, individuals and the community are interdependent entities, inconceivable apart from each other. Collective and individual identities and aspirations are complementary. As such, each entity is indispensable.

Therefore, equal opportunity is not merely a legal obligation to non-discrimination. It is an atmosphere where everyone's unique identity, aspirations, and obligations are recognized and accorded a complementary status within the whole. It is built on a consensual environment whereby everyone is accorded a voice, divergence is celebrated, both initiatives and chaos are leveraged, and hope against hope is midwifed. On the other hand, tendencies like control, rigidity, despair, and manipulation are discarded. Consensus building assumes the nature, character, structure, and function of life rather than merely a procedure. In this environment, OO6, a member of the Acholi diaspora, said that leadership is horizontal and is exercised in a flattened structure:

> You may have one leader leading you but even that leader needed to sit down and listen to the voices of the people he is leading. So in this case, decision making is collective, according to Acholi literature and culture. It is not hierarchical, whereby the voices of the people are silenced and only the king talks. In Acholi culture, there is a saying that *Ngonu*, which is being able to express your doubt loudly. Part of it is that I have heard you, but have you considered all options? Is this the only option we are left with? (OO6)

So, the hallmark of equal opportunity among the Acholi people lies heavily on respect for human dignity. In other words, acknowledging the inherent human dignity of everyone at all levels of interaction. No member is regarded as a mere number added up to constitute the group, because the whole is greater than the sum of the individual parts in their cosmology. The individual parts reflect the whole, both individually and collectively. According to NM, a human rights lawyer, in a flattened structure it is important to understand people you are dealing with.

> The chief can come and tell me that we need a contribution to a community project, and I will give my contribution if I agree, but he cannot dictate. So our cultural makeup is what informs our interactions with those who have political power, who control the State. We always insist that it is better to understand us, then you will know how to deal with us. Because if you don't understand us, you may think that we are a very difficult people. But we are actually not a difficult people. We just insist on being understood and it can be stated in one word, respect. (NM)

However, when NRA/M entered Acholiland in 1986, a new form of relationship between the state and the people unfolded in the entire region. Having conceded defeat, the Acholi people welcomed the NRA/M regime to the region peacefully with wide open arms. They complied with all the governmental orders. For instance, former soldiers responded to the order to assemble at a designated location with the hope of being reintegrated into the NRA or retiring peacefully. Despite all these overtures, LK, a researcher, observed that the NRA/M regime conducted itself as an adversary rather than a government. The first group of former soldiers that responded was taken to Kiburura in western Uganda, but to date nobody knows of their whereabouts. Furthermore, immediately after the Acholi people returned the guns, the NRA soldiers started committing unprecedented atrocities like mass murders and raping men and women in public. According to LK, "We have documented 86 men who were raped. We have been treating them medically and giving them psychosocial support. Many bad things happened during that period."

Since all the NRA/M responses were unprovoked, the Acholi people gradually realized that their peace overtures were not a priority in the NRA/M's military agenda. Instead, they noticed that the government was consistently imposing their unilateral preplanned agenda against the Acholi community without first understanding or involving the community. In response, using their cultural methods of talking to a violent group, the Acholi people took up arms and organized themselves under groups like the UPDA as a violent mouthpiece to convince the government to put down their arms. This sparked unprecedented war episodes, which the government pursued to disenfranchise the entire Acholi community.

Unlike the previous wars, which targeted only the war antagonists with the aim to attain or protect power, people, and property, the antagonists in the northern Uganda conflict targeted the masses indiscriminately without the aim to either capture or protect power. ZA, a member of the Acholi diaspora who was based in Germany, attributed the response of the Acholi people to the unconventional nature of the war the Ugandan government waged against the people in northern Uganda:

> So, we said, "Now, if the people are hoping in us, what can we do in this situation and the kind of war being waged in Uganda is different from the kind of problem Id Amin brought? There was no civil war, even in Acholi districts here in northern Uganda, there was no civil war that time. Id Amin had his obsession with foreign aggression. And inside here people could go to school, you go and do your work. And it might be only managers, medical officers who were being affected. A normal person, if he runs from town to the village, was not being hunted. But the opposite was true during Museveni time. In that actually, for him he lures those people who are potentially supposed to overthrow him, but destabilizes their roads from town to the village. The people in the village had been uprooted totally and put into the camps. There was no social base for any organization. They were economically depleted what Johan Galtung in Peace called structural violence. Education system was run down, economic system was run down. All the cattle looted. There was no economic base. (ZA)

Thus, the Acholi people reached a consensus that the war in northern Uganda was a ploy by the Ugandan government to destroy the Acholi community. They arrived at this conclusion because of the double standard the Ugandan government employed in dealing with the (LRA) war compared to other conflicts in which it intervened in the Greats Lakes region. Unlike its approaches in the other conflicts, which posed a real threat, the government did not engage the LRA with the same level of intensity. In the following excerpt, OO5, a career diplomat and an intellectual who engaged the international community, pointed out the government's double standard:

> Now regarding the episode of the war, there were some factors at play. One is, people knew that this was a false war. It was something that was really concocted because they did not really see the army engaging with the insurgency and they tell you so many stories of the insurgents coming this way and the army says, "Why don't you go and tackle them?" or "The army coming this way" and [the army] comes after [the rebels] have gone and say how come you are collaborating with them? So this was very much really a contrived situation. And they were intrigued that how come when the government was really interested in ending the real insurgency, like that of Lakwena, they fought hard and furious. Odong Latek, they fought hard and furious but this of Kony, a year, two years, three years, ten years, going twenty years, nothing. Now, so they knew that something wasn't right in this picture. And of course, they knew also that all the destruction taking place was in their area; you know, northern Uganda was being destroyed. Nobody was crossing Karuma. The government was not under a threat. So whether it is the government forces who rounded the people into the camps or committing atrocities, and massacres, it was against the Acholi. Whether it was Kony and his group coming to commit atrocities against the people. So either way, it is the Acholi who were the losers. So it did not matter so long as this war was going on, whatever was being exacted by the insurgents, it was the Acholi who suffered, exacted by the army it was against the Acholi. (OO5)

The government's cold feet coincided with the total collapse of government structures in the entire Acholi subregion. The absence of functional government structures denied the Acholi people opportunities to thrive as a community. As ZA put it, "Everybody was touched and agreed that this was not something you could sit on the side and see it being resolved."

Economically, the war destroyed the northern Uganda economy. The offices of the government programs in northern Uganda were relocated to central Uganda in favor of southerners. Moreover, on many occasions, the government declined to undertake developmental programs in the region under the pretext of the war. OO5 said that the Acholi people saw these excuses as a cover-up to exterminate them:

> So, people knew that kind of devices, the government was really playing a very contrived game. It was not genuinely interested in ending the conflict and they got to know about the corruption, the money that was being made in the war and the lie that was created in the rest of Uganda because each time anybody said, "There is corruption," Museveni would say, "We can't do this, we can't do X, we can't go multiparty democracy, because we are still prosecuting the war." So I think most people who were a little informed knew there wasn't something right with this picture. So they developed the conviction that if they themselves did not press and take charge, the normal party (the government) was not willing to take charge, because it had vested interest in this war. So I think they felt they themselves had to take charge. (OO5)

The war also influenced government policies on the natural resources in northern Uganda. Although northern Uganda has the largest share of the oil reserve in Uganda, OL the academician said that the government decided to build oil wells in Bunyoro, which is situated in southern Uganda. The Acholi people saw this as a governmental ploy to disenfranchise them of their fair share of the natural resources in Acholiland.

> For example, the oil well is being built in Bunyoro. There are five oil wells in Acholi. The oil well in Acholi will dry out in 50 years and that in Bunyoro will dry out in 12 years, and yet they are building a well in Bunyoro. According to the Acholi, the well should be built in Acholi subregion. This would create economic incentive to the people in terms of employment. So this is one of the red cards they want to wave at the President. (OL)

Communally, LK, a member of parliament and a researcher, pointed out that in rural areas, the entire Acholi community was forcefully uprooted from their homes and abandoned in the Internally Displaced People's camps, where they were forbidden from accessing their land and relatives in other camps. All their properties were forcefully confiscated and houses demolished. For over a decade the Acholi community remained idle, redundant, and isolated. For a people who were economically independent and community oriented, this was an intentional government policy to wipe out an entire community rather than a military strategy to end the insurgency, especially given that the Acholi people did not support the LRA. In the villages,

> The removal of cattle was the most fundamental assault to their economy. So the war took away all the cattle, which was the investment bank of the community. Commercial bank was things like chicken and goats. So the investment bank was destroyed. That meant that the economic resilience that supported the community to stand was destroyed. (LK)

The war did not spare the business community either. According to OO4, an elder, the general belief in Acholiland attributes the ambushes against the business people to some elements in the army. Many businesspeople lost their lives and merchandise in ambushes mainly on the Gulu-Kampala highway.

> Of course, this war was a mixture of many things. For instance, if you study vehicles shot on the highways, the majority of about 70–80 percent were coming to Kampala with prominent business people inside and you know they were shot on the way, you know the rumor was that wrong characters in the army would go to the bus parks and monitor who was boarding which vehicle. If they see prominent business woman or man boarding and they would use their walkie talkies then they would waylay them and shoot them, and in return, blame it on the rebels. Most them were coming to Kampala. (OO4)

As far as freedom of speech was concerned, the government declared northern Uganda a war zone and consequently banned freedom of press. According to NM, "We also did not have access to state media. The radio did not allow us to go and talk. And then the rebels were also not understanding us. The government was not understanding us." The news reporters and media houses that tried to report on the conflict underwent persecutions, in many ways such as arrests, imprisonments, torture, murder, and closures. Thus, for over a decade, the government managed to keep the world in the dark about the atrocities the security forces were meting out against the people. The information lacuna transformed the conflict into the most forgotten human crisis in the world. It is not surprising that the Acholi community felt abandoned by their own government and the international community. As a result, NM pointed out that the community members were "full of apathy" because they thought the government was insensitive to their sufferings and too strong for the ordinary people to counter.

Furthermore, prominent Acholis who committed their efforts to disseminating alternative information about the conflict, contrary to the official government propaganda, had their own share of persecution. The government revoked the citizenship of OO5, the Under-Secretary General of the United Nations. He could no longer compete for the United Nations Secretary General position. However, he stood firm in discrediting the government's official position on the conflict with substantial empirical evidence that changed the international community's perception and response to the conflict. During the interview, he shared his experience:

> Of course, of course, I was persecuted ferociously. They denounced my citizenship and denied there was any concentration camp. They said I am not even a Ugandan at that. They threw everything at me. I am told one time, while K was leading a meeting at the State Department in the U.S. was furiously swearing at the top of his voice saying, "This Olala man! This Olala man!" Because apparently in the meeting, they told him that, "But you are saying this and that, but here are some writing and documents written by so and so whom we know and respect, what do you say?" I think he could not answer. After leaving the meeting, he was furious, because in his perception, I was spoiling the good name of the government and then of the regime and spoiling a good story. They also got very furious after the summit, the Commonwealth meeting. I had told them that, "How come you are going to a country with people in concentration camps?" And that is partly how they [Western governments] brought the pressure to bear on the government in order for them to come. Otherwise they don't care about what Ugandans think. (OO5)

Finally, according to OO4, a prominent elder, the government curtailed people's freedom of movement. Nobody could travel without obtaining a travel permit from the president's special representative in the area and those allowed were restricted to specific hours. Upon their return, they were required to report back to the office to check out. Martial law turned the people into hostages in their country and land.

> And then do you know the army declared curfew, nobody could move before 9 am. Even buses were not allowed on the roads before then. And the movement stopped at 3pm. Wherever it finds you, regardless of what you are doing, you stop there. Personally, I slept in my pickup truck. So for all these years, people were not allowed to move out before 9 am and after 3 pm and you would not go from one camp to another. They were confined. Even

if your relative died in another camp, you were not allowed to go. And then coming here, particularly during the Tenyefunza thing, [a military operation named Operation Iron Feast] it was really a scorched earth policy. You could only travel after obtaining a document from Resident District Commissioner's office, and you were not allowed to exchange the document with anybody else. So my own nephew came with that travel document, and stayed with me two nights, but he refused to allow me photo copy it. You were required to take it back to the office to check out. Apparently, you cannot get a copy because the government collected them back. So business was paralyzed, even for those living in town. So there were many, many challenges. (OO4)

In a nutshell, the government's unprovoked unilateral decisions and actions nearly caused the extinction of the Acholi culture and people. OO6, a member of the Acholi diaspora, said that the government policy and actions in northern Uganda were ill-conceived and executed:

There were situations where the government did not consult like moving people to the camps and to this day I contend that moving people to the camps was a bad idea. I think there would have been other ways like the "Mayumba Kumi" ("ten cells"). It seemed to me that moving people to the camps almost cost us the entire culture. (OO6)

The most devastating impact of this policy was felt among the younger generation that grew up in the camps. OO4, a retired member of parliament, said that the children who were born and raised up in the camps lack moral compass:

So, children could not accept to sleep together with their parents. Children started to misbehave. They were undisciplined all this time, people were in the camps. Now they are going back [to how things were before]. They are starting afresh to educate the children who are being born. Children born in the camps are rebellious, they don't want to stay in the village. They want to ride "bodaboda" (motorcycle) and stay in town. So the destruction of culture was very, very big weapon against us. A very big weapon. The culture was interfered with because the people of Acholi were very, very strong because of the culture. They taught children from early age around the fire place and the girls when they are cooking with their mothers. (OO4)

However, despite the appalling level of economic disenfranchisement, social disruption, physical and psychological torture, and political marginalization, the Acholi people did not give up. They maintained their dignity through protracted, successful responses, which prevailed against the government and rebel schemes to wipe them out. For instance, they developed a narrative of peaceful conflict resolution, which overcame the government narrative of violent conflict resolution. The Acholi countermeasures to restore and preserve the Acholi values, which were at the verge of extinction were based on the consciousness and commitment to their dignity.

The Acholi human dignity is built upon the interaction between root factors and fruit actions. The root factors are discussed in chapter 6. The factors are divided into two categories. The first category is endogenous factors, which include character subdivided into attitudes, atmosphere, and core values. The second category is exogenous factors, which include things like context, culture, and education.

6

Findings on Followership Development: Root Factors

THIS chapter discusses the findings on root factors which interact with overt actions to form human dignity out of which followers develop their followership identities, roles, and behaviors in the context of everyday life experiences. So just as the interaction between root factors and fruit actions form human dignity, human dignity also influences human response to a stimulus, which in turn influences root factors. In this context, followership development is a continuous, seamless interaction among layers of factors in the context of daily life encounters as previously shown in Figures 2 and 3. The chapter is divided into three sections: core values, character, and exogenous factors.

ENDOGENOUS FACTORS

In the Acholi culture, overt human actions like observation and response are the tip of the iceberg, floating above layers of factors such as core values, characteristics, and exogenous factors like culture and education, whose knowledge is paramount in understanding people and their behaviors. This paradigm comes from the Acholi people's belief that human beings are embodied spirits, situated in a specific physical location. For that matter, humans have dual natures composed of tangible and intangible components. The components are complementary and inconceivable in isolation. OL, an elder, narrated that the Acholi people prioritize the intangible component of human nature over the tangible:

> Many times, there is a deeper understanding of a people than just what you think or read and sometimes it is not those big tangible things that matter. The intangible sometime turns out to be more valuable, and that has been the case in this particular conflict in Acholi. People did not care about being in power, just that our values were threatened, our dignity was threatened. That is what counted. (OL)

Thus, given the dual human nature, this study found out that the factors, which influenced the response of the Acholi people to the Ugandan government policy and approaches to the conflict, fall into endogenous and exogenous categories. Endogenous factors include core values and characteristics, which are divided into attitude and atmosphere.

Core Values

Acholi cultural core values are central to their self-consciousness, aspirations, and obligations. It is extremely difficult and even impossible to understand either the Acholi people or their behaviors without understanding their cultural core values, which include: inviolability of life, invaluability of life, interrelationships, and interdependence among others. In the next section, I will discuss inviolability of life.

Inviolability of Life

Among the Acholi, human life is a sacred gift of God's life packaged in a human body and situated in a specific physical location. While describing the divine nature of human life, YA, an elder, said, "You know, I owe it [life] to God. I owe it to the wisdom of our ancestors and elders who saw that life is a gift to be defended. Life has a value and this value cannot be wasted. It has to be defended." LK, a member of parliament, pointed out that like God, human life is eternal—and thus inviolable. That is, "Once you are born, your soul cannot die." Ultimately, the circumstances of life "don't matter because the matters of life and death are matters that are in the hands of God." Thus, humans can neither give nor take it away, regardless of what they do. God alone has the prerogative of giving life and taking it away. Any thought and attempt to harm human life mars the humanity of the offender. This is because human life is not a property, a possession, or a product, but rather a sacred treasure that must be cherished in order to enhance harmonious well-being. BO, a retired prelate, summed up the sanctity of human life in the following excerpt:

> One of them, one of their members, a child of God created in the image of God. That is why they accept you even though you have brought great shame and disgrace upon the community. They will still accept you. Two, it [dignity] symbolizes purity and sanctity of human life. Nobody in the world is allowed to violate or desecrate the purity or sanctity of human life. (BO)

For that matter, there is a clear distinction between the life of God in humans—the real life and the physical life. So, in their cosmology, human life is the spiritual life and the physical body is the house of the spiritual life the same way a building and its surroundings house the body. In that regard, the Acholi people consider humans as embodied spiritual personal beings situated in a physical environment.

Thus, first, human life is rooted in divine nature and life, and is multifaceted. It is composed of the spiritual, personal, social, physical, and ecological selves. Second, it is expressed in human vertical relationship to God and horizontal relationships to personal self, others, and the ecology. So a human being—*dano*—is a spiritual personal being, which can be understood properly only in its harmonious, seamless nature.

Horizontally, the human body and the ecology derive their immediate value and meaning from their connection to human life, which in turn finds its value and meaning in its connection to God. However, vertically they all ultimately derive their value and meaning from God, the Creator (*Lacwec*) or the daughter of Obanga (*Nyar Obanga*). In other words, God is the ultimate source, sustainer, and destiny of humans and the rest of the creation. In that case, human beings and the ecology ultimately are windows to the divine. OA2, a Roman Catholic prelate, explained the divine nature of human life and its implications in the following excerpt:

> Many of these troubles we have in the world, somebody was telling me I have not done the study of peace and so on deeply. Somebody was telling me, factors like identity that I belong to this tribe, this clan, religion or this kind of thing, some of them are the causes of fighting because this one would want his identity to supersede the identity of the other one. Then, we have the material resources and the issue of power comes in and cause tension and animosity among people to separate and begin to see the other as the enemy that should be eliminated so that you have monopoly. That is where the trouble is. If we can go and educate ourselves as humanity to go up and cross

over these artificial barriers and say that, after all, your identity and my identity we have common identity inherent in all of us. Localization of it or distributing the level of understanding one another because of language, location this and the other, these are secondary. (AO2)

Therefore, the divine nature of human life is the bedrock of the identity of the Acholi people. It is impossible to establish meaningful relationships with the Acholi people without understanding and respecting their cultural value of inviolability of life. The value of the inviolability is undergirded by specific principles and dispositions, discussed herein below.

Principles

The value of inviolability of life predisposes the Acholi people to a collective life built upon fundamental principles and dispositions. The principles include: common inviolable life, individual autonomy and authority, and collective expression. These principles permeate the fabric of the Acholi mental models and values, which in turn drive their responses.

Common Inviolable Life

Humanity possesses a collective identity derived from the common, inviolable (sacred) life whose well-being rests upon recognizing and preserving its inviolability. The Acholi people preserve human sacredness through a cultural ethos of human belongingness. In other words, humans are human because they ultimately share a common inviolable nature and life, rather than merely ethnicity, race, or nationality. In this context, human community is a synthesis of everyone, rather than merely a sum of the parts. The essence of human collective identity or belongingness is the common inviolable nature and life (humanity, or *"dano/Ubuntu"*), which makes everyone an indispensable, complementary member.

According to Roman Catholic prelate OA2's views, a human complementary nature implies that human community is a dynamic synthesis with a complex status, which subordinates secondary identities like ethnicity, race, class, age, and gender to a common nature and life. In that regard, individual members and the corporate community are complementary entities due to their common nature and life, which makes human community a phenomenon that is greater than the sum of its parts. In other words, for the Acholi people, the Acholiness in the corporate Acholi is not greater than an individual Acholi, and the humanity of a single human being is not lesser than its corporate humanity because the image of God in humans is inviolable, immeasurable, and indivisible. OA2 reiterates the importance of human common nature and life when he says,

> Mr. Ofumbi, what I can say here is this, if one wants to play a role of uniting people, he must go deeper than the two sides. The deeper level is to see the two people who are fighting as human beings [*dano—ubuntu*], because that is the common denominator. They are all human beings and therefore you must have the passion for humanity first then you will work as a mediator. (OA2)

For that matter, human responsibility is ultimately a bigger factor of human nature and life than office, age, or any other variable. The Acholi people esteem humanity and the values that undergird it above everything else, including their physical bodies. OA2 remarked that when the Acholi elders met Kony and his commanders in the bush, they impressed upon them the value of preserving the sacredness of human life as the basis for ending the conflict. In their address, they emphasized their impartiality and reverence for human sacred life:

> And for your information, I think it is also appropriate that I say this to you. When we went to see Kony with his team, even this man who was recently committed to The Hague for trial, Ongwen; I am saying I think God also put it somehow in me the courage to say it in his own territory, the camp. I said this in his own camp: I said, "Kony, you know, your life and the lives of those who are now in your hands, plus the lives of all Ugandans whatever categories they are in, and the lives of those in the Sudan, these are precious lives, they should not be destroyed. And if we have come all the way to you in the bush, it is for this reason. We would like that you sign the peace agreement so that this issue must stop to spare the lives. (OA2)

These were very daring words to a rebel leader in the jungle under his jurisdiction. However, emboldened by their reverence for the sacred human nature, OA2 stuck to his conviction, even though he was physically terrified of its ramifications. To their surprise and elation, Kony was tongue-tied.

> I am telling you Mr. Ofumbi, Kony did not say a single word to me. He heard these words from me, and he saw me like this, and he had no word. Then, I was now thinking within myself, is he going to react by assaulting us or what? Nothing! I think, first

of all, he did not expect any of us to say something like that, he did not expect. Second, I did not exclude his life. I took his life as precious. I took his life like the life of others. So really to put it in a more, maybe another way, to bring really a divided group together, you must be common [impartial] to both. If there are two common to both, if there are three, common to the three, if there are many, common to the many. They should feel you are for their good, for their good. And I think that way we could eliminate many things. (OA2)

According to OO3, a retired Anglican bishop, the Acholi people used the same paradigm to urge the government to embrace a peaceful approach to conflict resolution. At the beginning, the government was adamant, but through persistence and great mobilization efforts, the Ugandan government adopted the Acholi traditional method of conflict resolution, which prioritizes peaceful over violent approaches. In the quotation below, OO3 narrated their first encounter with the president:

You can't allow the people of God to suffer when you are there. The challenges we faced when we organized ourselves were enormous. The first time we met the President it was quite difficult. I like the way you are trying to study it. The President did not listen to us. That, if we want to talk we can talk to Kony, but not him. He [the president] will fight this man. But we told him, "Mr. President, you have been fighting this war for twelve years now and if this was a sickness I think the doctors would have prescribed something different. You cannot keep on treating somebody with the same medicine for twelve years. We are giving an alternative. You never know what will come out of it but give us the green light." He said, "Yes, go ahead." This was still a private meeting with the President, because by that time they were not interested in anybody talking peace with the rebels. So on the day of my consecration, he was there, and I told him that he must talk peace and he must unite with Acholi religious leaders, he must unite with the Acholi people to find a solution. The government would say no, we go this way, but we were consistent. Fight, talk peace, we will fight, talk peace, we will fight, talk peace, consistent! (OO3)

Furthermore, OO1, a member of parliament, said that their advocacy campaigns also targeted the international community, particularly the United Nations, the European Union, and the United States, because of their vested interest in the war and influence on the Ugandan government. Like the government, the international community also yielded to the peaceful approach to conflict resolution:

> Then we also did a lot to convince not only the Ugandan government and the LRA, but also extended our advocacy to the International body. We went to the UN. African Union we did not do much with them. We went to the U.S., Canada, Europe, European Union. We went there and we were making clear statement that please you governments of international influence try to influence the governments of Uganda and the Sudan, which hosted the LRA, to come back to the peace table. Bring them to the table and let them talk and resolve this issue. (OO1)

The common inviolable life gave the Acholi people the common platform and language to forge a united campaign to pursue a peaceful approach to the conflict's resolution. It also emboldened them to overcome the government's attempt to subjugate them into passive followership.

Individual Autonomy and Authority

In addition to common inviolable life, humanity possesses individual autonomy and authority derived from the sanctity of human nature and life. As OO6, a member of the Acholi diaspora, discussed, Acholi culture accords every individual a voice in the community because a community is not the sum of the individual members, but rather a synthesis of everyone based on the common image of God they share, which accords everyone both a transcendent and immanent, or spiritual/immaterial and physical/material, existence. The corporate community cannot subjugate individual members, and vice versa, because the individuals and the corporate community are inconceivable apart from the other. Instead, everyone is given a platform to make complementary a contribution commensurate with their distinctiveness. Individual autonomy and authority are relational rather than individualistic attributes. They can only be understood and exercised in the context of shared human belongingness, rather than individualism:

> In the Acholi culture, the idea of the individual in the collective is very strong. In other words, we want to hear; let people talk, but the notion of let people talk is not chaotic talking. People take time to chew on the ideas and to put across the ideas and through such talks, a central theme will emerge. And in that central theme, they will be some conclusions and some specific actions. (OO6)

According to OO6, the idea of a strong individual in the collective or individual autonomy and authority is the necessary antidote to oppression and exploitation by both the majority and minority. "That is our culture. For many cultures that experienced oppression, that was an obstacle to oppression." Thus, the Acholi cherish it to develop a harmonious society.

Collective Expression

Human sacred human life also possesses a collective identity with a collective expression. A synthesis of the individual members of the whole community, based on their common identity, shines a brighter light on their common identity. In other words, the members of the whole community are different than the sum of their parts because instead of a collection of parts, a synthesis is the outcome of the distillation of the distinct elements of each part, which expresses the common features the parts share. For example, whereas every member in Acholi is given a voice at public meetings, no one has a vote. Instead, a vote is the consensus, which emerges out of the synthesis of the individual voices. Thus, the outcome of the consensual process is greater than the sum of the greatest individual contribution or dictation of a section of the community. Consensus is the essence of common human identity, which accords everyone inviolable life, equality, interconnectedness, and interdependence.

In conclusion, for the Acholi people, a community is a dynamic synthesis of individual members possessing in common sacred life, individual autonomy and authority, and collective expression. Thus, human community is an open society built on individual and corporate conscientiousness, obligations, and aspirations which are congruent with the values that reflect the core human identity of inviolability and the invaluability of life. These values predispose them to specific dispositions. In the following section, I will discuss some of the dispositions they derive from the inviolability of life.

Dispositions

The common sacred nature and life predispose Acholi people to unique dispositions responsible for their response and well-being. Four identifiable dispositions are peaceful conflict resolution, optimism, circular rather than hierarchical social order, and value- rather than gain-driven life. These dispositions are seen in their response to the Ugandan government policy and approaches to the northern Uganda conflict. In the next section, I will discuss the dispositions.

Peaceful Conflict Resolution

First, the inviolability of life informs the Acholi people's disposition and approach to conflict resolution. According to BO, a retired Anglican bishop, the Acholi people believe that due to human frailties, human conflict is a normal human phenomenon expected to occur anytime and anywhere in the community. "More than anything else, the Acholi people realize that issues will always crop up in society. The question is how do you solve them? It is a way of life within the household, within the clan." In their context, conflict is a normal human phenomenon whose occurrence is taken for granted. However, NM, a lawyer, argued that whereas the occurrence of conflict is normal in a society, its degeneration into violence is abnormal and unacceptable. The Acholi culture defuses conflict before it degenerates into violence because the latter violates the inviolable life and thereby consigns both the perpetrator and victim to the same level of consciousness that caused the violence as well as marring their identity—a recipe for a spiral of perpetual violence:

> If you have harmed my child, it is because something has gone wrong with you to such an extent that you could do that. That which has gone wrong for you is now harming my life. It means I cannot be the kind of human being I want to be because you are no longer [acting as] human. So it is in my interest—my interest—as the victim, to assist you to get your humanity back so that I can become human again. (BO)

Furthermore, like any other human condition, no human conflict is permanent. So whereas they foresaw northern Ugandan conflict in the conduct of the National Resistance Army/Movement (NRA/M) officials and soldiers during and after the 1985 Nairobi peace talks, they situated it within a broader human conflict. NM concluded that, like other conflicts that have been resolved, northern Ugandan conflict was not exceptional, its unique nuances notwithstanding:

> For me, I knew for a fact that this was not a unique problem. There were other communities that had faced these problems like in the Middle East, the Jews, the South Africans. There are many resistance fighters who have resisted dictatorial regimes that are abusive. So I had to look for inspirations from the

experiences of other people from the rest of humanity and we always say that, you know, there is no condition which is permanent. (NM)

The insinuation here is that human conflicts have root causes, which require deeper analysis and appropriate measures to resolve. For instance, NM said that the Acholi people believed that the northern Uganda conflict was a political problem, which could only be solved by a political solution versus the military approach preferred by the government.

For that matter, voluntary dialogue plays a central role in conflict resolution. OO2, an elder and academician, remarked that the Acholi people "understand that nothing can move forward unless you sit down to talk about it. It is not going to solve itself. You cannot leave it for somebody else to solve for you. You must be willing to sit down and talk about things and move them along." MA, the oldest among the elders I talked to (102 years), told me that peace talks in Acholi are volitional actions of the heart, devoid of coercion and manipulation, which are based on honesty and truth-telling. Members feel free to express their opinions without any fear of retribution:

> He allows people to talk in turn and then concur, they never continue with dispute; that is honesty. Our people in the past don't bother about riches, no! They were sincere people who don't want to create enmity. I am one of those; I don't want to create enmity. If I can go down to the roots to bring peace, I will, and that is one of the reasons why I have lived longer [102 years]. The problems people bring to me, I talk to them honestly. (MA)

The inevitability of conflict and peaceful approach calls for consensuality and restorative measures rather than retribution. For instance, their culture of peaceful conflict resolution allowed them to mobilize the international community to influence both the Ugandan government and the rebels to abandon military confrontations in favor of a peaceful approach. According to ZA, "We advocated for reconciliation between the Ugandan government and rebels, the rebels and the people, the Ugandan government and the people and also among the different tribes that were involved in the conflict." This was an inclusive process in which every Acholi participated individually and collectively. OM2, a religious leader, reiterated the centrality of dialogue in conflict resolution:

> So, the interactions between us as their ambassadors while playing the role of leadership among them were based on listening to them and they were also listening to us. This is why we went

> very far and wide in that it is true we realized that our people in a way were commanding us their leaders to do what they wanted. And they wanted through us also to command the government and LRA. They spoke directly to the government about it for example amnesty. Amnesty was the wish of the people. (OM2)

Furthermore, peaceful approaches are derived from collective identity, which implies that an individual's life is woven into the life of the community to the extent that it is impossible to talk about an individual in isolation. Thus, violence occurs in community and can only be healed in a community. For that matter, in their context of restorative justice, collective identity is not a platform for either collective guilt or the abdication of individual accountability. Rather, the worst form of punishment in society is excommunication from the community because human life has meaning only in a community. According to NM,

> We think that everybody deserves fairness and that society should not just be based on who is stronger. I think there should be rules and that is the essence of community. So that is why even when we were growing up, we were taught that as the Acholis, we never had a death penalty. In fact, our idea of the gravest punishment was to ostracize somebody, because we felt that denying you that right to belong to the community was the worst punishment than death, and you cannot have peace without a sense of community. (NM)

So, the community shares in the sin of one of its members, only to the extent that the perpetrator is seeking restoration and the extent to which they are collectively accountable to each other. In those cases where the perpetrator is unwilling to seek reconciliation, the communities on both sides of the violence still conduct reconciliation ceremonies to regain the fractured relationship. However, the perpetrator is ostracized until he or she is ready to reconcile with the aggrieved party. Punishment in this context is meted out when the perpetrator is not willing to reform rather than merely because of committing an offense. OA2, a prelate, elaborated the communality of life among the Acholi people here:

> The principle among the Acholi stipulates that the individual should not be taken in isolation, whether for good or for a bad, because a person is always in a society. So when this person has made a mistake outside, he is still accountable to the people where he or she comes because as they say, "No man is an island." So if this is a matter of saying this person should be executed, it is a loss to this community here. They say no, instead of losing

> this life, we should gain this life back and they decide to have reconciliation with their counterparts who want to revenge on them through this member. So they accept the responsibility to account for the fault of this person as a community, because this man did not grow up "in the air." He grew up within the community. So the community may have contributed in one way or another for the negligence. You see, So because of this, they say no, the person here should not be executed in isolation. (AO2)

Restorative justice is compatible with their Christian beliefs. OO3, a religious leader, said that the Acholi culture of restorative justice rather than punitive justice is consistent with their divine nature and beliefs. As believers in God, they demonstrate their faith by emulating God's love for sinners. God forgives sinners who repent and restores them to himself and the church rather than condemning them to death. Condemnation is invoked only when the offender declines the offer of the grace to heal and be restored into fellowship with God.

> Now, if the Acholi people can forgive, what about Christians? I know also with Muslims, but I don't know much about Muslims. But from the Christian perspective, and we are the majority we know we serve a God of mercy, a God of love. God does not want a sinner to die in his sin. God has no pleasure in a sinner dying in his sin. God would not be happy. He believes in a sinner who turns away from his sins and lives. If we are serving this God, why don't we live by these values, this virtue of the God, the God of mercy? God is merciful he will forgive them. Let them come and renounce rebellion. He will forgive them. So when you look at the spiritual and the cultural, they are intertwined in our approach. (OO3)

Since their cultural values are compatible with their spiritual beliefs, the Acholi people redeem conflicts before they degenerate into violence, because violence causes a supernatural barrier until a ransom is paid and a rite of reconciliation is done. According to OO2, an elder, "Our understanding as Acholi is that when there is a feud between families, you cannot suppress it with force. What you can do is reconcile them." The reconciliation process requires honesty, repentance, reparation, forgiveness, reconciliation, restoration, and celebration. OO2 continued to narrate that the whole process is an act of the heart performed without coercion. "The process has a connection with the spirit world and it cannot be enforced by intimidating or keeping someone under control. People must do so voluntarily." They believe that only God can forgive sin and therefore forgiveness is the strongest antidote to impunity and the best tool for honoring life in a conflict situation because it enhances healing and restoration in a community.

Last but not least, their approach to forgiveness in a conflict situation is based on their practical life experiences over the years. As a society, they know that vengeance rather than forgiveness causes perpetual violence. For the sake of communal continuity and harmony, they prefer peaceful conflict resolution over violent approaches. There is a classic case of perpetual violence encapsulated in the story of the two brothers, Gipir and Labongo, who separated permanently and became separate tribes because they could not forgive one another. OO2 pointed out that violent conflict resolution perpetuates violence:

> Acholi believe in talking, because they know, if they continue fighting, they will kill everybody, because spear and spear, who will remain? Who will remain? So the elders must find a way of talking. So we know, the Acholi believe in talking to reach a solution to a violent conflict. So why can't the government talk with the rebels? We know the Acholi can forgive, we know it through the tradition known as *Mato Oput*. It has been there since Acholi came into being to save society, to sustain society. (OO2)

The conflict tested the Acholi resolve for peaceful conflict resolution, but they prevailed because of their belief in the inviolability of life. The challenges they endured gave them an opportunity to demonstrate that human conflicts can be solved peacefully as long as the parties to the conflict value inviolable human life and are ready to listen to each other.

Optimism

The inviolability of life predisposes the Acholi people to optimism based on justice and truth. Their optimism is driven by the transcendent, ultimate resources hidden in their inherent human potential, which is a mirror of the image of God in humanity. OO4, a retired member of parliament, shared the basis of this optimism: "We lost so many lives. But you know, God's things, it is very difficult to get rid of God's creation, it is very difficult. So once we are convinced of the justness of a cause, we are not afraid of physical death, which does not kill our spiritual self."

In a separate encounter, NM commented on Acholian optimism, saying, "In our culture, if you kill me for doing the right thing, they believe that once you are born, your soul cannot die." Regarding war, he said, "We believe that we cannot lose a just war. It is just a matter of time. We can have temporary setbacks and so on but ultimately we believe that victory will be ours because of the justness of a cause" (NM).

Therefore, the Acholi people measure optimism by the extent to which one adheres to cultural values rather than longevity because they believe that life encounters and circumstances are opportunities to bear witness to their divine nature. That is, optimism is a factor of being rather than doing.

Value Rather than Gain Driven

Third, the Acholi people are value driven rather than gain driven. Since they are embodied, spiritual, personal beings with inviolable lives, their well-being is tethered to their adherence to the core cultural values rather than a pursuit of gain. While on a campaign encounter with the community, OR2, a member of parliament, narrated the people's priorities and expectations during the conflict, saying, "They told me one thing. We just want you to go; we know that you are not going to bring roads but go and tell the truth. We want the whole world to know the truth and that is all." Being value driven enhances harmony and societal well-being, which leads to material gain. Thus, adherence to the cultural core values, rather than the pursuit of gain, is the basis for their well-being and longevity. He continued,

> The population wants to see honesty in their leadership and that you are attached to them. The people want to see it in their leaders, that you should remain principled by adhering to their values, protect their values, protect their dignity and can lead them to a better destination. Transition them through life from one stage to another. I have seen people have started coming. For example, this year there is nomination of candidates, there are people who started campaigning three years ago, they move with money, government sent them. I don't go. I withdraw. But on the day of my nomination if I speak out on a radio and announce everybody will come. (OR2)

For that matter, they guard their cultural core values above everything else, including their physical lives. The government strategy of reward and punishment would not work in the Acholi community, where people act from the heart, beyond any inducement or coercion. Inducement and coercion mar human identity and dignity. OL spelt out what they hold dear as a people:

> Public and official life is not divorced from private and unofficial life. You could talk of Acholi values. The values we hold so dear

are things like honesty, trustworthiness, honor and equality by birth and life. And if any of those are broached, we consider them almost inviolable and we do anything to uphold them. (OL)

When faced with the daunting task of convincing the Ugandan government, the LRA, and the international community to adopt a peaceful approach to conflict resolution, the Acholi people were neither afraid of the task nor doubtful of their capacity to bring their cultural core values to bear on the conflict. The issue was not the size of the challenge, but rather the justness of the cause as OO2, an elder, summarized: "Don't you think it is right for the people to tell the government what should be done to solve the problem?" In their mission, they were not seeking for any favor or gain, but merely an opportunity to demonstrate the authenticity of their cause, motive, and strategy. Acholiland was engulfed in a violent conflict that was violating the inviolable life of the Acholi people and nothing other than a peaceful approach could resolve it. Theirs was a mission to call upon humanity to recognize and preserve the dignity of the Acholi people, the rebels, the Ugandan government soldiers and officials, and the international community. OM2, a religious leader, summarized their mission:

> Our mission was very clear. We were just in the middle of two people fighting. We were in the middle to mediate. Mediation advocacy with the goal for forgiveness and reconciliation, because we don't believe that a human society can have a future without reconciliation. So we made our position very clear. Our response was not meant to gain any political post.

Tethered to their values, the Acholi people overcame the temptations to coerce them into a compromise to forfeit their heritage. As embodied, spiritual, personal beings situated in a specific physical location, they demonstrated their divine nature by upholding values over gains. This disposition endeared them to the pursuance of justice and truth until the conflict was resolved.

Harmony

A fourth common identity trait is harmony with oneself, others, the created world, and God. Harmony prioritizes collective identity, responsibility, and interest over individualism, self-interest, and passive followership. The interest of the other is put above secondary identity, passive followership, and self-interest to create the necessary atmosphere for complementary relationships rather than a mentality of survival of the fittest. In articulating it, religious leader OM2 said,

> The people had their way of living, and in their way of living, they value life, they value peaceful living, they value relationship amongst themselves and with the others and with God also. They value reconciliation: Why? Because for them relationship is better for the survival for human beings, any human being than what we call, "We fight by strength," I said, "No, we don't live that way. It is not the rule of the jungle to say survival of the fittest. Not like that for the people." The strongest must protect the weakest and the two must live together, you know.

Common human identity connects them vertically to God and horizontally to other humans and the rest of creation. In that regard, they are accountable to one another as unto God and the rest of creation. Thus, humans are embodied spiritual personal beings whose well-being is inextricably intertwined in their common sacred identity. Harmony is the accord humans derive from their common identity, which enhances their well-being.

Circular Rather than Linear Social Order

Finally, collective identity predisposed the Acholi people to circular rather than linear social order, which creates a structure in which collective voices are distilled to form a consensus rather than a dictation and manipulation of either the majority or minority. A lot of emphasis is focused on efforts that guarantee societal continuity rather than fractures. For example, they maintain a very strong bond between the dead and the living and among the living. Strong bonds reinforce the belief that human beings cannot survive without maintaining unbroken bonds because of their common identity. LK, a researcher, explained their orientation below,

> And life in Acholi is led not in a linear direction. The community believes that life is led in cyclic format: that a boy is born, a girl is born, you live your life, you become an elder, you give knowledge to people, and in the process, you progress into ancestry, but you don't die, even if you physically die. You inform the future by going into it. And therefore, that is why for everything that is done, the Acholi would first give to the ancestors. You cannot eat food without giving to the ancestors. The circle continues whereby life moves in a wheel, so that society is continually moving.

This social order is egalitarian in nature. There is reciprocity in the relationship between leaders and followers and the same order permeates the entire social strata of the society. The circular social strata are reinforced in cultural formation activities like dances and drama, and in cultural artifacts like building architecture and public meeting structures. According to NM,

> First, we believe in the equality of all human beings, egalitarianism. We believe in merit. If you are really a leader, people will follow you. We don't have to vote, because votes can be distorted. Our culture is manifest in our architecture. Our houses are round. That is a sign of egalitarianism. Our dances are in circles, that is egalitarianism.

OO2, an academician, narrated how the egalitarian structure works:

> We dance round [in circles] with women in the center. So several things inform it. This is how we are socialized. It means that we are all equal. When we call a meeting, we all sit in a circle. Normally in a meeting, we invite a neutral person to chair it. No matter where you come from, we are all equal. Equality is very important. So that also helped us in the cultural setting. For us, we sleep on a skin or one mat. One blanket is enough for everybody. People like egalitarian social set up rather than the hierarchical one.

MH, a Muslim leader, said that by following their cultural core values, the Acholi people reached a consensus that any further tolerance of perpetual violence in their lives, bodies or physical environment was tantamount to forfeiting their identity and well-being as a community. "In this war, it was not only one group or denomination participating, it was the entire community. We assumed the mediation role, seeing the people of God suffering and the life which God has given being taken away forcefully, without their will and without their consent." NM, reiterated that the whole of northern Uganda was uninhabitable. "This area that has been the epicenter of the conflict is my home. I think everybody would want a home that is peaceful. So whether I wanted to participate or not, I had no choice because this is my home."

Invaluability of Life

In Acholi cultures, human life is not only eternal. It is also invaluable. That is, life is not a commodity one can possess, attain or exchange. Life is priceless. It is ultimately who you are—one's very being. Therefore, it requires no human effort to attain it like a commodity or status. Instead, life is a gift already given. Humans simply live it out. In relation to human inviolable/eternal and invaluable/priceless life, human effort is understood as a conformation of values that reflect this inviolability and invaluability of life. Since human life is immeasurable, all human beings are equal and unique. For that matter, invaluability is the basis of human equality, which renders human abilities as complementary resources. OL, a member of parliament, recollected European explorers' impression of the Acholi people:

> Some of those colonial writing, I think it is that of Speke [Baker] when he described his journey in Uganda from the south up to the north. When he reached Patiko, the chief arranged seats in a circular manner, rather than in a hierarchical manner and they gave him a seat like that of the rest of the people. He said that these people think that they are our equals. For us, he is just another human being, nothing special about it. Life circumstances may be different, you may be wearing the best suit but that does not take away the fact that you are just another human being like us. Then these guys [NRA/M]; they came with all those deficiencies that we knew and they wanted to load it on us. That was extremely provocative. Even your own dad cannot dictate to you. We grew up knowing if I want something I will discuss with him. (OL)

For the Acholi people, life does not consist of what you possess or what you do; it is not found in what you attain or lose. Rather, life is the essence of who you are. It is measured by adherence to fundamental values rather than accomplishments and possessions. Some of these values, according to NM, are "brotherhood, solidarity, with all of us being God's children, all of us having a place under the sun. These are things, which are very much part of that tradition in which I grew up. And they form and inform what I do."

Human responses and actions emanate from and reflect cultural core values. The values inform the lenses the Acholi people use to interact with others. According to MA, an elder, "It takes time to both understand an Acholi and for an Acholi to love you wholeheartedly. Once they discover that you have similar values with them, then they befriend you. Once an Acholi befriends you, the relationship will remain permanent." So for the Acholi people, values are the source, force, and destiny of efforts, status, possession, position, and trust. For example, OR1 said that whereas the Acholi tended to prefer older to younger people when choosing leaders, there are times when young people are chosen over their elders because of the degree of adherence to Acholi values:

> In our cultures, we have a saying that when you are child, you cannot be a leader. You must follow certain footsteps because people wanted a leader with experience with exposure and everything. Now, what happened eventually those leaders with experience had betrayed the people and people were looking for a new chapter. So when I went to one place, people listened to me, and that was not even my clan. And the elders said, you know, "We need to give this young man a blessing." Our blessing is done using *Olwedo* tree and they talk over its leaves with their saliva and thereafter give you. But they told me one thing, you know what, "We just want you to go; we know you are not going to bring roads and all these things but just go and tell the truth. We just want the whole world to know the truth and that is all." After that, I went to our clan, they called me, they asked me, "Are you serious, you want to be a leader? Are you serious that you want to contest? Do you understand our values?" (OR1)

In some cases, even foreigners and paupers are preferred over older people or people of royal descent because of their adherence to the core values of the community. Human equality is a fundamental value in Acholiland, however, it is worth noting that equality in their context emanates from human inviolable and invaluable life, or the vertical realm of human life rather than the horizontal. Thus, the horizontal realm is a window to the vertical realm. OO3, a retired prelate, stressed their commitment to values:

> The Acholi are very particular about certain qualities. You can be the son of a pauper, or adopted within this family, or nephew or cousin, but if you have these qualities, they will say you are the one who will be our leader. You don't have to be from royal blood or this family to qualify as a leader, no; it is about the qualities. They will say this one we adopted is the best, give this. The qualities are very important. You know, there are Acholi who are very successful according to the Western standard, somebody like a person x, AAA is successful but is not respected in Acholi. (OO3)

In this egalitarian context, leadership is regarded as an aggregated phenomenon comprising everyone in the community. It is a collective phenomenon with shared life, interest, and responsibility. "*Rwot* is an embodiment of the community collectivity. It is an aggregated body which involves the whole society." Leadership in Acholi is not imposed on people by the rest of the people because "people don't see themselves as subjects. They are part and parcel of the chieftain." For example, at one chief's home there could be a big granary where people stock food in preparation for famine. Whereas the chief is mandated with the duty of supervising the production, storage, and distribution of food during famine, his responsibility does not dispossess, negate, or subjugate the role of the people. The chief is not a benevolent figure people look upon to rescue them. Instead, a chief is considered one among the people rather than one above or beside the people. A leader is one of, and with, the people. Here, OR2 described the Acholi understanding of a leader:

> Though we also have a saying in our culture that I am a king in my own home. Literally it shows how proud we are. You don't rely on a chief as much as he is your king. Symbolically, he is a cultural leader. You don't live by his providence. You can survive as a household. He is not the giver of your life, but you respect him as a cultural leader.

According to OR1, a leader's role is to capture the imagination and aspiration of the people and work together with the people as one of the people to attain that goal. A leader does not work for the people because his or her identity in the collective community places him or her among the people rather than beside or above the people.

> People were saying, "R, for us, we are now just praying for you because you are alone." You hear how they are talking? So you know, people want to see somebody who can capture their interest, their imagination, somebody who cannot be compromised. For me, that is the only way that is the rallying point. And by the way, that is not only about the Acholi, it is all over the world. (OR1)

A leader is recognized based on his or her adherence to societal core values and aspirations. Otherwise, people assert their own authority and autonomy to reject the leader who is considered a traitor. "I stand with him, but if that leader deviates, I am also a leader in my own right. There are some leaders in Acholi now who cannot command respect. They may have strong voice but they lack respect, because people see them as traitors." OO5, a diplomat, said,

> So, leadership is embedded in the cultural values. These values have practical values and people see their benefits. For example, the dignity of an Acholi is that I can be poor, but I have a home. I am the chief of my home; you cannot sleep with my wife. In Buganda, the King is called Sabasaja, meaning that he is the husband to all men. He can sleep with your wife and you praise him so much for that [modern kings no longer practice this]. (OO5)

During the conflict, OA2, a prelate, said that "the leaders and the people were together and this is what worked. If the leaders spoke contrary to what the people wanted, we would not have succeeded." Collective responsibility, based on the invaluability of life, permeates the Acholi social strata. It governs social interactions and the community's response to all challenges:

> People saw the way the conflict was conducted and everybody thought, that, "It is my responsibility to do something." And you know, when each person looked at the person next to them within the village, the leadership circle, being it religious or political or traditional, they said that the best thing we can do since we have the same objective is to rally ourselves together and speak the same language through our social settings. Let us take this matter to the elders so that they can confront or put this matter forward. (OA2)

The value of collective responsibility, which is anchored in individual autonomy and authority, flattens the social structure which in turn balances the power between the people and the leaders. The leaders acknowledge and enhance individual autonomy and authority in accordance with their values, which redeems them from degenerating into individualism. The people also redeem the power and authority culture accords to leaders to sustain the equality and harmony necessary for the effective participation of everyone. BA, a member of parliament, said that leaders understand their role as amplifying the collective voices of the people. "Actually, what brought me into politics was to give a voice to my people, which was completely lacking. I represent that voice, which is voiceless. [I am a leader,] as long as I am ready for it and am ready to die for it." Leadership is a collective responsibility of the community, rather than a position or status. OW1, a religious leader, confirmed BA's point:

> I think as per our culture, we are an acephalous society. The chiefs derive their power from the people, not the other way around. That is, the chief speaks and it goes down. For example, when the British came here and they wanted land, they went to the chief of Awic who told them that I am just a mere custodian. This is not my land; the land belongs to the people. So it is embedded in our culture. (OW1)

The egalitarian setup is built on precedents, which define the Acholi people. It is hereditary to the extent that the Acholi people consider it genetic, because it is ingrained in Acholi heritage, cultures, and practices. It has enabled the Acholi people to deal with life issues and abuses of power by both the people and their leaders. Whereas the people and leaders both have voices, neither has the vote. The vote is an outcome of a consensual process, which distills individual voices into a consensus that factors in precedents, cultural core values, and individual and collective societal interests to consider the issue at stake. Regarding the conflict, the Acholi people concluded that it was a genocide against the Acholi people, because it was destroying the social fabric of the society. OO1, a member of parliament, reiterated their resolve to uphold egalitarianism:

> So, the genetics brought that resolve and what we call egalitarianism, I am a king in my own house. So we are an egalitarian society. Even if we are given one million years, we shall not evolve to have a centralized system. There are several chiefdoms and fiefdoms but our strength arises from the organization at a micro level. So the organization at micro level brings an automatic check.

The Acholi's peaceful approach, unlike the government-preferred military approach, gave voices impartially to all the parties in the conflict. For the first time, the rebels were formally invited to present a human face to their story. Consequently, the collectiveness of the peaceful approach overcame the military micromanagement approach. It created a conducive atmosphere for truth-telling, rather than propaganda. JC, a member of the Acholi diaspora, ascribed their success to egalitarianism:

> It was a conference in the Western sense, but it was still collective. So in the meeting, all the groups were represented. It was the first time the face of LRA was seen. The LRA made its presentation and people were very excited because that was the first time a human face was put on the LRA in the diaspora. So even if it was a European style of meeting, it was still collective and inclusive.

The Acholi people root for a collective approach, because in their context of human equality, conflict does not merely cause physical harm or material loss. It ultimately disrupts relationships and harmony, which are the prerequisite for societal well-being and longevity. In their context, a community prioritizes holistic harmony over individualism. The harmony in this context is both horizontal and vertical. So OO2, an elder, said that conflicts fracture vertical relationships with God as well as horizontal relationships. The barrier is supernatural and permanent unless a way is paved for reconciliation and restoration:

> So, our restorative justice is intended to restore the lost love, the lost peace, the lost relationship. We restore it back not by committing another atrocity or by destroying another life. This is important, because you know, people lived in community and you can't live in broken relationship. For example, when it comes to building community road you do it together, or when it comes to hunting you do it as a community, or if a robber attacked me, the whole community must respond. (OO2)

YA, an elder, pointed out that the conflict almost destroyed people's ways of life, which is far worse than the loss of property or lives. The Acholi people concurred that the conflict was a Uganda government scheme to destroy the Acholi people. Thus, they responded to protect their identity and destiny as a people. It is not surprising to note that the Acholi people risked their lives to stop the war because they believed that the Ugandan government military policy and approach to the conflict was a ploy to destroy them:

> My interest was just this; can we really continue like this as Acholi, and can we remain human beings in our area? If that is because of the war, why can't I talk to the fellow who is our boy, our son, and then we give also a message to the government. I was arrested for that one many times, thirteen times. The last one was 2002. I was branded a rebel collaborator, but I did not give up because of the problem. I just continued to talk to Kony until he accepted. (YA)

OG1, cultural leader, said that the government used a dualistic social order, which has been fighting for supremacy since the British introduced it in the formal sector during the colonial era. It prioritized state hegemony over community autonomy and authority, and projected the state as benefactor to the society and thus subordinated the role of the people. On the other hand, the Acholi people used their seamless approach to demand a complementary role for the state and community in order to resolve the conflict. OG1 said that complementarity in Acholiland is built on the principle of collective identity and responsibility:

> It applies more to our situation than these laws we are passing in Uganda now, the constitutional law. The law of natural justice is more suitable for our society, because our society looks at the issues of collective responsibility, the issues of relationship building, the issue of togetherness, we still want to be together as a people, we look at the interaction more than anything else. You

know, crime disrupts interaction and therefore if it spoils interaction, our major preoccupation is to build relationship. (OG1)

The egalitarian view and way of life was one of the fundamental values that informed the response of the Acholi people. The lack of a proper understanding of the Acholi ways of life by the Ugandan government led it to develop a wrong diagnosis of the war and to misunderstand the Acholi response. It also enhanced its war propaganda until the Acholi peace narrative saw the light of day, following a successful advocacy and despite stiff opposition and persecution.

Interrelationship

In Acholiland, human life is not only inviolable and invaluable. It is also interrelated and interdependent. Human beings are interconnected because of the nature of their lives. The interconnection is an ontological reality derived from collective common identity. There is ultimately no dichotomy and compartmentalization between leaders and followers, just like there is no dichotomy and compartmentalization between God and people, or spiritual life and physical life, or physical life and the environment. Whereas there are distinctions between and among distinctive entities like God, human beings, and the environment, there is an underlying bond connecting them as interconnected and interdependent entities. Thus, the interconnection refers to the underlying bond among distinctive entities, which permeates the explicit binaries so that the distinctive parts are fully reflected in the whole and the whole in the distinctive parts. While describing the integrated cosmology, OO2, an elder and self-taught academician, said,

> Conflict creates supernatural barriers. We don't eat or share anything with them. The killer is not forgiven by mere mortals, but our rulers were linked to the spirit world that was the cause of harmony. Our government was linked with the spirit world. We comply with the demands of the spirit world. We had many chiefdoms here. We did not have centralized chiefdoms. But if any outsider invaded us, all the chiefdoms unite to defend themselves as the Luos. You scholars always think that societies were always presided over by kings but among the Luo, this was the opposite. We had an integrated system of the physical and the spirit. (OO2)

Human interrelationship signifies the togetherness and commonness of human life, which identifies the people as collective individuals. The

Acholi people express interrelationship in the communality of the society. For example, during the conflict, the Acholi people communalized the challenges at stake. According to OA2, a prelate, they were inspired by the common identity of the antagonists and victims, which enabled them to develop a collective ownership of the challenges, saying things like, "You know my problem" or "your problem is our problem."

They also overcame the inherent differences within and between the respective entities involved in the conflict resolution, to establish a processual framework for consensus building, by prioritizing the common values that unite them. As a result, they gained the trust and confidence of the people, antagonists, and the international community. For instance, OA2, a prelate, said that the religious groups overcame their differences when they realized their commonalities:

> That is how the religious leaders' peace initiative started. Because we came together and prayed together with the Muslims. Our Christians friends were not amused. They said "Why do you pray together with the Muslims? If you were Anglicans praying with the Catholics, is it okay?" We said, "Wait, we have a lot of commonalities in life. Peace, unity, do we need to be only Christians to have peace? No, all humanity need peace, unity and harmony." You know, eventually we convinced our people and now the religious prayer later became the Acholi Religious Leaders' Peace Initiatives. Now, we have public trust or public credibility in the eyes of the people. We have that even with the international community, even with the Ugandan government and the rebels. They all later realized that we were neither on the side of the rebels nor the government [impartial]. (OA2)

They used the pillars of interrelationship as the basis for forging a common bond that allowed them to develop a common goal while maintaining their differences. First, in their culture, truth-telling is the cornerstone of conflict resolution. They establish truth after exhausting the available facts, opinions, doubts, and intuitions of all members. So they sought for and disseminated the truth about the conflict instead of the propaganda that the Ugandan government preferred:

> In other words, where the truth is that is where the majority is. It is not because government said that but where is the truth. That is why we say *oyoo m'opilo too pi litino ne* [the striped rat dies for its offspring]. It means that the love that we have for the people must override all other interests. That is why we don't want to

become sycophants or to do what we call *rwot oneka*, you see to please people. (OW1)

Second, OW1, a religious leader, continued and said that they used their cultural ethos of collective responsibility based on equality rather than the Ugandan government approach of monopoly and manipulation. Consequently, their collective approach created a flat structure, which enhanced popular participation:

> Even wars that are fought, they are fought as alliances rather than have superior command. I come with my soldiers, you come with yours, and attack the other bad guys because our interests are the same, not because you are now supervising all the others. So the leaders and the people were together and this is what worked. Because if the leaders were speaking different voices from what the people wanted, we would not have succeeded. That is also with religion. They believed that human beings are equal. That belief was very strong before Christianity. It was very strong. (OW1)

In interconnectedness, they involved all the stakeholders, including the rebels. This inclusive approach produced mutual trust, which enabled them to create a platform for constructive dialogue that resulted in the Juba peace talks. The inclusive approach is consistent with their cultural concept of holistic peace, which they used to frame an alternative narrative of the conflict—a narrative which ultimately overcame the Ugandan government's war narrative.

Interdependence

Among the Acholi people, interdependence, like interrelationship, is an ontological feature of human nature. Whereas interrelationship focuses on common features among distinctive entities, interdependence focuses on complementary strengths and uniqueness among distinctive entities. According to OO6, an academician based in Canada, the Acholi people derive the culture of interdependence from human distinctiveness and the complexity of human challenges, which demand combined efforts to identify and address them:

> Human beings have many problems, but nobody is endowed with the capacity to solve them. But they work together as a community. While the chiefs preside over meetings, the decision is arrived at by consensus. You know, we had a Parliament,

which sits in a circle. We start with a role call to ensure that everybody is present. When everybody is confirmed present, the meeting starts. (OO6)

According to OA1, a prelate, the Acholi people developed the culture of interdependence from life encounters across generations: "These norms of living in community as individuals stem from strong historical background of long struggle for existence." Interdependence predisposes them to open-mindedness and freedom, which flattened the social structures that govern their relationships across social strata. For example, BA said, "They are not shy; they call a spade a spade. And that is the cultural norms that you don't hide your opinion and feelings. You can tell a chief that you are naked." According to her, these norms are entrenched in the cultural values they esteem, beyond any "monetary values or temporary survival means."

The culture of interdependence is responsible for the collective system, which endears the Acholi people to consensus democracy of chiefdoms rather than a monarchy or the Western majority democracy. According to OW1,

> For something to be done to the society, you table your proposal and let it be discussed by all, until it becomes accepted by all for it to become an Acholi idea, because we believe in taking initiatives. We believe that we are masters of our destiny and that if there are problems, we can confront them ourselves." (OW1)

They undertake local initiatives collectively because they believe that they are stronger together. For example, BA attributes her accomplishments to the confidence and trust the people have placed in her, "the belief my people have in me. I am strong with my people. I don't speak [for my] own gain, [or] for myself; I speak on behalf of the people and they believe in me and they make me proud."

Interdependence characterizes their response to challenges. For example, during the East African Revival movement, the northern stream adorned Acholi cultural values and forms, unlike the southern stream which discarded native cultural values and forms altogether. For instance, whereas women played an active role alongside men in northern Uganda, the movement was led by men in the south. OO6, a disciple of the movement, narrated the contrast:

> You see the northern stream of the East African Revival was much more militant, much more independent, very African rooted with African idiom and expression. They challenged the colonial missionaries frontally. It set a strong practice of women

participation alongside men on equal footing and there were some issues they debated and brought to the table, which were not present in the south. (OO6)

During the conflict, the Acholi used the interdependence approach to challenge the government's unilateral policies and approaches to the conflict. Armed with alternative proposals, replete with facts and actionable steps, they overcame the Ugandan government's preference for a centralized approach. They opposed the Ugandan government policy of recruiting Acholi youth into local militias to fight the rebels alongside established security forces. Rather than recruiting the youth into counterinsurgency militias, SM, a Muslim cleric, said that the Acholi people asked the government to use the established security institutions because they looked at the recruitment as an attempt to divide the community.

> We have the institution of the army, why again train civilians to participate in the war? And it was not easy, because we were not speaking the same language with the government, to the extent that the President called our chairman by that time the Archbishop of the Gulu Archdiocese. He addressed him as Odama. He had to swallow it as a leader. These are some of the challenges we went through. At times, the government did not actually love to hear what we were saying, but we never feared to say because we were not working alone. We were working with our community, the community was behind us, the people were within us, the international community was in full support. (SM)

When the government attempted to compromise a few leaders to support its unilateral policies, a new crop of leaders emerged who pledged to adhere to Acholi cultural values. According to OM1, the Acholi people replaced all the leaders who were susceptible to compromise:

> The framework of social dignity that is embedded in the values of the culture of the people. So as the war intensified, the Acholi people stood firm on their demands. They stood firm and told President Museveni in his face that "You are wrong." So many leaders, most of these leaders got compromised. They turned around and started telling people, "Please talk slowly. Don't abuse the President." You know, let us change our tone. Acholi people kicked out all these leaders. This was now the population dictating what leaders should offer, why? Because of the environment, because of the cultural values, because of the social values that they cherish. (OM1)

Interdependence culminates in collective responsibility. The cardinal principle among the Acholi people prohibits unilateral decisions on behalf of the people. Instead, they rely on the collective efforts of everyone, in accordance with their respective skills, to promote the common good. OA2, a prelate, said that the Acholi people depend on one another:

> Husbands and wives, children and parents, or children amongst themselves [are interdependent] and so on. The same applies also to those who are leaders. They can't live in isolation, and neither can people live in isolation. Therefore, we support one another. And therefore, we should be constantly communicating and listening to one another. You see, often leaders make that mistake of thinking that the people don't matter. (OA2)

During the conflict, the Acholi people used their cultural approach of interdependence to frame a theoretical construct and strategies which they used to mobilize and convince all the stakeholders to prevail upon the antagonists and abandon violent approaches. OA2, a prelate, described their approach:

> After mobilizing the community in the Acholi subregion, we worked together with all the stakeholders. That was our approach. We worked as a team. We worked with the local councils from one to five. We worked also with Resident District Commissioners. We worked closely with members of Parliament, we worked closely with the United Nation agencies that were in this place and all other stakeholders, which enabled us to convince the government and the rebels to listen to the people's voice. (OA2)

In their cultural system, they work in teams using one language, message, and goal persistently and consistently. Their collective engagements are undergirded by inclusivity, impartiality, and truth-telling among others, which lend credibility to their efforts. For example, OF, an academician, said that war in Acholi requires the participation of all community members, including the women:

> Ladies are involved in war. They are the ones who decide whether there is going to be war or not. While men play a great role in the real war, women are called upon to bless it with the leaf of *Olwedo*. But if she is not satisfied, she would say *kun chwo kun chwo*, meaning that both sides are going to face casualties. (OF)

For instance, the women played a pivotal role in mobilizing women across Africa by initiating the Peace Torch walk, which started in Kenya and ended at the peace talks venue in Juba. According to OR2, "even men were inspired. The cultural institution was behind us. The religious institution was part and parcel of us. And then, collectively we demanded for some form of negotiation as a means of ending that conflict." The women also advocated for and facilitated the restoration of traditional institutions because chiefs play special roles in conflict resolution among other cultural duties. OR2, who mooted the idea of restoring traditional institution, narrated how she conceived it:

> If this thing [a conflict resolution ceremony presided over by clan leaders] has been happening, our traditional leaders have been doing this without external support. Why don't we revive them? Why don't we revive the cultural institutions and the chiefs, so that they take strategic leadership of their own clans because that is what we are? We have chiefdoms whereby chiefs are the leaders of their own respective clans. So that is how we initiated it. So we prayed to God and asked the cultural institutions to give us blessing. If you go to war without a cause, you lose. We believe in blessing and respect the voice of elders, which is now limited. We are still fighting to restore respect for elders. For example [as an elder], I always tell Kony what is wrong without fearing his gun. (OR2)

Their collective approach overcame the government's dualistic approach and efforts to divide the Acholi community. Thus ON said they attribute the prevailing peace in northern Uganda to the collective efforts of all the stakeholders—children, women, leaders, the government, and the international community—as a testament to Acholi egalitarianism:

> That is why nobody can wake up and say, "I brought peace." Nobody, not even the archbishop can get up, say "I brought peace," not even the Acholi religious leaders can get up and say, "We brought peace," not even the paramount chief can say that. Not even the government can get up and say, "I brought peace." We can only say that we thank you for the enabling policy that allowed us to enjoy the peace we have. But no single person can get up because everybody contributed to it, everybody contributed to it. And if you begin to line up people and ask them everybody has contributed. This is a very important and interesting study that will inform how people worked together to bring peace. There was a collective responsibility. The musicians were singing songs, you remember South Africa? Others were composing poems and talking about peace. Woman groups were also singing for peace. Drama groups and the like. Therefore, nobody will stand up and tell you, "I brought peace." The peace was not

brought by anybody but everybody worked for it and that is the peace we have today. I think the voice of the innocent [the night commuters] became so powerful. (ON)

Interdependence is a hallmark in Acholi cosmology. They used it during the conflict resolution to foster unity, which enhanced mutual trust and harmony where there was mistrust and division between the people and the government. Among other things, it demonstrated the importance of the strength of unity in diversity over the strength of power.

Character

The response of the Acholi to a stimulus is predicated on a unique attitude and atmosphere. The mental and moral qualities that form and inform responses among the Acholi people are undergirded by an atmosphere characterized by impartiality, truthfulness, competence, collectivity, and consensuality. The atmosphere is enforced by personal attitudes, which are directed at self, others, and the task at hand. The self-attitudes include prudence, temperance, and meekness. The other attitudes include justice, humility, patience, and charity. The task attitudes include fortitude, diligence, faith, and hope.

Atmosphere

The Acholi people have unique qualities which create a unique atmosphere in their relationships toward themselves, others, and their tasks. These are derived directly from cultural core values like the inviolability and invaluability of human life. Thus, it is imperative to understand the Acholi people's cultural atmosphere, which explains why they responded the way they did during the conflict resolution.

Impartiality

Impartiality permeates social interactions among the Acholi people at all levels of the social strata. It is grounded in the self-consciousness of and commitment to human dignity. In a conflict situation, it is likened to a stick (*rio tal*) used to separate warring factions from hurting each other. In this context, impartiality is based on the cultural inclination that, whereas human conflicts are inevitable due to the complexity of human nature, they should never be allowed to degenerate into violence. Thus, they advocate for

FINDINGS ON FOLLOWERSHIP DEVELOPMENT: ROOT FACTORS   185

peaceful conflict resolution because violence escalates rather than resolves conflicts. Given the inevitability of human conflict, conflict resolution strategies should be restorative, volitional, and proactive, rather than punitive, coercive, and reactionary.

Thus, impartiality refers to the atmosphere, which seeks the best interests of both the feuding parties and the victims in order to amicably resolve the conflict. It offers a restorative, voluntary, and proactive environment, which acknowledges and guarantees the best interests of everyone, under all conditions. When the rebels asked the religious leaders to mediate between them and the Ugandan government, they used the word *rio tal*, which signifies neutrality. In other words, they were tasking the religious leaders with the responsibility of creating a neutral atmosphere which would acknowledge and guarantee the best interests of the feuding parties and the victims of the conflict. OA2, a Roman Catholic prelate, reflected on his conversation with one of the rebel leaders about this mediation process:

> And during the meeting, one of rebel leaders, in fact it was the vice chairman of the rebels called me on the phone. I was here (conference room in his residence and referring to a meeting attended by Jan Egeland, the former UN Under-Secretary General for Humanitarian Affairs and Emergency Relief Coordinator), he said he wanted to talk to me. Now, I found myself with this crowd here, the government minister was here, I said, "Hon. Minister, you will excuse me." I called another bishop to chair the meeting in my place. When I went out, I realized that the one who was calling me was a junior officer. He said, "Now please talk with my senior," and who did I hear? Vincent Otti. He called me first by my name. He said, "OD, we would like you, the religious leaders, to mediate between us and the government." He used a technical word, *rio tal*, which refers to a stick used to separate warring factions from hurting each other. When two people are fighting you put a log between them. When one wants to beat the other, you raise it up and when the other one wants to beat in return you raise it up so that that one does not injure this one and vice versa. So I said, "This is a good idea, but where do we find you?" He said, "If you want, we can arrange to meet you. But we want to find out from you if you are willing and ready to do this." Yeah. So he told me, "It is not difficult to contact us. If you are serious, we shall tell you where we are." I said, "Okay, we shall find time to come to you." (OA2)

The rebels knew that in the context of conflict among the Acholi people, impartiality is restorative and for that matter, it allows the feuding parties to discover and develop a mutual ground to relate to each other through their differences, rather than using them to escalate the conflict. Initially, the antagonists were stuck in entrenched, biased positions, which inclined them to using their differences as grounds for antagonism rather than mutuality. However, when the stakeholders adopted the Acholi cultural atmosphere of impartiality, they found a common ground as the level playing field, which enabled them to join efforts toward ending the conflict without the fear of either incrimination or loss. According to ZA, a member of the Acholi diaspora, they relied on neutrality to develop a common ground:

> There was a point when all the Acholis were connected, we had a discussion list in the internet, and then started saying as much as some of them were in the diaspora and others at home, we were divided. Some of them supported the rebels. Others never. And some of us we felt we were neutral, but that was our feeling. I think other people might have also associated us with either the government or the rebels. Now, we wanted to get a common position because the hopes of the people who were here at home were on those who were in the diaspora. The precedent was set when Id Amin was here it was the people who went in exile in Tanzania and other places who chased Id Amin away. (ZA)

So in their impartiality, the feuding parties acknowledge their mutual humanity, which in turn enables them to develop the capacity to resolve conflicts without personalizing them. For example, prior to the big meetings (*Kacoke Madit*) organized at home and in the diaspora, the Ugandan government had refused to recognize the LRA group as rebels. Instead, they portrayed the conflict as an internal problem and the LRA as a ragtag group suffering from ignorance and a lack of objectivity. The government justified the war as a necessary measure to discipline and civilize the entire Acholi community. The government narrative won international approval easily, because it was constructed within the still-popular Western narrative of political conflicts in Africa, which was used to justify the imperial subjugation and Christianization of Africa at the expense of their adverse consequences. ZA described the biases the stakeholders harbored and how they overcame them:

> The main aim was to come first of all to a neutral place where everybody is supposed to talk. We even called opinion leaders including those Acholis in government, like MPs [members of parliament], like religious leaders, cultural leaders, but we wanted them to meet. Even the extreme cases, those who were totally opposed to the government or those who were in total support

> of the government and even including the representatives of the rebels. Let them meet in a neutral ground, where they don't have any fear incrimination and arrest. Our main aim was to set the ball rolling and to ask everybody who was supposed to come and present what they thought was our way forward. Because the kind of war or the situation we were facing was different from what we faced before. So that was the moment when I started actively participating in the conflict resolution efforts. I am also happy that this was actually the first time that [the Ugandan government acknowledged that the LRA is a rebel group]; the Ugandan government had never called these people rebels—those are internal problems, illiterate, they don't know, ah rag tag. So the world had dumped the issue and they could not even capture the highlights of the Western press. But immediately after the meeting, we actually started to tell the whole world about the gravity of the matter. What was taking place in northern Uganda came to light. Because like, from 1991, the government had declared northern Uganda incommunicado. Whatever was being done here, the atrocities committed here were not known anywhere. People were just saying, "Those are savage people; they need to be disciplined, educated and brought to civilization." That is all. Like when Christians who came here from Europe said they we are going to take civilization to Africa, and whatever took place here is now history. (ZA)

Furthermore, impartiality enables the feuding parties to build mutual trust and confidence, which creates a platform for unity of purpose and action. The greatest impediment to the northern Ugandan conflict resolution stemmed from mutual suspicion between the Acholi people and the Ugandan government, the Acholi community and the LRA rebels, and the Acholi community and the rest of Uganda and the international community. For a long time, the Ugandan government rejected the Acholi people's denunciation of rebellion, and in turn the Acholi people interpreted the government's negligence and reluctance to end the war as a scheme to wipe them out, especially following the government's abrogation of the 1985 Nairobi Peace Accord. OO4, an elder, said,

> The government was suspecting the population of supporting the war and those of us who were there told the government that the people of Acholi were not supporting this war. We had several meetings with the President, we told him if they were supporting the war, Kony would not be abducting them. They would just voluntarily join. But, the President was not listening to us and I personally attribute the peace negotiation to the late

JG. Even my colleagues did not know this and we did not want to reveal it. (OO4)

However, following the impartial intervention of the Acholi people, the feuding parties and the victims established mutual trust and confidence which enhanced the development of a common ground in favor of peaceful conflict resolution, which was devoid of the personal vendetta that culminated in the direct peace talks at Juba. According to OM2, a religious leader,

> We chose these approaches because we took the government and rebels as our children, saying we must make sure that they don't kill each other. That is what we were encouraging. And that is why they were a little bit obedient to us when we were saying something. In the beginning, they were a little bit suspicious, but later, when they saw that we were consistent with them, they began to say yes; in some critical cases, the government would call us if they wanted to talk to the rebels, and then the rebels would also call us if they wanted to talk to the government. So we learned some of these things, as they say, on the job. (OM2)

Impartiality overcame the divisions inherent in the differences between Christian and traditional cultural values, and among the different religious groups. Thus, religious leaders and traditional leaders found a common ground which united them into a single force that championed the wishes of the people. OF, an academician, narrated the impact of impartiality:

> Another group that came on board was the Acholi Religious Leaders Peace Initiative. That became a very big voice and surprisingly or amazingly they worked with the traditional leaders. They worked together without despising that this is *jok* (witchcraft. They said, "What we want is peace." If we can work with one voice, because they could be heard. They were heard more than elected leaders who were in the opposition. So being neutral, the government could listen to them better. They influenced further peace talks. (OF)

Impartiality fostered an atmosphere of transparency, which encouraged the free flow of information. The Ugandan government declared northern Uganda incommunicado since the inception of the conflict, and thus swept the atrocities and sufferings meted out on the Acholi people by the government security forces and rebels under the carpet of national and international news media. For over a decade, neither the government nor the rebels had articulated the cause, conduct, consequences of, or a concrete viable solution to the conflict. However, when the Acholi people established a neutral ground, all the stakeholders began to voluntarily share and listen to each other's views about the conflict and its possible resolution. ZA remembered that when they established a neutral atmosphere, the government held itself accountable by volunteering information to the stakeholders:

> That is when the government found out that these things might bring them problems, because we were now exposing them. We had actually contacted very many countries. Those who were in Sweden approached their government and explained the situation using the *Kacoke Madit* resolutions. Those in the mainland Europe traversed the entire Europe and met with development organizations and government organizations. And then in the USA, they were doing the same. Somewhere, somehow, the government started feeling the pinch. Somewhere people started to ask them about what they were actually concealing. Then they started realizing these things were going to bring them problems. It has to be stopped. First, it started to actually portray us as anti-government, and on the other side, the rebels were saying we were pro-government, because we were actually talking for neither the government nor the rebels. We were trying to bring them together to explain to us why they were doing that [fighting] and why they could not talk. (ZA)

The free flow of information fostered by the Acholi people revealed that the northern Uganda conflict was an international conflict laden with confluences of interests at the local and international levels. Thus, it required global rather than merely local efforts to ameliorate the suffering of the people and to end it. Among other things, they established that the war had become a profit-making venture for the local politicians and soldiers. Internationally, many countries had vested interests in the war to the extent that the conflict was a proxy war for other countries instead of only impacting the direct antagonists. According to ON, a journalist, the war was global:

> Journalist fight battles, we fought battles to put ourselves in the forefront to get information in the hardest way to try to get the world informed. Then the issue of the Acholi war ended. People were able to see that it was a regional problem and a global problem. No, indeed it is a global problem, Central African Republic, there are other nations involved. The effects of the LRA conflict went beyond the scope of Uganda. (ON)

The free flow of information enhanced two-way communication among all the stakeholders. For example, the government volunteered information to the Acholi and international communities. In return, the rebels also started to volunteer information. In 1998, a high-profile government delegation met with the LRA rebels in Spain for the first time:

> They themselves found that they [the rebels] had to get in touch with us to put their position for us to understand that they are not bad. And we also asked for the government representative to come; and they met for the first time in 1998, in Spain. It was Dr. O and Hon. M. It was too much for the government. The information flow that we established made us very strong. (ZA)

Furthermore, ZA noted that the voluntary flow of information dispelled mistrust, selfish interest, vendettas, and propaganda, and depersonalized the rationale for the war. For example, they invited all the stakeholders to all their meetings and dispatched copies of the resolutions to relevant authorities at home and abroad. The *Kacoke Madit* resolutions were distributed to the European and American governments and other relevant international agencies. They also gave out copies of the resolutions to the local government and the rebels. Since the resolutions were binding, the antagonists adhered to them:

> One thing is that we knew what was going to happen. There were some strategies we laid out to make us work. We made sure that the government and the rebels knew that we were transparent. When we called the rebels, we told the government representative that we are going to approach the rebel representative and vice versa. So whoever is coming back to say these people are pro this and that, could not do so because we already informed them we were going to approach so and so. So that transparency was kept. But all the same, we were now sure that through transparency alone these people would know that we were neutral. You know, once we did something, we sent out copies to the governments, rebels, international development partners, US-AID, Seed in Sweden. In our communications according to the *Kacoke Madit* protocol, we included a list of all the people who attended—the government representative, the religious leaders. Now, the government started seeing, because in the meeting where their representative attended it was decided like this and the government has been informed about the resolution. How do you again turn aside and say these are rebel groups that are supporting the rebels, when you sent your representatives to the meeting, and a copy of the resolution is given to the President? They knew we were transparent and could not say, "This guy went on his own, we never sent him when he is a government sitting minister." And we made sure we published it and we

> invited the representatives of the Commonwealth, governments and agencies including the Uganda embassies. For me, when I came back to the mainland Europe in Germany, I distributed [this information] to other governments. It came to a time when wherever the Ugandan government went, they would ask them, look at this resolution, have you implemented it? So that strategy was one of the greatest weapons. Everywhere they went, the information about northern Uganda was already there. (ZA)

On their part, the religious leaders devised a strategy of neutrality in their mediation. They asked the antagonists to communicate with each other in writing and restricted themselves to delivering the letters and the corresponding replies between the antagonists until they established direct contact ahead of the formal talks in Juba. Thus, OA2, a prelate, said that they avoided being compromised by the antagonists:

> And our principle was, we are not going to allow either the government or the rebels to use us as their spokespersons. We always went with papers. When we were there, we gave them papers and pens, and asked them to write what they want to say to the President. We take this letter to the President and ask him to write down what he wants to tell the rebels in return. After we have given the letters, we wait for them to give their answers. We say, write to each other. We remained neutral and remained nonpartisan to both sides and that thing continued until the time when these people were called to the table talks in Juba. (OA2)

There is no doubt about the importance of impartiality in conflict resolution. In the northern Ugandan conflict resolution, the religious leaders attributed the trust and goodwill they used to convince the government and the rebels to come to the negotiation table in Juba to the atmosphere of impartiality.

Truthfulness

In Acholiland, truthfulness is derived from a sense of inherent human dignity. They believe that truth-telling is a normative ingredient in the well-being of a society, and an expression of the acknowledgment of human dignity. Therefore, it is one of the hallmarks of humanity that has sustained their unity for generations. It signifies an atmosphere of a volitional disposition toward disclosure, which is a voluntary act of the heart devoid of coercion or inducements. Thus, it is an atmosphere of vulnerable/naked transparency whereby no information is withheld from or held against each other at both the organizational and personal levels. NM said that truthfulness in is integral to human dignity:

> Usually, you know, when M visits places, you hear speeches, telling him lies. Here people will tell him exactly the truth. Because we believe in our inherent human dignity and it does not matter who you are and that is why we say *Arwot ki ioda*, which means I am a chief in my own homestead. The authority of the chief stops at the boundary of my homestead. (NM)

The Acholi sense of human dignity endears the people to truth-telling as a mark of individual autonomy in a community. Thus, every community member is held to the same standard without exception. This explains in part why their social stratum is horizontal rather than hierarchical. "The people don't see themselves as subjects. They are part and parcel of the chieftain." According to OR1, a member of parliament, the Acholi people developed this understanding following experiences, which resulted in their unwavering resolutions to uphold truth-telling in their code of conduct. For instance, somebody who tells lies is worse than one who has admitted to committing murder. Telling lies is inexcusable in Acholiland, because no one is incriminated for truthfulness regardless of the content of the truth. This applies even to someone who has committed murder and is ready to tell the whole truth about it. Lying is tantamount to a repudiation of the Acholi magnanimity, which acknowledges redeemable human weaknesses.

Thus, in an environment where corrective measures are restorative rather than punitive, lack of truth impedes efforts to discover the root causes of problems and hinders the healing process. Truthfulness enhances harmonious community well-being because it holds society accountable to cultural core values. It also facilitates the restoration of wayward members and broken relationships in the larger community. OO2, an elder, narrates the centrality of truth-telling:

> Actually, anybody who does anything wrong, the issue is that you don't prove yourself innocent. But you declare that you did something wrong. So truthfulness was at the core of societal life, and that is what drove the community, so that whatever you do, make sure that it is the truth; that will help you. (OO2)

As a matter of principle, the Acholi people inculcate the discipline of truthfulness in their members from childhood. Every Acholi knows that he or she is supposed to tell the truth without any fear of retribution. It

FINDINGS ON FOLLOWERSHIP DEVELOPMENT: ROOT FACTORS 193

is therefore not surprising that the Acholi people have the audacity to tell truth to power. As they put it, "We can tell the chief that you are naked."

In the following excerpt, OO2, an elder, explained that truth-telling is a voluntary act of the heart. It signifies acknowledgment of and respect for human dignity, which calls for corporate and individual accountability and mutuality.

> You cannot stop them from killing or fighting. The only thing you can do is to sit down with them to find out what causes conflict. We know that violence cannot solve anything. We have our elders who help to establish the root cause of conflict. According to our culture, even before this war, if one man from one clan kills another person from another it causes supernatural barrier until the killing is paid for and a rite of reconciliation is done. So our understanding as the Acholi people is that when there is a feud between families, you cannot suppress it with force. What you can do is to reconcile them. The process requires truthfulness and repentance. (OO2)

Truth is not synonymous with facts. Whereas facts refer to all the pieces of information available about the subject under consideration, truth is the summation of all the facts available on a subject, including doubts, intuitions, and attitudes. So truthfulness is a volitional responsibility expressive of one's commitment to societal values and well-being. It engenders boldness, frankness, thinking outside the box, inclusivity, consensus, and multiple perspectives among others. It is ultimately a communal attribute that enhances unity, harmony, and longevity.

During the conflict, the Acholi people gathered the facts about the war through different mediums and forums over a long period. Then they assembled them into a concrete body of information upon which they established the root cause of the conflict and the campaign for the adoption of peaceful conflict resolution strategies rather than the violent method the government preferred. They used workshops, meetings, seminars, and conferences to exchange information that informed a joint position on the conflict and its resolution. OO1, a member of parliament, said that their resolutions emanated from exhaustive consultations and research across the board.

> So, we came up with joint mandates through workshops, meeting, seminars and conferences. The process was defined by the agreements of the various sections and then the condition in which people were. So we designed a work plan, and moved to all the districts of Uganda including the Acholi subregion. We

also traveled to Sudan and most capitals of the world, persuading them that peace was possible. (OO1)

On a more personal level, individuals shared the information they obtained with the whole community in order to empower them. In the following quotation, OB, a journalist, listed the sources he consulted in order to get his information, and discussed how he shared the information with the rest of the society:

> I got information through media, through the constitution. We have our rights in the constitution. There are others who don't want to open the constitution and read. I bought Local Government Act, I bought other law books. I bought the constitution. I used to consult other people who were more knowledgeable than me. I also used to sit down with government agents and argue with them. Because, when I argue with them, they want to teach me so that when I understand I may change and support them. So this information that I always get from them and other sources, I could share with the people and say, this is what it is and this is wat the government wants. (OB)

Traditionally, truth in Acholi involves contrasting the facts about their culture with other cultures to develop a comprehensive picture of the issue at stake. OM2, a religious leader, said that when they compared their restorative traditional method of conflict resolution with the Western punitive method, they chose their method for many reasons. First, the latter continues to perpetuate conflict, which degenerates into war. Second, by its very nature, the punitive approach is more costly and destructive than the peaceful approach. Third, war also alienates the antagonists, unlike the peaceful method, which seeks to reconcile and restore broken relationships. Last, war humiliates the losers and mars the humanity of the feuding parties and the victims, whereas the peaceful approach restores and upholds the human dignity of the feuding parties and the victims:

> And we told them that the peaceful means is less costly than war and we told them that the peaceful means is less destructive, because when you dialogue with your fellow human, and at the end of it, whether you agree or disagree, you all go back intact, without destruction of property or something like that. And also, we told them that you know the warring parties will just alienate further. (OM2)

As a result, during the conflict, they invested in peace negotiation skills. They attended formal training on negotiation skills in Europe and the United States, as ZA noted: "I remember we were sent here to train traditional leaders on peace negotiation. We even took some religious leaders to Birmingham to train them on negotiation." Overall, as YA shared earlier, truthfulness allows them to interact with other cultures to improve theirs.

Following their culture of truthfulness, they asked the Ugandan government to create a genuine process of conflict resolution characterized by honesty, transparency, mutual respect, and reconciliation—something that took a long time to fathom and incorporate. However, after a considerable time, the government obliged the Acholi demand.

In the aftermath of the Juba talks, KL, a member of parliament, said that the Acholi people began calling for a national truth and reconciliation forum to heal the ethnic divisions that inflamed conflicts in the country and region. This is because they believe that there cannot be peace and healing without truth-telling, followed by admission of wrongdoing and commitment to reform.

> The Acholi people believe that for Uganda to be safe there must be a national healing process that can reconcile the different ethnic communities, but without telling the truth, without the leaders admitting what they did, Uganda cannot have peace. And that is the core of what they advocated for. (KL)

Although it is still too early to determine how the Ugandan government is going to respond, the Acholi experience has set a precedent that is impossible to ignore. Furthermore, the examples of a peaceful approach to conflict resolution in South Africa and Rwanda, among others, lend credibility to the Acholi traditional peaceful method of conflict resolution.

Competence

In the Acholi cultures, competence is ultimately a collective mutual capacity of the community to sustain itself. It is predicated on the self-consciousness of and commitment to human dignity, and is measured by the capacity to take the initiative to identify the challenge at stake, its root cause, potential remedies, and the desired response or responses. Competence aligns human dignity with existential conditions and locates its remedies in the human inviolable and invaluable nature, which demands interrelational and interdependent collaboration. Competence is the mark of human identity and innate potential that makes humans personally responsible beings over their well-being.

According to OW1, a religious leader, the Acholi people initiate solutions to their local challenges. Otherwise, any idea or project remains foreign to the community unless they localize the initiative, ownership, participation, and benefits. This is because human interrelationship and interdependence create an environment in which everyone can live up to their potential so that together they can achieve more than the sum of their individual contributions. It is expressed in phrases like: *Olomadilo matelo* ("a big man or a hero is pulled by skin of his or her back"). The essence of this proverb calls for self-initiative, based on human individual autonomy and authority, due to a shared identity and destiny.

In this context, people sit together with their leaders to develop a common stance and agenda. The chiefs have no mandate to talk on behalf of the people. For anything to become an Acholi idea, it must be agreed upon by the community, which then tasks the chiefs to execute it in conjunction with the people. OR2, a global peace award winner, described their resolve to uphold the strength of collective competence:

> What I have learned is that the Acholi people are so resilient and they have so much courage, because going through all what I have told you, we would not have done it. And what I know is that when they mean something, when they are clear about what they want to do, they will come together and do it, which is completely very different from other communities. Like at the moment, the country has been fragmented into many districts, which I see it as another form of divide and rule, so that people are split into small unviable groups. We, in the Acholi subregion, brought together the local leaders, the elected ones, the LC 5, the political leadership, the RDCs appointed by the government, and we, the civil society organizations, we are always saying anything regarding the Acholi, you have no prerogative of talking without asking us. So everything must go systematically and we must agree. (OR2)

For instance, they thwarted the Ugandan government's unilateral decision to award 40,000 hectares of the communal land to one of the investors in Uganda for growing sugar cane. Using their communal ethos of collective competence, they asked the government to allow investors to negotiate directly with the Acholi people about their land. OR2 said that they adopted the same approach in addressing how to handle the revenue from the oil that has been discovered in the Acholi subregion.

> We have already mobilized people and organized a conference where we said we want to discuss and understand what is going

> on about the Acholi land. So everybody from Kitgum, and the rest of Acholi, came together and came up with a resolution about our land and how it should be protected and all these. That is why the Madhvan thing cannot take off. Because instead of Madhvan the investor, recognizing that there are people who own the land, [Madhvan will] need to negotiate with them, it is the President that comes and orders, that this land, 40,000 hectares be given to Madhvan for cultivating sugar cane and it is the President who is on the frontline. And we keep on asking him, you are on the frontline as who? And we empowered the people to demand the President to tell them, whose land it is that he is going to give out? At the end of the day, I heard he said the land belongs to the people, and we said yes, that is the first statement. The land belongs to the people, it is the people who will decide what they want. We are not against investors. (OR2)

The Acholi people together consider themselves better than the best among them individually. During the conflict resolution, no one group claimed the credit for ending the war. Instead, they attributed it to the collective efforts of the entire local and international community. In the following excerpt, OW1, a religious leader, described the collective efforts they exerted in the peace process,

> Even our people here would not have spoken. It would have been the paramount chief talking, but that was not the case. And that is why when you look at the people who went for the peace talks, you cannot say that this is the structure of the people who attended. You will find it is made up of different groups of people from different walks of life. Why? This shows you the interdependent nature of our people. You will ask Owiny Dollo, are you a leader? He will tell you no. He was not yet a minister. You ask Oulanya, are you a leader? He will say no. But they were there, because the thing was touching them. If you ask me why did you go to Juba. I went because I raised a concern why do you relocate people from big camps to smaller camps? (OW1)

Therefore, they nurture competence in an environment where individual strengths strengthen the whole and vice versa. In the Gulu municipality, ZA said, "The councilors this time are highly educated. The minimum education they have is master's degree since the law allows them to hold two positions. Their purpose is to inform and strengthen the council. This has created a wave whereby what they discuss permeates the society." OR2 said that they used the Acholi ethos of collective competence to grow stronger together through mutual collaborations.

> So, in these meetings, we bring everybody: the judges, the former politicians, the current MPs [members of parliament] everybody would be part and parcel of us. And if we can get some from the diaspora they are just part of us. So we get the Acholis from all walks of life to speak one language. So we ask the Owiny Dollos of this world to interpret things from a legal perspective. Because we felt threatened, and it has helped to unify us. Although we have got major differences, but still at the end of the day, you would find this business of what do we do collectively as a people and how do we pursue this? I have learned a lot. And in that case, what we used to do as NGOs in terms of building networks, coalitions, collaboration, we are really now practicing in it at a larger level within the Acholi subregion, which is quite good. (OR2)

BA described the collective trust and support the people accorded her, which enabled her to play a unique role in the conflict resolution. She accepted the request to represent her people in parliament without the knowledge of parliamentary procedures, but her senior colleagues from the Acholi subregion mentored her:

> When I was approached then, it just came in as a request to serve my people: can you come and talk on behalf of your people in Parliament? And it was just a need awaiting. As much as I did not know the game, I had people to lean on. I had Hon. OR1 and Hon. OO4 and indeed they supported me into the national scene. (BA)

No single contribution is considered greater than another. Instead, each contribution counts in relation to the whole. These contributions count only in their mutual interrelationships and interdependence toward a common goal. There is neither a lone individual nor a lone contribution in the Acholi community or benefactor/beneficiary dichotomy. OO6 described the nuances of the collective competence in the following excerpt:

> So, it is that sense of coming together collectively, which makes us strong. And yet the focus is on the peace and goal is peace, how you get there may take time. Who is involved varies. Everybody knows that I may not speak, but I need to be here to help move this thing along. The notion is always being able to help move things along and not to keep it stagnant in a manner that does not help anybody. So the collective is important because it brings everybody together, but the individual voices, the center of the human person in the collective is still valued. But the goal

is; there is always a goal that people want to arrive at, whether it is land dispute or the issue of peace which had affected many lives and their homes. (OO6)

In this context, each member is satisfied with their respective role within the bigger picture. For example, when the Ugandan government yielded to the Acholi people's request to grant the rebels blanket amnesty, the community initiated a plan to restore the office of the traditional leaders in order to handle the traditional aspect of reconciliation, which was exclusively reserved for them. OR2 narrated the role she played in restoring and strengthening the cultural institution:

> That again was part of our strategy of seeing how we could mobilize the community effectively and make the traditional leaders take a lead in peace making and peace building. And again, it was from an insight I developed from the type of work I was doing. Because, one of the things I used to do was to go to these traditional leaders. The father of this man here, Rwot Achana the first was there somewhere in Pece. The traditional leaders used to work together with BB and all that. So I would attend their meetings to help them strategize. In fact, I was helping them learn how to strategize, how to move, how to do this and that. (OR2)

The entire society is preoccupied with enabling each member to become the best in their respective expertise, rather than fighting to outshine each other. For instance, OR2, a prominent female elder who played a leading role in ending the war, declined people's requests to run for a political office. According to the following excerpt, she declined the offer to focus on her areas of expertise:

> Like for me, I am contented with what I have and do. There are people, the local people who would want me to join politics and become an MP and represent them. But I keep on telling them that what I am doing is more crucial than going to Parliament. Because right now, I have got the trust of the whole world. (OR2)

Collectivity

The Acholi people's cultural understanding of humanity is relationality. They are human because they belong. According to OG1, a cultural leader, "I have been nurtured to think that I belong to a particular community and that is why we have these clan identities and activities reemerging: this

Payira clan, this Agaki clan, Alokolum clan. You know, we are now even going back further to these things." In their relationality, the individual is accorded autonomy and authority because human life is inviolable and invaluable. However, as noted earlier, individual autonomy and authority are relational variables with flexible boundaries, which enhance reciprocal interactions among them. In this context, a community is greater than the sum of individual variables. Individual variables reflect and affect the whole and vice versa. There is no dichotomy between the individual and the community. Individual autonomy and authority enhance collectivity rather than individualism. OG1 reiterated the Acholi people's commitment to collectivity:

> Our society looks at the issues of responsibility, the issues of relationship building, the issue of togetherness; we still want to be together as a people. We look at the interactions more than anything else. You know, crime disrupts relationship and therefore our major preoccupation is to build relationship. (OG1)

The Acholi people view human life and responsibility from the standpoint of collectivity, without which the essence of a community is inconceivable. In this setting, leadership neither subjugates, displaces, nor negates individual autonomy and authority. They regard leadership as a complementary role. Leaders are part and parcel of the community. The leaders and their roles are acknowledged in relation to adherence to the core cultural values rather than the importance of the office. Most of the current Acholi members of Parliament were elected when they were very young due to their adherence to societal values. OR1, one the people who became members of parliament at a young age, said,

> Today we speak as the politicians who are committed to the values of our society and we are listened to as core Acholi. People listen to you to guide them on what to do. And that is why some of us, at our very young age, we became enemies of the President. At one time, I told him, "But I am not your generation because people listen to us [more] than him and his sycophants who want to feed him on things he wants to hear. You know, people are being misled in situations like this but, for us, we are very vocal. I am telling you the truth . . . " And that explains why at our age, when the opponent of Museveni came to look for votes, for me, they used to tell me that I appoint leaders, that I tell people [to] vote for so and so. (OR1)

Thus, as OW1 shared earlier, leaders derive their power and authority from the consensus of the community. However, they enjoy individual autonomy and authority with flexible boundaries just like any other individual community members.

The collective approach is the Acholi way of life, which cuts across all the social strata. It is predicated on their disposition, and based on precedents and theoretical constructs, which have undergirded their self-understanding as a people for centuries. OO2, an elder, narrated how they have maintained unity as a people:

> So, it became everybody's responsibility that we should do this together, as we have been living together. And going back a little bit, the Acholis are made up of different chiefdoms, but together, we have never split. We have maintained ourselves under one tribal name, the Acholi. If you talk to the Acholi people, you will find that there are different clans, but we have maintained our unity based on that mutual agreement that if there is a conflict, we have to settle it before it goes haywire or something like that. (OO2)

The collectivity is both convergent and divergent. On one hand, they are convergent at the conceptual stage, when formulating goals through consultations. On the other hand, they are divergent in their methods of response once they have developed a common complex understanding of a phenomenon. FO described the process of consensus building:

> Yes, definitely the Acholi people consult very much through their local structures of what is good and bad. Normally, the Acholi people will never, for instance, approach anything without the presence of key people. If there is an issue, there should be a communal approach to it. If an issue comes up, somebody does not just go and begin handling it like that. The approach they use starts by saying, okay, if this issue has come up, we need so and so here available. We need to first sit down in a community meeting, you know, and discuss, and come up with a common position, and this is what was happening. When people got carried away with all this movement and going to the camps, discussions were going on and people were sharing their own experiences that look, we have a problem. They were seeing what was happening. Here was the army that could no longer protect them. Here they were under constant attack. As the saying goes, if you can't defeat the rebels, why can't you to talk to them? It is the cheaper option. So these were the things that men and women and younger children who were in the camps, who were constantly affected, were saying because it was really hard on them. So using consultative process through their local leaders and others, they said, "Please, this is the message

we want you to take to the government. Let them listen to us."
So in a way, that had an impact. (FO)

For instance, during the conflict, they held big inclusive meetings to develop a common understanding of and response to the war. FO, a religious leader, narrated that all the stakeholders to the conflict attended the meetings to develop a common understanding of the phenomenon and thereafter developed multipronged responses:

> They asked themselves, what can we do? And a big meeting was held here in Gulu called B*edo Piny* (sitting down) and we were all brought from various parts of Acholi and of various categories: politicians, religious leaders, civil societies, the chiefs, and we really came for the big meeting. I remember I was in Kitgum already, in the Catholic Church that side. We were picked up by a military helicopter and brought here in Gulu for that meeting. It actually came from the understanding that we cannot do it individually. This is a common enemy, a common thing; how do we jointly handle this thing? So we came for the meeting and that was the beginning. The Acholi people coming together from different categories, and I am sure you have seen some of documents. And it was not just an Acholi gathering, because the government was there, the military was there. So it was a very successful thing, putting aside all the differences that one might have: the political differences, the religious differences. I think this was the most important thing, that there is something that affects all of us and coming together and we did not just come in as Acholi people but we came as people, as Ugandans we engaged all categories of people who came together. Now for the Acholi religious leaders and the chiefs, we had always been in constant meeting sharing ideas to the point that our recognition was already high. (FO)

Following the big meetings, the Acholi people developed a counter-narrative, which informed their response to the conflict. Among other things, it informed the criteria for choosing new leaders and responding to the Ugandan government and the international community. Overall, it overcame the government press censorship and propaganda. It created a level playing field, which enhanced collective collaborations among all the stakeholders. OA2 summed it up:

> I would say that the people were not completely dependent, given the structures of how they work at different levels. There was a high level of consultation and organization in a way and

to a larger extent the leaders were conveying what the people were saying. And you would find that there was commonality in how people were thinking about the solution. You would not really get stark difference. People were resolute in their demands of what they wanted and this is what they impressed upon their leaders and I can assure you this was reflected in how they voted. It was uncommon to find anyone elected if you stood on the ruling party ticket. You were naturally compelled to state the government official position that look we need to go militarily. I can assure you that you would never be elected. It was uncommon. It was actually the opposition leaders who were elected. The government leaders would never be elected. (OA2)

In the aftermath of the conflict, OA2 said that the Acholi women are already replicating the collective approach at the national level. So far, the focus is on the government rehabilitation program under the prime minister's office. Unlike the government approach, which focuses on the hardware components of development, they focus on the software component, which prioritizes values and quality over figures and long-term impacts over short-term:

> So, in a way we are trying to replicate this type of thing—that it is very important to work collectively. So normally what happens is that the PRDP [Peace, Recovery and Development Plan for Northern Uganda] monitoring committee meets twice a year in the office of the Prime Minister, when they give their reports about the implementation. The women have elected me to be their representative in that forum. And the larger civil society is also there. So normally during the meeting, the government gives its report and they give space for civil society, and we, the women, have demanded that we want a space to give our own report. And we give our own report, which is very unique. It is about those practical things: you are telling us about your achievements, which is about those many health centers you have built. For us, if the health centers are built, they should not be white elephants; they should provide better services to the people. But you go to those health centers; they are just there lying without facilities. They are dysfunctional, there are no staff, no drugs, nothing! And how do you pride yourself to talk about so many health centers being built if they are not changing people's lives? So in my report, I would always quote from Teso, so many hospitals, the maternity ward don't have even a single bed, women deliver on floor. In Acholiland, this and that. In West Nile, this and this. So the donors and development

> partners have been following our reports very, very keenly. So they were not surprised when they learned of the massive theft. Because, we were now pointing out about the disadvantages of focusing on the hardware and leaving out the software. So in this process we as women coming together to do this is also one way of learning. So everybody is now learning. And we have got the women taskforce at national and the district level. So we have ours here and different districts have their own task forces and mobilizing women around it. And it will go. I think in a way it is even verbally speaking to many people but there are so many things we have been doing practically across the board with fellow Ugandans, which they can learn from. (OA2)

The women's initiative to monitor government programs has transformed itself into a national coalition of women interested in holding government accountable to the people for quality service delivery. Although it is still a young movement, its potential to spread over to other countries is a possibility because women already have strong cross-border networks.

Consensuality

Consensuality is a convergent agreement where each component is divergently complementing the whole in order to produce an outcome attributed to all. It stems from shared values and a common understanding of the issue at stake, which enhances the popular participation of stakeholders in a joint effort to address it.

Shared values stem from human common life, which accords everyone a complementary uniqueness. Thus, humans thrive in mutual complementarity rather than via monopoly, control, or competition, because they share common life and values which incline them toward mutual interrelationship and interdependence. Second, human challenges like conflict are complex phenomena which require complex understandings and approaches to address them. Quick fixes, as the Ugandan government preferred, target the symptoms rather than the root cause. OR1 said that the Acholis take time to develop a convergent understanding of the issues at stake and divergent means to address them:

> We see that every community, every people have something to contribute to humanity. I don't think that anyone has a monopoly of yardstick that if it is not in accordance with my yardstick then it is wrong. It only requires some humility to say that let me

understand what these people have to say in this situation and what are the values embedded in their practice? (OR1)

According to OO6, an elder, in this context, everybody has a voice, but no one has a vote. The agreement is a synthesis of all the voices. The notion of unilateral decision is inconceivable:

> So, whenever there is a conflict, the Acholi devise ways of initiating dialogue to negotiate. At least talking about it so that a solution is got before somebody goes ahead to declare war. So it is a process that is not decided by one person. It is a process that is built on the consensus of everybody else, because when you talk of conflict or war it does not target the person who initiates it. It targets their families, relatives, children friends, clansmen and tribesmen. (OO6)

Thus, contrary to the Ugandan government directive approach, the Acholi people chose the consensual approach to addressing the root of the conflict that had lagged on for decades and led to negative impacts on the Acholi people. OO6, a member of the Acholi diaspora, narrated this approach:

> So, the issue of moving the people to camps was a government directive. They had no say. But on the issue of engaging the LRA and the government in a series of discussions, especially beginning from 2004 to 2007, that was the classic style of Acholi way of doing things. The government would have said that we don't want to talk to Kony, but the Acholi civil society and leaders said no, we need to engage Kony and we also need to be able to talk about what we do with the children who were taken to the bush and transformed into children soldiers? These are our innocent children. If they are turned into child soldiers, but they are still our children. (OO6)

Consensus is necessary because human lives and circumstances are complex. For instance, the permanent and temporary aspects of life require collaboration and a constant act of balancing the tension between the need for preservation and transformation. As OR1, a member of parliament, narrated in the following excerpt, the Acholi people preserve their societal values without resisting inevitable changes:

> Life is on transition, even culture is on transition. Should we be able to modernize some of these values and then you move on? But you should also be able to preserve that society. So any leadership should be able to do that. That is why for us, when

Kony became extremely against the population we condemned him. We fought him because we wanted to preserve our people, otherwise our people were going to perish. (OR1)

Thus, the nature of an atmosphere influences the procedure and outcome of human effort. For the Acholi people, impartiality, truthfulness, competence, collectivity, and consensuality undergird their dignity, which in turn influences their responses. During the northern Uganda conflict, the aforementioned atmosphere enhanced their resolve to pursue a peaceful approach toward conflict resolution.

Attitude

Besides atmosphere, there are attitudes that undergird their responses. In the following section, I will discuss the attitudes that characterized the Acholi people's response to government policy and their approaches to the conflict. They are categorized into three subsections: self-attitude, other attitude, and task attitude.

Self-Attitude

Humans have predisposed mental and emotional dispositions that govern their responses either to self, others, or things. In Acholiland, some of the cardinal self-attitudes the society inculcates in its members include prudence, temperance, and meekness among others. Attitudes are important because they dictate human thought and actions. Self-attitude is the mental predisposition toward oneself. Below I will discuss prudence.

Prudence

Humans encounter tenuous challenges in their responses which require a firm intellectual capacity to discern between what is good and bad in a particular situation, and the ability to take appropriate actions instantaneously. It thus calls for clarity on the issues at stake and the mitigating actions. For example, during the conflict, some of the challenges that called for clarity and mitigating actions included a failed state, unending war, and unprecedented suffering amidst opposition, sabotage, ambiguity, and sheer malice. However, the Acholi people prevailed despite the challenges, partly because of their attitude. One of these necessary attitudes was prudence.

During the northern Uganda conflict, the Acholi people encountered numerous challenges, but they used forums referred to as *Kacoke Madit* ("big meetings") among other things to develop a consensus on how to address common challenges. In the following excerpt, ZA narrated how they identified and overcame the attempts by detractors who wanted to highjack the *Kacoke Madit* platform to advance their own selfish agenda. Whereas the Acholis, who had not yet secured their immigration status, wanted to use the platform to paint a negative image of Uganda, those opposed to the government wanted to use the forum to mobilize the international community against it. The Ugandan government did not want the forum to be used as a platform for disseminating information contrary to its propaganda. So he said that they grappled with the critical challenge of how to act impartially:

> For me, it was easy and you know, I am a person who interacts with people but it is tedious in that the experience is not good in that when you are organizing you take charge of organizing meetings and conferences and in all these things the first thing you see is the number of the people interested in it, their characters and motivations. You will make your assessment even before the meeting. Because when you tell the people in Germany that, look, *Kacoke Madit* is scheduled to take place. So I would like to compile a list of the people interested to participate. Now, who among you is interested or would like to tell others about it? Let me know who would want to present a paper. I say, yeah, bring your paper first. So before I compile the list, I go through their papers, because that will reveal their interests. So as the person organizing, you need to establish the interests of the person A and B. And you see, you are going to create enmity. The ones who have refused to relinquish their selfish interests will start accusing you of something. They will say that you were given a lot of money and embezzled it. These people are collaborators and they even go to Uganda and just want to know our names. These people are working with State intelligence agencies like Eso and will give them our names. So we had names, they gave us of all sorts of names. Others wanted the issues to be dramatized to paint a picture that Uganda is so bad. Nothing is happening there, because they had not secured their status as refugees. Once you say there is peace in Uganda, that would jeopardize their efforts to gain refugee status. There were vast categories of people with different interests. You can't fulfill all the interests. (ZA)

However, they used prudence to establish criteria which mitigated the challenges. First, they screened people's motives before they could participate in the forum. Second, they invited all the stakeholders without exception. Third, they invited the representatives of the stakeholders to participate in the writing, distribution, and publication of the resolutions to exonerate themselves from any false accusations. Finally, they declined to transform the platform into a formal organization. All of the platform members served on a voluntary basis to keep the primary focus on the forum's objectives rather than establishing it as an entity with privileged positions, which could have become soft targets of compromise.

The Acholi people also developed a comprehensive understanding of the conflict, which generated a consensus that the military approach was not a viable option. Their decision was informed by many factors. The war had gone on for far too long despite the superiority of the Uganda army. Furthermore, the suffering of the people was no longer bearable, and the roots of the conflict were political, so it could be resolved only by a political approach, not a military one. NM, a former member of parliament and a lawyer, described some of the factors which influenced their responses:

> But more importantly, the war had been going on for years. The government's counter insurgency strategy was based on forcing the people into concentration camps and using a military approach to confront the rebels and generally resisting any calls for peace talks with the rebels. I believed that this was an internal conflict, it was and still remains a conflict whose roots are political and therefore there was no military solution. And when I was elected to Parliament I was just about 28 years old. And the first thing I did was to join hands with other members of Parliament and we proposed a motion calling for a parliamentary inquiry into the conflict: Why it took long? What are the possible solutions? I was a member of the committee chaired by a member of Parliament from Nebi. The report of the committee did not capture what some of us wanted. So two of us, myself and Hon. O A decided to write a minority report and in the minority report, we called for direct peace talks with rebels, dismantling of camps, concerted response to the humanitarian crisis and human rights protection programs. But also, we called for the restoration of multiparty democracy. We thought that the roots of conflicts in Uganda are political and we needed rules that enhance fair competition. But more importantly, the intensity of the suffering here was no longer capable of being ignored. (NM)

Consequently, OO3, a retired bishop, said that after a prolonged analysis of the conflict, they resolved that its solution rested largely on the people who were suffering, rather than the government, or even the Acholi people in the diaspora. Therefore, they mobilized the international community to influence the rebels' and the Uganda government's perceptions and approaches to the conflict in favor of a peaceful approach:

> So, what was in my mind was how do we stop this war by using the people who are gravely affected? Not the government, not the government. The people who are running, who are in the camps have 85 percent of the solution to the problem. Now if the people have decided that we must talk, the government will have no way continuing with their gun. The power of the gun, no way! So we came together as Acholi religious leaders from Muslims, Catholics, Anglicans Pentecostal and Orthodox. Our coming together also encouraged the traditional leaders to come stronger. The political leaders also started to form their groups. (OO3)

Thus, instead of the Acholis at home relying on the military initiatives of the Acholis in the diaspora, as had happened in their previous conflicts during the Id Amin era, they took it upon themselves to spearhead a peaceful approach to conflict resolution in conjunction with the Acholis in the diaspora and the international community.

Temperance

Whereas prudence is an intellectual capacity, temperance is the moral capacity to restrain and moderate one's own desires from excesses. It involves nurturing authentic human desires to enhance the common good of the society, rather than indulging in excesses that compromise one's judgment and motives. It calls for chastity, contentment, integrity, and frugality. It affords one a clear conscience to wade through complex terrains without giving in to illicit desires for excesses.

The Acholi people witnessed both compromise and resilience in equal measures among their members. The compromises were witnessed especially among leaders who abandoned their people in favor of the government, in exchange for safety, monetary benefits, and job security. Nevertheless, it led to the emergence of new young leaders who preferred to stand by their people in accordance with their core cultural values and well-being against all odds. Ordinarily, when it comes to leaders, the Acholi people prefer older people over young people. However, following the betrayal by some of the former, the Acholis entrusted young people with leadership responsibilities because of their allegiance to cultural core values. OR1 narrated his journey into leadership as a young person who dedicated his commitment to Acholi cultural values:

> In our tradition, personally, I would not have become a leader at my age then. But I was a student activist when I was at the university. And I shunned our leaders, because they had become what I would call sycophants. They wanted to kneel before the President. And they would go and tell the people now you see, you know; they became the spokespersons of the government to the people and not people's spokesperson to the government. And people shunned them. So I emerged as a young leader with the likes of Mao who was also a young man. (OR1)

There were some people in leadership positions who endured intense pressure to demonstrate their loyalty to Acholi values. For example, on many occasions, RA, a cultural leader, was falsely accused of being a government collaborator. However, he consistently demonstrated his faithfulness to the people and their cultural values. According to him,

> People say *Rwot* X is pro government. No, I am pro nobody. I am pro people and I will do the things that are right for them. So that is how we all rose as the people of Acholi and not only the people of Acholi. We brought on board other people. You know, as a cultural institution, I do not have jurisdiction over the people from West Nile, but we brought their representatives on board. I brought the kingdom from Ankole, Lango Teso, Madi on board. We spent nights in the bush with them with the conviction that we are their [the rebels] cultural leaders. (RA)

Other members encountered the temptation to betray Acholi cultural values. OO2, an elder, refused to betray his commitment to the Acholi cultural value of integrity, even when a top government official offered to give him a huge amount of money in exchange for executing a sensitive mission. For OO2 and others, the temptation came in the form of persecution, which culminated in a revocation of his citizenship. While others might have surrendered to compromise in order to avoid persecution, OO2 remained loyal in his conviction to uphold the cause of the Acholi people against government machinations.

The government unleashed everything in its arsenal to compromise the Acholi people's temperance. For example, it slapped a rape charge on OR1 to clip his influence, because the government considered him a stumbling block to its goal of gaining a political foothold in the region. However, far from achieving its goal, the charge quadrupled the latter's popularity and appeal among the Acholi people and the international community, which came to his rescue:

> Yes, you see, Museveni looked at me as a big threat because I chaired the formation of the opposition party. Although I was not its leader, he looked at me as someone who was very influential in northern Uganda. And So the idea was that if we don't frame him with charges, he is going to cause us problems in the next election. The law of the land stipulates that when you are arrested on capital offense and put in prison, the minimum remand period is one year. So they arrested me one year prior, so that I would not participate in the election. They arrested me on framed up charges of rape. I actually laughed at them because they charged me at 6 pm past the official time. They took me to prison and locked me there. They also underestimated the influence I had. For the first time, the ambassadors of Western Europe dropped in a convoy of 16 embassies to see me in Luzira. When they reached there, they asked to see where I was sleeping. They mounted pressure for my release. I remember the American ambassador told me that don't worry you will be out soon. But I told him that you see I am not worried about myself. I want them to take me to court and we proceed. I am only worried because when I came here in Luzira I found so many people on remand. Within one month, I was released on bond and I was the first in this country to break the legal record for having attained release on bond on capital offense. My precedent opened the way for people like Kiiza Bisigye. So the arrest was basically political, but they underestimated the population. Because after the arrest, my popularity tripled. In that election, people wanted me to direct them who to vote for. (OR1)

The Acholi resolve to adhere to their convictions is grounded in their heritage and legacy as a people. Some of it came from the training they received growing up. MA, the most senior elder, recalled that the Acholis are trained to uphold a disciplined lifestyle and live a life of integrity at all cost. The religious leaders' resilience came from their vocational convictions, which oblige them to peaceful co-existence. From their convictions, they advocated for peaceful conflict resolution against the government's insistence on a military solution without compromise. The failure of the military options, despite the superiority of the government, emboldened them to impress upon the president the need to adopt a peaceful approach. OO3, a religious leader, described their encounter with the president:

> Mr. President, the situation on the ground is very bad. Provide security for the people. They have no food; they need to have food. Why don't you talk? You also attempt dialogue as way of handling this issue; then the fourth point was, we are available as religious leaders if you want us to help you out." Just straightforward like that, with clear points. Then his response was, "Okay, I give you 21 days." I don't know why he was saying 21). "I give you 21 days to get to these people"—he wanted us to get to the rebels. "If you get them and you can tell me what they want to talk to me about, I will be available to talk to them. If you don't get them, I will continue with my approach of the military. (OO3)

They were convinced that a peaceful approach to conflict resolution is Christ's preferred way of resolving human conflict. Consequently, they participated in the demands of the Acholi for the government to adopt a peaceful approach. Their advocacy targeted the international community, which also preferred punitive justice and military solutions to a political conflict. OM2 described the basis of their conviction:

> We were determined. Two, we knew ours was the right one. The right way because that is part of the proclamation of the gospel. So we were very much aware that our target is the target of Christ and we were not going to bend to any methodology, any approach that promotes violence. We were not going to bend to that. Ours was to follow the path of Christ, which is forgiveness and reconciliation. In Acholi, there is a technical term for reconciliation. We call it *mato oput*, which means that no more war but peace. And from now we are going to live as brothers and sisters. And that is what the world needs now. That is what Uganda needs. God has given us all these wisdoms, which we don't even pay for it, not even a dollar. You just need to open your heart. All you need to know is that the person I am talking to is my brother, created in the image and likeness of God. Any mission that is inspired, any mission to building peace, any mission to preaching reconciliation which is not inspired by God will not bear any fruit. That is why ARLPI, of which I am a member, is very proud of their support for peaceful conflict resolution. That is our uniqueness and that is our contribution to the world. We even challenged the ICC. The ICC does not believe so much in forgiveness. It believes in the punitive system of justice whereby you have got to pay for what you have done in the same measure and the same value. (OM2)

For OO1, it was the influence of his parents' legacy which inclined him toward a principled lifestyle despite the pains associated with it. Although he was the youngest among the people who assumed leadership at a young age, he maintained a life of integrity against all odds. Whenever faced with overwhelming challenges, he resorted to supernatural powers for wisdom and guidance for the course of action to take as he described in the following quotation:

> My parents were in the Democratic Party. So I have known that being principled pays. It pays. It may pain, but it pays. So when I say this is it that is it. And being from a religious background, I would meditate and reflect and ask for eternal wisdom that everyone is counting on me and I am just an individual. May what happen be done according to the wishes of the greater force [one of the many ways they talk about God]. So if you are in that situation where everybody is counting on you, that means you must listen and observe because the solution might be just outside the window. (OO1)

Overall, it took conscientious discipline and determination for the Acholi people to resist the temptation to compromise their resolve to advocate for the peaceful resolution of the conflict. The self-attitude of temperance restrained them from excessive desires and vices like corruption and compromise.

Meekness

It is the psychological and emotional aptitude which overcomes the resentment of and by others while pursuing a common goal. It is enhanced by conquering hateful anger and a victim mentality, while also cultivating patience. It also calls for a steady focus on issues without personalizing them, and empathizing with others even in their offensive weaknesses by focusing on each other's humanity. It calls for a resolve to be proactive rather than reactionary or rebellious. In the following excerpt, JO, a religious leader, narrated that the process of adopting a peaceful conflict resolution approach required patience because they needed time to build trust and confidence in one another. It took the Ugandan government a long time to accept that the conflict was a global rather than local Acholi problem. The government also needed time to own up to the failure of the military option to gain the trust and confidence of the Acholi people:

> On the part of the Ugandan government, it took northern Uganda conflict as a tribal thing, as the war of the Acholi, but we kept on telling the government that your Excellency, this is not an Acholi war, because the guy who went to the bush to wage war against your government did not go into the bush with our blessing to fight on behalf of the Acholi. When we talked like this and people heard that we were talking sense without any compromise. (JO)

In a similar vein, the people from the south needed time to deal with their resentment of the Acholi people, whom they blamed for their suffering during the Luwero-Triangle War, as the prerequisite for initiating peaceful conflict resolution. So according to OL there was need for patience:

> And therefore, moving from war to negotiation, we had to see in that negotiation process ingredients of honesty, that this is a genuine process. We needed in it—ingredients of atonement; that the blanket blame levied on us in the past was not justified and the ingredient of reconciliation. That took a long time, because the Museveni regime I would suggest, the group were highly vindictive; they still needed like, we must punish these guys, we must teach them, and we must show them this and that, and that is why the war went on for so long. So elements like convergence of interest that allowed for peace process to begin. I think the war had become a very tiring enterprise. Second, the dynamics of Southern Sudan had changed. A new regime there needed to be protected from further machination by the Arab north. (OL)

On the other hand, the Acholi people maintained a reconciliatory attitude, which earned them the right to demand a peaceful approach to conflict resolution. They conquered hatred and rage and displayed a positive attitude consistently. OR2, an elder, described how she maintained a positive attitude toward people who were plotting to harm her:

> And they tried all means to link me to the rebels by doing this and that, but I maintained my stand. And they even never came to understand that I knew what they were planning to do, because I never showed them that I knew their plans. So if it meant linking up with local leaders, I would continue doing it. If anything happened in the local community and I needed to report, I would go to the right people and report. I performed my role and I never cared, I never showed them I knew what they were doing. Some of them have died, like WO, without knowing that I knew what he was doing to me, and some officials up to now,

they don't know because I maintained my face; I maintained being friendly. I was focusing on doing the right thing and I did not want them to begin fearing. So the fact that my relationship with them did not change, they thought I did not know, but I knew, and I have never told them to date. (OR2)

OO3, an elder, adopted a pragmatic approach in dealing with the rebels and the government. He chose a personal approach toward the government and radio for the rebels. Whenever he had issues with the government, he would contact the respective authorities in person. He also talked to the rebels over the radio because he could not contact them in person:

> When rebels have done something bad, go over the radio and challenge them; they are listening to you. Don't bark down don't fear to challenge them they are listening to you. But if the government has done something bad, don't go over the radio. Go to the immediate authority and tell them. Otherwise, they will fight you. Be diplomatic. I got the best orientation nobody got when you find yourself in a war situation. What I used to do was to crosscheck with government officials, including the army commanders, what is happening here before I go public. (OO3)

So, the Acholi people maintained a clear focus on the issue at hand and took the appropriate reconciliatory actions needed to ameliorate it. Compelled by their sense of human dignity and their resolve to protect it, they convinced the Ugandan government, the rebels, and the international community to adopt the Acholi traditional approach to conflict resolution. According to OM2, they were compelled by their conscience, which cherishes the sanctity of human life:

> Human life and human dignity that was the driving force; saving lives and that is the mission of the Church. The church is prolife. That is why we stood very firm on that. You know, the conscience also; when we talk of an informed conscience, the voice, that voice in each of us, a normal a sound a heathy mind has that conscience that tells you in whatever you do, do good, because that is what you are born to do and to avoid evil. In Latin, we say, *quaerite bonum et declinare a malo et facere bonum ad omnes sumptus*. This is the basic principle, seek good, do good and avoid evil at all cost, you know, seek peace, avoid conflict that disorganizes the society. So the drive of that, the fundamental force in each one of us, led us to act in defense of the innocent life. That was the driving force. (OM2)

The war created horrendous living conditions in Acholi subregion. According to OL, at one time 1,000 children were dying per week in the IDP camps, without the attention of the media and the international community. However, despite the challenges, they pursued the peaceful approach relentlessly:

> But we disagreed. Why did we disagree? First, for how many years had this war lasted? By the time, we entered dialogue with the government, the war had lasted for nearly twenty years and, you know what it means, many lives were lost, many young people abducted into captivity, many people were forced out of their homes and so on and so on, the lives of the people were reduced to abject poverty. The life in the camp where you are just there no economic engagement because you are just there to protect your life. It was for this reason that we told the government that the military option was not the best solution. It is like putting out fire with fire. When you see your house burning, what you need is water. Violence with violence will not produce the desired effect that we need. So that is the area we disagreed for some time until the government saw that we were steady, and consistent and there were some positive results until the LRA agreed to enter the peace dialogue. (OL)

In their meekness, OM2 observed that the Acholis did not seek favors from either the government or the rebels. Instead, they called on them to accept that the military option was not feasible, and to commit to resolving the conflict peacefully so the Acholi people could regain their dignity:

> We made our position very clear. Our leadership [role] was not meant to gain any political post. Our leadership was meant to defend human fundamental rights, which were being violated. Because, the whole thing is about leadership and we wanted people to see that our effort was actually for their own good to bring peace, to bring hope, to end the bloody war so that northern Uganda becomes peaceful and people begin to live in harmony. (OM2)

These people were not simply acting as victims who were out to blame either the rebels or the government for the suffering of the people. Instead, they understood their response as an enactment of the consciousness of and commitment to human dignity, which demands a solemn obligation to protect and preserve human life. According to OM2, they sacrificed everything for the sake of peace and the dignity of the people:

That, we are not supporting the rebels, although even some of us had to suffer for that; we are not supporting rebels, we are not blaming the government totally, we were trying our best, we were really working for the best. I think this helped to build trust. Of course, the political parties and other entities were there, but we, the religious leaders, were not preaching politics. So I think our impartiality and consistency must have contributed to the trust and of course the developmental program by government, the way they handled issues also generated confidence in the people. (OM2)

Other Attitude

The Acholi people value their relationships with others based on the cultural ethos, which stipulates that humans are humans because they all belong together. Therefore, they inculcate disciplines like charity, justice, and humility to enhance harmony as the chief goal of all human interactions. They develop and enact these disciplines through the lens of the inviolability and invaluability of life, interrelationship, and interdependence, which all culminate in harmony.

Charity

Charity is an action of the heart. It flows out voluntarily because it is one of the marks of being human. Ontologically, it is an attribute of God, which centers in humans a predisposition to a shared common life, which calls us to honor people as humans above mere rights or merit. Thus, charity is the gateway to authentic human relationships and a harmonious community because it empowers members to love others as they love themselves, and to acknowledge and honor the humanity in oneself and others. As BO, a retired bishop, said, it is a natural outflow, devoid of coercion or inducement:

> Genuine accountability is the most difficulty thing for the people of the world to accept. And because they don't have that one they don't even have genuine reconciliation. That is why when they avoid the truth they come to punishment. Punishment is not part of our justice system. You see, completely! So when you reveal the whole truth; the whole truth comes from the offender's community. But the one who forgives is the one who is offended. The one who is offended, mercy and forgiveness is an expression of agape love or grace. The love of God comes from

the heart of the victim and it is this forgiveness. This mercy, this love brings complete difference in a situation of violence and death. And it is this difference, this full difference that is known as full justice. (BO)

BO's credentials on a peaceful approach to conflict resolution are unquestionable. Besides being a religious leader and a Christian, which obliges him to peaceful conflict resolution, the loss of his daughter and wife at the hands of the antagonists challenged him further to dedicate the rest of his life to work for human peaceful co-existence. In the following quotation, he narrated the ordeals that influenced his resolve to advocate for peaceful conflict resolution:

> I want to say that this war in northern Uganda here, affected me as a family and as a priest. When Id Amin was in power, we spent most of our time burying the dead and comforting the bereaved families. Time came when it was our turn. When I was in North America, my daughter was here with my mother-in-law. So she was picked up by the rebel group called Slim and gang raped. After that terrible ordeal, she took an overdose of chloroquine and died. After 10 years, my wife went to our home in Magoro, but on her way back, her car was hit by a land mine, allegedly planted by the LRA, and she was blown into pieces. She died together with another woman who was seated next to her and a man at the back of the car. So this was a personal experience as a family. It was very, very difficult for us, but it became a challenge, her death and the death of our daughter. It became a challenge to me to dedicate and commit my whole life to work for peace so that other people should not go through the same problem we experienced as a family. (BO)

Charity creates the capacity to empathize with others. The Acholi measure it by one's inclination to care for the needs of others above self. In his quest to organize a formal community response to the government's failure to protect and care for the people, NM mobilized the people based on their propensity to care for others. "I was not looking for members of either the Democratic Party (DP) or UPC; I was looking for anybody who cared. I was not looking for a particular religion. The only test was if they cared. So I connected with those people." Second, charity requires like-mindedness. When OO4, an elder, joined efforts to resolve the conflict, he sought like-minded people. "Is there anything I can do to join hands with like-minded persons to change this situation? To do that is to revive and salvage whatever we can for our society following what happened."

Charity played a central role during the conflict resolution. The community's unconditional forgiveness allayed the rebels' fears of incrimination. Consequently, they abandoned rebellion in favor of peace. It also impacted the initiation and implementation of the Amnesty Act, which allowed the rebels to return home without any fear of prosecution. Al explained her role in the rehabilitation of the abducted children who were rescued,

> I participated in the amnesty act through which they forgave their own children. My role was to make the children know that they were already forgiven and above all God had forgiven them. First, in World Vision, as a Christian organization, we use the biblical method. That is why we are having success story, because we use the Bible, because of the word of God, because of God, because of prayer, which is one of the healing therapy. And that is how it changes people's behavior. After a child has come out of the trauma and love experiences in the village, a child is now prepared to participate in the community. (A1)

Charity focuses on the future rather than the past or the present. The Acholi people forgave and integrated into the community, without incrimination, the rebels who renounced rebellion. Charity also facilitated reconciliation among different tribes that were affected by the war.

Justice

In Acholian culture, justice is neither merely a legal nor a moral concept tied to behavior. Instead, it is a fundamentally relational concept of being. It is an act of the heart, developed and practiced through habits that are primarily concerned with one's duty and obligation to others. It focuses on behaviors which reflect how humans ought to behave toward others, rather than merely behaviors contrary to how humans ought to behave.

Thus, it connotes dignity, respect, and fairness to oneself and others in tandem with the cultural core values or the obligations and rights we owe ourselves and others. According to JO, a religious leader, "The only thing that best exemplifies leadership is dignity and respect for others and fairness, which is not justice in the conventional legal sense, but fairness integrated in other aspects of our values system." In case of a moral lapse or behaviors contrary to how humans ought to act, it is concerned with restoration rather than merely punishment because it confronts both the corruption that causes moral lapses and the offenses the lapses create. The moral lapse injures the offender's being before it injures that of the offended.

A person with a marred being can neither give nor receive justice in its positive sense. In other words, he or she cannot give others what is rightfully due them or receive the same from others. So whereas the offender needs restoration, which requires an acknowledgment of the wrong, remorsefulness, reparation, and a commitment to desist from the offense, the offended must offer forgiveness to the offender for genuine healing and reconciliation to occur. The restoration process in turn leads to harmony and tranquility in society.

Thus, like charity, it is an act of the heart (voluntary), which reflects one's being—*Ubuntu-dano*—in relation to oneself and others. In their context, justice in its punitive sense is excommunication, which applies only in cases where the offender neither owns up to the offense nor commits to desisting from it.

Otherwise, in the context of a moral lapse, the offender is isolated from the community until the inception of the process of restoration, which begins with the offender affirming his or her willingness to embrace his or her true being by owning up to the wrong committed, and affirming his or her commitment to desist from it. This is followed up by volunteering the whole truth about the wrong committed as a sign of remorse, and commitment to live in accordance with the harmonious ideals of a society. In the excerpt below, BO explained that the offender's remorsefulness and the pledge to reform are the gateways to reparation, forgiveness, healing, reconciliation, and restoration. Since crime disrupts relationships, the goal of justice is a harmonious society. The Acholi enhance harmony through cultural rituals like *Mato Oput*:

> You know, crime disrupts relationship and therefore if it spoils relationship, our major preoccupation is to build relationship. And that is why even in politics if your family was earmarked for something wrong in the past, they will never vote you into office. They will bring all those issues. Those days your grandfather committed this and that. So that is why the folklore justice system comes on board. The *Mato Oput* comes on board, the reconciliation comes on board to harmonize the society, to make the society more cohesive so that we are able to move on. (BO)

OM2, a journalist, said that the Acholi people chose a peaceful approach to conflict resolution because the conflict distorted the meaning of a human community in according to the Acholi social fabric. In response, the Acholi people asserted their cultural ethos of peaceful conflict resolution to redeem their community.

> But why the war took long: when the government officials go on radio shows, they used to say that Kony only listens to the gun; we shall hunt him; we shall bring them dead or alive. So such words were not going well with the rebels. Whether you are a junior officer or abducted, as long as you don't surrender, we shall crush you. That is why the Acholi people came up strongly to demand for unconditional return. I want to appreciate the government. The government gave opportunity to the religious leaders to act as a point of contact for the rebels who wanted to renounce rebellion. They were receiving the returnees and in turn handed them over to the army for further investigation. That gave hope to the rebels and the whole of Acholi community. And that is what led to the resettlement to our homes. (OM2)

Humility

Humility at the human level is a disposition of accommodating others through acts like talking and listening to one another. Thus, it is the antidote to pride and envy, which create the kind of self-centeredness that ignites animosities and competition rather than cooperation and consensus. It calls for the capacity to acknowledge others and their points of view, which leads to a comprehensive understanding of issues at hand. According to OO3, a retired prelate, the capacity to listen to one another is the prerequisite for peaceful conflict resolution and community well-being:

> There is no conflict in the world that cannot be resolved peacefully if the parties are willing to talk and listen to each other. But if they are deaf, then you can't do much because they go parallel [antagonistic] like the religions I told you. They go parallel, you can hit them but cannot succeed. So what influenced me is my experience, my faith in Lord Jesus Christ who is the Prince of Peace, who made it clear that "Blessed are the peacemakers." So that is my foundational inspiration. That is even why I started a peace organization. (OO3)

Humility calls for celebrating others and recognizing human uniqueness or differences as the prerequisite for complementarity rather than competition. Even weakness is taken as an opportunity to shine light on the strength in others as a testament of human interrelationship and interdependence derived from common human identity. According to MA, an elder, the Acholi people are endowed with the gift of praising whatever is praiseworthy:

Acholi people are very proud of himself. And it is the only tribe that praises themselves to the maximum. Praising even relatives: I am son of so and I am son of mother so and so. My mother comes from this clan, a very powerful clan and that is what we call *mwoc*, you praise yourself. When you go out hunting and you spear an animal, you *mwoc*, you call the name of your clan and praise it. An Acholi is the only people with that gift. The Acholi people value themselves. And if I have a brother who is more powerful than me I praise him to the maximum. If I have a very powerful bull, I praise that animal to the maximum. (MA)

Humility is an indispensable attitude among the Acholi people. It enhances their societal harmony and well-being. During the conflict resolution, they used it to establish a conducive atmosphere for dialogue that led to the peace talks in Juba.

Patience

Patience is a commitment to walk alongside others in their life journeys. During the northern Ugandan conflict resolution, the Acholi people walked alongside the Ugandan government and the rebels, until they committed themselves to the peaceful approach to conflict resolution against the latter's preferred military option. They displayed patience persistently and consistently, which created room for dialogue and change. According to BM, a religious leader, patience required persistence and consistency:

> And I learned one thing in the experience of my life here; when you know what you want to do, be persistent and consistent you will reach there where you want. Be persistent and consistent with one message. So I learned when you want to bring a change whether from the ground to the government level, have one message and you will change the environment. (BM)

According to BO, patience also involves empathy. You must walk in the shoes of other people. The religious leaders showed solidarity with the children by spending four nights with them in the bus parks to draw the attention of the international community to their plight:

> We had to share the pain that our children were going through, the torture by rain which our children were going through. We spent there, three nights. Then the media people from all over the world were also invited and so they showed the whole world what was going on in northern Uganda. (BO)

In the following excerpt, OA2, a prelate, described the actions they took to demonstrate their solidarity with the children. For example, they walked from their respective homes to Gulu town and slept on mats just like the children:

> We would walk like myself, I would walk to the town, which about five kilometers. I walked for all four days. Like now [4 pm] this is the time we would start to walk to the town. Our sleeping mats, I had just a mat, a simple mat with a blanket that was all and put it in a paper bag and put on my shoulders like the children were carrying theirs. For them they were carrying papers and so on as their beds. So we would go to the town and in the evening the children would be there. (OA2)

According to OM2, in their solidarity, they were demonstrating their total commitment to the children to the point of shedding blood. In his narrative, he said that they were ready to die for peace. For example, when the rebels abducted students from his school, he pursued the rebels to the bush to demand for their unconditional release:

> And by the way related to this one is martyrdom. You see, any mission to preach the good news that Jesus preached, you must be ready to die, you must be ready to sacrifice your life for the others. And for us we knew what really was in front of us. Martyrdom stood in front of us. We knew that someday it would happen. I was here when the rebels came and abducted 41 of my seminarians on the May 11, 2002. (OM2)

Patience demonstrated the capacity of the Acholi people for restorative justice. They forgave the perpetrators of atrocities in northern Uganda—the rebels and government soldiers. Their magnanimity convinced the antagonists to adopt the peaceful approach to conflict resolution.

Task Attitude

The task attitudes the Acholi people used during the conflict resolution in an effort to withstand and overcome the impediments to the peaceful approach to conflict resolution included fortitude, diligence, faith, and hope among others. There is no doubt there are others, but these are the ones I could identify. Below I will discuss each one of them.

Fortitude

In Acholi culture, fortitude is one of the normative virtues which distinguishes one as an Acholi. Most of the participants regarded it as an inborn trait that governs their responses. In their own understanding, it is the mental ability to take a stand to pursue a course of action to its conclusion in full assurance of its justness, their competence, sufficiency, and certainty of success. Thus, it is an indispensable relational virtue exercised in the pursuit of a just cause. LM, an elder, in the following excerpt, attributed fortitude to an inborn trait that has characterized her responses:

> I am born courageous, I am born courageous! I am born courageous. That is how I grew up. Even my father I would tell him my father, "You are wrong. I don't want this. Why should you do this?" Even my mother, you are wrong, why should you do this. So that is how I was born. I am born not to fear. When I am on the right me, I stand for it. That was the day when [the President] sent some of his representatives to Gulu district saying why is it that the Acholi people are not giving him votes. That is when I said, "Stop calling Kony bandits [thugs]. Kony is taking our children." (LM)

Among the Acholis, it is a volitional nature that emanates automatically in the face of a challenge in conjunction with other virtues. NM considers this his nature, which serves as the antidote to fear. It empowers him to take a stand and pursue a worthy cause to its logical conclusion. "First and foremost, by my very nature I am not afraid of anybody. My character is a character that is really immune to fear." During the conflict, fortitude distinguished him as the bona fide representative of the Acholi people against the government's failures.

Fortitude is necessary because it enables the community to locate the solution to challenges within themselves and to initiate a course of action, rather than relying on others. As NM narrated earlier on, it inculcates in them the habit of developing well-thought out responses grounded on fundamental cultural values, obligations, and aspirations. Consequently, NM said that it is not easy to intimidate the Acholi people once they undertake a course of action. While describing their attitude toward war, NM said that, "we are not afraid to fight. We love peace but we are also not afraid of war. It does not mean that we are warlike or reckless, but we generally exercise our rights to say no."

In Acholiland, the will to respond is a collective responsibility, which emboldens the entire community. Thus, fortitude is expected of every Acholi

FINDINGS ON FOLLOWERSHIP DEVELOPMENT: ROOT FACTORS 225

as a mark of identity and dignity. That is, it is a proactive and volitional discharge of duty motivated by the conscientiousness of and commitment to human dignity regardless of either outcome or reward. It is exercised at both individual and corporate levels. OO6, an elder described how they exercise fortitude:

> We must be part of it and if we are part of it, then the results or the solution will be part of us and will last longer other than when somebody else initiated it and imposed on us. So in our culture, we want harmony and togetherness and that is how the resilience came in because once somebody has a problem, we take it upon ourselves and say as a family you are not left alone whether you have nothing, people will come around and give you support. (OO6)

So, this is the way of life in the Acholi society for all social strata. It is a predisposition to responsibility, which governs their well-being. Thus, any response in such circumstances is synonymous with a reflexive act. Second, the nature of certain human duties requires fortitude. For example, as a war correspondent, NO noted that he needed fortitude to execute his obligation of disseminating the truth about the conflict to counter government propaganda:

> As a war correspondent, as a war journalist, you have to stand firm and die for the truth. And for me, I believe that one of the tools was the truth. I tried as much as I could to put out the truth. Unless if it was from where I got information, you would get some lies, but if nobody lied to me, then I believed that it was the truth that I published. Bravery, you have to be brave, if you are not brave, you can't be there. Then you have to be balanced. Try as much as possible to get the other side, but of course it was not easy to get the rebels' side. First, where would you find them? (NO)

The northern Uganda conflict was a multi-layered one. It took the courage of people like NO to stand for what they believed was the most viable solution to the conflict. When the impact of the conflict became unbearable, the people were no longer afraid to speak their minds to the authorities. The Acholi people relied on their inherent dignity to overcome the numerous challenges which characterized the conflict. LM narrated that the women stood firm in their opposition to the government proposal to award their land to investors:

> One time I remember a situation where even the whole President had a meeting with the whole community including opinion leaders and civil society and so on. That was when there was this proposal to take away this land and give it away to Madhvan group to set up a sugar factory and there were women in that meeting. Women got up and even called out the President, that, "Mr. Museveni, now we know who you are, we can now understand that you took us deliberately to the camps, and after all this time, now when we are going home, you now want to bring investors to escort us to our homes by taking away our land." That is how bold the people were. You know when people are subjected to extreme suffering and brutality, they no longer fear. They will stand up for anything, even if their lives are at risk. And some of them lost their lives because of their courage. We had elders who were killed under suspicious circumstances because of spearheading the demand for the peace talks. We had elders who were killed like Olara Lagony, Ogony and many others. (LM)

Thus, fortitude is necessitated by human nature and the nature of human challenges. The implication here is that humans are created with an inherent ability to overcome the challenges they encounter. In this context, the Acholi people consider a lack of self-initiative and fortitude as either a betrayal or ignorance of human nature.

Diligence

Whereas fortitude conquers fear, diligence conquers sloth. Thus, it is the disposition to fulfill a duty without tiring until the end. The Acholi people encountered a pressing challenge, which required their response, and they resolved to pursue it relentlessly until it was resolved. As OJ, a member of parliament, narrated, diligence is the determination to accomplish a task relentlessly:

> But, you see, it is just a person whose feet are in deep waters who shouts loudest. I am struggling to understand. Anybody who has an issue, a pressing issue, would put that matter forward and pursue it for as long as the bridge or the suffering continues. They will pursue it. We have received petition here in Parliament by people coming from the population to direct Parliament to work on their issues. So for me it is not anything strange. (OJ)

According to OJ, the Acholi people demanded a peaceful approach to conflict resolution because the military option had failed for over twenty years amidst unprecedented suffering in the entire region. The antagonists lacked any concern for the welfare of the people. Instead, they perpetrated heinous atrocities against the people, contrary to the Acholi conventional understanding of war. In response, the Acholi sought to stop the war and deny the antagonists the opportunity to inflict further misery on the people:

> We had a war that had gone on for far too long. We had people who had suffered for far too long. We had a community that had been displaced. And because of their displacement, all sorts of suffering, ceaseless lack of amenities and social services, all those things. And looking at these people and the things they were saying, we said, but we can't be like this. We are not used to living like this. Can something be done about it? That was it. Anybody would do that. If you are concerned and you have pressing issue and it is bothering you, you come out and say so. And when they come say well this is it. And for us why did people opt for peace? They did not come out on day one, no they did not. The war took long, they fought for a long time but nothing was coming out and so they said, "Can you talk to these people?" (OJ)

Diligence is also a discipline of responsibility in moments of need. So, their response was nonoptional because the government abdicated its responsibilities to the citizen and instead committed atrocities against them in the same measure as the rebels. They asserted their autonomy and authority because the government had lost its authority in the eyes of the Acholi people, due to its failures to protect the people and their properties. In Acholi, when leaders lose respect of the people, it is incumbent upon the people to exercise their natural authority and autonomy to create a conducive environment for their own well-being. Thus, they understood their response as an indispensable moral challenge to the government to own up to its cardinal duty to the people of northern Uganda. The moral challenge according to NM, a lawyer, is based on the Acholi conviction that the government is accountable to the people for the security of their lives and property:

> I think we made an important contribution in changing the perception of the Ugandan government and the general population in the south about what was going on here. What we achieved was to pose a moral challenge to the M regime by saying, "Look, you are the government, children are sleeping in the shop

veranda, post office, hospital, do something, you are the government." So all we did was to pose that moral challenge. (NM)

For other people like RA, a cultural leader, it was an opportunity to demonstrate their commitment to defend and uphold their integrity as Acholi people. The people felt that is was their duty to act, despite the failures of the government. They could not let the community disappear under their watch. While sharing the rationale for participating in the conflict resolution efforts, RA said,

> I personally did not want to think of that. And therefore, together with the other chiefs, we told ourselves that this is our job regardless of what other people say. We are the ones who have the word Acholi written on our back and faces. The others are political and religious, but when they say Acholi, we are the traditional leaders, so we should work hard. And seeing the Acholi turned inside out, things that used not to happen in Acholi going on before our eyes, we wanted to reverse all that situation. We wanted Acholi to remain Acholi, despite what other people think of it, whether negative. We wanted Acholi to remain what we know, the good Acholi, culturally, traditionally everything. We did not want to be wiped out and no longer prominent among other tribes of Uganda. That is what motivated us to have the conviction we had. (RA)

OJ narrated that the Acholi people understood their response as their natural duty to convince the government and the rebels to stop the war against the people. They could not stomach passivity and compromise in the face of the suffering that engulfed their region at the hands of a callous government and lukewarm international community:

> You are just saying I have this situation. For example, when the amnesty law was proposed okay, and the government said, "No, we cannot have this." And the President said, "No, we cannot give this." We said, "No, no, we are the ones who are in trouble, you don't know what is going on here. If you give these people amnesty, many of these people are innocent. They will walk out on their own and come back." After some time, the President accepted. Of course, the people and the leaders, everybody including religious, cultural leaders, the politicians were working together and converged on this issue. They said, "No, this is a way of enticing these people back." The government eventually acceded to the amnesty law and it was enacted in 2002). All this is because of what was going on. It was not like some

> mobilization process where people were educated. No. These things were a result of somebody feeling the situation unbearable and they see ways that can settle it. (OJ)

Therefore, like the other attitudes, diligence is an inherent human quality that is nurtured and enacted as a reflex response in the context of need. As a mark of human nature, it equips community members with the responsibility to counter any challenges in society. They used it to mount a counterinitiative in favor of peace.

Faith

In the context of tasks, faith is the intellectual assurance derived from a conviction that human pursuit toward well-being is a divinely inspired cause anchored in divine presence and support. Culturally, the Acholi people believe in the transcendence and immanence of God, and as such, their actions are expressions of their reliance on and obedience to God. So their inspiration comes from a belief that God oversees everything. NM attributed his response to his family heritage, which is built upon a firm belief in the omnipotence of God:

> My grandfather was a lay Anglican preacher. He always taught us that God is in charge and he taught us to believe in the Bible. So my life was influenced by the Scripture, and it remains a major source of inspiration for me. So my Christian faith is based on our family tradition. (NM)

In all their undertakings, the Acholi are convinced that they are pursuing God's mission. As God's ambassadors, God guides their thoughts, attitudes, and actions. In the northern Ugandan conflict resolution, the sense of the presence of God emboldened them to undertake a relentless pursuit of the adoption of a peaceful approach to conflict resolution, despite all the hurdles they encountered. OM2, a religious leader, said that they felt the presence of God:

> You know we knew we were doing this work on behalf of God. So we felt we were not alone. We felt this was our mission. It is the mission of Christ who promised the apostles, that, "I will be with you," no matter what time, no matter which year, in which circumstance and situation come. "I will be with you" here means Christ will provide security to his apostles. So that is what sustained us that we were walking together with Christ. (OM2)

The assurance of the conviction emanates from the justness and rightfulness of the cause being undertaken with and on behalf of the innocent victims of an unjustified war. To their credit, OM2 said that the government eventually acknowledged the impartiality of the Acholi people and their contributions toward the conflict resolution:

> But we said no, we are determined because we see that this is the right thing to do and we continued to insist and remained a little bit stubborn. You know, when you see peace today, know that there were some stubborn people working in collaboration with the government. I think at the end of it, all the government was very appreciative that there were religious leaders and even today we made history that the world will remember. (OM2)

Finally, faith is ingrained in the Acholi way of life, which is inculcated in the members from childhood. Some of the fruits of faith include resilience and perseverance. Thus, they are resilient in the pursuit of a just cause. According to RO1, a member of parliament, everybody who witnessed the response of the Acholi people to the conflict marveled at their resilience and perseverance:

> I think it is by nature. I think it is creation. It is not something they invented. I think it is their creation. They are resilient; they can persevere. Everybody was wondering. In fact, even SS one day made a comment that he did not understand the Acholi. That despite all these sufferings, they were still walking with their heads up. I think it is creation. (RO1)

Hope

The Acholi people based their hope on the firm knowledge and belief that there is no permanent human condition. The northern Uganda conflict was not unique. For instance, they had encountered similar experiences during the Id Amin regime and they overcame them. Thus, they could not lose hope, lest they surrender to compromise. According to JI, a human rights activist, they were convinced that the conflict was temporary:

> In Acholiland, we were kind of in the diaspora within our own land; some went to Sudan but they eventually came back. I think it is fundamentally the conviction that that is the right thing. I think it bore fruits for us. And it might also be I don't know their character. This is kind of their nature–resilience. One could say it has been part of it. We just went and stayed around and

convinced ourselves that this thing will come to an end. During Amin regime, we had the same experience. People said, "When will this thing end?" and it came to an end, and if we compromise it will not end. (JI)

Second, hope amidst challenges requires a thorough understanding of the stakes involved and clear mitigating measures. In the northern Ugandan conflict, they concluded that there was no hope for military success for either the rebels or the Ugandan government. The geopolitical context surrounding the war had actually changed in favor of a peaceful conflict resolution! The Acholi people on whose behalf the antagonists were fighting were supporting neither the government nor the rebels. Southern Sudan had attained its independence from Sudan and was no longer interested in war, so they also encouraged the Ugandan government to accept a peaceful approach. The global nature of the war had been established, so the government propaganda, which portrayed it as an Acholi war, was no longer believed. It was now in the government's interest to end the war. Finally, the international community rejected the government's narrow war narrative in favor of the Acholi global war narrative. Both the rebels and the Ugandan government subjected themselves to the global will, and in return vouched for a peaceful approach to conflict resolution. One of the former rebel commanders said that he opted for a peaceful approach because the conflict had gained international attention:

> I realized that I am fairly educated and, you know, at least I have some human feelings. I found the world has turned against us. Even the very people we thought we were fighting for were also blaming us and others were already calling off the war, but the boss said continue. Then, I had to make a very difficult decision. Finding that very many people were being killed in battle, which could have been saved, and also to continue allowing this kind of loss of life to continue because of one person or two or three. Then I said, "No, if my coming out of the bush would influence other officers or even other soldiers, we would have solved the war in a different way. (LB)

Finally, the Acholi people expressed their hope through a firm conviction that the power of their unity possessed the commanding authority to shift the direction of the conflict toward a peaceful approach to its resolution. The strength of unity in the pursuit of a just cause shone a bright light on their assurance of victory. OO3 summed up the power of their unity: "He can't arrest us religious leaders, he can't shut our mouth, our mouth is big, when we put our mouth together, it becomes very big. Because when we talk, everybody hears."

So, for the Acholi people, hope was not a mere fantasy or whimsical desire for peace. Instead, it was an assurance of victory built on concrete knowledge that human predicaments are temporary challenges that call for precise, relentless actions derived from their consciousness of and commitment to their human dignity.

EXOGENOUS FACTORS

The exogenous factors that influenced the response of the Acholi people to the Ugandan government policy and their approaches to the northern Ugandan conflict and resolution included context, culture, education, experience, expectation, faith, people, reason, research, and technology. I will discuss each of them in the following pages.

Context

The context of the Acholi people's response to the Ugandan government policy and approaches to the conflict was characterized by a callous government wielding favorable international good will, a pessimistic international community, atrocious war precedents, and community apathy amidst prolonged, intense suffering and structural betrayal. However, despite this seemingly insurmountable bottleneck, the Acholi people created a counter-narrative which galvanized both friends and foes toward a peaceful settlement of the conflict.

The Acholi people encountered a callous government that relied on insidious political propaganda it constructed according to a Western ideological understanding of the conflict in Africa. Consequently, using its propaganda, the government won international good will, which cemented its legitimacy against any suspicions of misconduct associated with an autocratic, and atrocious regime. According to ZA, the Ugandan government enjoyed international good will:

> This is almost obvious. One of the eight presidents in Uganda who began at the weakest level is Museveni. Yoweri is one of the presidents that has enjoyed the international good will, because, for him, he had top propaganda. Much as he talks a lot, but he depends so much on the international good will. If you may know Uganda is one of the top poorest countries in the

> world and it definitely depends on foreign countries. So using economic muscles or political muscles, if we involve foreign countries, Uganda can be brought to its knees. And that is the reason why we cornered it where it goes for begging. We know Britain is one of the great donors; So if we involve those organizations like Department of International Development, Commonwealth which gives money to Uganda, USAID, GTZ, and if these people come to our meeting and find out that the issues we are talking about are genuine, when Uganda now comes to them we want money for this, they will say you would not have needed money for this if you had done this. You should not spend much money on the military. Uganda survives on donor support and we used the donors to push for our cause. (ZA)

Buttressed by international good will and news censorship on the conflict, the Ugandan government abdicated its state responsibilities and perpetrated abuses for over a decade instead of protecting the people in northern Uganda. NM, a human rights lawyer, spoke about the government's negligence and atrocities committed against the people:

> But even the government soldiers who were supposed to protect them were raping women, they were doing all sorts of things, even killing people. And of course, when people were killed, they would say it is by accident and so forth. But there was cumulative cross violation meted on the people. But more importantly, for years the war had been going on without any sign of the end in sight. (NM)

Consequently, the Acholi people lost trust and confidence in the government because it acted as an occupying force, rather than a government. The erosion of trust in the government started before the NRA/M government seized power and continued throughout the duration of the conflict. For example, although the Acholi people welcomed the government in northern Uganda peacefully, they still subjected the Acholi people to prolonged, unprecedented suffering. In the following excerpt, LK, a researcher, highlighted the sequence of events which eroded the people's confidence in their government:

> Well the people had no trust in the government at all, because, as I said, they were seeing what was happening as a sort of plan. So they lost confidence completely in the government and their trust continued to get lost because of the government action toward the people. When the new government of the NRA/M came here to Acholiland, they entered without a single bullet.

> Nobody fought them, nobody resisted them. So when they came, they immediately started asking the people who were in the armed forces to return their guns to the government and the people responded and all of us participated and sensitized the people that the best thing we could do was to get rid of the guns that were brought in our communities. So people were encouraged to go to local leaders [and] religious leaders to take back their guns and most of them did. Soon after we returned the guns, the government summoned all the former soldiers to assemble in a designated place. The first group that reported were taken to Kiburura in western Uganda from where they disappeared. (LK)

However, despite having their backs against the wall, the Acholi people posed a moral challenge to the government. They created a counternarrative in favor of peaceful conflict resolution, which superseded the government propaganda and callousness.

The Acholis also encountered a misinformed, uncaring, and pessimistic international community that was sympathetic to the government's propaganda. Rather than using the Acholi lens to understand the Acholi traditional peaceful method of conflict resolution, the international community, particularly the West, stuck to their own punitive approach, which favored violent conflict resolution. For years they resisted the Acholi campaign for the adoption of peaceful approaches to conflict settlement. According to FO, a religious leader:

> We as religious leaders we stood very firm on dialogue as the way to peace and not the use of arms to resolve a political conflict . . . Talking and dialogue is the right way. Definitely, it may not have been understood within a certain section of the population, even here in Uganda. The people from the West and many others had a kind of general perception that war must be stopped by war. For me, for example, I had had a meeting with members of Parliament I don't remember whether it was from the Netherlands, and they asked us questions, which sounded to us funny. That, "How can you shake hands with somebody who has, for example, killed your father, your mother and your sons?" It is not understandable and that is an indication that our approach seems to be strange. And of course, there were some who tried to water it down—our Acholi system of *Mato Oput*, whereby the one who has committed atrocities is brought face to face with the victim to reconcile, which is ingrained in our culture and it works. (FO)

However, after a protracted campaign, the Acholi people used their cultural atmosphere of truthfulness, impartiality, competence, inclusivity, and consensuality to overcome the pessimism and apathy of the international community against their traditional peaceful approach to conflict resolution, which they insisted was different from the transitory justice system. Second, the international community changed their attitudes toward peaceful approaches when they were adopted in the settlement of conflicts in other places like South Africa and Kosovo.

Furthermore, compared to two major atrocious war precedents of the Arabs in the nineteenth century, and Id Amin in the twentieth century, the atrocities the rebels and the government meted out on the Acholi people during the conflict were unprecedented. Thus, the prolonged attendant suffering and structural betrayal created a communal apathy which posed one of the greatest challenges to the Acholis' response. In this context, NM narrated that most of the Acholi people were on the brink of giving up:

> Many people in the community thought that the government was too strong to be confronted by someone who was not a soldier, someone who did not have money. So they felt that I was risking too much. Even my own family members thought that I was daring too much. We also did not have access to State media. The radio did not allow us to go and talk. And then, the rebels were not also not understanding us. The government was not understanding us. The community was full of apathy, thinking that, look, this is just our lot, we should just adjust to the problem, rather than solving the problem. Those were the main problems that we faced. (NM)

Overall, although the Acholi people paid a price for challenging a callous government and a pessimistic international community, they retained their dignity as a people which they used as the platform to create a counternarrative of the conflict that changed the Ugandan government's and the international community's perception of the Acholi people and the conflict.

Culture

The Acholi people attribute their existence to their culture. The Acholi cherish their culture and are inclined to protect, preserve, and pass it on to the next generation. Culture gives them a sense of identity and dignity as a people. It is therefore the basis upon which they build their obligations and expectations for themselves and the larger community. Thus, culture is the embodiment of their heritage, which makes them Acholi, as BA affirmed:

> You know, first, I am an Acholi woman. My culture is embedded in me. We are a proud people; we are a straightforward people. I grew in that culture and it is still in me. Two, me, I am a Catholic and my faith has 80 percent of me. My conscience cannot allow me [constrains my behavior]. It disturbs me. Really, what makes me what I am is my culture, my cultural norms and values, and then my faith. (BA)

However, the conflict pushed the Acholi culture to the brink of extinction. It halted all the cultural rituals and ceremonies of enculturation and acculturation. The implications were far reaching. A whole generation of Acholi children, who grew up in the camps, were never oriented to the Acholi ways of life. In the eyes of the Acholi people, this was tantamount to the depersonalization of the Acholi people. The consensus on the negative impact of the conflict on the Acholi culture is summarized by OO4, a retired member of parliament and an elder:

> Life was meaningless. People were dying and being buried in the camps. In fact, even the graves, we went to Anaka and we found the dogs were eating the dead bodies. First of all, people were very, very weak, so they could not dig deep graves. They did not have enough food and energy. In fact, if you went to the camps you would shed tears when you see the people. And you know, the biggest thing is that it destroyed our culture. The children who grew up in the camps were totally detached from our culture. And you know, that the culture made the people, and without the culture, you are no longer a person. So you know the girls started misbehaving. Because they were given one tent for a family of eight and whether you have girls who are already ... So they could not accept to sleep together with their parents. Children started to misbehave. They became undisciplined. All this time, people were in the camps. Now they are going back. They are starting afresh to educate the children who are being born. Children born in the camps are rebellious, they don't want to stay in the village, they want to ride *boda bodas* [motorcycles] and stay in town. So the destruction of culture was a very, very effective weapon against us, a very big weapon. The culture was interfered with because the people of Acholi were very, very strong because of the culture. (OO4)

Thus, inspired by their own cultural norms in which human conflict is expected, coupled with a strong predisposition toward and the belief in a peaceful approach to conflict resolution, they employed their core cultural values in the way they responded to the conflict in order to salvage their culture and rescue their people from depersonalization. OO5, a diplomat, herein summarized the resilience of the Acholi people:

> I think also what I can say is that the Acholi people traditionally speak their mind and that is how many of them are oriented in their upbringing. They are not this type of people who would be easily be intimidated; you know they are brought up with some high level of integrity to appreciate that this is wrong and this is right. They are people who never take bribes. For instance, somebody would say, "Let me rather die poor than being bought off." I recall they were leaders who stood up against the government excesses; some of them were working in the government. You remember the twenty people, including OA and the rest, who were roughed up by T and even incarcerated in Luzira prison. They defied intimidation and harassment. They said, we will say the right things. The government slapped treason charges on them and so on, and they said, "Look, we stand by what we said." Fortunately, the court acquitted them and the government paid them colossal amounts of money for wrongful charges. This tells you the type of leaders that were there. Otherwise if they were other kinds of leaders, they would have been bought off, they would have accepted those trumped up charges, in exchange for certain whatever, but they stood firm. That was just the reflection of the values people wanted. The people of Acholi were very, very clear of what they wanted and they also wanted their leaders to emulate them. So culturally, that is how the people were brought up in terms of what they would demand in such a situation. (OO5)

Thus, culture played a significant role in the formation of the Acholi people's identity and informing their responses to the conflict. When the Ugandan government abdicated its responsibility to the Acholi people, culture empowered them to assert their own authority to demand the adoption of a peaceful approach to resolve the conflict.

Experience

Experience gave the Acholi people both the inspiration and the urgency to respond to the government's policies and approaches to the conflict. The Acholi relied on precedents from their own experiences and the experiences of others, which they used as the necessary evidence to conclude that, like other human conflicts, the northern Ugandan conflict was neither unique nor permanent. NM shared the experiences of the people who fought and defeated dictatorial and oppressive regimes in South Africa and the Middle East, which inspired their response.

The prolonged suffering in the Acholi subregion also influenced the people to develop the unity and urgency needed to respond, confident that the victory was theirs. BA, a member of parliament, attributed their response to the discontentment the Acholi people harbored against the Ugandan government because of its negligence and callous attitude:

> Up to now, 30 years later, a government in power and you find economic disparity between the north and south. What has gone wrong? I just came back from the village the other day and I was asking people even if the development of Museveni could be carried on the head [like luggage] and you walk to the North without a vehicle, thirty years later, [development] would have reached here. What has gone wrong? Those are the stands we took. And if you see us politically behaving the way we are doing; we are being coerced to accept the government of NRM, but not because we are happy that this is the government for us. We are looking at what is happening elsewhere. (BA)EXT]

Thus, surrounded by precedents of successful campaigns against dictatorial regimes and deplorable economic conditions, in which the people survived on food supplies from the World Food Organization, the Acholi people took it upon themselves to change the status quo. This was the most painful experience they endured as industrious people who were used to fending for themselves.

Expectations

The nature of the northern Ugandan conflict violated the Acholis' expectations of a government, of war, and of the international community. When the NRA/M overthrew General Tito Okello's military junta and established a government, the Acholi people conceded defeat. However, they cautiously observed the behavior of the new regime in comparison to the conduct of the previous regimes like that of Id Amin. Contrary to their expectations, when the government soldiers reached northern Uganda, they conducted themselves as occupying forces, rather than like a government. OR1, a member of parliament, detailed the predicaments that led to the outbreak of armed conflict in the region:

> So, this was the background to it. That the war would not have broken out if Museveni's men did not start humiliating the

Acholi people. Museveni's people went and massacred people in Amakura, they went massacred people, they put roadblocks, they humiliated them, they arrested former soldiers, they would mock them when they saw any Acholi woman putting on *Gomes*. they would say, "This is what you looted in Kampala when you were in power. You are backward; you are not supposed to put on this cloth." (OR1)

The war shattered conventional expectations. The nature of the conflict, which engulfed the Acholi subregion for over two decades, was unprecedented. The government targeted the entire Acholi community as the enemy alongside the rebels. Consequently, it declared the entire region incommunicado. At one point, the entire society was forced into IDP camps where they were misplaced and abandoned. OA2, a prelate, in speaking about the predicament of the Acholi people in the camps, said, "More than 1.2 million people were in IDP camps and life was horrible there, where 60,000 would be gathered in one place and the army was placed in the middle, making them easy targets." The experience shocked the entire Acholi community.

But the Acholi culture expects them to uphold positive attitudes amidst any challenges. In their cosmology, human challenges are phenomena bound to occur due to human weaknesses. However, whereas they also believe that no human phenomenon is permanent, they are cognizant of the fact that no phenomenon solves itself without deliberate concerted efforts. So rather than caving in, the Acholi people rose to fulfill their cultural expectations of self-initiative, by responding to the conflict the Acholi way. RA, one of the traditional leaders said that they decided to participate in the conflict resolution to restore political stability:

> That is a big mandate. Culturally, you are the head of the clan, you have to protect your clan; you have to see that they are healthy, they are happy, they are prosperous. Everything is good about them. And as such, you cannot just look at them when they are suffering, when they are being killed, when they are being abducted, when they are being denied their rights. You must step up. But that takes a lot of courage and sense of responsibility to do that. (RA)

Therefore, the Acholi response was an expression of their consciousness of and commitment to the Acholi ethos of life. In a context where the government had failed to end the war and the resultant sufferings, the Acholi people assumed their cultural expectation of fearless response in the face of danger to end the conflict. Their response was a fulfillment of the cultural expectation of self-initiative in the face of a challenge rather than a mere reaction.

Education

Education was one of the central factors that motivated the Acholi people to adopt a peaceful approach to conflict settlement. The Acholi people used the exposure they acquired through education to analyze the nature of the conflict and military approaches the government preferred. After considerable effort, they concluded that a peaceful approach was the most effective conflict resolution approach. OF, a military officer who retired from the army to pursue an academic career, summarized his own experience. "They were saying that how can we be defeated. I was in the army for 24 years. I realized that the pen is mightier than the gun. There was general lack of knowledge. The metaphysics came in." Consequently, they used the knowledge they obtained to educate the entire community, including the rebels, on peaceful conflict resolution. For instance, OF spearheaded the initiation of a peace center at Gulu University, which become the think tank for the peaceful approach to conflict resolution.

For their part, the opposition leaders shared relevant information with the community, which the latter used to engage the government on peace issues. Consequently, they managed to develop a common ground and undertook a concerted effort to demand change. According to MO1, an NGO director:

> First, many leaders from this side were not pro government. So they knew that if they come closer to the people and give the community positive ideas, the [community] would understand. So politicians from the Acholiland and other leaders were going to the people and explaining to them technical stuff. When the government people would come to the people, the people talked to them as technical people in peace process. So people were very courageous to talk to the government. I remember even the President could at times come and call some individuals and take them to the barracks and people could talk to him as experts. I remember one elder just came up and said, "Museveni, if you don't want to talk peace, just resign from presidency." So people were very courageous and were prompted to say those kinds of words with the guidance of the political leaders. (MO1)

The Acholis in the diaspora also solicited funds to train their fellow Acholis concerning peaceful conflict resolution. In their training, they were exposed to topics like preventative diplomacy, which focuses on peaceful conflict resolution. According to SM,

> As religious leaders, we are saying militarism is not the way the world is going to be transformed and get peace. So briefly that is why we are strong even though we are local traditional leaders in this region of Acholi. We still stand and say that peaceful means of ending conflict is the best means. I studied in the U.S. in 2005). It was sponsored by the U.S. State Department. My topic was preventative diplomacy and conflict resolution. I acquired a certificate in it. So preventative diplomacy is what the world is lacking. (SM)

Following the training, they pursued the peaceful approach as the only viable solution to the conflict. For instance, the peace movement among the religious leaders emanated from the inspiration they obtained through education where they learned that dialogue is the antidote to violence. OO3 explained how he prompted the religious group to spearhead the demand for a peaceful settlement of the conflict:

> You know, I was exposed to peace work when I went for my studies in journalism. From there, I was invited to be on the panel at a peace discussion. So in my research, I prepared myself. I learned that when I come back, I could do something for my country, particularly on reconciliation. So when I came back, I initiated a branch of an international organization in Uganda. We called it Jamia Upatiniswa. I founded it in 1998, with the aim of teaching children how to resolve conflicts peacefully. We based it on memory of what happened to children in Hiroshima where the children floated in the river. The children were telling the leaders that, "Let us not float like the children in Japan." Then, I started this education for teachers to teach their children how to resolve conflicts peacefully. So with that exposure when I became a bishop, I knew I could do something here.... So what influenced me is my experience, my faith in the Lord Jesus Christ, who is the Prince of Peace, who made it clear that blessed are the peacemakers. (OO3)

The rebels also benefited from the training. The women organizations strengthened the capacity of the rebels during the peace process. OR2 described how they supported the rebels throughout the peace process in Juba:

> We were acting as Uganda women because Uganda women umbrella was broader. We then acted together with organizations such as FIDA. We have got among ourselves experts from civil

society organizations. We got people who could do training on mediation, negotiation and all that. So we fell back on that. So in our meeting in Kampala, we decided on who should be on different training teams: the legal team, who should be what. So we maintained our presence in Juba. We looked for our own external resources and maintained our presence in Juba... That is how we informally strengthened the capacity of the LRA on mediation and negotiation. They were very, very weak on it. Our women lawyers were looking at the draft agreements they wanted to sign, and if they saw any loophole they would point them out. And we became very, very instrumental again, even though we did not go into the house [peace talks room]. (OR2)

The lack of education delayed the response of Acholi in diaspora until they acquired sufficient education and legal status. ZA contended that the *Kacoke Madit* conference could not have begun before 1997, because members were still pursuing further studies. For example, he fled the country with a high school diploma and thereafter he delayed his participation in conflict resolution until he completed graduate studies:

> What we call talks before talks. Things were discussed like where to meet on daily basis. It could not be done before 1997). And, people who went without enough education had already caught up. Me, I left when I had just completed high school, but by 1997, I was already having my master. So if it was in 1987, I would not have participated in that. So for the period of about ten years since the conflict started, Kacoke Madit could not be done the way it was done. (ZA)

In the same vein, Kony is hesitant to renounce rebellion, because he cannot sustain the clout and privileges he enjoys in the bush due to lack of education. In a conversation with JI, a human rights activist, he told her about one of the reasons why he is hesitant to renounce rebellion:

> One reason why this war took so long and even at time people said the Acholi people are fighting themselves is lack of education... Everybody asked and I said nothing will change this land apart from education, because it is not leadership which is lacking, it is education. In 2008, I talked to Kony and he told me that he is not coming out of the bush, because he thinks he is not going to take up any leadership role. "I cannot be the vice president, nor can I be the LCV [Local Council 5] or the RDC [Resident District Commissioner] due to lack of education. Now tell me, J,

if I come out, tell me what are you going to do for me. You want me to come and beg you for food for my children?" (JL)

However, overall, education gave the Acholi the confidence to organize and the language to express their conviction about peaceful conflict resolution. It also gave them a high level of consciousness, commitment, and accountability beyond a mere sense of duty. Finally, it gave them autonomy from government control and manipulation. In the following excerpt, ZA described how education empowered the people in the diaspora:

> But what actually gave us strength is the fact that we were not depending on the government of Uganda for education, shelter, food, livelihood and anything. For example, I was doing my master degree in Frankfurt University and working in Frankfurt. I could travel to London anytime. I didn't need anything from the government apart from passport which is my constitutional rights anyway to have it and I could renew it from the Uganda Embassy [in Frankfurt]. Even my security, I did not depend on the government or the rebels. I was autonomous in everything I did. That one cleared my brain. That is why we could push the *Kacoke Madit* in the diaspora forward . . . You know, some of us were already [exposed] how do you call it in German? We were exposed, we were educated, we were knowledgeable, we could do research and we knew we could point out exactly this is bad. This is bad according to European standard, in American standard, this is bad. (ZA)

Thus, education played an instrumental role in informing the response of the Acholi people to the conflict. Among other things, it empowered them to develop alternative constructs of the conflict, which exposed the fallacies in the Ugandan government's propaganda.

Belief

Belief is a central pillar in the lives of the Acholi people. It gives people a sense of hope beyond death; commitment beyond their secondary identities of tribe, gender, or religion; and motivation beyond educement or coercion. Through belief, they can express the life of God in their obedience to the will and dictates of God. The Acholi believe that human life is a window into the divine. Thus, belief is the means through which humans renounce self-sufficiency to depend on God wholeheartedly and each other complimentarily. For example, the Acholi people conducted prayer rallies until the war stopped. LB, a former rebel who renounced rebellion, attributed the end of the conflict to people's faith in God:

> The Acholi people knew that the rebels went to the bush because of the way the NRA came. So they went to the bush to defend the Acholi people against the NRA attacks. So I think to me it was God, it is purely God who came into their [rebels] hearts for the war to end. Because before I renounced rebellion, we learned that they were conducting so many prayers rallies. Many people came from Kenya and other parts of the world. They wanted the war to end and God answered their prayers. (LB)

Furthermore, when they were faced with circumstances beyond their innate abilities, they resorted to divine support for wisdom and guidance. When OO1's constituents encountered challenges like constant mysterious fires in the camps, they sought divine wisdom and intervention. "And being from a religious background, I would meditate and reflect and ask for eternal wisdom, because everyone is counting on me, but I am just an individual. May what happens be done according to the wishes of the greater force."

Belief gave them a sense of commitment beyond a mere sense of duty. In this way, they focused on their mission without yielding to the temptation of succumbing to self-interest. Thus, they became the moral compass and voice of conscience which galvanized trust and support across the board. They pursued a peaceful approach, partly because they were convinced that it was God's preferred approach for conflict resolution. They concluded that their participation in the peace process was a means of enacting God's love and will. OF, an academician, reiterated this:

> I forgot to mention the role of the religious organizations. You know, predominantly the Acholi and people in the north are Christians. Apart from culture, you find that religious leaders play powerful roles in the community. It is one place where you can see culture and religion intermingle very, very well. So I cannot forget that angle. You would find Archbishop Odama, Onono and others very instrumental in conveying what the people wanted and they have continued doing that without fear or favor. They are still very instrumental today. And the support of the community also sustained us. But above all, the hope that it will happen because its happening is not in our own power, it is the power of God. We never gave up, because, you know, it was not an ordinary business, it was a vocation. You know, not a career, but a vocation, which comes from God and he has chosen you. (OF)

Finally, belief enabled them to develop a very strong bond to pursue the common good. For example, the unity exhibited by all the religious organizations and Christian denominations enabled them to speak with one voice as the testimony of their credibility and assurance of God's presence. OM2 described their unity in the following excerpt:

> So, that is what sustained us that we were walking together with Christ. We were not alone and we were actually doing his mission. So that is one. We were so united for the common good; you are a Muslim, yes. You are a Catholic, yes. When the time comes for you a Muslim, to go and pray, you go and pray. When the time comes for a Catholic to pray, you pray, but you bring the common thing that unites us together, that is what we want. We can bear all these names Muslim, Catholic, etcetera, but something that unites us is the mission of God. (OM2)

The unity of religious bodies was replicated throughout the Acholi subregion. For example, traditional institutions formed an umbrella organization to mobilize different communities in Uganda to advocate for the adoption of peaceful approaches to conflict resolution. The unprecedented demonstration of unity in and beyond the Acholi subregion influenced the Ugandan government and the rebels to adopt peaceful approaches to conflict resolution.

People

In Acholiland, humanity signifies belongingness. Humans are human because they belong. Therefore, they derive strength from mutual trust and support as BA stated: "I am strong with my people. I don't speak for my own gain or on my behalf. I speak on people's behalf and they believe in me and they make me proud."

In that regard, when you are alone, you are considered a nobody because the strength of an individual is derived from a common identity, which has its fullest expression in a community where love for others overrides all other interests.

The Acholi act as a community because conflict affects all categories of people due to human interrelationship and interdependence. As OA2 stated earlier, "It is a process that is built on the consensus of everybody else, because when you talk of conflict or war, it does not target the person who initiates it. It targets their families, relatives, children, friends, clansmen, and tribesmen."

The rebels who renounced rebellion came out of the bush because of the assurances people gave them. For instance, LB expressed a profound satisfaction he derived from the people's support for the rebels who returned from the bush. "What helped me most was to ask for forgiveness and people forgive you. If you repent and people forgive you, you start feeling different and you see the result, how people behave toward you. And many assistance people [rendered] us also gave us more assurance."

Thus, the people's power heightened the unity of the Acholi people and the confidence they place in mutual interrelationship and interdependence to advance a common cause. According to OA2, a prelate, "Our being together helped us a lot. Then, our meetings with various people in various places helped us to learn some of these things as we were moving around. Our being together made us always to sit and reflect, you know strategize." The people's power overcame gun power.

Reason

The Acholi used logic to analyze and frame their response to the conflict. For example, when NM analyzed the government's justification of the war, he concluded that it was mere propaganda based on false charges. For instance, the government incriminated the entire Acholi community for what had gone wrong in Uganda. In response, NM mobilized the people to reject the propaganda and challenged the government to identify and prosecute individuals who might have committed crimes in their individual capacities rather than as a community. Second, he challenged the government to protect the people against the rebels and the wrong elements in the army who were meting out atrocities in the Acholi subregion.

The rebels who renounced the military approach to conflict resolution based their decisions on the context of the war. For instance, KS decided to renounce rebellion because the context of the war had changed. First, the war gained global attention when other stakeholders like the United Nations joined it. Second, the local population on whose behalf they were purportedly fighting no longer supported a military approach. Consequently, he decided to desert the LRA in favor of peace, arguing,

> Because a brain like me, if I decide to leave, would it influence others? If I leave, can other people sense and follow me, and in the end LRA would be weakened, and the war come to a halt? Or if I come out, maybe if I am killed, maybe it will also strengthen the remainders to continue fighting. (KS)

In his analysis, he concluded that his desertion would advance their cause to either end or win the war, whether he was killed or not. When they came back from the bush after renouncing rebellion, the government and the people accorded them a warm reception and positive treatment. They in turn made appeals to their colleagues who were still in the bush to follow their example. In the following excerpt, LB narrated that their decision to renounce rebellion convinced the international community to support the peaceful option to conflict resolution and many rebels deserted the LRA in favor of peace:

> So, he [the President] left me, I spoke to the people [diplomats and elders] for a very long time like from this time (4m.) up to about midnight. We were about five. Then, the people started agreeing that the war will end. So when I finihsed talking, the President told us to go to radio Mega and call all the other people who were still in the bush to come back home. When the commanders heard my vioce they started coming back like K and O. (LB)

Furthermore, the Acholi people examined the conduct, impact, and duration of the war, and concluded that the military approach was not a viable solution. When they met the president, they impressed upon him the need to acknowledge that the military option was not viable. They pointed out the advantages of the peaceful approach over the military approach. For instance, they pointed out that the military option was costlier and more destructive and it would alienate rather than unite the antagonists.

Research and Publication

The Acholi people used research and publications to counter the government's propaganda. They liaised with international agencies to document and publish personal oral testimonies about the war, which exposed the atrocities the government troops and rebels meted out on the people. Thus, the international community and media developed a keen interest in learning more about the conflict beyond the government's propaganda. RO narrated the impact of oral testimonies:

> So, one time, ACORD [Association for Cooperative Operations Research and Development] organized an international conference at Gulu University. At that time, I documented men's oral testimonies. So I wrote it and gave it to a man to present, but on the paper, the man said he was doing it on my behalf, because

the title indicated I was the author. So he presented all those things that men were saying, and nobody could dispute them, because they were the realities about people's experiences. There were army men there who ran to me, saying, "R, we know what you are doing. But now instead of talking to us in this forum, why don't you come to us?" I just laughed at them and I said, "Did you understand what they whole thing was about? It was not about me; it was about those people who talked. I am just a channel airing their stories. Those are not my stories, there are their stories." For the subsequent research projects, we lobbied international agencies for funding and once we completed the projects, we gave them to publish. So we worked with organizations like ISSI International, Women in Kampala, ACORD and the Foundations for Human Rights Foundation to document and publish people's experiences of the war after 1996. (OR2)

Institutionally, they established a Center for Conflict Management and Peace Studies at Gulu University, which later became the Institute for Peace and Strategic Studies with a focus on academic inquiry and action-oriented research in the fields of peace and conflict. Among other things, the center hosted conferences on peace and conflict and furthered research in the same field. It also developed data for public dialogue with governments and international agencies. According to OF, the founding director,

I was now in Gulu University and then in one of the meetings; because every evening the night commuters [children] were sleeping on the university building verandas. When the religious leaders joined them in protest, the news exploded. So I said, "We are here. What are we going to do as a university?" I asked them for what we were going to do about the conflict surrounding us. They discussed and saw the need for an institute. I was appointed the director straight away. We lobbied for funding through government institutions and started hosting research forums and conferences to understand what went wrong and to create a data for engaging the government and the international community. It influenced a lot of issues. We invited development organizations and they came. Messages started reaching the government. Advocacy groups came in and a ceasefire resulted. There was pressure on the government. Through Gulu University, we linked up with USAID which created Northern Uganda Social Action Fund (NUSAF. This enabled us to get funds, the military stances softened. The President met people and made changes in the structure of the army. People would now complain and he would listen. He met with elders at night. We started seeing some changes. (OF)

Globally, the Acholi people conducted research and published data, which they used to show the correlation between the people's conditions at the camps and concentration camps and genocide in order to dismiss the government's attempt to portray the camps as People's Protected Camps. One of the leading Acholis who called the attention of the U.S. State Department and the Commonwealth Secretariat to the conflict made an empirical argument that the northern Ugandan conflict was genocide and labeled the camps as concentration camps. The following is his analysis of the war:

> I was not personally involved in the actual process that led to the discussion in Juba. Mine really was mainly of critic, analysis and narrative of the war. What was the war about? What was the logic of the war? What were the interests at play? I was seeking to pierce through the very fake infrastructure of this war. And two of course I did play probably the leading role in calling attention to the concentration camps and describing them as exactly what they were and getting the international community to do something about it. That was the most important single role I played. I was the first to name the situation by its very proper name. They danced around, did not want to call it concentration camp, did not want to call it genocide. I said this is genocide, these are concentration camps and the facts these are what they show. They did everything to destroy the facts and my life. Today, I am still here walking and talking having life despite their efforts to have me obliterated and they did everything. (OO6)

OO5 was particularly credited for mounting pressure on the international community to influence the government to disband the camps. He narrated that the international community was lukewarm because they don't care about the plight of Ugandans unless it has a direct impact on their domestic affairs:

> They also got very furious after the summit, the Commonwealth meeting. I had told them that how come you are going to a country with people in concentration camps? And that is partly how they brought the pressure to bear on them to disband the camps. Otherwise, they (international community) don't care about what Ugandans think. But their own public will know that they came here to a meeting presided over by Museveni and his regime while people are in the camps. So they said, look you want us to come to the Commonwealth it is difficult for us to

come if this situation is still there. It is difficult for us. Our Parliament, our media, our public will not take it lightly. And that is partly what largely actually led to the dismantling of the camps. Museveni was not remotely ready to dismantle the camps. He was not. It was the direct international pressure and the campaign I was involved in which is all out in the public domain. I had all my evidence and everything set up. (OO5)

At the governmental level, they influenced the parliament to institute an inquiry to explore why the conflict took so long to end and to suggest possible solutions. The main report did not capture the sentiments of the Acholi people, but two members of the committee who hailed from northern Uganda wrote a minority report, which the government initially rejected but later adopted and implemented. One of the architects of the report described its impact:

> Our minority report was rejected by the Parliament, but it stood as a testament of what we believed to be the right cause. And I am happy that as we talk now, everything that we proposed was actually implemented by the government. So I participated in the peace process in the pursuit of my belief in those ideas that I first tabled in Parliament. (NM)

Lastly, the Acholi in diaspora held several international forums on the conflict in London, which were attended by different dignitaries from Europe and America, as well as the Ugandan government and rebel representatives. Like other forums, they used the resolutions to attract the attention of the international media to the conflict. One of the coordinators said that many international organizations developed interest to get more information about the conflict:

> So, from that conference, one of the people who happened to work for the UK Department of International Development is the one who dispatched letters to different people. From there, journalists picked interest in what was happening in northern Uganda. Then, they started to get their way to northern Uganda after that conference. The people were really interested to find out whether these things were happening in northern Uganda. They went to find out more for themselves. (ZA)

In response, the international media joined the local efforts to advocate for the peaceful approach to conflict resolution which culminated in the Juba peace talks and the dismantling of the camps. Furthermore, the Ugandan government abandoned its propaganda in light of the Acholi counternarrative of the conflict and joined hands with the Acholi people to foster dialogue.

Technology

The acquisition of technology like the internet and mobile phones enabled the Acholi to circumvent state restrictions on both the media and the people. For instance, when the Acholi people acquired the skills and devices to document oral testimonies of the people and their experiences, they shared them directly with the international community through organizations like Foundations for International Human Rights, which published them. According to OR2, they used technology to circumvent governmental obstructions:

> [Government agents] intimidated the people who were documenting the evidence of people's experiences we used to tell the whole world about what was going on here. I was intimidated so many times, but I maintained what I was doing. Instead of getting these people views and summarizing them, I would go and document their oral testimonies. So if there was a Rose out there, I would use the first name to protect the person. I would not use the last name. So it became another way of circumventing the harassment and news censorship. (OR2)

The government employed its monopoly of the state media to disseminate its propaganda without any challenge before the Acholi people acquired electronic devices. However, the advent of modern technology heralded a new dispensation of communication. For the first time, people could mobilize local and international communities at will, without state interference. The Acholi in the diaspora used the internet to initiate the *Kacoke Madit* forums across Europe without any interference. ZA summarized the impact of technology on mobilization:

> There was a point where all the Acholis were connected to the net. We posted a discussion list in the internet and then engaged those in the diaspora and at home. First and foremost, technologically, internet did not start until 1987). Internet actually helped us a lot to link up the discussion groups. So we had Acholi forum/Acholi discussion groups. Such that you would sit in your safe workplace and talk to somebody in Canada. That one, we could not do it before. (ZA)

Locally, the community gathered data on the atrocities the antagonists committed daily, which they shared with members of parliament and other relevant organizations. They used the evidence they collected as the basis for influencing some of the major policies the government implemented. For instance, the Amnesty Act emanated from the pressure the Acholi people mounted on the government to encourage the rebels to renounce rebellion. OA1, a journalist, summarized their sentiments and resolve to demand amnesty for the rebels:

> But our people were saying that the government was keeping closed eyes, deaf ears; it is not seeing the problem. So leaders like NM would come here to give us information and in return took information from us. How many were killed, how many were injured, how many were abducted daily? NM gave us his fax line for sending data from the community daily. That is before the mobile phones were introduced. Mobile phone was introduced in Gulu in 2001). I remember there was debate about amnesty in Parliament, which the government resisted until the community and the MPs [members of parliament] mounted pressure using the data we collected. (OA1)

Furthermore, the participation of international news media like the BBC, CNN, the Voice of America, and other foreign organizations like Invisible Children, attracted global attention to the conflict. The Invisible Children documentary drew the attention of key players like the U.S. State Department and the U.S. Congress, which later passed a resolution that led to the relocation of the rebels to Sudan and the subsequent ceasefire. OJ said that the Invisible Children documentary made the plight of the people visible:

> The Invisible Children also helped us to raise the profile of northern Uganda. We were invisible until the Invisible Children came. For the first time, they said, "We must put an end to the atrocities of the LRA. We went to Washington DC to meet with the U.S. government officials at the State department." We asked them, "Where were you all this time, from 2002 to 2012? Where were you when people were dying in northern Uganda on daily basis?" (OJ)

The intervention of the global news media also drew attention to the plight of the children. For the first time, the international agencies responsible for children's affairs responded after religious leaders staged a demonstration when they slept among the children on the streets for four nights. The government also provided security for the children thereafter. A religious leader said,

> They provided security. The bus park was sealed off. Journalists from all over the world were there. I think they heard about it. Thereafter, the children stopped sleeping on the streets. Organizations provided shelters, the government provided soldiers and police to protect the children who were being abused in the camps . . . Therefore, we had it rough sleeping in the bus park. And that sent a signal to the world far and wide. The BBC, Voice of America, CNN and many others broke the news that the whole Archbishop and other religious leaders are sleeping among the children who were the victims of abduction. (OM2)

Finally, the local FM radios provided the main platform for engaging the rebels in the bush. For example, when the rebels who renounced rebellion used FM radios to appeal to their colleagues who were still in the bush to renounce rebellion and return home, over 2,600 rebels renounced rebellion and returned home within the course of a single week.

Exogenous factors gave the Acholi people the enormous resources needed to develop a comprehensive understanding of the conflict and the ability to frame and pursue a successful response to the Ugandan government's policies and approaches to the conflict. Above all, it gave them the agency to resolve the conflict as subjects rather than victims.

7

Findings on Followership Enactment: Fruit Actions

FOLLOWERSHIP enactment, like its development, is a unique process, which requires a separate section to describe it. In this section, the study uses tree and staircase analogies to report the findings on followership enactment, along with the terms "human dignity," "root factors," and "fruit actions." The enactment occurs in three seamless steps, namely: observation, analysis, and response.

The study uses a tree analogy to illustrate the mental model driving followership development among the Acholi people and the staircase analogy to illustrate followership enactment. The image in Figure 4 is a tree growth circle, which illustrates a seamless mental model envisioned in the tree analogy. According to the image, a tree goes through several stages of growth to bear fruit. First, fruit begins as a seed beneath the ground, which then goes through seamless and continuous interactions and growth until it becomes a tree composed of different parts that collaborate to produce fruits. Second, the different parts of a tree are outgrowth of a seed rather than independent entities in and of themselves. Thus, a fruit is a product of the seamless interactions of tree parts that are the outgrowth of a seed. The tree parts are dependent on the seed as the essence, but independent in form and interdependent of each other in function, respectively. That is, they are simultaneously the same in essence, unique in form, and complementary in function, a feature which makes their interactions context-specific, seamless, and continuous. Thus, a fruit-bearing process is a seamless and continuous interaction of internal and external factors that are organically interlinked in a context. The study uses this analogy to explain how followers develop and enact followership identities, roles, and behaviors.

Figure 4: Tree Growth Circle Depicting a Seamless Mental Model

Like a fruit, the enactment of followership identities, roles, and behaviors is an outgrowth of human dignity, which emanates from context-specific, seamless, continuous interactions between layers of root factors (core values and characteristics that inform and are informed by exogenous factors) and fruit actions (a consensus-building process of observation, analysis, and response). The actual enactment occurs in a consensus-building process characterized by observation, analysis, and response.

The image of a tree in Figure 2 (see page 135) illustrates that followership identities, roles, and behaviors are an outgrowth of human dignity which emanates from context-specific, seamless, continuous interactions between layers of root factors and fruit actions. Followership factors are like the tree parts that are simultaneously the same in essence, unique in form, and complementary in function. Thus, followership identities, roles, and behaviors are the tip of the iceberg which emanate from confluences of underlying factors rather than a mechanical response. In the image below, root factors interact with fruit actions to form human dignity, which in turn informs responses to a stimulus in a context relative to other contexts across time and space. Similarly, leadership variables are also supposed to emanate from and reflect an essence (a unique purpose), rather than functioning as entities in and of themselves.

Per the findings, there is a lot at stake when followers encounter a stimulus. First, human response has the potential to either form or deform human dignity. That is, when humans encounter a stimulus, their responses can cause them to either lose, maintain, or transform their dignity and the underlying factors which form and inform it regardless of what the short-term outcome might portray.

Thus, followers' responses demand careful observation and analysis before action because followership is a factor of human dignity, rather than merely a rank or role. It is fundamentally an outgrowth of self-consciousness and a commitment to human dignity, rather than being a merely passive object of the leaders' active influence. It comes from the understanding of oneself as a human being, one who carries a clear sense of aspirations and obligations toward human actualization and holistic well-being. In this context, human response is the criterion of being and becoming rather than merely duty and existence. Human response to a stimulus is primarily meant to reveal and affirm human nature and life rather than merely to sustain human material well-being. A proper understanding and enactment of human nature guarantees material well-being both in the short and long term. In the next section, I will describe followership enactment processes.

The followership enactment circle image (see Figure 3 on page 136) demonstrates how the Acholi people applied their human dignity to the stimulus of the Ugandan government policy and approaches to the northern Uganda conflict. Dignity undergirded both the process and outcome of their response. Thus, the findings propose that followers' responses are an outgrowth of human dignity rather than merely their duty, needs, or status. For instance, whereas the conflict caused an unprecedented humanitarian crisis, the Acholi people were proactive rather than reactionary in their response. Instead of succumbing to a victim mentality trap, or resorting to rebellious countermeasures, they developed a counternarrative based on their human dignity to highlight the flaws in the government narrative and to offer the case for a peaceful approach to the conflict's resolution, which eventually won the support of the antagonists and the international community. The response, vis-à-vis fruit actions, was composed of three pivotal episodes: observation, analysis, and response.

In Figure 3, the response (observation, analysis, and response) is represented in the picture by the stairs' steps. It is based on human dignity, which is represented in the picture by the newel post. Dignity is established by endogenous and exogenous factors, which is represented by the concrete in the picture.

OBSERVATION

In the observation phase, the focus is on establishing patterns of overt and covert words, actions, attitudes, and moods which characterize the phenomenon under observation. The criteria include: first, identifying the factors at play, such as the actors and recipients involved; second, naming the events, context, situations, and narratives being advanced to support them; third, ascertaining the stated objectives against the actual procedures and outcomes, and ascertaining how the gaps and bridges are rationalized; and fourth, establishing the structural and systemic issues and patterns at play. The procedure takes into consideration multiple perspectives and accounts to ensure objectivity, transparency, competence, inclusivity, impartiality, and consensus. For example, the Acholi people viewed the conflict from multiple perspectives and accounts and engaged multiple stakeholders with transparency, competence, inclusivity, and impartiality.

Observation, like analysis and response, takes place through the lens of human dignity and is based on multiple layers of factors in direct interaction with a stimulus. Without the consciousness of and commitment to human dignity, the observation outcome might become a projection of subjective biases and assumptions, rather than a conscientious experience. The image on Figure 3 on page 136 summarizes this observation.

Thus, a thorough observation requires enough time to allow clear patterns about the stimulus to emerge, and to consult widely to acquire the necessary insider and outsider perspectives to frame the emergent patterns according to accurate themes/subject areas. In their case, three things stood out in their observation: a failed state, unending war, and unprecedented suffering.

A Failed State

In their observation of the conduct, structure, and consequences of the conflict, the Acholi people noticed that when the NRM government reached northern Uganda, it committed deliberate errors of commission and omission, which disqualified it as the state. They categorized the NRM conduct as that of an occupying force rather than a government. The government agents perpetrated heinous atrocities against the people they were meant to protect, until the people could not differentiate between the state and the rebels.

The NRM government did not fulfill the obligations the citizens expected of a government. The government failed to protect the people and their properties against rebel incursions even within the camps it purportedly created to protect the people. Second, it was adamant in acknowledging the failures of its war policies in northern Uganda. Thus, as NM noted earlier, the people concluded that the government was callous and uncaring.

For instance, the NRM government censored media coverage of the atrocities in northern Uganda, except for its own propaganda. For over a decade, there was a news blackout regarding the conflict. OJ said that the government declared northern Uganda incommunicado deliberately to propagate its propaganda. So, the Acholi people asserted themselves to lift the veil off the thick curtain of intrigue and blackmail to expose the hidden infrastructure of the conflict:

> Northern Uganda was sealed off from the international media. So, we had to do something here to expose the suffering of the people. So, we called the big meeting in 1997. The theme of the conference was the consultation process and the government accepted to send representatives. (OJ)

For example, according to OA2, a prelate, the government used the concept of "Protected Camps" to force people out of their homes and into camps. Unfortunately, the conditions of life in the camps fell below the conventional standard of protected camps. In response, the Acholi people counterargued that the camps were IDP camps, where the government displaced and misplaced people without protection or provision.

Worst of all, the government was adamant in their refusal to accept any alternative views on the conflict or options for its resolution, even when it was abundantly clear that its policies had failed for over two decades. It sabotaged the Acholi people's initiatives, which it subsequently branded as collaboration and a conspiracy to overthrow the government. Those who initiated alternative views and options were classified as perpetrators and summarily charged with treason. Thus, the government abrogated the cardinal hallmarks of the state.

Unending War

In yet another observation, the Acholi people noticed that the conflict had become an end without any end in sight. OO6, a diplomat, observed that, "It took very, very long because the war itself became a source of wealth, especially to some government soldiers. The government army at that time was using the war to mobilize resources which would never go down for good purposes." The government was reluctant to pursue the conflict with the same vigor it exhibited in other conflicts it executed in the region like Rwanda and the Democratic Republic of Congo. Furthermore, BA, a member of parliament, said that the government was adamant in its refusal to either admit its failure to end the conflict despite its superior advantage over the rebels or seek external support:

> Others would say go and kill them; these are rebels. But you need to go into the details and find out what they are fighting for. This is a political conflict; could it have a political solution? Does it need a military option to solve it? The military option has failed. That is why it took twenty years, two decades and failed. Can't you find another way out? That is why the war became a business. How can Museveni explain how they toppled governments in Rwanda, Burundi and the Democratic Republic of Congo, the conquerors, and yet failed to win the war in northern Uganda? Isn't that deliberate that we people in northern Uganda should suffer? How could they topple government in Rwanda and fail to subdue rebellion internally? And besides, if they could not subdue the rebellion internally, then why did they not come out and say we are constrained, so that we would have been helped by outsiders? (BA)

The people noticed that the antagonists had no clear achievable goals. The government was not threatened by the conflict because the rebels were not interested in toppling the government. But the government was also not interested in protecting the people. Thus, it became obvious to the people that the government was pursuing a false war with a hidden agenda. Instead, the government was diversionary in its tactics. It would punish the people for not reporting rebel presence but then branded them as collaborators when they did report. Either way, the people realized that there was something wrong about the war, because the government was not interested in ending it.

Overall, government agents acted in a manner which cast doubts on their actions and words. They were indiscriminately inclined to the pursuit of revenge against the Acholi people for the mistakes of past regimes, even though the Acholi people were not the only people who constituted them. Therefore, the Acholi people concluded that the government was using the war to pursue a sinister goal that required further analysis.

Unprecedented Suffering

The conflict caused widespread suffering in northern Uganda. According to NM, the suffering had surpassed a magnitude that anybody could ignore. It is true that the Acholi people have suffered before during the slave trade and the Id Amin era. However, the suffering during the NRM era eclipsed all their previous sufferings:

> The intensity of the suffering here was no longer capable of being ignored. I felt that government was uncaring and callous. And if you have a problem which is affecting you and your people, you have to step forward. To me, it was therefore an act of responsibility and it was not based on any particular position I was holding because one can be responsible even if you are not holding any position. (NM)

NM's sentiments were echoed by other participants. For example, OO4 observed that there is no village in Acholi without causalities from the conflict. Altogether, they reiterated that the conflict had pushed the Acholi community at the verge of extinction:

> You know, they were seeing their children getting finished [dying]. So they came up to say that the gun has failed, why can't we try negotiation? Actually, every village in Acholi has got a grave of this war, every village. So I mean the war, I mean the gun was failing, and they said, "Why don't we try this?" I tell you Museveni was very, very adamant. (OO4)

Economically, the region was a pale shadow of the boom being experienced in other parts of the country. OO3, a religious leader, shared the hardship he encountered working in northern Uganda during the conflict, which made him question whether the Acholi people were truly Ugandans and why he was one of them.

> Uganda was sharply divided between the South and the North. The economy was growing by double digits in other parts of the country, while we were in poverty. Why were we put in this part of the world? Were we really Ugandans? Actually, I was angry being in leadership in such a situation. It is not good. Actually, I was in mission in the wreckage, it is not easy. I should have written a book about it. I did not like it. (OO3)

The observation raised hard questions which prompted further analysis to gain a comprehensive understanding of the conflict. In the following section, I will discuss the analysis phase, which sought to establish the meanings and implications of the outcome of the observation, vis-à-vis the failed state, enduring war, and unprecedented suffering.

ANALYSIS

In the analysis phase, the intent is to establish the meaning and implication of the observation outcomes about the stimulus at hand. It is divided into two sections: diagnosis and prognosis. This phase determines how the stimulus correlates with normative life patterns in a certain context and whether a response is inevitable. Thus, the observation outcome is analyzed through the filter of human dignity and its underlying determining factors. This stage is the threshold, which determines the impact of the stimulus at hand on the dignity of the people in question. It determines whether the stimulus is neutral, destructive, or constructive to normative life values. Each case prompts a different response.

Diagnosis: War Designed to Finish Off the Acholi People

When diagnosing, the focus is on correlating the observation outcomes to normative life values and patterns cherished by the people in question. In this case, the stimulus can be either neutral, destructive, or constructive. In the case of neutrality, there is no need for a response. In the case of destructiveness, there is need for a response to protect and sustain the normative values and patterns they cherish. In the case of constructiveness, there is need for a response to transform the normative patterns and values.

In the case of the Acholi people, the diagnosis of the observation outcomes showed that the conflict was characterized by values and patterns which were unwanted by the people and destructive to their dignity. In their own diagnosis, they discovered that the conflict was designed to finish off the Acholi people. Thus, any effort toward pursuing the military option to resolve the conflict only helped the government to achieve its sinister goal of finishing off the Acholi people. For example, it did not matter whether the government was fighting the rebels or committing atrocities against the people, because the victims were still the Acholi people. This is because the conflict was waged in Acholiland and the majority of the LRA rebels were children abducted against their will because the government did not protect them. Besides, as OR2 shared earlier, the war occurred in people's compounds and the antagonists targeted the ordinary people indiscriminately.

The statements attributed to the president and other cadres of the state confirmed the sentiment of the Acholi people. In one of his statements, the president likened the Acholi people to grasshoppers trapped in a bottle, which can escape by eating each other. BA said that the Acholi people understood it to mean that the government created a war situation for them to kill each other:

> We moved a motion in Parliament here that northern Uganda should be declared a disaster area twice, but the government refused. Isn't it deliberate that we die? How do you explain this statement by the head of the State: President Museveni said, "They will die like grasshoppers in a bottle?" In other words, put them in a situation of war and let them kill themselves. (BA)

Therefore, when the Acholi people had analyzed the conflict, they concluded that the government was pursing the war to finish off the Acholi community to consolidate its grip on political and military control. In that context, the pursuit of war benefited the Ugandan government rather than the Acholi people.

Prognosis: Stop the War to Secure Stability

A prognosis is designed to establish a viable proposal for the restoration or transformation of normative values and patterns, depending on whether the stimulus is destructive or constructive. When the Acholi people analyzed the dynamics of the conflict in comparison with the previous conflicts, they discovered that the context of the conflict was unique. Thus, the approach they used to solve the previous conflicts was not appropriate. Whereas there was internal economic and social stability during the Id Amin era, there was none during the Museveni era. Therefore, they unanimously agreed that the remedy to the conflict required political stability that could only be achieved by stopping the war, not by winning it.

RESPONSE: PEACEFUL CONFLICT RESOLUTION

The response phase is designed to develop a concrete roadmap for the implementation of the prognosis proposal. There are three possible options depending on the impact of the stimulus on the normative values and patterns of the people. First, when it is neutral, you respond with no action—maintain the status quo. Second, when the stimulus threatens dignity, you respond to restore and preserve it. Third, when the stimulus is constructive, you respond to improve upon the current normative values and patterns, which undergird dignity.

In the case of the Acholi people, the stimulus posed destructive threats to their dignity. As shown in the image in figure 3, the Acholi response was designed to stop the war in order to restore political stability so that they could address the challenges of the conflict. Thus, after a thorough discussion, they agreed that a peaceful approach was the most viable option to stop the war.

The response, like observation and analysis, is executed through the filter of human dignity and must contain the sparks, which are consistent with the normative values and patterns of the people in question. For example, both the activities they engaged in and the organization format they used to respond to the stimulus contained normative values and patterns which were consistent with the tenets of their dignity. So just like the observation, the response must be subjected to a rigorous analysis to ensure that it preserves human dignity. It is thus a proactive phenomenon which requires careful scrutiny. For example, the Acholis in the diaspora thwarted numerous attempts to turn the *Kacoke Madit* forum into a formal political organization for illicit purposes.

When the stimulus contains constructive values which have the potential to improve upon normative values and patterns, the Acholi people scrutinize their cultural values to transform them. The need for transformation is informed by the inclination that life is not static. Hence, they engage stimuli with the hope of improving upon their dignity.

Thus, enactment of followership identities, roles, and behaviors is a proactive phenomenon which requires careful observation, rigorous analysis, and effective response rather than a passive response driven by the active influence of leaders. Whereas leadership influence is necessary, it does not negate or subjugate the active role of followers because it is the outgrowth of human dignity.

Therefore, the enactment of followership identities, roles, and behaviors is a proactive response which is informed by human dignity according to fundamental cultural values. It requires careful observation and analysis before any actions can be taken. The actions taken must be consistent with human dignity. For that matter, the enactment of followership identities, roles, and behaviors is the consciousness and commitment to human dignity.

8

Discussions and Summary

IN this qualitative study, I explored how followers develop and enact active followership using the case of the active followership of the Acholi people in the resolution of the northern Ugandan conflict. The necessity of the study arose from the discovery that whereas scholars like Robert Kelley, Ira Chaleff, and Barbara Kellerman identified followership identities, roles and behaviors, and Carsten et. al. established factors influencing followership development and enactment, how factors influence followership development and enactment remained unknown.[1] So it is a pioneer study on how factors such as culture influence followership development and enactment. I began with the literature review. It showed that during the industrial era, organizations used individualistic and dualistic leadership theory, which regarded followers as objects of leaders' influence to socialize them into passive followership irrespective of context and outcome. Consequently, active followership was condemned as a toxic behavior that sabotages organizational processes and outcomes. However, the emergence of relational leadership theory in the information era, which regards followers as subjects of their own behavior has heightened the demand for active followership in organizations. Nonetheless, studies on followership are still in their infancy and for that matter we don't know how followers develop and enact such followership.

Thus, using a grounded theory case study approach, I asked thirty-nine participants to share with me their followership identities, roles, and behaviors; factors influencing how they develop and enact them; and how

---

1. Kelley, *Power of Followership*; Chaleff, *Courageous Follower*; Kellerman, *Followership*; Carsten et al., "Exploring Social Constructions of Followership."

such factors influence the ways in which they develop and enact them. From the analysis of the data, I found out that their followership identities, roles, and behaviors are the outgrowth of a conscious commitment to human dignity, which emanates from context-specific, seamless, continuous interactions between layers of root factors and fruit actions. They enact it through a context-specific, seamless, consensus-building process of observation, analysis, and response. Human dignity animates human consciousness, aspiration, expectation, and obligation toward a common goal for human well-being. Depending on the impact of a stimulus on dignity, the response can either solicit no actions or actions to uphold or change the status quo. The response comes in the form of delegation, obedience, and deference devoid of subjugation, dispossession, negation, and acquiescence; volitional participation alongside leaders; or intervention, especially when leaders are ineffective, malevolent, or ultra vires. So active followers' responses to leaders depend on their agency to develop and optimize the potential to thrive, their inherent human worth, and the environment for equal opportunity for all rather than merely reward or punishment.[2] For example, when leaders are effective, amiable, and intra vires, followers respond by first, standing down for the leaders through either delegation, obedience, or deference, and second, standing up for and with leaders through volitional participation. But when leaders are either ineffective, malevolent, or ultra vires, followers stand up to leaders through intervention to restore and preserve organizational normative environments. However, when leaders are blatantly obstinate, followers stand up against them. Therefore, active followers' responses to organizational leaders are an enactment of their being rather than merely actions toward an organizational outcome motivated by either a quest for rewards like promotions and salary raises or fear of punishments like dismissal.

For instance, although they had strong reservations about the government's policies and approaches to the conflict, they sanctioned it to implement them until their inability to resolve the conflict was no longer debatable amid unbearable sufferings. So, while they recognized the government's exclusive constitutional mandate to manage national conflict on behalf of its citizens, they did not abdicate their inherent authority. For example, when they were convinced that the government policies and approaches to the conflict were counterproductive and the government was adamantly unwilling to acknowledge it, despite their failures to yield any positive result for over a decade, they intervened with alternative viable proposals which led to the resolution of the conflict. They overcame the

2. Lundin and Lancaster, "Beyond Leadership," 36–44.

government's skepticism about their goodwill and ability to offer a viable alternative approach to the conflict's resolution. Thus, even the government's exclusive constitutional mandate to manage national armed conflict on behalf of its citizens did not subjugate the people's inherent authority to defer, delegate, participate alongside the government, or intervene. In addition, they intervened in a manner which did not subjugate, dispossess, or negate the government's role.

Followership among the Acholi people and followership literature struck a stark contrast. Whereas, organizations whose cultures are still dominated by the industrial-era organizational cultural paradigm are struggling to adapt to the information-era organizational culture, the Acholi people, who have always embraced active followership, exude confidence and excitement because the information-era organizational cultural paradigm is compatible with theirs. Thus, while organizations whose cultures are still dominated by the industrial-era organizational cultural paradigm must change the old paradigm that vilified followership to adapt to the dynamics of the information era, the new-era organizational cultural paradigm has emboldened the Acholi people to consolidate their culture of active followership. Therefore, knowledge of the development and enactment of active followership among the Acholi people, who have preserved and adapted their cultures of active followership to new contexts without losing their essence, is imperative to organizations that want to make active followership the normative behavior of followers. In the following section, I will discuss the findings in relation to followership literature, followership development and enactment, leadership theory, further research, and application.

FINDINGS AND FOLLOWERSHIP LITERATURE

These findings advanced followership theory because it established how factors like schema and culture facilitate followership development and enactment, which in turn sheds light on the processes of followership development and enactment and why individuals act in consistence with their role convictions under all circumstances. In their research on social construction of followership, Carsten et al. established factors influencing followership development, but did not explore how factors influence followership development and enactment, which would have explained the process of followership development an enactment and "the circumstances under which individuals' actions are consistent with their beliefs about their role responsibilities even though the context does not overtly support their actions."[3]

---

3. Carsten et al., "Exploring Social Constructions of Followership," 543–62.

However, according to the findings in this study, followership development and enactment are the outgrowth of the conscious commitment to human dignity, which emanates from context-specific, seamless, continuous interaction between root factors and fruit actions relative to other contexts across time and space. Specifically, root factors (endogenous and exogenous) interact with fruit actions (observation, analysis, and response) to form human dignity out of which followers develop their followership identities, roles, and behaviors in the context of everyday life experiences. Human dignity in turn influences human response (observation, analysis, and response) to a stimulus, which also influences root factors. Furthermore, they enact followership through a seamless consensus-building process of observation, analysis, and response. Human dignity in the context of leadership comprises potential, worth, and opportunity. The Acholi consider these features of human dignity as attributes of human nature rather than merely objects of organizational output. In the same vein, followership characteristics like dynamic (rather than a static) position,[4] proactive (rather than passive),[5] collaborative (rather than acquiescent),[6] and relational (rather than objects of influence),[7] are inherent human attributes that followers use in their ranks or roles to enact their being. As such, followership should be dynamic, proactive, collaborative, and relational because such followership abets the development and optimization of potential, reverence for human worth, and the rendition of unfettered equal opportunity for all. Conversely, reactive, passive, and acquiescent responses impede the advancement of dignity. So, whereas followership has been discussed in the context of what followers do in relation to leaders, the Acholi locate followership in who followers are. For instance, they emphasize both the human and the machine sides of followers,[8] and derive leadership from fundamental principles and values (philosophies) that characterize human nature and life, rather than from merely the observation of the actual human interactions in an organization guided by disciplines like sociology.[9] Therefore, the Acholi understand and practice leadership and followership as offshoots of who humans are rather than merely what they do, because to them doing is an enactment of being. For that matter, the Acholi act in consistence with their schema under all

4. Uhl-Bien et al, "Complexity Leadership Theory," 109–38.
5. Hirschhorn, "Leaders and Followers," 177–96.
6. Potter et al, "Leading the New Professional," 145–52; Burns, *Leadership*.
7. Hollander, "Processes of Leadership Emergence," 19–33; Hollander, *Leadership Dynamics*.
8. Hirschhorn, "Leaders and Followers," 177–96; Ilinitch et al., "New Organizational Forms and Strategies," 211–20.
9. Sorenson, "Intellectual History of Leadership Studies."

circumstances because they regard their actions/responses as the enactment of their being in which case they are not motivated by merely either external reward or punishment. They act not merely to obtain a result but because response is an opportunity to enact their being, which produces results as a natural outflow. In that regard, followership is an enactment of being, which is the basis and goal of human engagement and well-being. So it is easier to understand who the Acholi are by looking at what they are doing, and likewise understand what they are doing by understanding who they are.

The findings correlate with existing studies in various ways. First, they offer an answer to the question that Carsten et al. raised in their study on how individuals respond when their schema conflict with organizational environment.[10] Per the findings, when individuals encounter a conflict between their schema and organizational environment, they observe, analyze, and respond to it depending on its impact on their dignity. The response involves either creating an environment that is compatible with their dignity, or transforming their schema accordingly. In the case of the need to change the environment, their response includes the following steps: observation of the conflict to collect comprehensive data about it; analysis of the observation outcome to identify the problem (diagnosis) and thereafter offer a remedy (prognosis); and establishment of a strategy to implement the remedy (response), which is pursued relentlessly without fear or favor as an enactment of being rather than merely as an effort to obtain a result. If the leadership is effective, amiable, and intra vires, followers either stand down or stand up for and with leaders to remedy the conflict. On the other hand, if leaders are ineffective, malevolent, and ultra vires, followers either stand up to leaders or against them depending on how leaders respond to the suggested mitigation measures.

Second, the findings offer empirical evidence to the findings by Uhl-Bien et al. and Carsten et al. that followership, like leadership, is complex and multifaceted,[11] and as such can be understood only as a process involving layers of factors that engage each other in a way whereby each factor influences and is influenced by the corresponding actions of the others rather than as isolated actions, as demonstrated on Figure 1.[12] So leadership variables are complementary and inconceivable in isolation.[13] While each variable is distinct, such distinctions exist in forms that bear the essential features of the common essence that necessitates them to function

---

10. Carsten et al., "Exploring Social Constructions of Followership," 543–62.
11. Carsten et al., "Exploring Social Constructions of Followership," 543.
12. Uhl-Bien et al, "Followership Theory," 83–104.
13. Rost, "Followership," 53–66.

complementarily. In that case, variables ought to be conceptualized as the same in essence, different in form, and complementary in function. That is, they are all dependent on the common organizational goal, which accords each factor a complementary independent feature that functions interdependently. For example, factors like followership and leadership are complex and multifaceted partially because they simultaneously function as theories as well as variables. However, seamless mental models simplify their complexity because they regard their interactions as complimentary phenomena.

In addition, these findings also support Arend et al.'s study in which they identified human dignity as the "ultimate common, animating organizational goal in the service of humanity."[14] In support of their argument, this study found out that followers' responses to organizational leaders is an outgrowth of their human dignity. So their responses as delegation, obedience, deference, volitional participation, intervention (in cases of leaders' ineffectiveness, ultra vices, and malevolence) are an enactment of human dignity. However, unlike Carsten et al.'s study[15] that designated followers' behaviors like obedience and deference to leaders as passive followership, this study found out that deference, delegation, and obedience are acts of active followership provided the organizational construct and context in question are devoid of subjugation, dispossession, negation, and acquiescence. This is particularly true in organizational constructs and contexts like that of the Acholi people where active followership is regarded as an enactment of being and as such leadership and followership are flexible roles followers and leaders play interchangeably.[16] Thus, deference or obedience per se don't make followers passive. Instead, it is the degree of agency individuals exercise in their responses and the commensurate respect and honor accorded them that make them either followers or subordinates or active or passive followers respectively.[17] For instance, while commenting on followers' agency and respect among the Acholi, NM said that, the Acholi people obey leaders only if they agree with the directives a leader issues: "The chief can come and tell me that we need a contribution to a community project and I will give my contrubution if I agree but he cannot dictate. We always insist that it is better to understand us then you will know how to deal with us." This is because, among the Acholi, leadership also serves as an identification

14. Arend et al., *Human Dignity and the Future*, 123.

15. Carsten et al., "Exploring Social Constructions of Followership," 543.

16. Heller and Van Till, "Leadership and Followership," 405–14; Hollander, "Processes of Leadership Emergence," 19–33; Mead, "Problem of Leadership," 7–12; Williams and Miller, "Change the Way You Persuade," 65–73.

17. Uhl-Bien et al, "Followership Theory," 83–104.

role in which a leader is regarded as the embodiment and expression of a people's collective identity, aspirations, and obligations, rather than the exclusive executive authority and power vested in the person holding a position of leadership. Thus, among the Acholi, leadership focuses on the participation of everyone rather than merely influence by leaders as it is in the West. In their context, leadership is preoccupied with enhancing the capacity, environment, and space for the participation of everyone out of their being in relation to others rather than merely a position of subjugating influence. This view is consistent with studies that highlighted the necessity for volitional obedience rather than blind obedience in contexts like banking and the military that require obedience as a virtue for effectiveness.[18] It is also consistent with Uhl-Bien et al.'s definition that regards followership as a volitional construct, role, and behavior, unlike subordinance.[19] So while it is true that in authoritative cultures, deference, obedience, and delegation are tools of domination and control,[20] in a relational culture, these behaviors and roles are flexible, interchangeable tools that accord agency and honor to both followers and leaders. Therefore, the passivity and proactivity of followers depends on leadership constructs and the environment they create in an organization.

In the current study, the participants primarily attributed northern Ugandan conflict to the Ugandan government's ignorance of the Acholi culture. Therefore, the findings in this study highlight the need for understanding the prevailing environment in organizations that want to make active followership a normative behavior. The prevailing philosophical foundations and perceptions of leadership and followership and how they play out in an organization offer an entry point, otherwise adopting active followership without adequate information on the prevailing system may end up creating change without transformation by conforming to organizational cultures. This is particularly relevant in organizations that aim for personal transformation. The knowledge of the existing leadership perceptions and structures offers a solid foundation for creating long-lasting impacts in an organization.

Finally, these findings offer a seamless paradigm, mental model, and mind set for relational leadership, which subverts the underlying assumptions of the analytical categories of difference associated with the dualistic mental model that polarizes classes of difference, like leaders and followers,

---

18. Medcof, "Followers and Followership."

19. Uhl-Bien et al., "Followership Theory," 83.

20. Milgram, "Some Condition of Obedience," 57–76; Milgram, *Obedience to Authority*; Uhl-Bien and Pillai, *Romance of Leadership*.

into absolute opposites despite their seamlessness. The seamless paradigm is suitable for relational leadership because it locates followership in being instead of doing, and for that matter, human response (doing) is ultimately the enactment of being. In this context, being rather than merely the material accomplishments of organizations and individuals is the basis and goal of human response and well-being. It also regards leadership as a phenomenon about participation out of one's being in a harmonious engagement involving acts of doing and relating in a context toward a common goal for human well-being, rather than merely the influence of leaders on followers toward a goal.[21] Therefore, whereas most studies attribute active followership to technological advancement, globalization,[22] and higher education,[23] this study locates it in being, which emphasizes both the human and machine sides of leaders and followers.

Therefore, followership studies should adopt seamless mental models and empirical paradigms to avoid the limitations of current followership studies, which impose Western methodological and empirical paradigms on other contexts. Seamless paradigms will expand followership theory and practice beyond the dichotomies that absolutized the differences among leadership variables at the expense of their seamlessness. For example, whereas current followership studies tend to portray active followership as being confrontational, the Acholi people regard it as the normative followership identities, roles, and behaviors, which become confrontational only when a leader is ineffective and malevolent and is unwilling to change, most especially in a retributive culture. So the major difference is context specific. While followership studies in the West are undertaken in organizations whose cultures are still either dominated by or struggling to break the shackles of the industrial-era organizational cultural paradigm, the Acholi culture is based on a seamless paradigm in which active followership is the normative followership identity, role, and behavior.

FINDINGS AND FOLLOWERSHIP DEVELOPMENT AND ENACTMENT

Considering the findings in this study, the efforts toward making active followership the normative identity, role, and behavior of followers in organizations in the new era call for the establishment of a seamless mental

21. Collinson, "Dichotomies, Dialectics and Dilemmas," 36–55; Hirschhorn, "Leaders and Followers," 177–96.
22. Fisher-Yoshida and Geller, *Transnational Leadership Development*.
23. Dixon, "Exploration of the Relationship."

model to replace individualistic and dualistic ones which polarized differences among leadership variables into absolute opposites. It also requires a shift in followership studies and practice from actual to ideal followership, individual to corporate followership attributes, and dualistic to seamless structures and atmospheres.

Seamless Mental Model

D. A. Norman argued that people's mental models dictate their perceptions, expectations and obligations: "People's view of the world, of themselves, of their own capabilities and of the tasks that they are asked to perform or topics they are asked to learn depends heavily on the conceptualization they bring to the task."[24] Thus, a mental model, or people's cognitive picture of the realities of their surroundings, determines how they make decisions and act. In the same vein, mental models shape leadership studies and practices. So far, two mental models are associated with leadership theory: a dualistic mental model, or systems thinking, vis-à-vis an integrated model. The former dominated leadership theory during the industrial era, which lasted for over one century. As already discussed in chapter 2, the industrial era derived its mental model from Descartes's mind/body dialectical language,[25] which conditioned human thinking and relationships to individualistic and dualistic tendencies. The tendencies prioritized differences and similarities over seamlessness.[26] Descartes's mind/body dialectical language formed the basis for leadership research, education, and practice. Thus, leadership scholars and practitioners subjugated variables like followers under leaders as mere objects of influence.

However, following the emergence of the information era, the relational model is taking center stage in leadership theory. Pertinent to it is systems thinking which, as discussed in chapter 4, is a mental model that regards things like systems that influence each other within a whole.[27] It considers interrelationships among different variables rather than merely distinctive similarities and differences associated with the dualistic model.[28] Unlike the dualistic orientation, which considers relationships from the standpoint of individuals as independent, discrete entities, the latter

24. Norman, "Some Observations on Mental Models," 7–14; Gentner and Stevens, *Mental Models*.
25. Collinson, "Dichotomies, Dialectics and Dilemmas," 36.
26. Frye et al., "Embracing Spiritual Followership," 243–60; Senge, *Fifth Discipline*.
27. Senge and Sterman, "Systems Thinking and Organizational Learning," 137–50.
28. Senge, *Fifth Discipline*, 1.

DISCUSSIONS AND SUMMARY 273

orientation considers variables as integrated entities by starting with a process rather than variables, and views them as byproducts of a process.[29] Thus, it maintains analytical categories of difference without reifying its bifurcating tendencies.[30] In that case, it offers followers agency because it subverts the underlying assumptions of the analytical categories of difference that polarizes classes of difference into absolute opposites.[31]

However, despite a clear distinction between a dualistic model and systems thinking, they share a common feature of dispensationalism. That is, they are both era-specific. For instance, whereas the industrial era created the dualistic model, the information era is responsible for systems thinking. Second, they both regard variables as distinct entities in and of themselves. While the former focuses on entity independence, the latter is preoccupied with entity interdependence. That is, the parts have meaning in isolation and within a chain, respectively.

The two paradigms have huge implications for change dynamics. In the former, a change requires a reconfiguration of the entity and whereas consistency impedes progression, progression disrupts consistency. In the latter orientation, the parts interrelate as autonomous entities in and of themselves to the extent that the spheres and entities presumed unrelated are ignored. Like the former paradigm, consistency can impede progression and progression can disrupt consistency.

On the other hand, the seamless mental model illustrated in the image on Figure 4 on page 283 is based on the "Logic of Essential Seamless Seams," which envisions a fundamental essence with constituent outgrowths that are dependent on it, and which are both independent of and interdependent on each other. The parts reflect the essence separately and collectively, and as such are not entities in and of themselves because the essence, vis-à-vis the whole, is greater than the sum of the parts. The nature of the essence influences the interactions of the parts and their outcomes to reflect it. The essence is greater than the sum of the parts because it is indivisible, inexhaustible, inviolable, and invaluable. Thus, a change in this model is the progressive revelation of the consistent essence. So consistency and progression are compatible. Thus, the variables are simultaneously the same in essence, different in uniqueness and integrated in function.

29. Hosking and Bouwen, "Organizational Learning," 129–32; Hosking et al., *Management and Organization*.

30. Prasad, "Beyond Analytical Dichotomies," 567–95; Senge and Sterman, "Systems Thinking and Organizational Learning," 137.

31. Alcoff, "Objectivity and Its Politics," 835–48; Prasad, "Beyond Analytical Dichotomies," 567.

So, unlike the dualistic model and the integrated model, which polarize and integrate the parts as distinct entities in and of themselves, the seamless model juxtaposes and integrates the parts as outgrowths of the essence, which makes them seamless and mutually inclusive variables because of their absolute dependence on the fundamental essence.

At the organizational level, the essence can be likened to organizational common goals and the constituent parts are the entities needed to fulfill them. At the human capital level, it is the common human nature which endows everyone with complementary distinct features, which call for independence and interdependence. So they work together complementarily because they are different sides of a coin with an inherent value greater than the sum of the sides. The common essence necessitates differences/independence and interdependence among the parts because of the seamless seams of the essence. Neither one part nor a collection of the parts exhausts the whole. Instead, the collective and individual parts reflect the whole collectively and individually. So unlike the seamless model, the dualistic and integrated models don't have a common essence as their springboard. The seamless model gives a wholistic picture of the parts as an outgrowth of the essence rather than the sum of the parts. It has seamless seams and hence the term "logic of essential seamless seams." The seams of the constituent parts reflect the distinct parts of the seamless essence, which makes the parts also seamless. In other words, the differences among the parts are the distinct attributes of the essence, which necessitate independence and interdependence among the parts to shine a brighter light of the essence collectively.

Thus, the seamless model allows for the exploration of leadership factors as both disciplines and variables that stand as systems, individually and collectively, beyond themselves rather than in and of themselves as it is with the other models respectively. Consequently, leadership factors are simultaneously dependent, independent, and interdependent variables whose differences and similarities are complementary rather than polar opposites. Figure 5 illustrates the three models: (A) represents the dualistic mental model, as it categorizes things as either/or entities; (B) illustrates the integrated mental model, which categorizes things as both/and entities; and (C) the seamless mental model, which categorizes things as all in one and one in all.

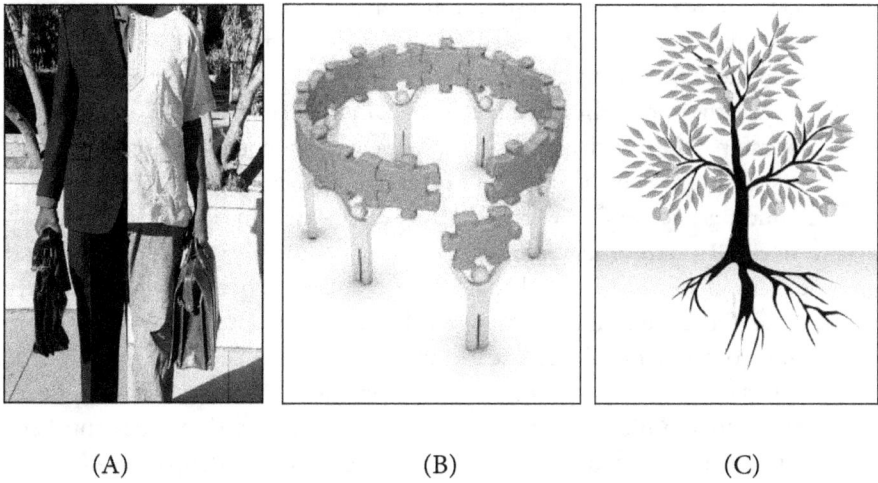

(A)   (B)   (C)

Figure 5: Three mental models: (A) represents the dualistic mental model. It categorizes things as either/or; (B) illustrates the integrated mental model, which categorizes things as both/and; and (C) the seamless mental model which categorizes things as all in one and one in all.

Note. Image B. From Puzzle Clipart Integration, moziru.com, Image #1665 of 2888. Retrieved from http://moziru.com/images/puzzle-clipart-integration-3.jpg. Reprinted with permission.

Actual to Ideal Followership

The followership theory is a young discipline (it began in 1988) compared to leadership theory. The seminal followership theorists established it on the premise that followers develop and enact followership identities, roles, and behaviors as subjects rather than mere objects of leaders' influence. Subsequently, several studies have supported it by highlighting the actual followership identities, roles, and behaviors and some of the factors influencing their development and enactment. But the empirical studies on ideal followership identities, roles, and behaviors, their rationale, and how followers develop and enact them, are scanty.[32]

The paucity of literature on ideal followership is a setback to the efforts toward making active followership the normative identity, role, and behavior of followers in organizations in the information era. For instance,

---

32. Carsten et al., "Exploring Social Constructions of Followership," 535.

whereas some of the seminal studies like that of Chaleff, identified courageous followership as a desired followership behavior (ideal followership behavior), they did not give either the rationale or explain how followers might develop and enact them.

Furthermore, these studies have painted a rigid picture of active followership. Most of the time, it is portrayed as a confrontation when it is in fact context specific.[33] This study addresses some of the anomalies. Per its findings, active followership degenerates easily into a confrontation in a retributive atmosphere/culture where it is difficult to acknowledge and address ineffectiveness and malevolence amicably because of its punitive stance. Otherwise, in a restorative culture/atmosphere, active followership is not confrontational because its atmosphere of impartiality, truthfulness, competence, inclusivity, and consensus enhance the resolution of failures and conflicts amicably. For that matter, active followership is not antithetical to deference, obedience, delegation, or followers' participation alongside leaders if there is no subjugation, dispossession, acquiescence, and negation depending on the context. Second, Chaleff portrayed courage as a stand-alone characteristic in followership enactment, but in the findings, it is one of the attitudes active followers possess. Thus, it is difficult to understand as well as develop and enact ideal followership identities, roles, and behaviors without a clear understanding of how the dynamics of factors influence the process.

For instance, in terms of rationale, the findings situate it in human nature. Humans possess inviolable and invaluable life, which makes them vertical, dependent beings who are horizontally independent and interdependent entities with common sacred life, inviolable autonomy and authority, and a collective expression. These dynamics form and inform high levels of consciousness, obligations, expectations, and aspirations which are congruent with the values of the inviolability and invaluability of human life. Thus, followership identities, roles, and behaviors are the outgrowth of the consciousness of and commitment to human dignity, rather than merely ranks, roles, rewards, reprimands, or even interactional relationships. It emanates from context-specific, seamless, continuous interactions between layers of root factors and fruit actions, and it is enacted through a context-specific, seamless, consensus-building process of observation, analysis, and response. Thus, an ideal followership behavior takes into consideration layers of factors.

Human dignity in this context comprises potential, worth, and opportunity, So active followership abets the development and optimization of

---

33. Kellerman, *Followership*.

potential, the estimation of human worth, and the rendition of unfettered equal opportunity. Whereas the practice or application of ideal followership is context specific, its essence and necessity are neither optional nor passive because they are ingredients of the fundamental human identity whose subjugation, dispossession, acquiescence and, negation violate humans' inviolable and invaluable nature, which can only be expressed in a simultaneously vertical dependence and horizontal independent and interdependent relationships. In that case, a shift from actual to ideal followership identities, roles, and behaviors is necessary because it is a measure of human self-awareness and actualization in the context of human efforts toward a common goal for human well-being.

Individual to Corporate Attributes

Organizations that want to make active followership the normative identity, role, and behavior of their followers must change their understanding of followership attributes as merely individual attributes to corporate attributes expected of its members, just like passive attributes were required of followers during the industrial era. Most studies on followership were undertaken in organizations dominated by industrial-era organizational cultural paradigms where active followership is still marginal. As such, most studies depict it as inherently confrontational without spelling out the factors that turn active followership into a confrontation. The lack of a clear understanding of the nonconfrontational side of active followership will make it difficult to change its attributes from individual to corporate behaviors expected of members across the entire organization. Active followership becomes confrontational only in unconducive atmospheres like a retributive culture where there is no peaceful method of resolving differences.

Individualistic and Dualistic to Seamless Structures

Passive followership flourished under dualistic tendencies during the industrial era, which regarded followers as objects of leaders' influence. Structurally, organizations developed dualistic cultural tendencies and structures to entrench passive followership. So since organizational structures are outgrowths of mental models, active followership requires a seamless mental model and the accompanying infrastructure to provide an enabling atmosphere for its development and enactment. For most organizations, it means developing new mental pictures and structures as well as cultures. For example, in a church setting, it calls for a discipleship/leadership model which empowers the body of Christ beyond leaders and organizational structure, that acknowledges the complementary role of followers beyond the four walls of the church to mobilize and equip the whole church to take the whole gospel to the whole world. This also calls for the provision of an environment consistent with human inviolable and invaluable nature, which makes humans simultaneously dependent, independent, and interdependent beings who thrive in an organic harmony.

FINDINGS AND LEADERSHIP THEORY

In this section, I will discuss how Acholian active followership relates to leadership theory. I explore the relationship by comparing the Acholi perception of leadership to four other lenses of leadership: African, Asian, Muslim, and Western. The findings pose three theoretical challenges to leadership theory: first, what is the philosophical basis of leadership or how is leadership framed cross-culturally? Second, how is leadership perceived and actualized cross-culturally? Third, whose theoretical paradigms of inquiry are leadership researchers and practitioners using?

The perception of followership, like leadership perception, is an outgrowth of people's mental models which come from context-specific philosophical foundations and perceptions.[34] The mental model that governs the Acholi perception of leadership is seamless thinking. It is derived from the philosophical foundation that drives their self-understanding, aspiration, obligation, and well-being.

As discussed in chapter 6, the Acholi people believe that humans are embodied spiritual personal beings located in a specific physical location. This means that they are spiritual beings living in physical bodies in a physical location. Human life comprises the spiritual, personal, social, physical, and ecological selves. In this context, human labor has spiritual, personal, social, physical, and ecological dimensions. At the spiritual dimension, human labor is the process of being and becoming spiritual at personal at social as well as physical and ecological levels. At the physical level, it is the means of sustaining the physical and ecological selves. So human labor is not merely a physical action whose result is measured in merely quantitative and social terms.

In their context, the goal of human labor is measured by its ability to form and reflect human spiritual nature and life through actions and processes that enhance societal harmony and well-being rather than merely the

---

34. Boyacigiller and Alder, "Parochial Dinosaur," 262–90; Den Hartog and Dickson, "Leadership and Culture," 249–78; House, "Leadership in the 21st Century."

material possessions and accomplishments of individuals. In other words, human life and labor are ultimately the consciousness and enactment of one's being through daily life actions pursued in relation to one another. So societal harmony and well-being reflect human spiritual nature and life, and human spiritual nature and life are the basis and goal of societal harmony and well-being. Human actions and relations cannot be understood in isolation from human spiritual nature, life, societal harmony, and well-being.

Thus, among the Acholi people, leadership comprises being, doing, and relating. Doing and relating emanate from being. Whereas being deals with the personhood of people, which includes human nature and capacities, doing deals with the activities people engage in, and relating deals with the structures and processes involved in executing activities. For that matter, leadership is regarded as a participatory process which engages the personhood of everyone in acts of doing and relating toward a common goal. So the emphasis is put on the participation of everyone out of their being in relation to one another. The Acholi understanding is shared by other ethnic groups in Africa. For example, Chiku Malunga stated that, in the indigenous African understanding, leadership is regarded as a participatory process based on human nature toward societal harmony and well-being.[35] In the following quotation, Nelson Mandela gave a practical example of the participatory nature of leadership among the Tembu people of South Africa:

> Everyone who wanted to speak could do so. It was democracy in its purest sense. There may have been a hierarchy of importance amongst the speakers, but everyone was heard ... Only at the end of the meeting as the sun was setting would the regent speak. Its purpose was to sum up what had been said and form some conclusions among the diverse options. But no conclusion was forced on those who disagreed.[36]

For that matter, among the Acholi people and other indigenous African communities like the Tembu people of South Africa, the central focus of leadership is the capacity and structure of participation of everyone rather than unidirectional influence, which is reserved for leaders.

On the other hand, when John Antonakis, et al. reviewed Western leadership literature, they discovered that, in the West, leadership is understood as a process of influence:

> Leadership can be defined as the nature of the influencing process—and its resultant outcomes—that occurs between a leader

---

35. Malunga, *Understanding Organizational Leadership through Ubuntu*.
36. Mandela, *Long Walk to Freedom*, 20.

and followers and how this influencing process is explained by the leader's dispositional characteristics, and behaviors, follower perceptions and attributions of the leader, and the context in which the influencing process occurs.[37]

Their finding is consistent with the findings on the emergence of leadership theories I discussed in chapter 2. According to the findings, the dominant theme among the respective theories centered on the direction of the flow of influence between leaders and followers. In the leader-centric era, the direction of influence was unidirectional from leaders to followers. In the leader-centered era, opinions about the direction of the flow of influence started to shift in favor of reciprocity. In the complexity era, in which active followership was formally accepted, followed by the emergence of followership theory, consensus emerged that the direction of the flow of influence between leaders and followers is reciprocal. So although there were multiple views of leadership like the top-down rational approach represented by Chester I. Barnard,[38] human-relatedness approach represented by Mary Parker Follett,[39] and integrated and value-laden approach represented by Christopher Hodgkinson,[40] Barnard's top-down model dominated leadership theory for over a century. The sudden change in the perception of the direction of the flow of influence between leaders and followers in the West and other regions needed a comprehensive explanation.

So far, in the West, active followership is attributed to technological advancement, globalization,[41] and higher education.[42] This explanation is consistent with the findings from Georgia Sorenson's historical review of leadership that in North America, leadership is driven by psychology, social science, and business management, rather than philosophy.[43] The limited interest in the role of philosophy in leadership studies and practice by Western leadership scholars and practitioners poses a challenge to cross-cultural understanding and the application of leadership and active followership. For example, how have leadership scholars and practitioners been addressing leadership dynamics in contexts other than their own? Second, which

---

37. Antonakis et al., "Leadership," 3–15.
38. Barnard, *Functions of the Executive*.
39. Follett, *Essentials of Leadership*.
40. Hodgkinson, *Philosophy of Leadership*.
41. Fisher-Yoshida and Geller, *Transnational Leadership Development*; Halal and Taylor, *Twenty-first Century Economics*, 218–24; Hitt, "Presidential Address," 7–19.
42. Dixon, "Exploration of the Relationship"; Smith, "Followership Behaviors."
43. Sorenson, "Intellectual History of Leadership Studies."

philosophical foundations, epistemological perceptions, and theoretical paradigms of inquiry are at play?

In the Asian context, the flow of influence between leaders and followers is based on paternalistic reciprocity in which the leader is the fountain of authority, benevolence, and morality, and followers reciprocate with subordinate responses of indebtedness expressed through dependence, compliance, gratitude, and repayment.[44] Like the West, leadership in Asia is understood as a process of influence which is characterized by hierarchical loyalty. Therefore, the perceptions of leadership in Asia and the West have some similarities and differences. For example, whereas the goal of leadership in Asia is geared toward societal harmony and well-being, in the West the goal is personalized at an individual level.[45] Second, like the West, Asia is experiencing a rapid increase in active followership, and this phenomenon is attributed to higher education and modernity.[46] However, whereas for the Asians this is a major issue because the shift represents a departure from their philosophical foundations which govern mental models like Confucianism, in the West the perception is not linked to any philosophical explanation as noted above.[47]

Furthermore, although some Western leadership studies have tried to contrast leadership theories from the West and Asia, studies now show that Asian and Western leadership theories have a lot in common.[48] For example, a study on the relationship between transformational leadership and paternalistic leadership discovered that the main features of paternalistic leadership like "benevolence, authoritarianism and morality" correspond to the main pillars of transformational leadership like "individualized consideration, high performance and modeling."[49] In their conclusion, Cheng et al. observed that the main differences between paternalistic leadership and transformational leadership lie in context and application rather than principle.[50]

However, when I looked at the Asian philosophy of human nature, I discovered it has some similarities with the Acholi culture even though the language and expressions are different. Unlike the Acholi people, Asians

---

44. Cheng et al., "Paternalistic Leadership and Subordinate Responses," 89–117.

45. Cheng et al., "Paternalistic Leadership and Subordinate Responses," 89.

46. Ho and Chiu, "Components of Individualism," 137–56; Yang, "Psychological Transformation of Chinese People," 279–498.

47. Lee, "Chinese Conception of Management."

48. Cheng et al., "Paternalistic Leadership and Subordinate Responses," 89.

49. Cheng et al., "Paternalistic Leadership and Subordinate Responses," 93.

50. Cheng et al., "Paternalistic Leadership and Subordinate Responses," 94.

don't perceive God as a transcendent spiritual personal being over and above humans. Human life is traced to impersonal spirits of heaven and earth—cosmic creative forces. Therefore, humans possess the same intrinsic potential inherent in spirits and for that matter can replicate the heaven and earth of the spirits through the development of culture and morality. However, for humans to do that, they must develop a higher level of mind and intelligence. So "the ultimate goal of life is to strive for self-realization in moral cultural creativity" derived from the internal creative force.[51] The cosmic nature of the common creative force among humans and between humans and the spirits of heaven and earth makes human interconnectedness, societal harmony, and well-being both the basis and goal of doing and relating.

However, despite the perception of human nature discussed above, active followership in Asia is still attributed to education and modernity. Second, like the Acholi culture, the Asian philosophy of human nature gives no justification for condescending relationships because it locates the cosmic creative force in everyone. Therefore, my conclusion here is that the condescending element in human relationships in Asia is contextual rather than ontological. In that case, a change in context (globalization, technological advancement, and higher education) affects the direction of the flow of influence between leaders and followers. The same conclusion on active followership in Asia holds true for active followership in the West. However, a philosophical explanation is needed to avoid the error that created the condescending relationships in leadership.

In Islam, leadership is subordinated under submission to Allah, which covers all human relationships and responsibilities with the sole purpose of bringing out the best in an individual to love God and one's neighbor.[52] Everyone is a vice-regent of Allah. So, leadership in Islam is characterized by participatory followership in the path of righteousness toward human proximity to God and service to one another rather than a position. So like the Acholi people and Africa, Islam situates active followership in the human-divine connection even though it does not stress human-divine nature and life, which are pronounced in the Acholi and African context.

Therefore, whereas active followership is gaining universal acceptance, there is still no consensus on the basis of its source. While the West and Asia trace active followership's source to globalization, technological advancement, and higher education, in Africa its source is attributed to the common human spiritual nature and life. The application of active followership

51. Shun, "Philosophy of Human Nature," 555–58.
52. Mir, "Leadership in Islam," 69–72.

without a comprehensive philosophical justification is going to pose a major challenge for its development and application locally and cross-culturally. Second, active followership poses a challenge in leadership theory and practice because it represents a new paradigm in leadership that current leadership theories don't offer. For example, whereas Asian leadership theory is based on the authority, morality, and benevolence of a leader, all of which are equivalent to the main features that characterize Western leadership theories like transformational and servant leadership, active followership assigns self-care, ownership, and moral obligation to followers.[53]

Second, in active followership according to the Acholi model, the roles (doing and relating) that members of an organization play are based on human common nature and life (being), which makes followers and leaders simultaneously dependent, independent, and interdependent partners. In this context, leadership and followership roles are governed by the principle of complementarity, which is devoid of subjugation, dispossession, negation, or acquiescence. Whereas the current dominant leadership theories justify subjugating structures based on leaders' roles, the emergence of active followership calls for a change in both the perception of the roles followers and leaders play and how the roles play out. For instance, whereas both leaders and followers need support and time to grow, leadership theories like servant leadership have used the necessities of growth and support to justify subjugating structures that subordinate followers under leaders even when we now know that followers who have grown (active followers) are fully empowered like leaders offer support to leaders.

In an era where followers work beyond contractual obligation at their own expense to deliver organizational goals, subjugating structures are hindrances rather than tools of facilitation. Organizations need a comprehensive philosophical construct to develop their theories of leadership and followership that transcend and transform cultural imperatives associated with human transient weaknesses that are used to justify condescending elements in human relationships. The Acholi model of active followership offers a platform for exploring alternative philosophical foundations for leadership and followership theories that reconcile the tensions between human strengths and weaknesses without entrenching condescending tendencies.

Therefore, there is need for establishing the philosophical basis of active followership or how active followership is framed cross-culturally, how active followership is conceptualized and actualized cross-culturally,

---

53. Hirschhorn, "Leaders and Followers," 177–96; Hughes et al., *Leadership*; Kellerman, *Followership*; Rajan and Wulf, "Flattening Firm."

and the theoretical paradigms of inquiry that leadership researchers and practitioners are using to avoid the errors of either imposing one's theoretical biases on others or misrepresenting and misunderstanding one's own culture, or that of others. For example, the Ugandan government developed its narrative of the conflict using the Western concept of civil wars in Africa to win the support of the global community. However, its narrative misrepresented the nature and impact of the conflict. For instance, the government referred to the camps as protected camps when they were in fact internally displaced people's camps. Second, Western communities opposed the Acholi peaceful method of conflict resolution until the Western version, known as transitory justice, was developed. So, Western communities used their own perception of peaceful conflict resolution to support the peaceful process in northern Uganda instead of that of the Acholi people—a practice the Acholi people protest to date.

FURTHER RESEARCH

The participants in this study were drawn from one ethnic group and the research topic focused on an event pertinent to them collectively. It is necessary to explore the perspective of people from other ethnic groups and regions on followership development and enactment. Particularly it would be good to compare the perceptions of people from different ethnic groups within Africa and other regions across the world, especially in this era of multinational corporations which regularly facilitate people movement across their borders of ethnic orientation. Since studies show that people can hold different paradigms, in this era of internationalism people do not only need to understand how others frame reality and perceive leadership and followership, but also need to have the capacity to understand reality from different paradigms as well as use different theoretical perspectives to understand how these realities work in different contexts. It would also shed more light on the basis of passive followership if we got the perspectives of government officials and organization owners other than leaders who expect passive followership from followers. Also, we need to find out how people who exemplify passive and toxic followership develop their perspectives and find out their effectiveness.

It would also help to find out if people hold the same view when they step out of their social context. For example, do the Acholi people uphold active followership in their places of work outside of the Acholi subregion, where there is no strong collective social accountability? This would shed light on Robert Kelley's suggestion that active followership varies according to the intensity of the issues people are dealing with. How does it apply where there is disagreement among followers? For example, are there times when active followers choose passive followership over active followership?

This study focused on a case of active followership involving bad leadership and therefore it did not focus on how it works in a setting where good leadership exists. We need a separate study, in an atmosphere of good leadership and where active followership is the normative behavior, to show how it works. For example, there is a need for an ethnographic study of active followership in Acholiland to understand its dynamics in an atmosphere of good leadership. I focused on active followership by intervention, but the other forms of active followership did not feature. For example, when do followers need to stand down for leaders in obedience, and how do they do it without creating subjugating tendencies? Or how do followers stand up for and with leaders without undermining leadership roles and positions? The current followership studies are conducted in organizations where active followership is still marginal.

There is also a need for understanding the prevailing conditions in organizations that want to develop active followership. What philosophical foundations and perceptions of leadership and followership do they hold, and how do they play out in their organization? This will work as an entry point; otherwise adopting active followership without adequate information on the prevailing system may end up creating change by conformation to organizational cultures without transformation. This is particularly relevant in organizations like churches that aim for personal transformation. The knowledge of the existing perceptions and structures creates a long-lasting impact. These studies will enable researchers to know whose theoretical paradigm of enquiry they are using, and to enhance their capacity to develop appropriate paradigms for each context so as to avoid the dangers of imposing their own paradigms or misunderstanding and misrepresenting other paradigms.

APPLICATION: THE POWER OF ACTIVE FOLLOWERSHIP

Whereas active followership has been part and parcel of leadership, leadership theorists and practitioners attributed it to leadership qualities, characterized it as insubordination, or just ignored it for over a century. However, since the advent of the information era, the demand for active followership has been gaining an upper hand even in regions like Asia[54] and Russia,[55] that were thought to favor passive followership because of their culture of a high-power distance based on Hofstede's 1982 findings.[56] Unfortunately, the increasing demand for active followership has not been matched with followership development because for two decades since the inception of followership theory, theorists focused on establishing the theory as a distinct academic discipline rather than establishing active followers. Thus, the demand for active followership is acute.

Furthermore, the active followership of the Acholi people presents a theoretical challenge of the importance of understanding the philosophical foundation underpinning leadership theories and the theoretical paradigms of inquiry, which are always context specific. The response to this challenge will pave the way for developing alternative theoretical paradigms of enquiry appropriate for respective contexts. This will mitigate the limitations of the dominant tendencies of using a theoretical construct developed within a specific cultural context to conduct studies in other contexts or to develop theories for other cultures. The findings from this study have far-reaching implications for leaders, individuals, communities, and organizations in equal measures. The Acholi people overcame one of the worst forms of bad leadership and callous regimes in Africa, using the power of their human identity and dignity rather than countering brutal power with brutal power. Oppressed by their own government and abandoned by the international community, the Acholi people sought refuge in their own culture, out of which they developed a counternarrative of the conflict that they used to persuade an uncaring government and a skeptical international community to adopt a peaceful approach to resolving the conflict that sought to subjugate them into passive followers. Therefore, the Acholi model of active followership has some practical applications for leaders, followers, organizations, and communities that face challenges like extinction, change and growth, toxic leadership and followership, and breaking new frontiers. In the following section, I will discuss these implications.

The Church

Paul Hiebert discovered that there is a gap in Western thinking which has created a hole in their perception and application of the gospel.[57] This asser-

---

54. Cheng et al., "Paternalistic Leadership and Subordinate Responses," 89.
55. Tolstikov-Mast, "Followership in Russia," 100–10.
56. Hofstede, *Cultures and Organizations*.
57. Stearns, *Hole in Our Gospel*.

tion was affirmed by the framers of the Lausanne Covenant, that Christians "have sometimes pursued church growth at the expense of church depth, and divorced evangelism from Christian nurture,"[58] and Christian nurture from socioeconomic transformation.[59] Thus, the church is clamoring for a discipleship model that empowers the body of Christ beyond leaders, and a leadership model that acknowledges the complementary role of followers beyond the four walls of the church[60] to "mobilize and equip the whole church to take the whole Gospel to the whole world."[61] The Acholi mental model of seamless thinking offers a tool kit that the church can use to dissolve the dichotomous tendencies that have compartmentalized human thinking and behaviors, and thus regain its unique nature, voice, and place in order to fulfill its purpose on earth. Otherwise, efforts toward mobilizing and equipping the whole church to take the whole gospel to the whole world will remain a dream.

Africa

Over three decades ago, Chinua Achebe observed that a crisis of poor leadership is the foremost challenge of Africa, which accelerated leadership development programs across sectors as a panacea.[62] However, according to the Acholi model, Africa's foremost challenge is poor leadership theory, which casts a larger-than-life image of leaders in the minds of leaders and followers, rather than merely poor leadership. Consequently, leaders act as benefactors and followers as beneficiaries. This theory stifled the efforts toward the development and optimization of Africa's potential to relate to God, each other, nature, and the rest of humanity as a co-creator rather than a beneficiary.[63] Hence, African scholars and the educated elite could use insights from this study to inform their demand for active followership, and to overcome the challenges of poor leadership theory and leadership failures so they can unleash Africa's potential.

---

58. Stott, "Education and Leadership," 1; Hanciles, "Conversion and Social Change," 157–80.
59. Ntamushobora, "From Transmission to Transformation."
60. Allen, *Future Church*.
61. Stott, "Education and Leadership," 1; Allen, *Future Church*.
62. Achebe, *Trouble With Nigeria*.
63. Ogbonna, "Followership Imperative of Good Governance," 65–80.

ORGANIZATIONS IN GENERAL

In the early 1980s, when organizations encountered abrupt changes which required new paradigms, skills, and structures, they discovered that the structures they had relied on for years were ineffective because they were created for a context which had ceased to exist without their knowledge. So organizations need living cultures to leverage the challenge of continuous and discontinuous changes, which have become so rampant in the era of globalization, technological advancement, and skilled workers. Whether an organization needs a change in the of course of direction, or is breaking new frontiers or facing extinction, the Acholi model offers one of the tool kits organizations need in their quivers in order to achieve their goals.

Leaders, like followers, are human beings full of strengths and weaknesses. The bad news is that the image of leaders as larger-than-life individuals that developed the hope of a new world, especially in Africa, has turned out to be a mere illusion.[64] The truth of the matter is that there are bad leaders and good leaders just as there are bad followers and good followers. Furthermore, leadership theories and practitioners have discovered that both good leaders and good followers are both born and made. For that matter, good leaders need good followers, and vice versa. The case of Acholi active followership offers a model of good followers who know when to stand down for a leader, when to stand up for and with a leader, and when to stand up to a leader without going against them or organizational goals. In this era, when organizations have discovered that they cannot move forward with workers who cannot go the extra mile beyond contractual obligations and existing structures to cope with the challenges of toxic leadership and rapid continuous and discontinuous changes, the Acholi leadership construct, which supports active followership, is a gold mine for leaders who want good followers, followers who want good leaders, and organizations that want to build living cultures.

SUMMARY

This study demonstrated that followers develop active followership out of the consciousness of and commitment to human dignity, which emanates from the interaction between root factors and fruit actions in the context of daily life encounters, using a comprehensive understanding of the stimulus at hand. Such endeavors call for ascertaining the philosophical foundations

---

64. Oloka-Onyango, "'New-Breed' Leadership, Conflict," 29–52.

used to frame the issue at hand, the perception, and theoretical paradigm of enquiry at play.

Theoretically, active followers have been examined from individualistic and dichotomous standpoints as a segment of followers among other categories of followers in organizations. For that matter, followership studies are preoccupied with actual followership identities, roles, and behaviors, rather than the ideal attributes followers ought to have in an organization, especially following the emergence of the information era which demands active followership throughout the organization. Thus, organizations need to make active followership the normative followership identity, role, and behavior. This requires a seamless mental model and structures to create an enabling environment for its development and enactment. The Acholi followership is a good model for organizations that want to make active followership the normative behavior of their followers.

Appendix A
Demographic Data on Participants

Pseudonyms	Gender	Age Range	Education*	Group
BA	F	55–60	Master	MP
OJ	M	45–50	Master	MP
OR1	M	45–50	Master	MP
KL	M	45–50	Master	NGO
OM1	M	45–50	Master	NGO
OO1	M	40–45	Master	MP
OL	M	60–65	PhD	Elder/cultural
OW1	M	45–50	Master	Religious
BL	M	75–80	Master	Rebels
OR2	F	70–75	Master	NGO
OO2	M	85–90	PhD	Elder
OA1	M	50–55	Bachelor	Press
AY	M	70–75	Bachelor	Cultural
ZA	M	45–50	Master	Diaspora
OW2	M	50–55	Bachelor	Press
LB	M	50–55	Master	Press
LA	F	60–65	Bachelor	Women
MS	M	50–55	Master	Religious
ON	M	40–50	Bachelor	Press
KS	M	45–50	Master	Rebels
OO3	M	70–75	Master	Religious
JI	F	35–45	Master	NGO
ML	F	55–60	Bachelor	Women

Pseudonyms	Gender	Age Range	Education*	Group
AA	M	80–85	Master	Elder
OA2	M	80–85	PhD	Religious
OG1	M	50–55	Master	Cultural
OM2	M	60–65	PhD	Religious
FO	M	50–55	PhD	Religious
AM	M	100–105	Bachelor	Elder
OB	M	80–85	Master	Religious
OO4	M	80–85	Master	MP
OF	M	50–55	PHD	NGO
OO5	M	60–65	PHD	NGO
MN	M	50–55	Master	MP
AR	M	50–55	Master	Cultural
KK	M	45–50	PhD	NGO
JS	M	50–55	Master	Diaspora
OO6	M	50–55	PhD	Diaspora
OG2	M	50–55	Master	Press

Note. **MP=Member of Parliament; NGO=Member of a nongovernment organization; Rebels= LRA member; Cultural= Cultural leader**

*Highest educational degree obtained

Appendix B
Interview Guide

1. Thinking about the northern Ugandan conflict, may you please describe the issues which were at stake that influenced your decision to participate in the conflict resolution process?
2. Thinking about your role in the northern Ugandan conflict resolution process in relation to the position and approaches of the Ugandan government to the conflict, in what specific ways did you find yourself engaging more in independent or dependent-type orientations and behaviors?
3. Please, may you describe the factors that informed and influenced your orientation, role, and behavior in relation to the Ugandan government's policy and approaches toward the conflict?
4. Would you please describe the specific ways in which you responded to the Ugandan government policy and approaches to the conflict?
5. Would you please describe what you experienced because of the independent or dependent orientation and role you adopted in response to the Ugandan government policy and approaches to the conflict?
6. Would you please describe how long it took you to make the decision to respond to the Ugandan government policy and approaches to the conflict?
7. Would you please describe how you decided, organized, and executed your independent or dependent-type response to the Ugandan government policy and approaches to the conflict?
8. Is there something else you would like to add that we have not covered?

Bibliography

Aboukhalil, Robert. "The Rising Trend in Authorship." https://thewinnower.com/papers/the-rising-trend-in-authorship.

Abrahamsen, Rita. *Disciplining Democracy: Development Discourse and Good Governance in Africa*. London: Zed, 2000.

Abudu, Francis. "Work Attitudes of Africans, with Special Reference to Nigeria." *International Studies of Management and Organization* 16.2 (1986) 17–36.

Achebe, Chinua. *The Trouble With Nigeria*. London: Heinemann Educational, 1984.

Acholi Religious Leaders Peace Initiative. *Let My People Go: An Assessment Carried Out by the Acholi Religious Leaders Peace Initiative and the Justice and Peace Commission of Gulu Archdiocese*. Gulu, Uganda: Peace Commission of Gulu Archdiocese, 2001.

Adupa, Cyprian Ben. "Conflict Continuous: The Historical Context for the Northern Uganda Conflict." PhD diss., Indiana University, 2006.

Adyanga, Onek C. "Modes of British Imperial Control of Africa: A Case Study of Uganda, C 1890–1990." PhD diss., University of Connecticut, 2009.

———. *Modes of British Imperial Control of Africa: A Case Study of Uganda, C.1890–1990*. Newcastle-upon-Tyne, UK: Cambridge Scholars, 2011.

Afako, Barney. *Northern Uganda: Justice in Conflict*. London: African Rights, 2000.

Agho, Augustine. O. "Perspectives of Senior-level Executives on Effective Followership and Leadership." *Journal of Leadership and Organizational Studies* 6.2 (2009) 159–66.

Ajulu, Deborah. *Holism in Development: An African Perspective on Empowering Communities*. Monrovia, CA: MARC, 2001.

Alcoff, Linda M. "Objectivity and Its Politics." *New Literary History* 32.4 (2001) 835–48.

Alcorn, David S. "Dynamic Followership: Empowerment at Work." *Leadership and Organizations Development Journal* 33.1 (1992) 9–33.

Alford, Fred C. "Whistleblowing as Responsible Followership." In *The Art of Followership: How Great Followers Create Great Leaders and Organizations*, edited by Ronald E. Riggio et al., 237–51. San Francisco: Jossey-Bass, 2008.

Allen, John L. *The Future Church: How Ten Trends are Revolutionizing the Catholic Church*. New York: Doubleday, 2009.

Allen, Louise A. *Management and Organization*. New York: McGraw-Hill, 1958.

Allen, Tim. *Trial Justice: The International Criminal Court and the Lord's Resistance Army*. London: Zed, 2006.

Angucia, Margaret. "Children and War in Africa: The Crisis Continues in Northern Uganda." *International Journal on World Peace* 26.3 (2009) 77–95.
Antonakis, John, et al. "Leadership: Past, Present and Future." In *The Nature of Leadership*, edited by John Antonakis, et al., 3–15. Thousand Oaks, CA: Sage, 2004.
Arend, Anthony Clark, et al. *Human Dignity and the Future of Global Institutions*. Washington, DC: Georgetown University Press, 2014.
Ashby, William Ross. *Design for a Brain: The Origin of Adaptive Behavior*. New York: Wiley, 1960.
Ashforth, Blake E. "The Experience of Powerlessness in Organizations." *Organizational Behavior & Human Decision Processes* 43.2 (1989) 207–42.
Associated Press. "Northern Uganda 'World's Biggest Neglected Crisis.'" *The Guardian*. October 22, 2004. http://www.guardian.co.uk/world/2004/oct/22/2.
Atkinson, Ronald Raymond. "The Evolution of Ethnicity among the Acholi of Uganda: The Precolonial Phase." *Ethnohistory* 36.1 (1989) 19-43.
———. *The Roots of Ethnicity: The Origins of the Acholi of Uganda before 1800*. Philadelphia: University of Pennsylvania Press, 1994.
Avolio, Bruce J., and Rebecca J. Reichard. "The Rise of Authentic Followership." In *The Art of Followership: How Great Followers Create Great Leaders and Organizations*, edited by Ronald E. Riggio et al., 325–37. San Francisco: Jossey-Bass, 2008.
Azar, Edward. E. "The Analysis and Management of Protracted Social Conflict." In *The Psychodynamics of International Relationships*, edited by Vamik D. Volkan et al., 109–26. Lexington, MA: Lexington, 1990.
Baines, Erin. "Accountability, Reconciliation and the Juba Peace Talks Beyond the Impasse." *Field Notes* 3 (October 2006) 1–10.
———. "The Peace Process in Northern Uganda." Liu Institute for Global Issues. http://epe.lac-bac.gc.ca/100/200/300/liu_institute/peace_process_north_uganda.pdf
Baker, Susan D. "Followership: The Theoretical Foundation of a Contemporary Construct." *Journal of Leadership & Organizational Studies* 14.1 (2007) 50–60.
Baker, Susan D., et al. "The Fluid Nature of Follower and Leader Roles." In *Followership: What is it and do People Follow?*, edited by Laurent Lapierre and Melissa K. Carsten, 73–88. London: Emerald Group, 2014.
Barge, Kevin J. "Pivotal Leadership and the Art of Conversation." *Leadership Quarterly* 10.1 (2014) 56–78.
Barnard, Chester I. *The Functions of the Executive*. Cambridge, MA: Harvard University Press, 1938.
———. "The Theory of Authority." In *The Great Writings in Management and Organizational Behavior*, edited by Louis E. Boone and Donald D. Bowen, 92–104. New York: McGraw-Hill, 1987.
Barrs, Jerram. *Shepherds and Sheep: A Biblical View of Leading and Following*. Downers Grove, IL: InterVarsity, 1983.
Barth, Fredrik. "Ethnic Groups and Boundaries: The Social Organization of Culture Difference" In *Ethnicity*, edited by John Hutchinson and Anthony J. Smith, 9–37. Oxford: Oxford University Press, 1996.
Bass, Bernard M. *Bass and Stogdill's Handbook of Leadership*. New York: Free Press, 1990.
———. *Leadership and Performance Beyond Expectations*. New York: Free Press, 1985.
Bass, Bernard M., and George Barrett. *People, Work, and Organizations: An Introduction to Industrial and Organizational Psychology*. Boston: Allyn & Bacon, 1981.

Bass, Bernard M., and Ruth Bass. *The Bass Handbook of Leadership: Theory, Research, and Managerial Applications*. New York: Free Press, 2008.

Bass, Bernard M., and Ronald E. Riggio. *Transformational Leadership*. Mahwah, NJ: Lawrence Erlbaum, 2006.

Baum, Jennifer. "Competing in the 21st Century: Globalization Is Shaping the Way We Do Business." https://www.thefreelibrary.com/Competing+in+the+21st+century%3b+Globalization+is+shaping+the+way+we+do...-a0183650545

Bayart, Jean-Franqois "Civil Society in Africa." In *Political Domination in Africa*, edited by Patrick Chabal, 118-132 Cambridge: Cambridge University Press, 1986.

Behrend, Heike. *Alice Lakwena and the Holy Spirit: War in Northern Uganda, 1985-97*. Kampala, Uganda: Fountain, 1999.

Bennis, Warren. "The Art of Followership: Great Followers Create Great Leaders." *Leadership Excellence* 25.4 (2008) 4-12.

———. *Managing the Dream: Reflection on Leadership and Change*. New York: Perseus, 2000.

Berg, David N. "Resurrecting the Muse: Followership in Organizations." In *The Psychodynamics of Leadership*, edited by Edward B. Klein et al., 27-52. Madison, CT: Psychosocial, 1998.

Berger, Peter L., et al. *The Homeless Mind: Modernization and Consciousness*. New York: Random House, 1981.

Bernard, Luther Lee. *An Introduction to Social Psychology*. New York: Holt, 1926.

Bettis, Richard A., and Michael A. Hitt, "The New Competitive Landscape." *Strategic Management Journal* 17.13 (1995) 7-19. doi:10.1002/smj.4250160915.

Bettis, Richard A., and C. K. Prahalad. "The Dominant Logic: Retrospective and Extension." *Strategic Management Journal* 16.1 (1995) 5-14.

Bjugstad, Kent., et al. "A Fresh Look at Followership: A Model for Matching Followership and Leadership Styles." *Journal of Behavioral & Applied Management* 7.3 (2006) 304-19.

Bligh, Michelle C., et al. "Charting the Language of Leadership: A Methodological Investigation of President Bush and the Crisis of 9/11." *Journal of Applied Psychology* 89.3 (2011) 562-74.

Bloch-Hoell, Nils E. "African Identity: European Invention or Genuine African Character?" *Mission Studies* 9.1 (1992) 98-107.

Boisot, Max H. *Knowledge Assets: Securing Competitive Advantage in the Information Economy*. Oxford: Oxford University Press, 1998.

Bolino, Mark C. "Citizenship and Impression Management: Good Soldiers or Good Actors?" *Academy of Management Review* 24 (1999) 82-98.

Boyacigiller, Nakiye A., and Nancy J. Alder. "The Parochial Dinosaur: Organizational Science in a Global Context." *Academy of Management Review* 16.2 (1991) 262-90.

Boyett, Joseph H., and Henry P. Conn. *Workplace 2000: The Revolution Reshaping American Business*. New York: Dutton, 1991.

Bradbury, Hilary, and Benyamin M. B. Lichtenstein. "Relationality in Organizational Research: Exploring the Space Between." *Organization Science* 11 (2000) 551-64.

Branch, Adam. "The Political Dilemmas of Global Justice: Anti-civilian Violence and the Violence of Humanitarianism, the Case of Northern Uganda." PhD diss., Columbia University, 2007.

Brown, Arnold. "The New Followership: A Challenge for Leaders." *Futurist* 37.2 (2003) 68-75.

Brown, D. Andrew, and W. T. Thornborrow. "Do Organizations Get the Followers they Deserve?" *Leadership & Organization Development Journal* 17.1 (1996) 5–15.

Brown, James A. C. *The Social Psychology of Industry: Human Relations in the Factory.* Harmondsworth, UK: Penguin, 1954.

Bufford, Rodger K. *The Human Reflex: Behavioral Psychology in Biblical Perspective.* San Francisco: Harper & Row, 1981.

Buganda Kingdom. "The Uganda Agreement of 1900." http://www.buganda.com/buga1900.htm

Buijs, Gina. "Arms to Fight, Arms to Protect: Women Speak Out About Conflict." *DISASTERS* 20.2 (1996) 160–65.

Burger, Jerry M. "Replicating Milgram: Would People Still Obey Today?" *American Psychologist* 64.1 (2009) 1–11.

Burkirtt, Ian. *Social Selves: Theories of Social Formation of Personality.* London: Sage, 1991.

Burns, James M. *Leadership.* New York: Harper & Row, 1978.

———. "The Structure of Moral Leadership." In *Corporate Ethics and Corporate Governance*, edited by Walther C. Zimmerli et al., 87–94. Berlin: Springer, 2007.

Burns, James M., et al. *Encyclopedia of Leadership.* Thousand Oaks, CA: Sage, 2004.

Caesar, Felix A. "The Impact of Followership as Related to Leadership on Organization Performance in a Canadian Chartered Bank." PhD diss., University Microfilms International, 1998.

Carlyle, Thomas. *On Heroes, Hero-Worship and the Heroic in History.* London: Chapman & Hall, 1888.

Carsten, Melissa K., and Mary Uhl-Bien. "Ethical Followership: An Examination of Followership Beliefs and Crimes of Obedience." *Journal of Leadership and Organizational Studies* 20.1 (2013) 49–61.

———. "Follower Beliefs in Co-production of Leadership: Examining Upward Communication and the Moderating Role of Context." *Zeitschrift für Psychologie* 22.4 (2012) 210–20.

Carsten, Melissa K., et al. "Exploring Social Constructions of Followership: A Qualitative Study." *The Leadership Quarterly* 21 (2010) 543–62. doi:10.1016/j.leaqua.2010.03.015.

Carsten, Melissa K., et al. "Reversing the Lens in Leadership Research: Investigating Follower Role Orientation and Leadership Outcomes." Paper presented at the Southern Management Association Annual Meeting, New Orleans, LA, December 2013.

Chai, David H. "Leading as Followers: A Followership Study of the Korean Congregational Leadership of the Presbyterian Church (U.S.A.)." PhD diss., Spalding University, 2010.

Chaleff, Ira. *The Courageous Follower: Standing Up to and for Our Leaders.* San Francisco: Berrett-Koehler, 1995.

———. *The Courageous Follower: Standing Up to and for Our Leaders.* 2nd. ed. San Francisco: Berrett-Koehler, 2003.

———. "Creating New Ways of Following." In *The Art of Followership: How Great Followers Create Great Leaders and Organizations*, edited by Ronald E. Riggio et al., 67–88. San Francisco: Jossey-Bass, 2008.

Chan, David K. "The Concept of Human Dignity in the Ethics of Genetic Research." *Bioethics* 9.4 (2015) 274–82.

Charmaz, Kathy. *Constructing Grounded Theory: A Practical Guide through Qualitative Analysis*. Thousand Oaks, CA: Sage, 2006.
Cheng, Bor-Shiuan., et al. "Paternalistic Leadership and Subordinate Responses: Establishing a Leadership Model in Chinese Organizations." *Asian Journal of Social Psychology* 7.1 (2004) 89–117.
Child, John. *Industrial Relations in the British Printing Industry: The Quest for Security*. London: Allen & Unwin, 1967.
Cilliers, Paul. "Boundaries, Hierarchies and Networks in Complex Systems." *International Journal of Innovation Management* 5.2 (2001) 135–47.
———. *Complexity and Postmodernism: Understanding Complex Systems*. London: Routledge, 2002.
Ciulla, Joanne. *The Ethics of Leadership*. Belmont, CA: Thompson Wadsworth, 2003.
Civil Society Organisations for Peace in Northern Uganda. "Counting the Cost: Twenty Years of War in Northern Uganda." https://www.oxfam.org/sites/www.oxfam.org/files/uganda.pdf.
Clinton, J. Robert. *Leadership Emergence Theory: A Self-Study Manual for Analyzing the Development of a Christian Leader*. Altadena, CA: Barnabas Resources, 1989.
———. *A Short History of Modern Leadership Theory*. Leadership Series. Altadena, CA: Barnabas, 1992.
Collier, Paul, and the World Bank. *Economic Causes of Civil Conflict and Their Implications for Policy*. Washington, DC: World Bank, 2000.
Collins, James C., and Jerry I. Porras. *Built to Last: Successful Habits of Visionary Companies*. 1st ed. New York: Harper Business, 1994.
Collinson, David. "Dichotomies, Dialectics and Dilemmas: New Directions for Critical Leadership Studies?" *Leadership* 10.1 (2014) 36–55.
———. "Rethinking Followership: A Post-structuralist Analysis of Follower Identities." *The Leadership Quarterly* 17.2 (2006) 179–89.
Courtright, John A., et al. "Interaction Patterns in Organic and Mechanistic Systems." *The Academy of Management Journal* 32.4 (1989) 773–802.
Creswell, John W. *Qualitative Inquiry and Research Design: Choosing among Five Approaches*. Thousand Oaks, CA: Sage, 2013.
Creswell, John W., and Vicki. L. Plano. *Designing and Conducting Mixed Methods Research*. Los Angeles: Sage., 2011.
Cross, Robert L., and Andrew Parker. *The Hidden Power of Social Networks: Understanding how Work Really Gets Done*. Boston: Harvard Business School, 2004.
Crossman, Brian, and Joanna. Crossman. "Conceptualizing Followership: A Review of the Literature." *Leadership* 7.4 (2011) 481–97.
Crotty, Michael. *The Foundations of Social Research: Meaning and Perspective in the Research Process*. Los Angeles: Sage, 1998.
Dale, Robert D.. (1987). "Leadership-followership: The Church's Challenge." *Southwestern Journal of Theology* 29.2 (1987) 23–28.
Dansereau, Fred, et al. "Vertical Dyad Linkage Approach to Leadership Within Formal Organizations: A Longtitudinal Investigation of the Role Making Process." *Organizational Behavior and Human Performance* 13.1 (1975) 46–78.
Davis, Louse. E., and Gerald. J. Wacker. "Job Design." In *Handbook of Human Factor*, edited by G Salvendy, 431–94. New York: Wiley, 1987.

De Cremer, David, and Eric Van Dijk. "When and Why Leaders Put Themselves First: Leader Behavior in Resource Allocations as a Function of Feeling Entitled." *European Journal of Social Psychology* 35.4 (2005) 553–63.

Den Hartog, Deanne N., and Marcus W. Dickson. "Leadership and Culture." In *The Nature of Leadership*, edited by John Antonakis et al., 249–78. 3rd ed. Thousand Oaks, CA: Sage, 2004.

Densten, Iain. L., and Judy H. Gray. "The Links between Followership and the Experiential Learning Model: Followership Coming of Age." *Journal of Leadership & Organizational Studies* 8.1 (2001) 69–76.

DePree, Max. *Leadership Jazz*. New York: Doubleday, 1992.

———. "The Leadership Quest: Three Things Necessary." *Business Strategy Review* 4.1 (1993) 69–74.

DeRue, Scott D., and Ashford, Susan J. "Who Will Lead and Who Will Follow? A Social Process of Leadership Identity Construction in Organizations." *Academy of Management Review* 35.4 (2010) 627–47.

De Vreis, Reinout E., and Jean-Louis Van Gelder. "Leadership and the Need for Leadership: Testing an Implicit Followership Theory." In *Implicit Leadership Theories: Essays and Explorations*, edited by Birgit Schyns and James R. Meindl, 277–304. Greenwich, CT: Information Age, 2005.

Dinh, Jessica E., and Robert G. Lord. "Implications of Dispositional and Process Views of Traits for Individual Difference Research in Leadership." *The Leadership Quarterly* 23.4 (2012) 651–69.

Dixon, Eugene N. "An Exploration of the Relationship of Organizational Level and Measures of Follower Behaviors." PhD diss., The University of Alabama in Huntsville, 2003.

Dixon, Gene and Jerry Westbrook. "Followers Revealed." *Engineering Management Journal* 15.1 (2003) 19–25.

Dolan, Chris. *Social Torture: The Case of Northern Uganda, 1986–2006*. New York: Berghahn, 2011.

Doom, Ruddy, and Koen Vlassenroot. "Kony's Message: A New 'Koine'?: The Lord's Resistance Army in Northern Uganda." *African Affairs* 98.390 (1999) 5–36.

Dvir, Taly, and Boas Shamir. "Follower Development Characteristics as Predicting Transformational Leadership: A Longtitudinal Field Study. *The Leadership Quarterly* 14.3 (2003) 327–44.

Dwyer, John Orr. "The Acholi of Uganda: Adjustment to Imperialism." PhD Diss., Columbia University, 1973.

Eden, Dov, and Uri I. Leviatan. "Implicit Leadership Theory as a Determinant of the Factor Structure Underlying Supervisory Behavior Scales." *Journal of Applied Psychology* 60.6 (1975) 736–41.

Epitropaki, Olga, and Robin Martin. "Implicit Leadership Theories in Applied Settings: Factor Structure, Generalizability and Stability Over Time." *Journal of Applied Psychology* 89.2 (2004) 293–310.

Eriku, James, and Jimmy Kwo. "Museveni Apologizes for Army Atrocities." *Daily Monitor*, 10/26/2012. https://www.monitor.co.ug/News/National/Museveni-apologises-for-army-atrocities/688334-1598436-bvp856/index.html.

Erlandson, David A., et al. *Doing Naturalistic Inquiry: A Guide to Methods*. Newbury Park, CA: Sage 1993.

Fairhurst, Gail T. *Dualisms in Leadership Research*. Thousand Oaks, CA: Sage, 2001.

———. *The Power of Framing: Creating the Language of Leadership*. San Francisco: Jossey-Bass, 2011.
Fairhurst Gail T., and David Grant. "The Social Construction of Leadership: A Sailing Guide." *Management Communication Quarterly* 24.2 (2010) 171–210.
Fairhurst, Gail T., and Mary Uhl-Bien. "Organizational Discourse Analysis (ODA) Examining Leadership as a Relational Process." *The Leadership Quarterly*, 23.6 (2012) 1043–62. http://dx.doi.org/10.1016/j.leaqua.2012.10.005.
Fairhurst, Gail T., et al. "Inertial Forces and the Implementation of a Socio-Technical Systems Approach: A Communication Study." *Organization Science* 6.2 (1995) 168–85.
Fairhurst, Gail T., et al. "Manager-subordinate Control Patterns and Judgments about the Relationship." In *Communication Yearbook 10*, edited by Margaret L. McLaughlin, 395–415. Newbury Park, CA: Sage, 1987.
Fiechter, Jean-Rodolphe W. "The Role of Traditional Justice in Uganda, Given Rwanda's Experience of Gacaca." http://works.bepress.com/jean_rodolphe_fiechter/2.
Fielder, Fred Edward. *A Theory of Leadership Effectiveness*. New York: McGraw-Hill, 1967.
Finnegan, Amy C. "Forging Forgiveness: Collective Efforts Amidst War in Northern Uganda." *Sociological Inquiry* 80.3 (2010) 424–47.
Finnström, Sverker. *Living with Bad Surroundings: War, History, and Everyday Moments in Northern Uganda*. Durham, NC: Duke University Press, 2008.
———. "Wars of the Past and War in the Present: The Lord's Resistance Movement/ Army in Uganda. Africa." *Journal of the International African Institute Africa* 76.2 (2006) 200–20.
Fisher-Yoshida, Beth, and Kathy Dee Geller. *Transnational Leadership Development: Preparing the Next Generation for the Borderless Business World*. The Adult Learning Theory and Practice Book Series. New York: AMACOM, 2009.
Fiske, Alan P., and Nick Haslam. "Social Cognition is Thinking about Relationships." *Current Directions in Psychological Science* 5.5 (1996) 143–48. doi:10.1111/1467-8721.ep11512349.
Fiske, Susan T., and Shelley E. Taylor. *Social Cognition: From Brain to Culture*. New York: McGraw-Hill, 1991.
Follett, Mary P. *The Essentials of Leadership*. London: Management Publication Trust, 1949.
———. "Leader and Expert." In *The Psychological Foundations of Management*, edited by Henry C. Metcalf, 220–43. Chicago: Shaw, 1927.
———. "Management as a Profession." In *Classics in Management*, edited by Harwood F. Merrill, 1–17. New York: American Management Association, 1960.
Foss, Sonja K., and William J. C. Waters. *Destination Dissertation: A Traveler's Guide to a Done Dissertation*. Lanham, MD: Rowman & Littlefield, 2007.
Foucault, Michel. *Discipline and Punish: The Birth of the Prison*. London: Allen Unwin, 1977.
Frese, Michael, and Doris Fay. "Personal Initiative: An Active Performance Concept for Work in the 21st Century." *Research in Organizational Behavior* 23 (2001) 133–87.
Frew, David R. "Leadership and Followership." *Personnel Journal* 56 (1977) 90–97.
Friedman, Thomas L. *The World Is Flat: A Brief History of the Twenty-First Century*. New York: Farrar, Straus and Giroux, 2006.

Frye, Joshua, et al. "Embracing Spiritual Followership." *Communication Studies* 58.3 (2007) 243–60.

Galton, Francis. *English Men of Science: Their Nature and Nurture.* London: Cass, 1883.

———. *Hereditary Genius: An Inquiry into Its Laws and Consequences.* Cleveland: Meridian, 1900.

Gardiner, Alfred G. *The Life of Sir William Harcourt, Vol. II.* London: Constable & Company, 1923.

Gardner, Howard. *Changing Minds: The Art and Science of Changing Our Own and Other Peoples Minds.* Boston: Harvard Business School, 2006.

———. *Leading Minds.* London: Harper Collins, 1996.

Gardner, William L., et al. "Can You See the Real Me? A Self-Based Model of Authentic Leader and Follower Development." *The Leadership Quarterly* 16.3 (2005) 343–72.

Gass, William H. "Kind of Killing-the Flourishing Evil of the Third Reich." *Harper's Magazine* 45.3 (2009) 75–82.

Gentner, Dedre, and Albert L. Stevens. *Mental Models.* Hillsdale, NJ: Erlbaum, 1983.

Ghai, Dharam. "Participatory Development: Some Perspectives from Grassroots Experiences." *Journal of Development Planning* 19 (1989) 79–115.

Giddens, Anthony. *The Constitution of Society: Outline of the Theory of Structuration.* Berkeley: University of California Press, 1984.

Gilbert, G. Ronald. "Building Highly Productive Work Teams through Positive Leadership." *Public Personnel Management* 14 (1985) 449–54.

Gilbert, G. Ronald, and Albert C. Hyde. "Followership and the Federal Worker." *Public Administration Review* 48.6 (1988) 962–68.

Gioia, Dennis A. "From Individual to Organizational Identity." In *Identity in Organizations: Building Theory through Conversations*, edited by David A. Whetten and Paul C. Godfrey, 17–32. Thousand Oaks, CA: Sage, 1998.

Girling, Frank K. *The Acholi of Uganda.* London: Lit Verlag, 1960.

Gitari, David. "The Claims of Jesus in the African Context." *International Review of Missions* 71 (1982) 12-19

Glaser, Barney. G. *Theoretical Sensitivity: Advances in the Methodology of Grounded Theory.* Mill Valley, CA: Sociology, 1978.

Goffee, Rob, and Gareth Jones. "The Art of Followership." *European Business Forum* 25.5 (2006) 22–26.

Gordon, Gregory S. "Complementarity and Alternative Justice." *Oregon Law Review* 88.3 (2009) 621–702.

Graen, George B., and Mary Uhl-Bien. Relationship-based Approach to Leadership: Development of Leader-member Exchange (LMX) Theory of Leadership Over 25 Years: Applying a Multi-level, Multi-domain Perspective." *Leadership Quarterly* 6.2 (1995) 219–47.

Graen, George B., and Terri. A. Scandura. "Toward a Psychology of Dyadic Organizing." *Research in Organizational Behavior* 9 (1987) 175–208.

Graen, George B., et al. "Effects of Leader-member Exchange and Job Design on Productivity and Satisfaction: Testing a Dual Attachment Model." *Organizational Behavior and Human Performance* 30.1 (1982) 109–31.

Graham, Jill W. "Chapter 3 Commentary: Transformational Leadership: Fostering Follower Autonomy, Not Automatic Followership." In *Emerging Leadership Vistas*, edited by James G. Hunt et al., 73–79. Lexington, MA: Lexington, 1988.

Graham, Pauline. *Mary Parker Follett Prophet of Management: A Celebration of Writings from the 1920s*. Edited by Pauline Graham. 1995. Reprint. Washington, DC: Beard, 2003.
Grant, Adam M., and Susan J. Ashford. "The Dynamics of Proactivity at Work." *Research in Organizational Behavior* 28 (2008) 3–34.
Grant, Adam M., and David A. Hofmann. "Role Expansion as Persuasion Process: The Interpersonal Influence Dynamics of Role Redefinition." *Organizational Psychology Review* 1.1 (2011) 9–31.
Grant, Adam M., et al. *Getting Credit for Proactive Behavior: Supervisor Reactions Depend on What You Value and How You Feel: New Perspectives on Organizational Change*. Thousand Oaks, CA: Sage, 2009.
Grant, David., et al. *The Sage Handbook of Organizational Discourse*. London: Sage, 2004.
Greenleaf, Robert K. *Servant Leadership: A Journey into the Nature of Legitimate Power and Greatness*. New York: Paulist, 1977.
Gronn, Peter. "Leadership: Who Needs It?" *School Leadership and Management* 23.3 (2003) 267–90.
Gudykunst, William B. *Bridging Differences: Effective Intergroup Communication*. 4th ed. Newbury Park, CA: Sage, 2004.
Gyekye, Kwame. *African Cultural Values: An Introduction*. Philadelphia: Sankofa, 1996.
Habecker, Eugene B. *The Other Side of Leadership: Coming to Terms with the Responsibilities that accompany God-Given Authority*. Wheaton, IL: Victor, 1987.
Hackman, Richard J., and Ruth Wageman. "Asking the Right Question about Leadership." *American Psychologist* 62.1 (2007) 43–47.
Halal, William E. "From Hierarchy to Enterprise: Internal Markets are the New Foundation of Management." *Academy of Management Executive* 8.4 (1994) 69–83.
Halal, William E., and Kenneth B. Taylor. *Twenty-first Century Economics: Perspectives of Socioeconomics for a Changing World*. New York: Macmillan, 1999.
Hall, Douglas T. "Protean Careers of the 21st Century." *The Academy of Management Executive (1993–2005)* 10.4 (1996) 8–16. doi:10.2307/4165349.
Hall, Stuart. *Modernity: An Introduction to Modern Societies*. Cambridge, MA: Blackwell, 1996.
Hampton, Laura Lynn. "The Deification of Man: A Comparison of the Doctrine of Soul in Thomas Aquinas and René Descartes." PhD Diss., The University of Dallas, 1994.
Hanciles, Jehu. "Conversion and Social Change: Review of the Unfinished Task." In *Christianity Reborn: The Global Expansion of Evangelicalism in the Twentieth Century*, edited by Donald M. Lewis, 157–80. Grand Rapids: Eerdmans, 2004.
Hansen, Theodore. L., Jr. "Management's Impact on First Line Supervisor Effectiveness." *SAM Advanced Management Journal* 52.1 (1987) 41–45.
Harter, Nathan. "Leadership as the Promise of Simplification." *Emergence* 8.4 (2006) 77–87.
Havins, Marwin H. Jr. "An Examination of the Relationship of Organizational Levels and Followership Behaviors in Law Enforcement." PhD diss., Northern Arizona University, 2010.

Heckscher, Charles. "Defining the Post-Bureaucratic Type." In *The Post-Bureaucratic Organization: New Perspectives on Organizational Change*, edited by Charles Heckscher and Anne Donnellon, 14–62. Thousand Oaks, CA: Sage, 1994.

Heifetz, Ronald A. *Leadership Without Easy Answers*. Cambridge, MA: Harvard University Press, 1994.

Heifetz, Ronald A., and Martin Linsky. *Leadership on the Line: Staying Alive through the Dangers of Leading*. Boston: Harvard University Press, 2002.

Heller, Trudy, and Jon Van Till. "Leadership and Followership: Some Summary Propositions." *The Journal of Applied Behavioral Science* 18.3 (1982) 405–14.

Henman, Linda D. "Leadership: Theories and Controversies." https://www.researchgate.net/publication/265035920_Leadership_Theories_and_Controversies.

Henrich, Kim T. "Follower Propensity to Commit Crimes of Obedience: The Role Leadership Beliefs." *Journal of Leadership & Organizational Studies* 14.1 (2007) 69–76.

Herold, David M. "Two-way Influence Processes in Leader-Follower Dyads." *The Academy of Management Journal* 20.2 (1977) 224–37.

Hersey, Paul, and Kenneth H. Blanchard. *Management of Organizational Behavior: Utilizing Human Resources*. Englewood Cliff, NJ: Prentice-Hill, 1977.

Hiebert, Paul G. "The Flaw of the Excluded Middle." *Practical Anthropology* 10.1 (1982) 35–47.

———. *The Missiological Implications of Epistemological Shifts: Affirming Truth in a Modern/Postmodern World*. Harrisburg, PA: Trinity Press International, 1999.

Hinrichs, Kim T., and Andrew T. Hinrichs. "Comparing Followers and Subordinates: Accounting for the Effects of Organizational Hierarchy." In *Followership: What Is It and Why Do People Follow?*, edited by Laurent M. Lapierre and Melissa K. Carsten, 89–108. Bingley, UK: Emerald Group, 2014.

Hirschhorn, Larry. "Leaders and Followers in a Postindustrial Age: A Psychodynamic View." *The Journal of Applied Behavioral Science* 26.4 (1990) 177–96.

Hitt, Michael A. "Presidential Address: Twenty-first Century Organizations: Business Firms, Business Schools, and the Academy." *The Academy of Management Review* 23.2, (1998) 218–24.

Ho, David Yau-Fai, and Chi Yue Chiu. "Components Ideas of Individualism, Collectivism, and Social Organization: An Application in the Study of Chinese Culture." In *Individualism and Collectivism: Theory, Method, and Applications*, edited by Uichol E. Kim et al., 137–56. London: Sage, 1994.

Hodgkinson, Christopher. *The Philosophy of Leadership*. New York: St. Martin's, 1983.

Hofstede, Geert H. *Cultures and Organizations: Software of the Mind*. New York: McGraw-Hill, 2005.

———. *Management Control of Public and Not-for-profit Activities*. Luxembourg, Austria: International Institute for Applied Systems Analysis, 1982.

Hogan, Robert, et al. "What We Know about Leadership: Effectiveness and Personality." *American Psychologist* 49.6 (1994) 493–504.

Hogg, Michael A. "Social Identity Theory of Leadership." *Personality and Social Psychology Review* 5.3 (2001) 184–200.

Hogg, Michael A., and Scott A. Reid. "Social Identity, Self Categorization and Communications of Group Norms." *Communication Theory* 16.1 (2006) 89–106.

Hollander, Edwin P. "Conformity, Status and Idiosyncrasy Credit." *Psychological Review* 65.2 (1958) 117–27.
———. "The Essential Interdependence of Leadership and Followership." *Current Directions in Psychological Science* 1.2 (1992) 71–75.
———. "Leadership and Power." In *The Handbook of Social Psychology*, edited by Gardner Lindzey and Elliot Aronson, 485–538. New York: Random House, 1985.
———. *Leadership Dynamics: A Practical Guide to Effective Relationships*. New York: Free Press, 1978.
———. "Leadership, Followership, Self and Others." *Leadership Quarterly* 3.1 (1992) 43–54.
———. "Legitimacy, Power and Influence: A Perspective on Relational Features of Leadership." In *Leadership Theory and Research: Perspectives and Directions*, edited by Martin M. Chemers and Roya Ayman, 27–47. San Diego: Academic, 1993.
———. "On the Central Role of Leadership Processes." *Applied Psychology* 35.1 (1986) 39–52.
———. "Processes of Leadership Emergence." *Journal of Contemporary Business* 3 (1974) 19–33.
———. "Style, Structure and Setting in Organizational Leadership." *Administrative Science Quarterly* 16.1 (1971) 1–9. doi:10.2307/2391280.
Hollander, Edwin P., and James W. Julian. "Contemporary Trends in the Analysis of Leadership Processes." *Psychological Bulletin* 71.5 (1969) 387–97.
Hollander, Edwin P., and Lynn R. Offermann. "Relational Features of Organizational Leadership and Followership." In *Measures of Leadership*, edited by Kenneth E. Clark et al., 83–97. West Orange, NJ: Leadership Library of America, 1990.
Hollander, Edwin P., and Wilse B. Webb. "Leadership, Followership, and Friendship: An Analysis of Peer Nominations." *Journal of Abnormal and Social Psychology* 50.2 (1955) 163–67.
Hollenbeck, John R., et al. "Beyond Team Types and Taxonomies: A Dimensional Scaling Conceptualization for Team Description." *Academy of Management Review* 37.1 (2012) 82–106.
Holmquist, Ford, and Michael Ford. "Kenya: Slouching toward Democracy." *Africa Today* 39.3 (1992) 97–111.
Homans, George C. *The Human Group*. New York: Harcourt Brace & World, 1950.
———. *Social Behavior*. Rev. Ed. New York: Harcourt Brace Jovanovich, 1974.
Hoption, Colette B., et al. "Submitting to the Follower Label: Followership, Positive Affect and Extra-role Behaviors." *Journal of Psychology* 220.4 (2012) 221–30
Horner, Melissa. "Leadership Theory: Past Present and Future." *Team Performance Management* 3.4 (1997) 270–87.
Horsfall, Chris. "Real Leaders Make a Difference in Raising Achievement." In *Leadership Issues: Raising Achievement*, edited by Chris Horsfall, 44–56. London: Learning and Skill Development Agency, 2001.
Hosking, Marie D., and Rene Bouwen. "Organizational Learning: Relational Constructionist Approaches: An Overview." *European Journal of Work and Organizational Psychology* 9.2 (2000) 129–32.
Hosking, Marie D., and Stephen Fineman. "Organizing Processes." *Journal of Management Studies* 27.6 (1990) 583–604.
Hosking, Marie D., et al. *Management and Organization: Relational Alternatives to Individualism*. Brookfield, VT: Ashgate, 1995.

House, Robert J. "Leadership in the 21st Century: A Speculative Enquiry." In *The Changing Nature of Work*, edited by Ann Howard, 411–50. San Francisco: Jossey-Bass, 1995.

———. "A Path-Goal Theory of Leader Effectiveness." *Administrative Science Quarterly* 16.3 (1971) 321–39.

———. "A Theory of Charismatic Leadership." In *Leadership: The Cutting Edge*, edited by James G. Hunt and Lars L. Larson, 22–37. Carbondale: Southern Illinois University Press, 1976.

House of Commons. "Hansard, House of Commons 4 Series Ii." Edited by House of Commons. London: Great Britain, 1891-92.

Howell, Jane M., and Boas Shamir. "The Role of Follower in the Charismatic Leadership Process: Relationships and Their Consequences." *Academy of Management Review* 30 (2005) 96–112.

Howell, Jon P., and Maria J. Mendez. "Three Perspectives on Followership." In *The Art of Followership: How Great Followers Create Great Leaders and Organizations*, edited by Ronald E. Riggio et al., 45–55. San Francisco: Jossey-Bass, 2008.

Hughes, M. L. *Keeping Your Job While Your Bosses are Losing Theirs*. Binghamton, NY: William Neil, 1998.

Hughes, Rebecca C. *Africans in the British Missionary Imagination, 1910–1965*. Ann Arbor, MI: University of Washington, 2010.

Hughes, Richard L., et al. *Leadership: Enhancing the Lessons of Experience*. Homewood, IL: Irwin, 2001.

Huizing, Russell L. "The Importance of Ritual for Follower Development: An Intertextural Analysis of Leviticus 23 in the Pauline Corpus." PhD diss., Regent University, 2013.

Human Rights Watch. "ICC: Investigate All Sides in Uganda." https://www.hrw.org/news/2004/02/04/icc-investigate-all-sides-uganda

———. "Justice for Serious Crimes before National Courts: Uganda's International Crimes Division." https://www.hrw.org/sites/default/files/reports/uganda0112ForUpload_0.pdf

Hurwitz, Marc, and Samantha Hurwitz. *Leadership Is Half the Story: A Fresh Look at Followership, Leadership, and Collaboration*. 2015. Toronto: University of Toronto Press, 2015.

Hutchful, Eboe. "Military and Militarism in Africa: A Research Agenda." Presented at *Dakar Council for the Development of Economic and Social Research in Africa (CODESRIA)*, Dakar, Senegal, 1989.

IBM Global CEO Study. "Capitalizing on Complexity." www-935.ibm.com/services/us/ceo/ceostudy2010/index.html.

IBRD. "Tenth Annual Review of Project Performance Audit Results." http://documents.worldbank.org/curated/en/351561468327397931/Annexes-and-tables

Ilgen, Daniel. R., and John. R. Hollenbeck. "The Structure of Work: Job Design and Roles." In *Handbook of Industrial and Organizational Psychology*, edited by Marvin D. Dunnette and Leartta M. Hough, 165–207. San Dieg: Consulting Psychology, 1991.

Ilinitch, Anne Y., et al. "New Organizational Forms and Strategies for Managing in Hypercompetitive Environments." *Organization Science* 7.3 (1996) 211–20.

International Bank for Reconstruction and Development. *Tenth Annual Review of Project Performance Audit Results, Vol 2: Sector Reviews*. Washington,

DC: World Bank Group, 1985. http://documents.worldbank.org/curated/en/445831468332048001/pdf/multi-page.pdf.

International Crisis Group. *Northern Uganda: Understanding and Solving the Conflict*. Nairob: International Crisis Group, 2004.

Isis-WICCE. "Women's Experiences of Armed Conflict in Uganda, Gulu District 1986-1999," part 1). Isis Women's International Cross-Cultural Exchange. Kampala, Uganda: Isis-WICCE, 2001. https://newbooksinpolitics.com/political/women-s-experiences-in-armed-conflict-situations-in-uganda-gulu-district-1986-1999/

Johnson, Craig. *Ethics in the Workplace: Tools and Tactics for Organizational Transformation*. Thousand Oaks, CA: Sage, 2007.

Judge, Timothy A., et al. "The Forgotten Ones? The Validity of Considerations and Initiating Structure in Leadership Research." *Journal of Applied Psychology* 89.1 (2004) 36–51.

Kalu, Ogbu U. "African Christianity: From the World Wars to Decolonization." In *The Cambridge History of Christianity: World Christianities c. 1914 - c. 2000, Vol. 9*, edited by Hugh McLeod, 120–22. Cambridge: Cambridge University Press, 2006. 120-122

Kanungo, Rabindra N. "Culture and Work Alienation: Western Models and Eastern Realities." *International Journal of Psychology* 25.3-6 (1990) 795–812.

Kanyogonya, Elizabeth, et al. *Sowing the Mustard Seed: The Struggle for Freedom and Democracy in Uganda*. London: Macmillan, 1997.

Kaplan, Robert D. "The Coming Anarchy: How Scarcity, Crime, Overpopulation, Tribalism, and Disease are Rapidly Destroying the Social Fabric of Our Planet." https://www.theatlantic.com/magazine/archive/1994/02/the-coming-anarchy/304670/

Katz, Daniel, and Robert L. Kahn. *The Social Psychology of Organizations*. New York: John Wiley and Sons, 1978.

Kaufman, Stuart J. "Social Identity and the Roots of Future Conflicts." A paper presented at the US Government National Intelligence Council 2020 Project, 2003. http://indianstrategicknowledgeonline.com/web/kaufman_panel2_nov6.pdf.

Keegan, John. *War and Our World*. New York: Vintage, 2001.

Kellerman, Barbara. *The End of Leadership*. New York: Harper Business, 2012.

———. *Followership: How Followers are Creating Change and Changing Leaders*. Boston: Harvard Business School Press, 2008.

———. "What Every Leader Needs to Know about Followers." *Harvard Business Review* 85.12 (2007) 84–91.

Kelley, Robert E. *In Praise of Followers*. Boston: Harvard Business Review Case Services, 1988.

———. "Leadership Secrets from Exemplary Followers." In *Leading Organizations: Perspectives for a New Era*, edited by Gill Robinson Hickman, 193–201. Thousand Oaks, CA: Sage, 1998.

———. *The Power of Followership: How to Create Leaders People Want to Follow, and Followers Who Lead Themselves*. New York: Doubleday/Currency, 1992.

———. "Rethinking Followership." In *The Art of Followership: How Great Followers Create Great Leaders and Organizations*, edited by Ronald. E. Riggio et al., 5–15. San Francisco: Jossey-Bass, 2008.

Kelman, Herbert C. "Informal Mediation by the Scholar/Practitioner." In *Mediation in International Relations: Multiple Approaches to Conflict Management*, edited by Jacob Bercovitch and Jeffery Z. Rubin, 64–96. New York: St. Martin's, 1992.

———. "Violence Without Moral Restraint: Reflections on the Dehumanization of Victims and Victimizers." *The Journal of Social Issues* 29.4 (1973) 25–53.

Kennedy, Robert. *The Rise and Fall of the Great Powers*. New York: Random House, 1987.

Kerr, Steven., and John M. Jermier, "Substitutes for Leadership: The Meaning and Measurement." *Organizational Behaviour and Human Performance* 22.3 (1978) 375–403.

Kitching, Arthur Leonard. *On the Backwaters of the Nile: Studies of Some Child Races of Central Africa*. London: T. Fisher Unwin, 1912.

Komakec, Ayaa Cynthia, and Fatuma Ahmed. "The Quest for Governance, Conflict Transformation and Development in Africa: A Case of Study of the Acholi in Northern Uganda." PhD diss., Universitat Jaume I, 2010.

Komakec, Michael. "Making Peace (Peacemaking) in Uganda: Theological Underpinning and Pastoral Ministries." PhD diss., Duquesne University, 2010.

Komakech, Daniel. *Reinventing and Validating the Cosmology of and Ontology of Restorative Justice: Hermeneutics of Traditional Acholi Justice System in Northern Uganda*. African Perspectives on Tradition and Justice. Edited by Tom W. Bennett. Portland, OR: Intersentia, 2012.

Komarn, Abraham K. "Consideration, Initiating Structure and Organizational Criteria: A Review." *Personnel Psychology* 19 (1966) 349–61.

Korostelina, Karina V. "Identity Salience as a Determinant of the Perceptions of Others." In *Identity, Morality, and Threat: Studies in Violent Conflict*, edited by Daniel Rothbart and Karina V. Korostelina, 100–50. Lanham, MD: Lexington, 2006.

Kougniazondé, Christophe Codjo. *Militarization and Political Violence in Tropical Africa*. South Bend, IN: Notre Dame University Press, 1998.

Kunnath, Harish. *Followership: A Way Forward*. Mumbai: Frog, 2015.

Lapat, Anyeko Kevin. "The Role of the Structures of the Archdiocese of Gulu in Providing Reconciliation and Healing: The Case of Pre-War, War, and Early Post-War in Northern Uganda." PhD Diss. Gulu Catholic Archdiocese 2007.

Lapierre, Laurent, and Melissa K. Carsten. *Followership: What Is It and Why Do People Follow?* London: Emerald Group, 2014.

Larsson, Magnus, and Susanne E. Lundholm. "Talking Work in a Bank: A Study of Organizing Properties of Leadership in Work Interactions." *Human Relations* 66.8 (2013) 1101–29.

Latour, Sharon M., and Vicki J. Rast. "Dynamic Followership: The Prerequisite for Effective Leadership." *Air & Space Power Journal* 18.4 (2004) 102–10.

Layder, Derek. "Understanding Social Theory." Sage, https://epdf.tips/understanding-social-theory-2nd-edition.htm

Lee, Siew Kim. "A Chinese Conception of Management: An Interpretive Approach." PhD diss., University of Massachusetts, Amherst, 1987.

Leggett, Ian. *Uganda: Oxfarm Country Profile*. Oxford, UK: OXFARM, 2001.

Liden, Robert C., et al. "Leader-member Exchange Theory: The Past and the Potential for the Future." In *Research in Personnel and Human Resource Management, Vol. 15*, edited by Gerald R. Ferris, 47–119. Greenwich, CT: JAI, 1997.

Lincoln, Yvonna S., and Egon G. Guba. *Naturalistic Inquiry*. Beverly Hills, CA: Sage, 1985.

Lipman-Blumen, Jean. *The Allure of Toxic Leaders: Why We Follow Destructive Bosses and Corrupt Politicians--and How We Can Survive Them*. Oxford: University of Oxford Press, 2005.

Litzinger, William, and Thomas. Schaefer. "Leadership through Followership." *Business Horizons* 25.5 (1982) 78–81.

Locke, Edwin A., and Shelley S. Kirkpatrick. *The Essence of Leadership: The Four Keys to Leading Successfully*. New York: Maxwell Macmillan International, 1991.

Lopez, George A. "National Security Ideology as an Impetus to State Violence and State Terror." In *Government Violence and Repression: An Agenda for Research*, edited by Michael Stohl and George A. Lopez, 76–90. Westport, CT: Greenwood, 1986.

Lord, Robert. G. "Followers' Cognitive and Affective Structures and Leadership Processes." In *The Art of Followership: How Great Followers Create Great Leaders and Organizations*, edited by Ronald E. Riggio et al., 255–66. San Francisco: Jossey-Bass, 2008.

———. "Four Leadership Principles that are Worth Remembering." Paper presented at the Australian Industrial-Organizational Psychology Conference, Perth, Australia, October 2013.

Lord, Robert. G., and Douglas. J. Brown. "Leadership, Values, and Subordinate Self-concepts." *The Leadership Quarterly*, 12.2 (2001) 133–52.

Lord's Resistance Army Disarmament and Northern Uganda Recovery Act of 2009. Pub. L. No. 111-172, 124 Stat. 1209 (2010).

Luckham, Robin. "Armaments, Underdevelopment, and Demilitarisation in Africa." *Alternatives* 2 (1980) 179–245.

———. "The Military, Militarization and Democratization in Africa: A Survey of Literature and Issues." *African Studies Review* 37.2 (1994) 13-75

Lundin, Stephen C., and Lynne C. Lancaster. "Beyond Leadership: The Importance of Followership." *The Futurist* 24.3 (May/June 1990) 18–22.

Luttwak, Edward N. "Give War a Chance." *Foreign Affairs* 784 (1999) 36–44.

Malakyan, Petros G. "Followership in Leadership Studies: A Case of Leader-follower Trade Approach." *Journal of Leadership Studies* 7.4 (2014) 6–22.

Malunga, Chiku *Understanding Organizational Leadership through Ubuntu*. London: Adonis and Abbey, 2009.

Mamdani, Mahmood. *Citizen and Subject: Contemporary Africa and the Legacy of Late Colonialism*. Princeton, NJ: Princeton University Press, 1996.

———. *When Victims Become Killers: Colonialism, Nativism, and the Genocide in Rwanda*. Princeton, NJ: Princeton University Press, 2001.

Mandela, Nelson. *Long Walk to Freedom: The Autobiography of Nelson Mandela*. London: Little, Brown, 1994.

Maxwell, John C. *Developing the Leaders around You: How to Help Others Reach Their Full Potential*. Nashville: Thomas Nelson, 1995.

———. *The 21 Indispensable Qualities of a Leader: Becoming the Person Others Will Want to Follow*. Nashville: Thomas Nelson, 2007.

———. *The 21 Irrefutable Laws of Leadership: Follow Them and People Will Follow You*. Nashville: Thomas Nelson, 1998.

Maxwell, Joseph Alex. *Qualitative Research Design: An Interactive Approach*. 1st ed. Thousand Oaks, CA: Sage, 2005.

———. *Qualitative Research Design: An Interactive Approach*. 2nd ed. Thousand Oaks, CA: Sage, 2013.
Maynard Smith, John. *Evolution and the Theory of Games*. New York: Cambridge University Press, 1982.
Mbiti, John. S. *African Religions and Philosophy*. Garden City, NY: Doubleday, 1970.
———. *Introduction to African Religion*. Portsmouth, NH: Doubleday, 1991.
McKelvey, Bill, and Max H. Boisot. "Transcendental Organizational Foresight in Nonlinear Contexts." Paper presented at *INSEAD Conference on Expanding Perspectives on Strategy Processes*. Fontainebleau, France. 2003.
McLellan, David. *Karl Marx: His Life and Thought*. New York: Harper & Row, 1974.
Mead, Margaret. "Problems of Leadership and Mental Health." *World Federation for Mental Health Bulletin* 1.6 (1949) 7–12.
Medcof, Thomas Max B. "Followers and Followership: An Exploration of Follower Prototypes, National Culture, and Personality." PhD diss., York University, 2012.
Meindl, James R. "On Leadership: An Alternative to the Conventional Wisdom." *Research in Organizational Behavior* 12.4 (1990) 341–63.
———. "The Romance of Leadership as a Follower-centric Theory: A Social Constructionist Approach." *Monograph in Organizational Behavior and Industrial Relations* 24.B (1998) 285–98.
Meindl, James R., and Sanford B. Ehrlich. "The Romance of Leadership and the Evaluation of Organizational Performance." *Academy of Management Journal* 30.1 (1987) 91–109.
Meindl, James R., et al. "The Romance of Leadership." *Administrative Science Quarterly* 30.1 (1985) 78–102.
Merriam, Sharan B. *Case Study Research in Education: A Qualitative Approach*. San Francisco: Jossey-Bass, 1988.
———. *Qualitative Research: A Guide to Design and Implementation*. San Francisco: Jossey-Bass, 2009.
———. *Qualitative Research and Case Study Applications in Education*. San Francisco: Jossey-Bass, 1998.
———. *Qualitative Research in Practice: Examples for Discussion and Analysis*. San Francisco: Jossey-Bass, 2002.
Milgram, Stanley. *Obedience to Authority: An Experimental View*. New York: Harper & Row, 1974.
———. "Some Condition of Obedience and Disobedience to Authority." *Human Relations* 18.1 (1965) 57–76.
Miller, Darrow L. *Against All Hope: Hope for Africa*. Nairobi: Samaritan Strategy Africa Working Group, 2005.
Mir, Ali M. "Leadership in Islam." *Journal of Leadership Studies* 9.3 (2010) 69–72.
Mitchell, Michael R. *Leading, Teaching, and Making Disciples: World-class Christian Education in the Church, School, and Home*. Bloomington, IN: Cross, 2010.
Mitroff, Ian I., et al. *Framebreak: The Radical Redesign of American Business*. San Francisco: Jossey-Bass, 1994.
Mokyr, Joel. *The Lever of Riches: Technological Creativity and Technological Progress*. New York: Oxford University Press, 1990.
Mumford, Michael, et al. "Charismatic, Ideological, and Pragmatic Leadership: Multi-level Influences on Emergence and Performance." *The Leadership Quarterly* 19.2 (2008) 144–60.

Mung'oma, Stephen Masette. "Revitalization in the Church: A Study of Leadership in the Anglican Diocese of Kampala, Uganda." PhD diss., Fuller Theological Seminary, 2003.

Mutibwa, Phares M. *Uganda Since Independence: A Story of Unfulfilled Hopes.* Trenton, NJ: Africa World, 1992.

Nampindo, Simon, et al. "The Impact of Conflict in Northern Uganda on the Environment and Natural Resource Management (PDF)." Wildlife Conservation Society, U.S. Agency for International Development, 2005, August. https://albertinerift.wcs.org/DesktopModules/Bring2mind/DMX/Download.aspx?EntryId=11632&PortalId=49&DownloadMethod=attachment

Nannyonjo, Justine. "Conflicts, Poverty and Human Development in Northern Uganda." *The Round Table* 94 (2005) 473–88.

Natulya, Paul. "Exclusion, Identity and Armed Conflict: A Historical Survey of the Politics of Confrontation in Uganda with Specific Reference to the Independence Era." In *Politics of Identity and Exclusion in Africa: From Violent Confrontation to Peaceful Cooperation*, edited by Konrad-Adenauer-Stiftung, 81–92. Johannesburg: Konrad-Adenauer-Stiftung, 2001.

Ndongko, Theresa M. "Management Leadership in Africa." In *Management of Organizations in Africa: A Handbook and Reference,* edited by Julius Waiguchu et al., 89–123 Westport, CT: Quorum, 1999.

Nibbe, Ayesha Anne. "The Effects of a Narrative: Humanitarian Aid and Action in the Northern Uganda Conflict." PhD diss., University of California, Davis, 2011.

Nkrumah, Kwame. *Neo-Colonialism: The Last Stage of Imperialism.* New York: International, 1966.

Nkurunziza, Deusdedit R. K. "Insurgency in Northern Uganda: A Challenge to the Church in Amecea." *AFER* 45.4 (2003) 314–28.

Nonaka, Ikujiro, and Toshihiro Nishiguchi. "Introduction: Knowledge Emergence." In *Knowledge Emergence: Social, Technical, and Evolutionary Dimensions of Knowledge Creation*, edited by Ikujiro Nonaka and Toshihiro Nishiguchi, 3–9. Oxford: Oxford University Press, 2001.

Norman, Donald A. "Some Observations on Mental Models." *Mental Models* 7.11 (1983) 7–14.

Northern Uganda Crisis Response Act. Pub. L. No. 108–283, 118 Stat. 912 (2004).

Northouse, Peter Guy. *Leadership: Theory and Practice.* Thousand Oaks, CA: Sage, 2010.

Ntamushobora, Faustin. "From Transmission to Transformation: An Exploration of Education for Holistic Transformation in Selected Christian and Public Universities in Kenya." PHD diss., Biola University 2012.

Ntarangwi, Mwenda. *Jesus and Ubuntu: Exploring the Social Impact of Christianity in Africa.* Trenton, NJ: Africa World, 2011.

Nyongesa, Alfred. "$300b Lost in Conflicts Yearly." *Daily Monitor*, September 22, 2010. http://www.monitor.co.ug/News/National/-/688334/1015608/-/cnmruxz/-/index.html.

Obote, Apollo Milton. "Notes on Concealment of Genocide in Uganda." http://www.upcparty.net/obote/genocide.htm.

Oc, Barak, and Bashshur, Michael Ramsay. "Followership, Leadership and Social Influence." *The Leadership Quarterly* 24.6 (2013) 919–34.

Offermann, Lynn R. *Leadership Followership Focus Group: Leading and Empowering Followers.* Baltimore: Kellogg Leadership Studies Project, 1997.

Ofumbi, David W. *Identity and Transformation: A Study of the Significance of African Christianity in Christian Community Transformation*. Maitland, FL: Xulon, 2012.

———. "Significance of the Humanity of the Other in Peacemaking: An Acholi Perspective." *William Carey International Development Journal* 1.1 (2012) 50–61.

Ogbonna, Chijioke E. "Followership Imperative of Good Governance: Reflection on Nigeria's 'Second Chance' at Democratizatio." *International Affairs and Global Strategy* 4. 4 (2012) 65–80.

Ogot, Bethwell A. *History of the Southern Luo*. Nairobi: East African House, 1967.

Ojera, Latigo James. "Northern Uganda: Tradition-Based Practices in the Acholi Region." In *Traditional Justice and Reconciliation after Violent Conflict: Learning from African Experiences*, edited by Luc Huyse and Mark Salte, 85–120. Stockholm: International IDEA, 2008.

Okello, Lucima. "Kacoke Madit: A diaspora role in promoting peace (2002)" https://www.c-r.org/accord-article/kacoke-madit-diaspora-role-promoting-peace-2002.

Okumu-Alya, Fabius. "The Regional Dimensions of the War in Northern Uganda." https://www.files.ethz.ch/isn/124038/CPRDNORTHERNUGANDA.pdf

Olango, Willy. "Christian Leadership in Relation to Conflict in the Great Lakes Region with Special Focus on Northern Uganda." A Paper Presented to the *Africa Pilgrims*. Gulu, Uganda, 2007.

Olara A. Otunnu, "The Secret Genocide." *Foreign Policy* 155 (2006) 44–46.

Oloka-Onyango, Joel. "'New-Breed' Leadership, Conflict, and Reconstruction in the Great Lakes Region of Africa: A Sociopolitical Biography of Uganda's Yoweri Kaguta Museveni." *Africa Today* 50.3 (2004) 29–52.

Oloya, Opiyo. *Child to Soldier: Stories from Joseph Kony's Lord's Resistance Army*. Toronto: University of Toronto Press, 2012.

Omara-Otunnu, Ogenga. "Causes and Consequences of War in Acholiland." In *Protracted Conflict, Elusive Peace: Initiatives to End the Violence in Northern Uganda*, edited by Okello Lucima, 40–55. London: Conciliation Resources and Kacoke Madit, 2002.

———. "The History of Political Crisis in Uganda: The Legacy Facing the Museveni Regime, 1986 to the Present." PhD diss., Saint Mary's University, 1989.

———. "The Struggle for Democracy in Uganda." *The Journal of Modern African Studies* 30.3 (1992) 443–63.

Onyango-Ku-Odongo, Joel. M. *The Central Lwo During the Aconya*. Kampala, Uganda: East African Literature Bureau, 1976.

———. "Uganda: The Root of the Regression from Light to Darkness." Unpublished manuscript. 2015. Microsoft Word file.

Osaghae, Eghosa. "The Limits of Charismatic Authority and the Challenges of Leadership in Nigeria." *Journal of Contemporary African Studies* 28.4 (2011) 29–44.

Osland, Joyce S. "Broadening the Debate: The Pros and Cons of Globalization." *Journal of Management Inquiry* 12.2 (2003) 137–54.

Oyetunji, Christianah O. "The Relationship between Followership Style and Job Performance in Botswana Private Universities." *International Education Studies* 6.2 (2013) 179–87.

Padilla, Antonio, et al. "The Toxic Triangle: Destructive Leaders, Susceptible Followers and Conducive Environments." *The Leadership Quarterly* 18.3 (2007) 176–94.

Pain, Dennis. *"The Bending of Spears": Producing Consensus for Peace and Development in Northern Uganda*. London: International Alert, 1997.

Parker, Sharon K. "From Passive to Proactive Motivation: The Importance of Flexible Role Orientations and Role Breadth Self-efficacy." *Applied Psychology* 49.3 (2000) 447–69.

Parker, Sharon K., et al. "That is Not My Job: Developing Flexible Employee Work Orientation." *Academy of Management Journal* 40.4 (1997) 899–929.

Parks, Sharon Daloz. *Leadership Can be Taught: A Bold Approach for a Complex World*. Boston: Harvard Business School Press, 2005.

Parliament of the Republic of Uganda. *Report of the Committee on Defense and Internal Affairs on War in Northern Uganda*. Kampala, Uganda: Parliament of Uganda (Hansard), 1997.

Patterson, Kathleen. "Servant Leadership Roundtable." In *Servant Leadership Research Roundtable Proceedings*, edited by Dirk Van Dierendonck, 1–13. Virginia Beach, VA: Regent University Press, 2003.

Perkins, John M. *Beyond Charity: The Call to Christian Community Development*. Grand Rapids: Baker, 1993.

Pfeffer, Jeffrey, *The Ambiguity of Leadership*. Boulder, CO: Westview, 1984.

Phillips, James S., and Robert G. Lord. "Causal Attributions and Perceptions of Leadership." *Organizational Human Performance* 28.2 (1981) 143–63.

Phillips, Nelson W., and Cliff. Oswick. "Organizational Discourse: Domains, Debates, and Directions." *The Academy of Management Annals* 6.1 (2012) 1–47.

Pittman, Thane S., et al. "Followers as Partners: Taking the Initiative for Action." In *Contemporary Issues in Leadership*, edited by William E. Rosenbach and Robert Lewis Taylor, 107–20. Boulder, CO: Westview, 1998.

P'Lajur, John Muto-Ono. "The Challenge of Reporting the Northern Uganda Armed Conflict." In *Media in the Situations of Conflict: Roles, Challenges and Responsibility*, edited by Adolf E. Mbaine, 30–41. Kampala, Uganda: Fountain, 2006.

Poblicks, Nyeko Caesar. "Kacoke Madit: A Diaspora Role in Promoting Peace." http://www.c-r.org/accord-article/kacoke-madit-diaspora-role-promoting-peace-2002.

Postlethwaite, John. R. P. *I Look Back*. London: T. V. Boardman, 1947.

Potter, Earl H., III, and William E. Rosenbach. "Followers as Partners: Ready When the Time Comes." In *Military Leadership: In Pursuit of Excellence.*, edited by Robert L. Taylor and William E. Rosenbach, 91–102. Boulder, CO: Westview, 2005.

Potter, Earl. H., III, et al. "Leading the New Professional." In *Military Leadership: In Pursuit of Excellence,* edited by Robert L. Taylor and William. E Rosenbach, 145–52. Boulder, CO: Westview, 1996.

Prasad, Ajnesh. "Beyond Analytical Dichotomies." *Human Relations* 65.5 (2012) 567–95.

Prisca, Tanui Too. "An Analysis of the Rebel War in Northern Uganda." *African Ecclesial Review* 45.4 (2003) 335–45.

Przeworski, Adam, and Frank Salomon. *On the Art of Writing Proposals: Some Candid Suggestions for Applicants to Social Science Research Council Competitions*. New York: Social Science Research Council, 1988.

Putnam, Linda L., and Gail T. Fairhurst. "Discourse Analysis in Organizations." In *The New Handbook of Organizational Communication,* edited by Fredric M. Jablin and Linda L. Putnam, 78–136. Thousand Oaks, CA: Sage, 2001.

Rajan, Raghuram., and Julie Wulf. "The Flattening Firm: Evidence from Panel Data on the Changing Nature of Corporate Hierarchies." National Bureau of Economic Research Working Paper No. 9633. doi:10.3386/w9633.

Ramsbotham, Oliver, and Tom Woodhouse. *Humanitarian Intervention in Contemporary Conflict: A Reconceptualization.* Cambridge, MA: Polity, 1996.

Ravlin, Elizabeth C., and David C. Thomas. "Status and Stratification Processes in Organizational Life." *Journal of Management Studies* 31.6 (2005) 966–87.

Reuther, Cindy, and Gail T. Fairhurst. "Chaos Theory and the Glass Ceiling." In *Rethinking Organizational and Managerial Communication from Feminist Perspectives,* edited by Patrice M. Buzzanell, 236–56. London: Sage, 2000.

Riano-Alcala, Pilar, and Erin Bainesy. "The Archive in the Witness: Documentation in Settings of Chronic Insecurity." *International Journal of Transitional Justice* 5.3 (2011) 412–33.

Ricketson, Rushton S., Sr. "The Development of the Biblical Followership Profile." https://mafiadoc.com/the-development-of-the-biblical-followership-profile-foundation-of-_59f9a6791723dd317a5fd84c.html

Ricketson, Rusty. *Follower First: Rethinking Leading in the Church.* Cumming, GA: Heartworks, 2009.

Riggio, Ronald E., et al., eds. *The Art of Followership: How Great Followers Create Great Leaders and Organizations.* San Francisco: Jossey-Bass, 2008.

Rodney, Walter. *How Europe Underdeveloped Africa.* Washington, DC: Howard University Press, 1981.

Rohner, Dominic, et al. "Seeds of Distrust: Conflict in Uganda." *Journal of Economic Growth* 18.3 (2013) 217–52.

Rosenbach, William. E., and Thane. S. Pittman. "Performance and Relationship Questionnaire (Survey Instrument)." http://www.leadingandfollowing.com/documents/PRQSample.pdf

Rost, Joseph C. "Followership: An Outmoded Concept." In *The Art of Followership: How Great Followers Create Great Leaders and Organizations,* edited by Ronald E. Riggio et al., 53–66. San Francisco: Jossey-Bass, 2008.

———. *Leadership for the Twenty-first Century.* New York: Praeger, 1991.

Rousseau, Denise M. "Psychological and Implied Contracts in Organizations." *Employee Responsibilities & Rights Journal* 2.2 (1989) 121–39.

Rush, Michael C., et al. "Implicit Leadership Theory: A Potential Threat to Internal Validity of Leader Behavior Questionnaire." *Organizational Behavior and Human Performance* 21.1 (1977) 93–110.

Russell, Megan. "Leadership and Followership as a Relational Process." *Educational Management & Administration* 31.2 (2003) 145–57.

Samovar, Larry A., et al. *Communication between Cultures.* Boston: Wadsworth Cengage Learning, 2009.

Sanchez, Ron. "Strategic Flexibility in Product Competition: An Options Perspective on Resource-based Competition." *Strategic Management Journal* 16.1 (1995) 135–59.

Sanford, Fillmore H. "Authoritarianism and Leadership: A Study of the Follower's Orientation to Authority." Philadelphia: Institute for Research in Human Relations, 1950.

Sashkin, Molly. "Transformational Leadership Approaches." In *The Nature of Leadership,* edited by John Antonakis et al., 171–96. Thousand Oaks, CA: Sage, 2004.

Schneider, Marguerite. "A Stakeholder Model of Organizational Leadership." *Organization Science* 13.2 (2002) 209–20.
Schriesheim, Chester A., et al. "The Folly of Theorizing 'a' but Testing 'b': A Selective Level-of-analysis Review of the Field and a Detailed Leader-member Exchange Illustration." *The Leadership Quarterly* 12 (2001) 515–51.
Schyns, Birgit, and James R. Meindl. *Implicit Leadership Theories: Essay and Explorations*. Greenwich, CT: Information Age, 2005.
Seeley, Troy A. *Followership: The Missing Link: Followership Dimensions, Affective Commitment, and Performance*. Saarbrucken, Germany: VDM Verlag, 2009.
Senge, Peter M. *The Fifth Discipline: The Art and Practice of the Learning Organization*. New York: Doubleday/Currency, 1990.
Senge, Peter M., and John D. Sterman. "Systems Thinking and Organizational Learning: Acting Locally and Thinking Globally in the Organization of the Future." *European Journal of Operational Research* 59.1 (1992) 137–50.
Shamir, Boas. *From Passive Recipients to Active Co-Producers: Followers' Roles in the Leadership Process*. Greenwich, CT: Information Age, 2007
———. "Leadership Research or Post-leadership Research: Advancing Leadership Theory Versus Throwing the Baby Out With the Bath Water." In *Advancing Relational Leadership Research a Dialogue among Perspectives*, edited by Mary Uhl-Bien and Sonia Ospina, ix–xxxix. Charlotte, NC: Information Age, 2012.
Shamir, Boas, and Jane M. Howell. "The Role of Followers in the Charismatic Leadership Process: Relationships and Their Consequences." *Academy of Management Review* 30.1 (2005) 96–102
Shun, Kwong-loi. "Philosophy of Human Nature." In *Encyclopedia of Chinese Philosophy*, edited by Antonio Cua, 554–58. New York: Routledge, 2003.
Siedman, Irving E. *Interviewing as Qualitative Research*. New York: Teachers College, 1998.
Sivasubramaniam, Nagaraj, et al. "In the Eyes of the Beholder: Folk Theories of Leadership in an Academic Institution." *Journal of Leadership Studies* 4.2 (1997) 27–42.
Smith, Archie. *Siblings by Choice: Race, Gender, and Violence*. St. Louis: Chalice, 2004.
Smith, George D., and Davis Dyer. "The Rise and Transformation of the American Corporation." In *The American Corporation Today*, edited by Carl Kaysen, 28–51. New York: Oxford University Press, 1996.
Smith, John S. "Followership Behaviors among Florida Community College Faculty." PhD diss., University of Florida, 2009.
Smith, John Maynard. *Evolution and the Theory of Games*. New York: Cambridge University Press, 1982.
Sorenson, Georgia. "An Intellectual History of Leadership Studies: The Role of James MacGregor Burns." Presented at the Annual Meeting of the American Political Science Association, Washington, DC, 2006
Speke, John H. *Journal of the Discovery of the Source of the Nile*. New York: Harper & Brothers, 1968.
Stake, Robert E. *The Art of Case Study Research*. Thousand Oaks, CA: Sage, 1995.
Starcher, Richard L. "Qualitative Research in Missiological Studies and Practice." *Dharma Deepika* 15.2 (2011) 54–63.

Stearns, Richard. *The Hole in Our Gospel: What Does God Expect of Us?: The Answers That Changed My Life and Might Just Change the World*. Nashville: Thomas Nelson, 2010.

Steger, Joseph A., et al. "Following the Leader: How to Link Management Style to Subordinate Personalities." *Management Review* 71.10 (1982) 22–28.

Stewart, Frances. "Horizontal Inequalities as a Source of Conflict." In *From Reaction to Conflict Prevention: Opportunities for the UN System*, edited by Fen Osler Hampson and David Malone, 105–36. Boulder, CO: Lynne Rienner, 2002.

Stogdill, Ralph Melvin "Personal Factors Associated with Leadership: A Survey of the Literature." *The Journal of Psychology* 25 (1948) 35–71.

Stott, John R. W. "Education and Leadership." https://www.lausanne.org/content/covenant/lausanne-covenant.

Strauss, Anselm. *Qualitative Analysis for Social Scientists*. Cambridge: Cambridge University Press, 1987.

Strauss, Anselm, and Juliet M. Corbin. *Basics of Qualitative Research: Grounded Theory Procedures and Techniques*. Thousand Oaks, CA: Sage, 1998.

Strebel, Paul. "Why Do Employees Resist Change?" *Harvard Business Review* 74 (1996) 86–92.

Sturges, Paul. "Information and Communication in Bandit Country: An Exploratory Study of Civil Conflict in Northern Uganda." *Information Development* 24.3 (2008) 204–12.

Sy, Thomas. "What Do You Think of Followers? Examining the Content, Structure, and Consequences of Implicit Followership Theories." *Organizational Behavior & Human Decision Processes* 113.2 (2010) 73–84.

Tagoe, Michael. "Followership or Followersheep? Searching for Transformational Leaders for Accelerated National Development in Ghana." *Journal of Asia & African Studies* 46.1 (2011) 87–103.

Tan, Sharon. "Reconciliation as Political Ethic: From Religion to Politics to Law." PhD diss., Emory University, 2003.

Tanoff, Gregg. F., and Cassie B. Barlow. "Leading and Followership: Same Animal, Different Spots?" *Consulting Psychology Journal* 54.3 (2002) 157–67.

Taylor, Fredrick W. *The Principles of Scientific Management*. New York: Norton, 1911.

Tepper, Bennett J., et al. "Personality Moderators of the Relationship between Abusive Supervision and Subordinates' Resistance." *The Journal of Applied Psychology* 86.5 (2001) 974–83.

Tepper, Bennett J., et al. "Subordinates' Resistance and Managers' Evaluations of Subordinates' Performance." *Journal of Management* 32.2 (2006) 185–95.

Thody, Angela. "Followership in Educational Organizations: A Pilot Mapping of the Territory." *Leadership and Policy in Schools* 2 (2003) 241–56.

Thomas-Slayter, Barbara P. "Structural Change, Power Politics, and Community Organizations in Africa: Challenging the Patterns, Puzzles and Paradoxes." *World Development* 22.10 (1994) 1479–85.

Tindifa, Samuel B. "Listen to the People: Towards an Inclusive Approach to the Peace Process in Northern Uganda." A paper presented at Human Rights and Peace Center (HURIPEC) working paper no. 3 at Makerere University, Kampala, Uganda, 2010.

Tjosvold, Dean, et al. "Cooperative and Competitive Relationships between Leaders and Subordinates." *Human Relations* 36 (1983) 111–24.

Tolstikov-Mast, Yulia. "Followership in Russia: Understanding Traditions and Exploring Meaning of Current Reality." *Journal of Leadership Education* 13.4 (2014) 100–10.
Tutu, Desmond, and Douglas Abrams. *God Has a Dream: A Vision of Hope for Our Time*. New York: Doubleday, 2004.
Uhl-Bien, Mary, and Raj Pillai. *Romance of Leadership and Social Construction of Followership*. Greenwich, CT: Information Age, 2007.
Uhl-Bien, Mary, and Sonia Ospina. "Paradigm Interplay in Relational Leadership: A Way Forward." In *Advancing Relational Leadership Research: Dialogue among Perspectives*, edited by Mary Uhl-bien and Sonia Ospina, 537–80. Charlotte, NC: Information Age, 2012.
Uhl-Bien, Mary, et al. "Complexity Leadership Theory: Shifting Leadership from the Industrial Age to the Knowledge Era." In *Leadership, Gender, and Organization*, edited by Patricia Werhane and Mollie Painter-Morland, 109–38. Nijmegen, Netherlands: Springer 2011.
Uhl-Bien, Mary, et al. "Followership Theory: A Review and Research Agenda." *Leadership Quarterly* 25.1 (2014) 83–104.
Uhl-Bien, Mary, et al. "Implication of Leader-member Exchange (LMX) for Strategic Human Resource Management Systems: Relationship as Social Capital for Competitive Advantage." *Research in Personnel and Human Resources Management* 18 (2000) 137–86.
Useem, Michael. "Corporate Education and Training." In *The American Corporation Today*, edited by Carl Kaysen, 292–326. New York: Oxford University Press, 1996.
Van Vugt, Mark, et al. "Leadership, Followership, and Evolution: Some Lessons from the Past." *The American Psychologist* 63.3 (2008) 182–96.
Vecchio, Robert P. "Effective Followership: Leadership Turned Upside Down." In *Leadership: Understanding the Dynamics of Power and Influence in Organizations*, edited by Robert P. Vecchio, 114–23. Notre Dame, IN: University of Notre Dame Press, 1997.
Volti, Rudi. *The Sociology of Work and Occupation: Globalization and Technological Change Into the 21st Century*. Thousand Oaks, CA: Pine Forge, 2008.
Vroom, Victor H., and Arthur G. Jago. "On the Validity of Vroom-Yetton Model." *Journal of Applied Psychology* 63 (1978) 151–62.
Vroom, Victor H., and Philip W. Yetton. *Leadership and Decision-Making*. Pittsburgh: University of Pittsburgh Press, 1973.
Weber, Max. *Economy and Society*. Totowa, NJ: Bedminster, 1968.
Webster, Juliet. "Chicken or Egg? The Interaction between Manufacturing Technologies and Paradigms of Work Organization." *International Journal of Human Factors in Manufacturing* 3.1 (1993) 53–67.
Weick, Karl E. "Cognitive Process in Leadership in Organizations." *Research in Organizational Behavior* 1 (1979) 41–74.
———. *Sensemaking in Organizations, Vol. 3*. London: Sage, 1995.
Weis, Lois, and Michelle. Fine. *Speed Bumps: A Study-friendly Guide to Qualitative Research*. New York: Teachers College, 2000.
Westbrook, David. "The Torment of Northern Uganda: A Legacy of Missed Opportunities." *The Online Journal of Peace and Conflict Resolution* 3.2 (2000) 211–22.
Whiting, Steven W., et al. "Effects of Message, Source and Context on Evaluations of Employee Voice Behavior." *Journal of Applied Psychology* 97.1 (2012) 159–82.

Whitmire, Leslie. "The Creation and Evolution of the Acholi Ethnic Identity." MA Thesis. Clemson University.

Wilkinson, David J. *The Ambiguity Advantage*. New York: Palgrave Macmillan, 2006.

Willard, David. *The Spirit of the Disciplines: Understanding How God Changes Lives*. San Francisco: Harper & Row, 1988.

Williams, Brackette F. "Class Act: Anthropology and the Race to Nation across Ethnic Terrain." *Annual Review of Anthropology* 18 (1989) 401–44.

Williams, Gary A., and Robert B. Miller. "Change the Way You Persuade." *Harvard Business Review* 80 (May 2002) 65–73.

Williamson, Oliver E. *The Economic Institutions of Capitalism*. New York: Free Press, 1985.

Women's Commission. "Against All Odds: Surviving the War on Adolescents." https://www.womensrefugeecommission.org/youth/resources/445-against-all-odds-surviving-the-war-on-adolescents

Wortman, Max S., Jr. "Strategic Management and Changing Leader-Follower Roles." *The Journal of Applied Behavioral Science* 18.3 (1982) 371–83.

Wrzesniewski, Amy, and Jane. E. Dutton. "Crafting a Job: Revisioning Employees as Active Crafters of Their Work." *Academy of Management Review* 26.2 (2001) 179–201.

Yang, Kwan S. "Psychological Transformation of Chinese People as a Result of Societal Modernization." In *The Handbook of Chinese Psychology*, edited by Michael H. Bond, 279–498. Hong Kong: Oxford University Press, 1996.

Yin, Robert K. *Applications of Case Study Research*. 3rd ed. Thousand Oaks, CA: Sage, 2012.

———. *Case Study Research: Design and Methods*. Thousand Oaks, CA: Sage, 1994.

Yukl, Gary. *Leadership in Organizations*. Boston: Pearson, 2012.

Yukl, Gary, and David D. Van Fleet. "Theory and Research on Leadership in Organizations." In *Handbook of Industrial and Organizational Psychology*, edited by Marvin D. Dunnette and Leaetta M. Hough, 148–66. Palo Alto, CA: Consulting Psychology, 1992.

Yukl, Gary, and Richard Lepsinger "Why Integrating the Leading and Managing Roles is Essential for Organizational Effectiveness." *Organizational Dynamics* 34.4 (2005) 361–75.

Yukl, Gary, et al. "The Forgotten Follower." *Journal of Managerial Psychology* 21.4 (2006) 374-386.

Zaccaro, Stephen J., and Richard J. Klimoski. "The Nature of Organizational Leadership: An Introduction." In *The Nature of Organizational Leadership*, edited by Stephen. J. Zaccaro and Richard J. Klimoski, 3–41. San Francisco: Jossey-Bass, 2001.

Zaleznik, Abraham. "The Dynamics of Subordinacy." *Harvard Business Review* 43.3 (1965) 119–31.

Zierdan, William E. "Leading through the Follower's Point of View." *Organizational Dynamics* 8 (1980) 27–46.

Zoogah, David B. *Strategic Followership: How Followers Impact Organizational Effectiveness*. London: Kogan Page 2014.

Zoogah, David B., et al. "Determinants of Strategic Followership: An African Perspective." *Journal of International Business & Economics* 10.4 (2010) 137–48.

www.ingramcontent.com/pod-product-compliance
Lightning Source LLC
Chambersburg PA
CBHW050617300426
44112CB00012B/1549